Looking West?

Post-Communist Cultural Studies Series
Thomas Cushman, General Editor

The Culture of Lies
Antipolitical Essays
Dubravka Ugrešić

Burden of Dreams
History and Identity in Post-Soviet Ukraine
Catherine Wanner

Gender Politics in the Western Balkans
Women, Society, and Politics in Yugoslavia and the Yugoslav Successor States
Sabrina P. Ramet, ed.

The Radical Right in Central and Eastern Europe Since 1989
Sabrina P. Ramet, ed.

The Culture of Power in Serbia
Nationalism and the Destruction of Alternatives
Eric D. Gordy

Russia's Liberal Project
State-Society Relations in Transition from Communism
Marcia A. Weigle

Revolt of the Filmmakers
The Struggle for Artistic Autonomy and the Fall of the Soviet Film Industry
George Faraday

Twisted Politics
Readings of Bosnian Culture and Society
Rusmir Mahmutćehajić

Intimate Relations
History and Gender in the Russian Far East
Petra Rethmann

Looking West?

Cultural Globalization and Russian Youth Cultures

Hilary Pilkington
Elena Omel'chenko
Moya Flynn
Ul'iana Bliudina
Elena Starkova

THE PENNSYLVANIA STATE UNIVERSITY PRESS | UNIVERSITY PARK, PENNSYLVANIA

Library of Congress
Cataloging-in-Publication Data

Looking West? : cultural globalization and Russian youth culture / Hilary Pilkington . . . [et al.].
p. cm. — (Post-Communist cultural studies)
Includes bibliographical references and index.
ISBN 0-271-02186-1 (cloth : alk. paper)
ISBN 0-271-02187-X (pbk. : alk. paper)
1. Youth—Russia (Federation)—Attitudes.
2. Mass media and youth—Russia (Federation).
3. Globalization.
I. Pilkington, Hilary, 1964– . II. Series.

HQ799.R9 L63 2002
305.2350947—dc21 2002005318

Printed in the United States of America
Published by The Pennsylvania State University Press,
University Park, PA 16802-1003

It is the policy of The Pennsylvania State University Press to use acid-free paper for the first printing of all clothbound books. Publications on uncoated stock satisfy the minimum requirements of American National Standard for Information Sciences—Permanence of Paper for Printed Library Materials, ANSI Z39.48–1992.

In memory of Katya (1969–99),

without whom the future will be incomplete.

CONTENTS

FIGURES, DIAGRAMS, AND TABLES

Figures

Diagrams

Tables

ACKNOWLEDGMENTS

Academic research is all too often driven by what is "fundable" rather than by personally or collaboratively determined research agendas. The idea for the current book was a happy exception to this rule, having been developed as the logical continuation of the collaborators' earlier research with little real hope of funding being forthcoming. We are grateful in the first instance, therefore, to the Leverhulme Trust (United Kingdom) for its vision in supporting sociological research on Russia that mentions neither "marketization" nor "democratization" in its title. We are also grateful to Thomas Cushman, series editor, and Peter Potter, Editor in Chief, of Pennsylvania State University Press for their enthusiasm about the book in its outline and draft stages. Thanks also to Tom Cushman and to an anonymous reviewer for their comments on the manuscript. Photographs for the book were partly taken during the course of the research by project members, but some are the work of Moscow-based photographers Alexandr Tiagny-Riadno and Oleg Belikov, whom we thank for permission to reproduce their work. Thanks too to Paul Tann, who worked on the translation of first drafts of individual chapters of the book.

Over and above the final members of the writing team, the project drew upon the energies and resources of our wider work collectives, to whom we are grateful not only for their specific contributions, but also for providing a work environment that remains inspiring, despite the pressures brought by the increasing bureaucratization and commercialization of academic life. In Ul'ianovsk, in particular, we are indebted to Irina Fliagina, Irina Zudina, Zhenia Liukianova, Tat'iana Levagina, and indeed all the members of "Region," who contributed their skills to the project in the empirical data gathering and analysis phases. In Samara our research was facilitated by Irina Kozina and Irina Tartakovskaia of the Sociological Laboratory, Samara State Pedagogical University, and Vladimir Zvonovskii and colleagues at the Samara regional Social Research Foundation. In Moscow Aleksandr Tiagny-Riadno accompanied us to an apparently endless stream of clubs; inspiring us to fit still more into "the plan," when even we had run out of energy. Anna Kalinina-Artemova of the newspaper *Komsomol'skaia pravda* was also generous with her time and contacts. A number of postgraduate students of the Institute of Sociology, especially Ivan Klimov, participated in our mapping of the Moscow club scene and helped us find contacts with a range of youth groups across the city. In Birmingham, special thanks go to Nigel Hardware, Mike Berry, and Julian

Cooper for sharing relevant electronic and print media sources and to a number of research students—especially Erica Richardson, Apostol Apostolov, and Kyongwon Yoon—who have shared their respective knowledges on topics related to the research. Marea Arries and Tricia Carr provided technical and secretarial support throughout the project and coffee and chocolate at times of particular crisis. We are always indebted to them.

The findings of the research have been presented at numerous conferences and workshops in the United Kingdom, Russia, the United States, and other parts of the world. We are grateful to all those who have commented on the papers and participated in their discussion. In particular we would like to thank Richard Johnson for his constructive comments on the original project proposal and his contribution as a member of the "Global and the Local in Youth Cultural Practice" panel at the Crossroads in Cultural Studies Conference held in Birmingham in June 2000. Various aspects of the findings of the research were also presented and formally, and informally, discussed during the Summer School "Youth Cultures and Lifestyles" held in Ul'ianovsk, September 2000. We are grateful to colleagues and students who participated in the School for their comments and insights.

The work would not have been possible without the active participation of all our respondents. We thank all of them for their time, enthusiasm, and consideration in responding to our prompts to talk at length about themselves. In particular we would like to thank a number of individuals who took time out to introduce us to their friends and colleagues, arrange passes into clubs, agree interviews with others in the city, and to treat us as friends. These include Misha Tsabko, Andrei, Ania, and Lera (Samara); Maksim Matuk, Vasilii Markelov, Dmitrii Sergeev, Dmitrii Ezhov, "Adam," Masha Gatsenko, and Artem (Ul'ianovsk); and the two Nadias, Veronika, Anton, "Elvis," and Stanley Williams (Moscow). Our research experience bears testimony to the openness, articulateness, and hospitality of young people in Russia, which continues to inspire our research.

The intensity of the research conducted for this book sometimes meant our working lives dominated everything else. We are all deeply indebted to our families and friends for the love and support they give, which allows us this space. We also thank them for being there when we "surface."

Finally, the book is dedicated to Katya Spasskina who was tragically killed in Moscow in May 1999. Her friendship and support over the last ten years are irreplaceable, and the fun she brought to my own research is unforgettable. Her spirit runs through the pages that follow.

Hilary Pilkington
Birmingham, March 2002

INTRODUCTION

Hilary Pilkington

Russia has been "looking West" for philosophical and technological inspiration that might be applied at home since the time of Peter the Great. But can the concept of a unified West retain cultural significance in an era of globalization? What do Russians mean when they talk about "the West" today? And does the West still constitute a model for social and cultural emulation?

The current volume makes no pretension to charting the discursive configuration of "the West" in Russian history and culture over the last four centuries.[1] It presents, rather, an insight into the role of "the West" in shaping Russian cultural development at a specific moment in time—the last few years of the twentieth century. The "end of the century" has no intrinsic significance. In the cultural development of post-Soviet Russia, however, it was during these years that the dominant (official and popular) paradigm of the cultural relationship between Russia and the West—according to which the West was a model for economic, social, and political emulation—was dislodged. Moreover, the rapid increase in the inflow of cultural messages and artifacts into Russia from the West during the 1990s provided an unprecedented opportunity to engage in an empirical study of the relationship between Western cultural products and Russian youth cultural practice.

The story the book tells is that of how Russia's opening up to the West has been reflected in the cultural practice of young people. This empirical focus was clear from the inception of the collaborative research project upon which the book is based.[2] Finding an appropriate theoretical context for this narrative was more problematic, however, and involved negotiating the different intellectual agendas of members of the research team. For the Western academics the study naturally located itself within an emergent debate about the interaction of "the global" and "the local" in youth cultural practice. For the Russian academics, the research promised to help answer fundamental questions about how the younger generation—the first to grow up not only in "post-Soviet" Russia but in a globally incorporated Russia—would reconfigure images of "the West" and rework them in new concepts of "self." In the course of five years of ongoing dialogue, the research team has sought to understand how these two sets of research questions speak to each other. In the process, the British members of that team have had to acknowledge the Western-centric nature of globalization discourse, while the Russian research team has been forced to recognize the "inward-looking" nature of Russian cultural identity formation whereby the "other" is perceived primarily in terms of how it constructs "self." This has been a difficult, if ultimately liberating, process for the researchers involved in the project, and the decision to write this volume collaboratively should be seen as a conscious exposition of this discursive gap. We hope that the book shows the contribution genuinely collaborative research can make toward rendering studies of contemporary Russia meaningful to both Russian and Western academic publics. Evidently, and thankfully, differences between individual authors remain.

The first chapter of the book addresses directly the discursive chasm in debates on cultural globalization in Russian and Western academic literature. While in the West *cultural* globalization has been studied as a set of empirical cultural *flows* and social *processes* moving outward from "core" to "periphery," in Russia globalization has been interpreted as a political, or "ideological", project led by the West. The "global community" has been considered to be a *Western* idea, world culture equated with the Americanization of "peripheral" national cultures and economic and political globalization interpreted as a means of subordinating Russia (and the East) to the interests of the West, above all the United States. While, on the surface, this discursive gap might be explained by the political posturing of a "great power in decline," it is suggested in the chapter that it indicates something more significant; the inadequacy of the "core-periphery" model of cultural exchange and a deficit of "nation" in Western theorizing on cultural globalization. Taking a perspective from outside the dominant core suggests that processes of cultural exchange take place within a complex structure and that the subjective positioning of a particular nation state within the world order is central to making cultural sense of globalization processes. In the case of Russia this subjective positioning is highly complex, since themes of "catching up" with the West draw on both Soviet and pre-Soviet Russian cultural history but compete with past experience, memories, and imaginations associated with Soviet Russia's cultural isolationism and ideology of social superiority to the West. Considering the debate on cultural globalization as it appears from a vantage point on the "eastern periphery," therefore, is the first step in restoring Russia's subjectivity in processes of "cultural globalization."

The subjects of the research outlined in the current volume were the first generation of Russians growing up in a global information and media world. The second chapter of the book charts the positioning of Russian youth in the global information space. Drawing on quantitative and qualitative data, the chapter describes the diverse range of global, national, and local media encountered by young people in Russia and their relative accessibility and popularity. More importantly, perhaps, the chapter asks *how* contemporary media influence youth cultures in Russia. Through analysis of the content of media products and interviews with the producers of media messages—editors of youth journals and youth television and creative directors of advertising agencies—the chapter describes how young people in Russia were positioned ambivalently in global and domestic media discourses. The chapter also traces the interactions between youth-oriented media and youth cultural groups. The content, genre, and style of youth cultural texts, it is suggested, was no longer "pure," but reflected the complexity and cross-fertilization of contemporary youth cultural formations that drew on an ever-broader range of influences. Although it is not suggested that new youth media had created youth cultural trends, the use of video-clip aesthetics, interactive communications, and the virtualization of media interactions had revolutionized the contemporary media space in Russia and appeared to be crucial to understanding how youth cultural trends developed.

Chapter 3 looks more closely at the specific discourses of "the West" that were produced in the Russian youth media. It provides a detailed analysis of the thematic context—music, fashion, film, video, television, youth culture—in which images of the West were located. As a result, the youth media, it is suggested, acted to include young people in Russia in a "global" youth culture. However, when concrete cultural phenomena, social values, and characteristics of specific countries were discussed, the "global community" evaporated and the relationship between Russia and the West appeared more problematic.

While the youth media thus presumed a heightened openness to the West—and to global messages—among young people, they also reflected some of the ambivalences in this relationship. Chapter 4 specifically addresses some aspects of this ambivalence through an analysis of young people's images, stereotypes, and actual experiences of the West. The chapter reconstructs a "picture" of the Western world as a whole, as well as of the individual countries most readily associated with "the West." Although the chapter essentially describes the images articulated by young people, it also indicates how images of the West were reworked and reconstituted as they were filtered through layers of individual psychological makeup, own and others' experience, and changing cultural reference points. As this process is charted, it becomes clear that young Russians were acutely aware of the constructed nature of media images and that the images of the West they received via the media were significantly altered as they were filtered through the critical lens of family, teachers, and peer group.

The active critical faculty of young Russians exposes the lack of substance to Soviet ideological constructions of young people as acutely vulnerable to the divisive influence of the West and prone to "imitating" Western youth cultural styles and forms (Pilkington 1994).[3] Even in the perestroika period, the "infatuation of Soviet youth with the West, its style of life, its culture," was one of the most sensitive national issues (Shlapentokh 1989, 142). The collapse of Soviet paradigms of youth culture has allowed Russian sociologists to develop more complex understandings of the role of "the West" in Russian youth cultural practice, however. Such new thinking has led to suggestions that young people in the Soviet Union did not just copy Western sociocultural forms but reworked them and appropriated them selectively and in relation to Russian cultural tradition (Islamshina et al. 1997, 98). The growing openness of Russia to the West in the last decade has made it possible for Western researchers also to reflect on the relationship between Western cultural forms and Russian youth cultural practice in the late Soviet period, drawing, for the first time, on ethnographic studies (see, for example, Pilkington 1994, Cushman 1995, Pilkington 1996a, Rayport Rabodzeenko 1998, and Yurchak 1999).[4]

Chapter 5 explores how the newly reconfigured West interacted with other social cleavages of Soviet modernity through an exposition of the contours of the youth scenes in Moscow and two provincial cities in 1997–98. This chapter introduces readers to the range of cultural practices in evidence across the whole spectrum of the contemporary youth scene at the end of the 1990s. While the maps constructed are far from "representative" of even these city scenes, let alone Russia in general, by considering the whole urban youth cultural scene rather than focusing on "subcultural" groups alone, they provide a wider panorama of youth cultural practice than previously captured in academic studies.[5] In the course of this remapping exercise, the chapter traces lines of continuity and change on the Russian youth cultural scene over the last decade. Although acknowledging a rapid increase and diversification of stylistic and musical engagements—many originating in the West—the chapter questions the usefulness of interpreting this as evidence of the "Westernization" of young people in Russia, or their incorporation into a "global youth culture." It suggests rather that young people drew differentially on the global and the local in the generation of distinct youth cultural strategies. These strategies are defined as "progressive" (post-*tusovka*) and "normal" ("ordinary kids" and anti-*neformaly*). Young people adopting the former strategy had their roots in the old Russian *tusovki* ("subcultural" groupings) and in the new economic and political environment identified, at least partially, with translocal subcultural affiliations. Progressives tended to have more links with, and access to, Western cultural experience and products and consciously identified themselves as outward (westward)-looking, forward-moving individuals. The second strategy was adopted by the majority of Russian youth, especially outside Russia's capital cities. This "normal" or "non-*tusovka*" youth engaged in a wide range of youth cultural practices but consciously professed no subcultural identity; its cultural practice was demarcated territorially rather than symbolically (through style or music) and, in a minority of cases, was characterized by open hostility toward progressive youth.

It is, of course, tempting to read progressive strategy as an aspirant middle-class youth cultural strategy that employed media and material consumption to ensure incorporation into a wider global youth culture, and to read normal strategy as a working-class, local resistance to "Westernism." In the course of Chapters 6 and 7, however, it is argued that the peculiarities of consumer practices in post-Soviet Russia together with Russian sensitivities toward cultural globalization render such a reading impossible. In reality it was the progressives who were most critical of the West, while normal youth engaged with products for cultural consumption with relatively little concern for their origins or intrinsic meanings.

This conundrum is explored in Chapters 6 and 7 through an analysis of the cultural practice of young people across the youth scene at a microlevel. It is suggested that the global context of youthful negotiations of the post-Soviet social and cultural environment did not undermine established social stratifications, but reconfigured them according to "glocal"[6] dimensions. Global-local and core-periphery positionings, moreover, were not only reflected in youth cultural strategies; awareness of these positionings actually shaped those strategies.

In Chapter 6, the focus of analysis is on the people, places, and activities that constituted young people's daily cultural practice. The material position of the majority of young Russians was such that everyday activities surrounding home, school, college, work, and leisure were more locally framed than was their globally mediated cultural consumption. Even in this most domestic of spheres, however, young people appeared to inhabit cultural worlds with quite different horizons. While the pressures to study and earn money constrained leisure activities for both progressives and normals, what free time they had was structured differently. Normals tended to engage in a greater number of organized leisure activities of the "Soviet" type alongside unstructured "time-out" spent among territorially located peer groups. Progressives, on the other hand, had a greater propensity to combine leisure pursuits with study or part-time work, blurring the distinction between the two and creating the impression of a whole "lifestyle." In managing the "risks" of late modernity, progressives responded with an individually oriented discourse of choice, taking up the challenges of individual responsibility thrown at them while normals referred to group norms in managing the challenges of late modern diversity. For those with the social and cultural capital to permit them to claim a space in the center, therefore, the opportunities of post-Soviet society were mobilized in a progressive cultural strategy framed by broad horizons and characterized by a tendency to look outward and to seek new information and cultural stimuli. In contrast, young normals—having no pretension to a place "in the center"—used the depth of their local connections to seek to secure themselves a minimal material security that might facilitate global consumption.

Chapter 7 focuses on the specific engagements of young people with style and music and addresses the question of how "the West" and its cultural production signify in young people's stylistic and musical consumption and practice. It shows how points of access to, and modes of engagement with, the "global" were different for progressive and normal youth, resulting in multiple local narratives of global cultural forms (such as rave). These engagements, it is suggested, reflected neither a distinctive Russian imitation of Western forms nor a resistance to global musics and styles, but indicated how young people drew differentially upon both the global and the local as resources in the construction of progressive or normal lives. While specifically seeking to reveal the nonhomogeneity of the Russian youth scene at the end of the 1990s, both Chapters 6 and 7 highlight and explore specifics of Russian youth cultural practice that cut across progressive and normal strategies for how they might speak to Western theories of youth cultural practice. In Chapter 6, for example, it is suggested that it was communication (*obshchenie*), and not consumption, that acted as the substance of youth cultural groupings in Russian society. In Chapter 7, meanwhile, young people's distinction between meaning*less* "music for the body" (Western dance music and pop) and meaning*ful* "music for the soul" (Russian rock, bard music, and even Russian pop) is revealed to be a common mode of differential engagement with Western and Russian cultural forms.

Chapter 8 addresses directly the central question of the book: how are young Russians responding to processes of cultural globalization? It analyzes how young people perceived Russia to be positioned in current global flows of cultural exchange, their sense of Russia's place in the new global order, and how they managed "living with the West" as a daily cultural practice. It is suggested that young people, although receptive to them, considered Western cultural forms to be somehow intrinsically "global," while Russian culture remained peculiarly Russian and, as such, protected from "global" invasion. They thus described the cultural space they inhabited not as one fundamentally changed by globalization's one-way cultural exchange but as akin to a giant "mix and match" counter in which the global and the local existed simultaneously.

The empirical data drawn on in the book will require frequent renewal if they are to provide any kind of valid picture of cultural change in contemporary Russia. The empirical focus of the book, however, should not overshadow the aim of the authors to reflect back on theories of cultural globalization inscribed in Western academic literature. The research findings suggest that young people feel themselves to be included and engaged in a "global" information world to a degree unimaginable even ten years ago. This has been experienced, at the individual level, as liberating; new cultural spaces have opened up in which young people can engage in multiple and repeated constructions of self. At the level of national self, however, talk of the "global community" has undermined important markers of "here" and "there" and "us" and "them," which have anchored Russian narratives of self in the past. While some tentative suggestions about the significance of these processes are drawn in the concluding chapter, the current volume marks no more than a first attempt to expose the presence of such processes and indicate the first responses to them among Russian youth.

1 Cultural Globalization

A Peripheral Perspective

Hilary Pilkington and Ul'iana Bliudina

Cultural globalization is not new. Universalizing cultural processes can be traced from the early modern period, if not earlier, being rooted in the spread of world religions and imperial elite culture (Waters 1995; Held et al. 1999). However, cultural globalization is currently at an accelerated stage of development. The intensive development of new communications, media, and information technologies in the second half of the twentieth century has led to the extension, diversification, and acceleration of global cultural flows and an increase in the intensity, volume, and speed of cultural exchange and communication. This process has been accompanied by the emergence of new global infrastructures and the increasing dominance of a small number of multinationals in the sphere of cultural production and distribution of cultural goods; as a result, contemporary global interaction is conducted primarily through the media of Western popular culture and business communication (Held et al. 1999, 341).

The debate on globalization in Western academic writing is also in overdrive. Although the earlier writings of McLuhan (1964) lay dormant for a number of years, since the beginning of the 1990s there has been an explosion in writing on theories of economic, political, and cultural globalization. While all academic disciplines have been affected by this debate, it has, nonetheless, developed along a number of more or less disciplinarily bound tracks. Theorists of economic and political globalization have been inclined to build on "world-system" approaches, which overtly recognize the economic and political *structures* governing global interactions. *Cultural* globalization, in contrast, has been presented as a series of *processes* (Lash and Urry 1994, 306; King 1991, 1).

The emphasis on cultural *flows* in theories of cultural globalization has been driven by the concern *not* to reduce globalization to "Westernization" or "Americanization" where the latter envisages the "global" not as process but as a cultural *content* "dumped" upon other countries. While sociologists and cultural theorists alike would agree that cultural globalization cannot be equated to "Americanization" on a grand scale (Jameson 1998, 59), nonetheless, distinct disciplinary territories have emerged. Sociologists have been concerned primarily with the "global" (understanding the origins and forms of cultural flows emanating from the West) while "the local" has been conflated with the experience of nonwestern countries and thus ascribed to anthropology (Fardon 1995, 1–2). The focus on cultural flows also signifies a "postmodern" as opposed to a "modernist" approach—where the former is understood as the privileging of the spatial over the temporal in explaining social and cultural change—and lies within the domain of cultural studies as opposed to sociology (Featherstone and Lash 1995, 1).

These divisions are evident in the almost axiomatic typologies of theorists of cultural globalization as either "homogenizers" or "pluralizers" ("diversifiers"). According to this classification, the "homogenizers," also referred to as the "pessimists," envisage the process of cultural globalization as leading to a "global" homogenized culture as Western popular culture is exported around the world. The "pluralizers"—also known as the "optimists"—see the potential of greater center-periphery interaction to enable peripheral or minority cultural forms to transcend the local (Robertson 1995).

Models of cultural "homogenization" and of "diversification/differentiation" as outcomes of processes of cultural globalization are, of course, little more than ideal types; and theorists of cultural globalization who retain a connection to the field have sought more sensitive ways of conceptualizing the outcome of "one-way" cultural exchange via concepts of cultural "hybridization" (Hall 1990, 234; Bhabha 1990; Clifford and Marcus 1986) and "maturation" or "creolization" (Hannerz 1992, 264). The concepts of creolization and hybridization entail a process whereby the periphery receives but reshapes the metropolitan culture to its own specifications, thereby allowing for a model of cultural exchange in which the periphery shows culturally differentiated responses to the Western version of modernity being exported without ignoring the actuality of the power relations involved in economically driven, cultural globalization. For Held and colleagues this position is already a third pole of the debate—defined as a "transformationalist" position—which describes the "intermingling of cultures and peoples as generating cultural hybrids and new global cultural networks" (Held et al. 1999, 327).[1]

Another way in which the false dichotomy between the positions of "optimists" and "pessimists" concerning the benefits of globalization might be tempered is by reference to the different spheres upon which globalization impacts. In the sphere of ethnicity and nationhood, for example, globalization has been seen to *differentiate*, or celebrate difference; it has facilitated challenges to the nation state—or supranational state in the case of the USSR—which tends to conceal difference in the creation of an outwardly coherent national identity. In contrast, globalization is seen to *homogenize* above all in the sphere of popular or consumer culture.[2]

Theorists of cultural globalization rarely confront directly the question of structure.[3] Nonetheless, recognition of the unequal power in the "exchange" of cultural messages is implicit in their employment of the "core-periphery" model of cultural exchange. Such a model, it is suggested here, reflects a "centrist" standpoint that has little resonance with the experience of peoples on "the receiving end" of global trends (Howes 1996, 7). It posits a dominant, self-conscious, and confident core (established nation states of Western and northern Europe, North America, and Japan)[4] as the *subject* of cultural exchange against an atomized, self-ignorant, and absorbent periphery as the object of that exchange. Taking a perspective from outside the dominant core suggests that processes of cultural exchange take place, in fact, within a complex structure and require the reinstatement of the peripheral subject as an active agent in globalization. Russia, for example, is not newly exposed to cultural globalization but has a long history of complex interaction with Western ideologies and modes of thinking particularly in relation to Western scientific and philosophical paradigms.[5] Thus, while in the West the impacts of globalization may be just beginning to be felt, the West has been present (physically and symbolically) for those outside the core for much longer (King 1995, 123; Morley and Robins 1995, 217–18).

Cultural messages from the West today are neither simply absorbed nor complexly reworked in isolation. Rather, such messages are filtered through state-level ideology and the experiences, memories, imaginations, and fantasies that accumulate individually and collectively. Appadurai makes at least indirect reference to this when he notes that the "scapes" he describes are "deeply perspectival constructs inflected by the historical, linguistic and political situatedness of actors: nation-states, multinationals, diasporic communities, sub-national groups, villages and neighbourhoods"

(Appadurai 1990, 296). The subjective positioning of a particular nation state within the world order is thus central to making cultural sense of globalization processes. The global mass media—or "global imagination industries"—introduce people across the globe to visions of a greater range of possible lives, thereby bringing individuals' own lives and their imagined "possible lives" into ironical conflict with each other (Beck 2000, 53–54). In the case of Russia this is not just Bauman's "localized poor" confronting a "globalized rich" (Bauman, cited in Beck 2000, 55), however. The subjective positioning of post-Soviet Russia is, rather, highly complex as themes of "catching up" with the West draw on both Soviet and pre-Soviet Russian cultural history but compete with past experience, memories, and imaginations associated with Soviet Russia's cultural isolationism and ideology of social superiority to the West.

The reluctance of Russia to act out the new peripheral role apparently assigned it by the West is evident in Russian debates on cultural exchange between the West and Russia that barely interact with Western-centric theories of globalization. The latter, like the transnational, Western-based companies they so often critique, project their ideas as global when in fact they are local and specific. Russian debates, in contrast, have little space for globalization, but focus rather on Russia's place in the new world order, weighing up the legacies of past isolation alongside the potential benefits of forging a positive Russian national identity to combat the otherwise pervasive cultural presence of the West. Considering the debate on cultural globalization as it appears from the vantage point of an Eastern periphery, therefore, is the first step in restoring Russia's subjectivity in processes of cultural globalization. To take this debate seriously is to acknowledge that an exclusive focus on *process* to the detriment of *structure* in debates on cultural globalization seriously undermines the ability of globalization theories to understand and explain real cultural processes outside the Western world.

Power, the New World Order, and Cultural Exchange: Russian Debates

When globalization is addressed directly in Russian academic writing,[6] it appears not as a social or cultural process but as a political project "initiated and led by the West" (Simoniia 1996, 6). The formation of a global community is not understood as a consequence of, still less a condition for, modernity, but perceived to be rather a *Western idea*:[7] "World culture means above all the Americanization of the cultures of the peoples of this planet, foisting on them Western-oriented culture" (Zinov'ev 1995, 414).

Globalization in economics and politics is portrayed as a means of subordinating Russia (and the East) to the interests of the West, and above all the United States. This process preserves an asymmetrical integration into the world economy whereby all countries outside the West—referred to as the "non-West"—are drawn into the international division of labor in a neocolonial manner (Simoniia 1996, 6; Solonitskii 1996, 11). The argument that the West consciously seeks to "reinforce backwardness and dependence" (Khoros 1995, 123) among peripheral societies and is disinclined, therefore, to assist Russia in retaining its status and power, is commonplace (see, for example, D. Evstaf'ev 1997; Maksimychev 1997; Utkin 1995, 13; Khoros 1995, 123; Shliapentokh 1994; and Gubman 1994, 12). This is expressed starkly by Iusupovskii:

Why help Russian capitalism get off the ground, why create a partner-competitor for yourself . . . ? Supposedly [you don't help] because of concerns about eradicating socialism, guaranteeing democracy, and preventing any possible return to totalitarianism. . . . But surely it is not difficult to discern a thinly concealed desire to deprive Russia of the sources of its own development, to curtail the opportunity for the country to make its own choices, to determine its own fate? (Iusupovskii 1997, 22)

In the economic sphere, therefore, "globality" (*global'nost'*) is perceived to be maintained in the interests of the United States alone, since "global" financial and stock markets are tied to the U.S. dollar. The common portrayal of globalization as a "universal process" gradually incorporating the periphery into the global space is thus exposed as an "ideal-type" that fails to take into account the specifics of climate, demography, and human capital of different nations (Volodin and Shirokov 1999, 92). Thus economic globalization is characterized as "an uncontrollable accumulation of transnational short-term capital whose speculative character exacerbates the scale of market swings provoking national and regional financial crises and destabilizing political systems" (Volodin and Shirokov 1999, 84).

Occasional voices recognize the opportunities, as well as the threats, presented by economic globalization and call for Russia to work globalizing processes to the country's advantage (Mikheev 1999, 11). Even these voices, however, suggest that this more positive approach might be the most effective way to "counter American influence in the world economy and polity" (ibid.).

In political terms, the United States is characterized as seeking to isolate Russia while using the country as a buffer, separating China and the Muslim world from the West (D. Evstaf'ev 1997, 75; Brutents 1998, 62). Russia's "right" to act as "broker" in the post-Soviet space is contested by the West, it is argued, in order to prevent any potential challenge to American global hegemony (Brutents 1998, 60) based on America's role as "gendarme of the world," policing and securing interregional shipments (primarily of oil). At the same time, it is suggested, Western politicians exploit Russia's own sense of having a "unique path" as an argument for keeping Russia out of Europe (Maksimychev 1997, 86).

In the cultural sphere, Western "expansionism" is primarily attributed to America, in particular American pop culture (Solonitskii 1996, 11). The objection voiced is not to an "alien" culture invading Russian cultural space, but the "crude" form and ideological content of the cultural products produced by the West. While Zinov'ev's nostalgia for the Soviet era may be peculiarly strong, the sentiment concerning Western cultural inferiority is not: "Now you yourselves can go round the kiosks and see what a stinking flood, what a veritable cesspool of Western art has descended upon, has been directed toward, Russia. . . . The more genuinely talented the writer, the more difficult it is for him to emerge out of the cesspool. Phenomena like Maiakovskii or Sholokhov are just not possible there [in the West]" (Zinov'ev 1998, 20).

Global information networks are also envisaged as driven by Western countries and saturated by American culture (Zinov'ev 1995, 414). The head of Glasnet—one of Russia's primary internet service providers—is even reported as envisaging the World Wide Web as "the ultimate act of intellectual colonialism" (Anatolii Voronov, cited in Ellis 1999, 162). While Voronov is essentially referring to the English language medium of the Web, others root this new mechanism of cultural imperialism in the Internet's provision of yet another medium for the dissemination of American cultural influence: "It is not difficult to discern, behind the advertising and propaganda pressure of the Internet, the unerring efforts of the United States, not only to ensure its own superiority in the most important fields of basic and applied science and technology, but also to make it possible to dictate ideologically and to spread the United States's political and spiritual influence via modern telecommunications networks and systems" (Smolian et al. 1997, 44).

The current academic debate on globalization in Russia thus hinges less on charting the technological and economic forces driving global processes, or the social and cultural consequences of them, than upon the philosophical and historical aspects of geopolitical shifts. In contrast to Western debates, it follows, issues of *structure* and *power* are central to the discussion of globalization in Russia. The "global society" is considered to be a myth constructed in order to conceal the real relations of world power: "Global society is portrayed as consisting of tens of thousands of states—friendly, sovereign—sharing obligations . . . and struggling together against crime and so on. It is absolute nonsense. A real global society exists, but not in the form of a brotherhood of such states. Rather, as a multilayered vertical structure which has the whole planet caught in its tentacles" (Zinov'ev 1998, 26).

The "global community" is thus described as a "phantom" whose "will" is invoked to justify unilateral actions taken by the G7 and NATO and to amplify calls for mechanisms of "global governance" that might well prove "worse than any forms of totalitarianism to date" (Maksimenko 1999, 4). While it is difficult to assess to what extent this academic debate has resonance at a popular level, speakers at a meeting of over five hundred "antiglobalizationists" in Moscow in February 2001 reportedly declared globalization to be "one of the greatest threats of the new century" (Rosbizneskonsalting 2001). While the West has also witnessed active protests against aspects of global governance, most notably at the World Trade Organization meeting in Seattle, November 1999, the specific objection of the Moscow protesters was peculiarly Russian; according to speakers at the meeting "the creation of a single world government runs counter to the historic mission of Orthodox Russia" (ibid.).

Russia and the West: From Enmity to Mutual Disappointment

One might be forgiven for interpreting the works of those such as Zinov'ev as indicating the failure of Russian society to rid itself of the ideological hangover of the Soviet period, substituting only the word "globalization" for the traditional evil of "imperialism." In reality, however, relations with and rhetoric about the West have changed so dramatically over the last fifteen years that they have come full circle.

During the Gorbachev period (1985–91), the West became an object of devotion and the symbol of a "normal," almost ideal, life. This was facilitated by Russia's continued informational isolation and a mood of "masochistic self-criticism" in the country (Utkin 1995, 7). Indeed at the popular level, Soviet "heritage" was parodied by reference to the Soviet Union and Soviet citizen as *sovok* and the perceived distinctive Soviet "mentality" as *sovkovkii* (Pilkington 1994, 314). "The West" came to be equated with world civilization and considered as the standard of civilized behavior (*tsivilizovannost'*). What was termed a policy of "anti-isolationism" was, in fact, a policy of Westernization (*vesternizatsiia*) thinly veiled by the notion of "catch-up modernization" (*dogoniaiushchaia modernizatsiia*) (Utkin 1995, 8).

The real honeymoon period in relations between Russia and the West followed August 1991, when social consensus, so difficult to achieve in Russia on other policy issues, was established in relation to the West. The West at this time was perceived to be a model of political organization to which to aspire and the nucleus of world economic and scientific potential (Burganov 1995; Orlik 1995; Solonitskii 1996, 11). It was also considered a vital ally in implementing change in Russia, since it provided a key source of political support for the reformist elite and, it was hoped, might render real economic assistance (Utkin 1995, 13). The positive attitude toward the

West was manifest across Russian society. At the official political level, Yeltsin declared that "the spirit of the Cold War in relations between Russia and the West has been overcome once and for all" (Yeltsin 1992a, 73) and that "Russia has no enemies, even potential ones" (Yeltsin 1992b, 29). Popular perceptions of the West at the time, meanwhile, were associated with positive characteristics of Western society, such as "the inviolability of private property, efficiency, freedom of conviction and behavior, a professional attitude to business, the equality of all before the law, and the protection of political and social rights" (Orlik 1995, 12).

As Soviet isolationism was replaced by Russian integration into the global community, the mid 1990s saw a brief period in which relations between Russia and the West were characterized by "partnership" (Bocharova and Kim 2000, 2). Greater proximity to the West could not but shatter the ideal image of it, however. The early enthusiasm about the West began to be replaced by skepticism (Kustarev 1997; Utkin 1995) and renewed concern about Russia's great power status, uniqueness, and cultural potential (Bocharova and Kim 2000, 2). The shift was attributed to the association of the (Western) market model with the loss of social gains in health care, education, and science in Russia,[8] as well as with outward opulence against a background of growing poverty and moral degradation (Utkin 1995, 16). Utkin concluded that, for the first time in recent years, a mutual discontent could be detected between Russia and the West. The West felt disappointment with Russia and characterized it as "failing" in its "transition." From the Russian perspective, the West had not recognized Russia's geopolitical interests and rightful world status through either arrogance or continued mistrust (Utkin 1995, 49; Rogov 1998, 107). Moreover, the West had failed to assist Russia in this transition. Russia had not been assisted economically in the way both Germany and Japan had been following the Second World War, it was claimed, because Russia continued to be perceived as "the enemy" (Bestuzhev-Lada 1997b, 25). Worse still: "Instead of rapidly transforming Russia into a successful capitalist system, the West has acted as a giant magnet, pulling all its key resources—material and intellectual—out of Russia" (Shliapentokh 1994, 25).

This perception of the West was accentuated by a disappointment in Western politicians and publics, whose early flirtation with Russia in the second half of the 1980s had quickly dissolved into disinterest (Oleshchuk 1994, 52), allowing a "cold war" mentality to be reconfigured and to manifest itself in the Balkans (Fursov 1996, 22).

The growing skepticism about the West's attitude toward Russia is well reflected in public opinion data. A nation-wide survey carried out by the Russian Center for Public Opinion and Market Research (VTsIOM) in September 1994 suggested that 57 percent of Russian citizens believed that "the main aim of the West is to turn Russia into a third world country and exporter of natural resources." By August 1995, the proportion confirming this statement had risen to 62 percent (Bocharova and Kim 2000, 3), and in January 2000 the same proportion (62 percent) of the population felt that Western economic "aid" was in fact rendered in order to "gain political and economic control over Russia," compared to just 6 percent who believed such assistance was aimed at "stabilizing Russia."[9]

Popular images of the West deteriorated rapidly during 1998–99; by spring 1999 almost two-thirds (65 percent) of the population considered Russia to have "enemies";[10] 24 percent named this enemy as "Western industrial-financial circles"; 19 percent declared the enemy to be "the United States"; and 17 percent saw the enemy as "NATO" (Bocharova and Kim 2000, 4). Negative attitudes to the West peaked in spring 1999, determined clearly by the Kosovo crisis. Images of the United States were particularly negatively affected; in December 1998, 67 percent of respondents in VTsIOM polls had been declaring a positive attitude to the United States, but by April 1999 only 33 percent had such positive images (Bocharova and Kim 2000, 7). The Kosovo crisis, however, does not appear to have done irretrievable damage to relations with the West; by September 1999, positive attitudes to the United States had recovered significantly and were reported by 61 percent of respondents (Bocharova and Kim 2000, 11). While public opinion is evidently susceptible to short-term crises, it is clear that it is not so much that the West continues to be seen primarily as "the enemy" but that the power of the West is interpreted as a direct reflection of the weakness of Russia, and the latter is the fundamental concern of the Russian public.

Russia's Place in the World: Challenging Models of Linear Development

After a brief period firmly situated on "the periphery," Russia is challenging the global positioning it has been assigned. This does not mean a return to Soviet claims of economic "superiority" or denial of the existence of economic and technological lag between Russia and the West. On the contrary, Russian social scientists tend toward viewing Russia as engaged in ("catch-up") modernization (Krasil'shchikov 1996; Rashkovskii 1995; Simoniia 1996; Solonitskii 1996; Cheshkov 1996; Akhiezer 1994; Bestuzhev-Lada 1997b; Burganov 1995) and thus as positioned among a "second tier" of countries, alongside other states of Eastern and Southern Europe, Turkey, parts of Latin America and Japan (Krasil'shchikov 1996, 68). However, Russia is considered to be not "backward" per se but as suffering from developmental imbalances whereby postindustrial relations in the sphere of information and science coexist alongside other aspects of the economy and society which are still modernizing (Rashkovskii 1993, 63).

While in Soviet Russia the answer to economic lag was always rapid economic and technological development, a new element to the current debate is a questioning of traditional models of modernization and its accompanying globalization. Thus Iusupovskii invokes Wallerstein in arguing that the great illusion of modernization theory lies in the promise to make the whole system "a 'nucleus' without a periphery" (Iusupovskii 1997, 22). In fact, he argues, the "core" places in the world economy are already taken, thus whether or not Russia "remodernizes" successfully, only secondary and subordinate roles will be left for Russia. Thus globalization is portrayed, not as a strategy of global inclusion, but as an exclusive process leading to further division: "In the second half of the 1990s the world has been divided into those who enjoy the fruits of globalization and the rest, that is those who are pushed further and further out to the periphery of current processes. . . . The marginalization of whole regions poses a threat to world order" (Volodin and Shirokov 1997, 170).

As a developmental strategy, therefore, Russia's best hope, it is suggested, may be to ignore the pulls of globalization and to rely on the main counterforce to it—the nation-state (Simoniia 1996, 6). A notable exception to this argument is that put forward by Iurii Fedorov, who argues that the only way for Russia to evade peripheralization is to actively engage in, and meet the challenges of globalization. The first step toward this, he suggests, is to recognize that in the new transnational environment, new factors define great power status (Fedorov 1999, 1).

By rejecting the new "globality" as no more than a cloak for monopolarity, Russian academics (re)turn to the notion that both Eastern and Western "civilizations" are central to maintaining a healthy global balance. Thus, the Russian debate is distinguished from Western discussions of globalization in that it views the cultural realm as not just another dimension to globalization, but a potential challenge to it.

From this perspective "the West" is a particular path of civilizational development that formed in Europe in the fifteenth to seventeenth centuries as a synthesis of the classical world and the European Christian tradition. The outcome of this process was a technogenic civilization based on swift technical and technological progress, rapid changes in social ties between people, and the dominance of scientific rationality. The term "the East" refers to an earlier civilizational formation represented today by traditional societies and cultures. The social consciousness of Eastern societies is presented as "oriented toward charisma, a spiritual basis, religion or the ethical and philosophical search for the meaning of life, and the social ideal" (Besov 1998, 67). Eastern societies are also characterized by collectivism.

The significance of distinguishing these two alternative paths of civilizational development lies in the perception that historically there has been a clear "division of labor" according to which the West has supplied the world with innovative technologies (including social technologies), and the East has supplied *spiritual* initiatives (Panarin 1998, 69). Thus, Panarin suggests, grave consequences may follow any shift in the balance of power: "Westernizing the world—making it monopolar—is like making our brain mono-hemispherical, depriving it of its right side, its figurative, intuitive structure. Diminishing the status of the East in the world and weakening the impulses that emanate from it portends the universal triumph of a one-dimensional mass society" (Panarin 1998, 69). Attempts to create a "global civilization and world government" thus threaten to destroy the existing (binary) "world civilization system" (Anisimov 1996, 55; Cheshkov 1996, 15).

There is no agreement, however, on where Russia is placed in this civilizational binary. For some writers, Russia is firmly camped in the West because Russia belongs to the European and world Christian tradition (Shapovalov 1998; Maksimychev 1997; Panarin 1998; Lipkin 1995) and shares a common cultural root with Europe in the classical culture of the antiquity (Krasil'shchikov 1996, 69; Diligenskii 1997a; Solonitskii 1996). Authors taking this position also note the active role of Russia in European development, arguing that even the Tatar yoke, which isolated Russia from Europe, was in fact evidence of Russia's dedication to the European idea, since Russia's resistance to it absorbed the offensive power of the Mongol armies to the ultimate benefit of the rest of Europe (Maksimychev 1997, 90). In this paradigm of thought, the West appears as an ideal developmental model, deviation from which can only hinder progress (Burganov 1995, 20).

Those who point to Russia's difference from the West focus on the absence of civil society in Russia (Kholodkovskii 1996) and the development of Russia as a "closed" as opposed to "open" society. An open society is described as one founded upon "freedom," while a closed society is founded upon "coercion" (Bergson 1994). While from a Western perspective, this "closed culture" is something which requires remedy, from some Russian perspectives the introspection (*zakrytost'*) of Soviet society continues to act as a protective mechanism against American or Western cultural expansion. In the most extreme of arguments the Open Society (in particular as it is articulated by George Soros) primarily serves the purpose of leaving society open to the manipulation of individuals in the interests of "global governance" (Maksimenko 1999, 14). Attempts to create Russia in a Western image according to the recommendations of "Western experts," it is claimed, "have been received, always and at all times, negatively by the public" (Zobov and Kelas'ev 1995, 24). Thus the failures of the pro-Western policies of the post-Soviet Russian leadership are cited as evidence that Russia cannot integrate into Europe because Russia was "never a purely European state" (Tsygankov 1995, 15).

Measuring the degree of "Europeanness" or "Asianness" in individual and collective identities is extremely difficult. Certainly Russia's path of modernization suggests an increasingly European trajectory: although 75 percent of Russia lies in Asia, only 22 percent of the population lives there (Vishnevskii 1998, 126), while urban living and modern family formations inhibit the reproduction of traditional society. However, a sociological study in 1997 suggested that *European* identity remains at a very low level; only 1 percent of Russians identified themselves as "European," compared to 12.9 percent who still considered themselves "Soviet" (Avraamova 1998, 23). A more recent VTsIOM survey (January 2000) found many more "Europeans" (20 percent considered themselves "definitely" European) but there were almost as many "non-Europeans" (17 percent considered themselves "definitely not" European).[11]

Other writers see Russia as "somewhere in-between" East and West. This might be expressed temporally in theories of cyclical movement between Western and Eastern modes of development (Semennikova 1996). It also underpins the suggestion that, at any given point in time, Russian society contains the potential either to follow a "Western path" or to seek its own, "third" way. A VTsIOM poll conducted in 1994 found both strands of thinking among the population: 22 percent of the Russian population thought Russia should become like the West, while 52 percent considered it impossible and needless for Russia to copy Western experience (Sazonov 1994, 15). Subsequent sociological research (conducted in May 1996) addressing the question of popular attitudes to the West as a model for Russian development suggested the population was evenly split between the two positions; 41 percent of those surveyed were classified as "Western-oriented democrats," although 47 percent of this group believed that Russia would follow its "own path" to the "Western end point" (Kutkovets and Kliamkin 1997). In any case, public opinion is strongly against any return to Soviet isolationism: 68 percent of those polled in January 2000 were in favor of strengthening "mutually beneficial relations" with the West, compared to only 19 percent favoring a "distancing" from the West (Bocharova and Kim 2000, 11).

The historical and philosophical roots of this popular blend of European and Asian identity are deep, and it is beyond the scope of this volume to review the vast body of literature addressing the question of Russia's "Eurasian" identity (Bassin 1991; Ferdinand 1992; Kerr 1995; Tolz 1998; Smith 1999). In a discussion of globalization, it suffices to note that at the level of political discourse there are not one, but multiple "Eurasianisms" (Smith 1999, 55), and that at the popular level this "hybrid" state is experienced, not as a national schizophrenia, but as a distinct cultural identity rooted in the sharing of a common homeland by a large number of ethnic groups. This may, at least partially, explain why globalization discourse in contemporary Russia pays scant, indeed no, attention to theories of cultural hybridization in understanding contemporary cultural processes.

Russia does not position itself as a "peripheral receiver" of Western cultural messages but rather as the embodiment of alternative cultural values. Russian spirituality and sublimity are contrasted (opposed) to Western "ordinariness, down-to-earthness and rationality" (Guseinov 1996, 22; Klishina 1998, 156). This cultural and spiritual "wealth" and the contribution of the East in general, and Russia in particular, to current global development (Kopylov 1995; Panarin 1998) disrupts the core-periphery model of cultural exchange underpinning Western theories of cultural globalization. Objectively, in economic and technological terms, Russia places itself on the periphery. Subjectively, in terms of the country's global cultural contribution, Russia sees itself in a position of leadership: "The active intrusion of the East into global history that we are witnessing in this century is taking place with the powerful spiritual participation of Russia. The salvation of Russia lies in the vital moral strength of Russia's culture and its intransient values, which ensure a deservedly dignified place in the world" (Tol'stii, cited in Gubman 1994).

This produces a dual attitude to the West in Russia described as a "combination of sycophancy toward the West, verging on national self-humiliation, and hatred of the West, xenophobia, and self-aggrandizement" (*Kentavr pered sfinksom* 1995, 9). While both attitudes may be always present, the dominant mood depends heavily upon what the West's attitude to Russia is and *is perceived* to be. The swing from the former position to the latter in the last five years indicates how quickly the tide can turn and how different "one world" can look from the Eastern periphery and the Western "core." While in Europe, "globalization" may evoke periodic concerns about the power of transnational corporations to move production in and out of countries or destroy domestic cultural industries, from Russia it appears as a full-scale attack upon half the world's civilization:

Never before has encroachment upon the East as a phenomenon of world history and culture been on such a large scale and of such a blatant nature. Western modernizing missionaries are hard at work in every country, showing the local authorities and intellectuals how to eradicate traditional Eastern mentality and how to civilize peoples and continents as quickly as possible. . . . Western liberal ideology has usurped the right to speak on behalf of reason, truth, and justice. (Panarin 1998, 65)

From this vantage point, empirical processes of globalization appear as a "revolutionary ideology" of "globalism," borne of deeper spiritual crisis.

Youth and Cultural Globalization: Leading the Global Revolution?

Western globalization theories, focusing as they do on the forces driving globalization, rarely address questions of *differentiated* reception to global messages, or different levels of engagement with global processes. Individual and social identities in globalization literature are reduced to their expression in consumer practice. One exception to this rule is the discussion of migrants or diasporic peoples and professionals in the spheres of international finance, academia, advertising, and the media who are identified as key agents of globalization and physical embodiments of the deterritorialization of culture (Hannerz 1990; Waters 1995, 151; Appadurai 1990).

A less explicit exception is youth. Although structural constraints, family, and financial dependence may prevent young people from engaging in transnational movement, nonetheless they are seen as peculiarly receptive to global messages. Advertisers, for example, view the youth market as "the first truly international market in history" (Yovovich 1995). The wider cultural practice of youth appears to confirm a "global identity"; young people are major consumers of "popular culture," which is the aspect of culture most open to the transnational flow of cultural commodities (Hannerz 1992, 239). The American popular music industry, for example, has experienced such extensive transnationalization that it has undermined domestic industries in almost all other countries and acted as a medium for the transmission of a wider set of American youth and African-American cultural styles (Held et al. 1999, 353).[12] With specific regard to Russian youth, this openness to global messages is rendered as a particular receptivity to "Westernism" (Kosals, Ryvkina, and Simagin 1996).

Given that "globalization proceeds most rapidly in contexts in which relationships are mediated through symbols" (Waters 1995, 124), it is not surprising that young people appear to be leading the field; symbols—from hooded tops to piercings—are central to the creation of style and formation of microgroups by young people. Moreover, while older generations may struggle with the "information overload" of the twenty-first century, young people appear to move effortlessly between texts, in and out of real and virtual spaces, borrowing images, catchphrases, and symbols as they go and reinventing them in the ongoing process of identity formation.

Assumptions about the global engagement of young people are explicit in media images of "a global youth culture" and implicit in current (post-subcultural) theorizing of youth cultural practice. Such theories reread the connections between class, culture, and consumption drawn by the "modern" critics of the "massification" of culture through consumption (Hoggart 1957).[13] Drawing on theories of "individualization" in late (also known as "high" or "reflexive") modernity (Beck, Giddens, and Lash 1994), theorists of youth culture suggest that the decline in importance of social origins (ties with family and class-based community) means that young people are freer than ever to choose independently how they live and thus construct their own "lifestyles" through the exercise of consumer choice in the *global* market (Reimer 1995, 122). Indeed, individualization and globalization, Beck suggests, are two sides of the same process of "reflexive modernization" (Beck 1994, 14). Such cultural practice does not facilitate the construction of life-long social identities—for such have become redundant in a world driven by the need for "flexibility" (Bauman 1998b, 28). In a world characterized by "individualization," it follows, young people's successful "socialization" is not achieved through the internalization of given norms but through learning how to be self-reliant and to shape their lives as an "open process" (Beck 2000, 138). Young people thus forge identities with reference not to "real" communities (rooted in class, locality, ethnicity, race) but to taste communities or "lifestyle enclaves" in which consumption is practiced in the absence of communal regulation (Lash 1994, 160).[14] In this sense, "lifestyle" might be used to understand young people's cultural practices in late modernity, as David Chaney suggests, as a vocabulary of self-expression offering a means of differentiation at the same time as substantiating a sensibility or affiliation (Chaney 2001, 7). In this sense lifestyles do not constitute or substitute "identities" but represent identity (ibid.).[15]

The notion of cultural practice representing rather than constituting identity is perhaps the point at which the conceptual border between "late" modern and "post" modern society is crossed. In postmodern society, lifestyles are understood to be infiltrated increasingly by "tribalism"; the self-sufficient individual as the subject of the creation of lifestyle in modern society is thereby undermined (Maffesoli 1996, 97). Postmodernity, Maffesoli argues, is characterized by the formation of fluid microgroups that do not connect individuals to a particular community in a relationship of "belonging." Such groups, nonetheless, indicate the propensity to natural sociality and need for affect in contemporary society (76–80). It is this vision of highly fluid, scattered, and temporary formations—neotribes—which has proved appealing to researchers of contemporary urban youth cultural practice (see, for example, Malbon 1999, 56–57; Hetherington 1998; Bennett 1999b; and Muggleton 2000, 128). The prioritization of the "the affectual and the tactile" (Malbon 1999, 57) and the movement between consciousness of self and of submission of self to the "crowd" among clubbers, for example, sits uneasily with conceptualizations of youth cultural practice as located within the class-rooted, fixed, and stable subcultures of modernity. It has clear resonance, on the other hand, with Maffesoli's notion of disindividualization as manifest in the individual's submergence of self in a vast whole (Maffesoli 1996, 138).

To date, such "post-subcultural" theorizing has been developed primarily on the basis of youth cultural practices in Western "culture-producing" societies. An emergent debate on youth culture and globalization,[16] however, suggests that the interaction of the global and the local in youth cultural practice is beginning to be studied in a more sensitive way. Where youth "at the core" is concerned, discussion has focused on the exploitation of new technologies such as desktop and electronic publishing, computer graphics, animation and comic books, and Internet networking and chat rooms to enable the development of global, "multilocal" or "translocal" youth cultural forms (Richard and Kruger 1998; Leonard 1998; Hodkinson 2001; Newitz 1994). In some cases this translocality arises not from simultaneous transmission of youth cultural forms around the world, but through a complex process of the export, local reworking, and reimporting of cultural commodities by "producer nations." The result is hybrid cultural forms important to the construction of highly complex translocal youthful identities. Thus, in contemporary Britain, David Parker has shown how British Chinese youth draw on Hong Kong based "Canto-pop" to forge a distinctive cultural identity for themselves (Parker 1998). In America fans of Japanese animation (*anime otaku*) appropriate a peculiar Japanese cultural commodity, itself heavily influenced by Hollywood animation techniques, in order to distinguish themselves from the mainstream (Newitz 1994).[17]

Serious attention to the local meanings invested in global youth cultural forms is to be found primarily in writing concerning the local appropriations of various types of popular music as they are created through distinctive sampling and mixing practices and in specific ethnic, class, and gender contexts (see, for example, Robinson, Buck, and Cuthbert 1991; Taylor 1997; Bennett 1999a; Bennett 2000; Mitchell 1999; Huq 1999; and Condry 2000). Such studies sometimes lend empirical weight to theories of "syncretism," "creolism," or "hybridity" but always provide an important counterbalance to theories charting the logic of globalizing processes, by focusing on local articulations of global cultural forms. Indeed, "the local" in studies of "core" youth is not equated with any "national scene" but understood complexly as a contested space. Thus young people may draw on the same music and style but produce not a single style-based subculture but a variety of responses as a common set of knowledges relating to the local are differentially applied (Bennett 2000, 67).

While youth at the "core" is understood to be engaged in postmodern "being," youth on the periphery is described as being engaged with the global cultural economy in a process of "becoming." This is partly a result of the disciplinary territorialization noted above—whereby studies of the "local" are generally considered the domain of anthropologists—but it is rooted also in understandings of the logic of modernization and, in particular, associations made between the consumption of material and cultural commodities and the formation of youth cultural (and "subcultural") identities. In a global age, it is suggested, such youthful identities are forged in "modernizing" societies among an emergent middle-class youth as it links into transnational media and commodity flows (Liechty 1995) and imagines other possible lives rooted in different spatial contexts (Beck 2000,

53). Of course the engagement with things "out there" in shaping modern youth identities is not new; the specter of "Americanization" has haunted Europe since at least the beginning of the twentieth century. It was in the post-Second World War period, alongside the emergence of "the teenage consumer" (Abrams 1959) that fears of "Americanization" were discursively prominent. Dick Hebdige notes that concerns about "Americanization" and "Italianization" in Britain after the Second World War led to attempts to frame, contain, and limit the flow of imported goods and to determine their meanings and uses (Hebdige 1988, 9). In postwar West Germany the cultural influence of American movies and popular music was invoked by political and cultural conservatives to explain the emergence of disruptive teenage groups (*Halbstarke*) (Poiger 2000, 113). In France, fears about Anglicization—primarily via American cultural production—remain tangible. The implementation of the Pelchat Amendment in 1996 required most of France's 1,300 FM radio stations to broadcast music of "French expression" at a minimum level of 40 percent (Petterson 2000, 109).

The debate about "Americanization" may provide fascinating cultural histories, but appears theoretically restricting in a period of accelerated globalization. Is a movie with a British director and cast financed by Hollywood, an American or a British cultural product? Does rap performed by MC Solaar constitute an American or Senegalese influence in France? However, past debates about "Americanization" might inform current interpretations by globalization theorists of "peripheral" engagements with Western cultural production in at least two significant ways. Studies of the consumption of "other" cultural commodities suggest, first, that interaction with "foreign" cultural forms does not make everybody "the same." In the case of postwar Britain, far from leading to the homogenization of British culture, young people used American and Italian commodities to mark out aspirational *differences* among themselves through the invocation of an "America" of open roads and affluence, or a cool and sophisticated continental Europe (Hebdige 1988, 9). Second, such studies suggest that not only resistance of (as in the cases of the Soviet Union or Eastern Germany) but also reception to the consumption of American material and cultural commodities might be utilized in the formation, or reformation of a strong sense of nationhood. In postwar (West) Germany, for example, initial concerns about American influence were soon muted as the American model of mass consumption was recognized as an important mechanism for encouraging a nonclass and nonpolitical (nonideological) basis for youthful identifications in a post-Nazi Germany seeking to reintegrate itself into global modernity (Poiger 2000, 117). Likewise, in societies of the Pacific Rim, "global consumption" may become a marker of both second-wave modernization and a means of national assertion.[18]

Theorists of global-local interactions need to recognize, however, that such encounters are always framed within both the "commoditized logic" of modernity and the realities of power (Liechty 1995). Thus, where imaginations of "modernity" are rooted in national economic prosperity, global consumption may facilitate a near-universal middle-class identity and a growth in cultural diversity and opportunity.[19] However, in conditions of economic peripheralization, global commodity consumption may act rather to embed class differentiation while at the same time reinforcing dependent discourses of state modernism (Liechty 1995, 193). Such constraints upon youth cultural agency are inherent in the process by which young people form modern identities at the intersection of tradition and globalization, development, and consumerism (Wulff 1995, 9). This structural constraint is a factor recognized by Bauman when he distinguishes between the "globalized rich" and the "localized poor": "Residents of the first world live in *time*; space does not matter for them, since spanning every distance is instantaneous . . . residents of the second world, on the contrary, live in *space*: heavy, resilient, untouchable, which ties down time and keeps it beyond the residents' control" (Bauman 1998a, 88).

In the "transition" societies of Eastern Europe the interaction of discourses of modernity, consumption, and identity is complicated further by the uncoupling of the concepts of modernity and consumption. The prioritization of production over consumption until the 1970s, together with the inefficient distribution system in an economy of perpetual shortages, ensured that consumer choice was minimal or nonexistent (Wallace and Kovatcheva 1998, 161). In the absence of domestic production for consumption, Western imports took on an added cultural value and a heightened ideological significance. Thus while resistance to American (Western) cultural production was articulated via discourses of racial "primitiveness" and sexual "transgression" in a similar way to Western Europe (Poiger 2000; Pilkington 1996b), it also manifest itself in concrete policies designed to shield young people from the decadence of Western culture and to punish them if they, nevertheless, sought to consume or engage with it (Poiger 2000, 185–202; Pilkington 1998, 369–71). Lifestyle construction through consumption remains problematic as a way of conceptualizing youth cultural practice in post-Soviet Russia. Young citizens of Russia may be engaged primarily as "consumers" rather than producers in a way characteristic of late modern society (Bauman 1998a, 80), but, as Oushakine argues, young people do not as yet recognize themselves as subjects of post-Soviet consumption (Oushakine 2000b, 98). This suggests that local engagements with global culture by young people in post-Soviet Russia might defy the cultural logics of both "modernizing" and postmodern consumer societies.

Conclusion

Tracing the discursive fields in which answers to questions about the impact of "cultural globalization" on Russian youth cultural practice might be expected to be found reveals a discursive chasm. From Western academic literature, it is possible to formulate a clear picture of the way in which new technologies associated with the "digital age" have generated cultural flows that reach further than ever before into the global hinterland. This body of literature also presents evidence of how these flows have generated new institutional formations, in particular the growth of transnational corporations whose financial interests are served by a homogenization of taste or demand.

From this literature alone, it would have seemed appropriate to generate a preliminary hypothesis that Russian youth, more than five years into the "post-Soviet" era, would be *embracing* the West and already looking and sounding like its Western peers. However, Russian academic literature reveals a remarkable resistance to even the talk, let alone the practice, of globalization. This literature posits globalization as a Western ideology that seeks to ensure the integration of Russia (and the wider "non-West") into the world economy as a subordinate "periphery" to a dominant "core." Had this discursive context been the sole starting point of the research, the study might have anticipated that Russian youth would be either in conflict with their parents' generation or *resisting* Western cultural forms while actively constructing new Russian identities. The authors' attempt to root the empirical study of Russian youth and its cultural practice in *both* sets of literature made hypothesizing just what the impact of cultural globalization might be on actual youth cultural practice in Russia yet more difficult. Indeed this is not a problem peculiar to Russian studies. As Held and colleagues note, "it is a complex and exceedingly difficult task to interpret accurately the impact of this new form of cultural globalization on political identities, national solidarity and cultural values" (Held et al. 1999, 328).

This chapter has suggested that in order to understand these impacts, alongside the "flows" or processes of cultural globalization, it is essential that the subjective element, that is, the actual experience, of globalization, be studied. If real substance is to be given to theories of "hybridization" or "creolization," more knowledge of the social relations of consumption—that is, the logic by which goods are received (acquired, understood, and employed) in different societies—is required (Howes 1996, 2). For no cultural message crosses borders into a cultural vacuum, but must encounter an already existing frame of reference in the eyes of the consumer or receiver (Held et al. 1999). Given the social and cultural heterogeneity of contemporary Russian society and the range of interactions with Western cultural messages today, any number of subjects or sites could have provided rich research material; this study draws on just one social group (urban youth) and one site of cultural practice (experience of youth-oriented media as the mode of transmission of cultural messages).

The existence of global "borrowing" and "hybrid cultures," however, does not necessarily impact upon mainstream national cultures and national identities in any significant way (Held et al. 1999). Indeed, Bauman suggests that "hybridization" is what happens to cultures at "the globalized top" while the experience of people on the receiving end of globalization is reflected and articulated by "neo-tribal and fundamentalist tendencies" (Bauman 1998a, 3). "Nonwestern" societies open their doors to cultural influence from the West in the search of the higher living standards associated with the achievement of "modernity" (Lee 1994; Liechty 1995). However, familiarity with the West does not necessarily imply acceptance of it, and adoption of an economic and technical vision of Western modernization as a model for emulation may be accompanied by a suspicion of the Westernization of local values and cultures (Roniger 1995, 274). Thus for nonwestern societies the acceptance of Western goods or messages does not indicate that they have a globality (universality) or seductive (symbolic, technological, or aesthetic) power, capable of overcoming local differences; Western goods may simply be treated as such—as foreign goods—and as such not expected to conform to local values (Classen and Howes 1996, in Howes 1996, 182). This paradox, or cultural ambivalence, lies at the heart of this volume as it seeks to explain how globalization can be interpreted positively at one level, while being resisted at another. In the case of Russian youth, it is argued, globalization is welcomed insofar as it accelerates the eradication of Russia's isolated past and presents opportunities to realize levels of material comfort existing at globalization's "core." While young Russians aspire to Western standards of living, however, they do not seek to emulate Western standards of "being"; and where spiritual life is concerned, young people remain firmly rooted to the local.

2 On the Outside Looking In?

The Place of Youth in Russia's New Media and Information Space

Elena Omel'chenko and Ul'iana Bliudina

By the end of the 1990s, a new generation of Russians had emerged, a generation that felt itself incorporated into global information and media worlds. The nature and quality of young people's global "inclusion" was indeed mediated by this new information space, and this chapter traces its dimensions. It charts the diverse range and the relative accessibility and popularity of global, national, and local media encountered by young people in Russia at the end of the 1990s. It also describes how these media presented the West and its cultural products to their youth audiences.

More important, perhaps, the chapter asks *how* the media has influenced youth cultural formations in Russia. It explores the technologies and aesthetics of message production and dissemination in the Russian youth media and suggests that the art of "capturing" audiences and generating a sense of common identity around a particular lifestyle message was becoming increasingly sophisticated.[1] Just as youth cultural formations themselves drew on an ever broader range of influences and cross-fertilized to produce increasingly complex forms, so message producers had developed a multifaceted and polyphonic palette of new cultural texts targeted at youth audiences. The content, genre, and style of these texts was no longer "pure"; sources and contents of messages, images, and audiences were mixed and exchanged. The use of video-clip aesthetics, interactive communications, and the virtualization of media interactions, moreover, had revolutionized and complicated the Russian media space.

Although the actual reception to specific media images among Russian youth is addressed in Chapter 3, this chapter considers the interaction between the youth media and its audiences at a general level. It suggests that it was the way these audiences reproduced, or ignored, meanings and values reflected in the media that gave vitality to media messages and empowered information networks emanating from them. More specifically, it argues, new channels and means of disseminating information have changed notions of the public and private spaces of contemporary youth cultures; and as a consequence, perception of and involvement with such new texts has changed.

The Mass Media in Contemporary Society: New Images, New Theories

The mass media is no longer understood as a reflection of society, but increasingly as relatively autonomous of it. The rapid and ongoing development of new technologies has led to repeated public concerns over the power of the media to target and manipulate opinion among certain sections of society. Each new stage in the development of communications has been portrayed as a series of "losses" by society of ever more of the classical values of human discourse: direct contact, immediate response, the ability to clarify ambiguities, the balanced nature of dialogue, spontaneity, mutual interest in continuing the contact, and so on. These developments have been perceived as losses not just to communicative practice, but to culture more widely; and the resulting "moral panics" about cultural decline and moral degradation of society have focused on the impact of new media on youth in particular.

Television is an obvious case in point,[2] since, technically, television requires a simplification of the message being transmitted in order to provide sufficient visual interest. As television images have invaded life more and more,[3] it is argued, it has become difficult to detect the dividing line between show business and reality, for televisual delivery of material destroys the "deep" literary layers of artistic texts, waters down civic values, and turns even socially significant information into a theatrical show. Notions of the world have become formed through a constant stream of images, sometimes delivered without context. This interpretation—which envisages television as "dumbing down" its audience with a new type of social narcotic—has been particularly characteristic of debates surrounding youth and the media.

The era of commercial television—the development and conquest of the world's information markets by advertising—has generated no less panic. Spectacle, it is suggested, replaces reality with representation, real time becomes advertising time, and everything that is presented (or represented) becomes a commodity. Events are transformed into a kaleidoscope of symbols and a show-world of ubiquitous advertising. It is no coincidence that for Russian teenagers at the end of the 1990s the name "Rambo" signified a Hollywood character, but the name "Marx" was understood to refer to a chocolate bar (Mars).

While it is easy to criticize the slide into regurgitating moral panics, understanding the new forms of *power* that accompany new media technologies is far from straightforward. Althusser's work usefully distinguishes between the different forms of power invested in the *repressive* and *ideological* apparatuses of the state, positioning media among the latter. Unlike the political apparatus, which preserves the status quo by means of subjecting individuals to the political ideology of the state, the communications apparatus "saturates" each citizen with a daily dose of nationalism, chauvinism, liberalism, and moralizing, aided by the newspapers, radio, and television (Althusser 1994, 96). Ideology in media communications is not overt, but hidden in images and structures that may be taken for granted and thus assimilated unconsciously.

This understanding is not dissimilar to Jacques Lacan's idea that the individual, saturated with communications, is determined by the structure of the subconscious, which in the modern world is also determined by media culture. The erosion and substitution of the meanings being transmitted and the "concealment" of dictatorial pretensions of media messages take place under the "cover" of media discourse. Such "discourse" cannot be reduced to the editorial aims and motives of the publications, the objectives of the author, the presence (or absence) of censorship, or to state regulation. Discourse is more a way of thinking, characteristic of the culture of communication and the values established by the given community, which explicitly or implicitly determines the nature of the "delivery" and "presentation" of any individual piece of information (Nazarov 1999, 32).

The way in which the modern mass media have developed clearly casts doubt on—if not refutes—Adorno's belief that the consumption of mass information would lead to the erosion of individual difference and the atomization of society. For Adorno and Horkheimer, the producers of mass cultural forms proceed from the premise that audiences are homogeneous masses, which is why they are keen to preserve their passive and conformist qualities. Adorno's view that the mass media will lead to the atomization of society, on the other hand, is rooted in his belief that the "masses" are not a subject, merely an object of the "culture industry," receiving what is fed to them rather than that which they desire (Adorno 1991).

In fact the latest modern media offer ways of forming new virtual solidarities that eliminate not only spatial and temporal but also sociocultural differences (status, power, money, gender, sexual orientation, cultural level, national traditions) and thus, overcome to some extent social atomization. The way these solidarities are formed, however, always involves a qualitative loss in the value of the communication; telephone conversations, live radio dialogue between listeners, and Internet match-making remain incomparably different cultural practices from real-life meetings. Virtual images do not require real, every-day confirmation; they are entirely self-contained.

From a postmodern perspective, the issue of whether "the masses" are subjects or objects becomes irrelevant, since the subject is, in any case, "de-centered." The importance of the image, moreover, is accompanied by ever greater emphasis on appearance at the cost of depth and substance. The aesthetic style of postmodernism is characterized by Nazarov as consisting of inaccuracy, erosion, a tendency toward ambiguity, fragmentation; irony and a desire to eradicate established canons; carnivalization; intertextuality; and the generation of a multitude of conflicting versions (Nazarov 1999, 55). Cultural texts begin to exist almost in and of themselves, requiring or presupposing no correlation with reality.

The concept of reality multiplies—only what is presented in texts becomes real—and the text can only be understood in relation to how it is perceived and who perceives it at a given moment in time.

The notion of the communication chain changes accordingly. Past distinctions between the source of the information and its means of communication have been rendered meaningless. One text is transmitted via another text. This implies an enhanced role for cultural informational intermediaries, who by means of editing techniques (collage, bricolage, pastiche)[4] can change meanings and combine existing texts into something new. The French postmodern theoretician Jean Baudrillard considers the most important aspect of the new information world to be the unprecedented level of intermediaries in mass media experience. The huge volume of information means that culture is defined by certain simulation models. These models may not have clear referents, and meaning may be formed in correlation not to reality, but to other signs. A sort of unstable, aestheticized hallucination of reality is formed, a spectacle of images which have no innate meaning (Nazarov 1999, 60).

Russian Media and Youth Cultures in the New Information Space

The information space inhabited by contemporary Russian youth is best understood within the postmodern paradigm described above, for it is characterized by the use of spontaneity, a light-hearted attitude to reality, a new attitude to the surrounding world, a rejection of commonly accepted norms and stereotypes, a confirmation of universal tolerance of the many and varied manifestations of individuality, and the minimization and mobility of values and norms. This has been made possible by a phenomenal transformation of the Russian information space in the last decade.

In Soviet Russia media and information sources were mouthpieces of party and government opinion that claimed to articulate the ultimate truth. Negative or critical publications occasionally appeared but provoked serious repercussions; even constructive internal criticism might provoke administrative paranoia.[5] The primacy of ideological correctness over editorial stance in evaluating journalistic work—and the practice of making appointments to key posts through the highest party organs, commissions from city and regional committees, and the Committee for Television and Radio—effectively meant that the people who formed public opinion were political figures. The power of the spoken or written word was limitless. Criticism was cleared in advance, and praise prepared beforehand. Nowhere could one see Althusser's "secret power" theory being implemented so openly and consistently.[6] The reverberations of party and, later, state patronage were felt until quite recently. The launch of new magazines, television channels, and youth publications was always directed and supervised by the party and depended upon official decisions and official youth policy. Even when the first television programs involving "real" young people were initiated, they were done so in accordance with resolutions passed by the *Komsomol* Congress in line with the official program for working with informal youth groups.

The first phase of the "restructuring" of the media involved an exploitation of blatantly sensationalist themes as a consequence of the removal of censorship. Suddenly it was possible to talk and write about anything and everything; chasing new information and being first to discover topics, events, and names became paramount. In the second phase, this initial blanket approach was replaced by more selective methods. Media producers began to make their first tentative attempts to define an individual approach and carve out a particular audience. In the third phase, the media began to approach information selectively and to develop a conscious differentiation in style and artistic method. At the end of the 1990s, most Russian media lay somewhere between the second and third phases of development, although there remained a clear difference between "traditional" media and those new to the Russian information space. The first group included television and the press, while among the second were the new radio stations, glossy youth magazines, independent and foreign television and radio channels, and—the latest developments—video and computer networks.

In order to secure this new information space, both political and economic reform had been necessary. Commercial information, above all advertising, had to be developed and institutionalized, since the switch to self-financing by media outlets required the sale of advertising space, air time, brokering, advertising, and creative services. This also required the development of a legislative base for the media to allow it to function on a nonideological basis. Finally, at the political level, the media had to be removed from political, ideological, and party censorship. While pressure might still be brought to bear in some form or another on publications that strayed beyond the bounds of what was permissible, these bounds have become defined more diversely—by political engagement, the specific nature of the regional power hierarchy, financial interests, "moral" preferences, and covert political agendas. Certain publications and television channels had links with particular parties either because of "historical tradition" or as a result of preelection or longer-term agreements between editors and particular power structures. At the regional level "sympathies" were frequently linked to the personal preferences of the governor of the region, who backed certain publications and television channels, which, in turn, exclusively promoted the administration's views. Publications that pursued a different policy did not enjoy official protection and lay themselves open not only to criticism but to outright suppression. Financial involvement also amounted willy-nilly to political involvement, as was more than apparent during the presidential election campaign in 2000.[7]

By the end of the 1990s, the media was no longer seen to express truth in Russian society. With the collapse of the Soviet regime came a renunciation on the part of the state of any form of ideological or moral education; and although there remained some nostalgia for a publicly declared "truth," young people tended to be less concerned about the "source" of information than adult generations. Consequently, texts aimed at youth audiences often became a recreational, playful space beyond censorship, a carnivalesque space in which old and new values were exchanged and Russian and Western youth cultural models were amalgamated. This is not to suggest that young people put their faith in such texts; on the contrary, texts often served as objects of direct criticism and skepticism. Nevertheless, young people frequently and willingly used the wide range of cultural products transmitted by the media, and the messages contained therein, to form templates within which their perceptions of the world were framed and complemented by experience.

Youth Choices in the New Information Environment

Diagram 2.1 indicates the range of media sources from which young people in provincial Russia drew their information about the West at the end of the 1990s. It is based on data from a representative survey of young people aged between fifteen and twenty-five years conducted in Samara and Ul'ianovsk in November 1997 (see Appendix for details). The most widely

Diagram 2.1 **Sources of information about the West**

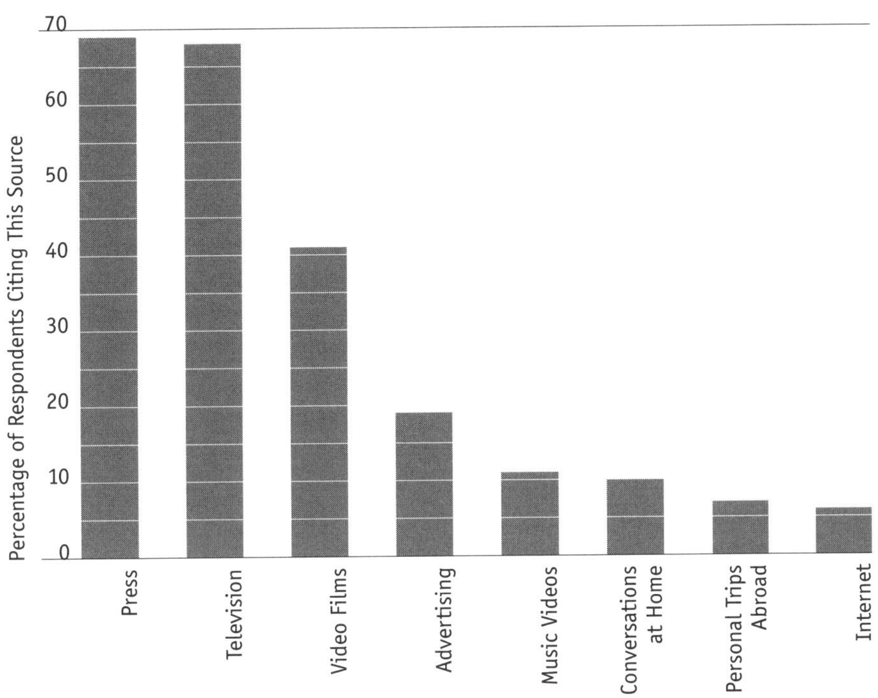

used media at the time of research were the press (newspapers and magazines), television, film and music videos, advertising and the Internet (see Diagram 2.1). The popularity of each of these media among youth—as well as radio, which enjoyed a revival of interest among youth after the period of empirical research—are discussed in the following sections of this chapter.

Television: A Thumbs Down for Youth Programming

Soviet television provided few programs targeted specifically at young people, the exceptions being *KVN, A nu-ka devushki*, and *A nu-ka parni*. These were all so-called competition programs designed to instill a "healthy" enthusiasm and optimism, and also to propagandize (advertise) the importance of specific professions. Thus the stars of these broadcasts tended to be young miners, steelworkers, hairdressers, nurses, and drivers. In the period prior to perestroika, Channel 1 established the first youth editorial team, which began broadcasting the social and current affairs program *12-ii etazh* (Twelfth Floor). This program pioneered the practice of talking live to young people themselves, which was subsequently used in almost all youth programs of the perestroika period. *KVN* continued to be broadcast,[8] and the first music programs began to appear, such as *50 na 50* ("Half and half").

Most youth programs being shown at the end of the 1990s dated back only to the post-perestroika period, however, and every channel had its own brand of music, entertainment, and information programs for young people. Such programs sought to attract their target audience by employing "youth-friendly" formats, including eyewitness reports, interviews with members of various subcultures, the appearance of music idols playing the latest music videos, and discussions of "taboo" topics such as sex, drugs, and AIDS. These programs—*Rok-urok, Dzhem*, and *Tin-Tonik*—described themselves as information and entertainment programs and were similar in form to the series *Do 16 i starshe* ("Up to 16 and Over"), which appeared in the late 1980s.

When the survey was conducted in November 1997, the most popular youth television program was *Do 16 i starshe* and among fifteen- to seventeen-year-olds, more than 50 percent of respondents said they watched the program frequently (see Diagram 2.2). Indeed, with the exception of *Dzhem*, all the programs mentioned were watched most frequently by the 15–17 age group. Other types of youth programs, such as those with an "educational" slant, like *Umniki i umnitsy*, which were supposed to promote further education among young people, and those which focused more specifically on such topics as computers, music, culture, sports, medicine, and travel were less popular. Each of them was watched by fewer than five people from the whole sample. New discussion programs appeared regularly, purporting to discuss those topics that were important to young people, but about which they found it difficult to talk; such topics were almost always sex, drugs, AIDS, homosexuality, and violence. Some such projects—for example, *Akuna motata*—had received substantial investment, but their popularity rating among youth groups remained fairly low.

Thus although television itself was an important media source, the results of the survey conducted in Samara and Ul'ianovsk suggested that *youth* programs did not figure prominently in the list of television programs young people preferred. Even the most popular youth program was preceded in popularity by twenty-five other named programs. These programs were those designed for general adult audiences: the news, films, entertainment programs, soap operas, information programs, and so on. Since the survey was conducted, the range of youth programs available has widened but the level of interest in specially produced youth programs has remained the same. The only exceptions were the "pure" music programs, such as those on Russian MTV[9] and its imitators, whose programs consisted entirely of music videos. This finding in relation to youth program-

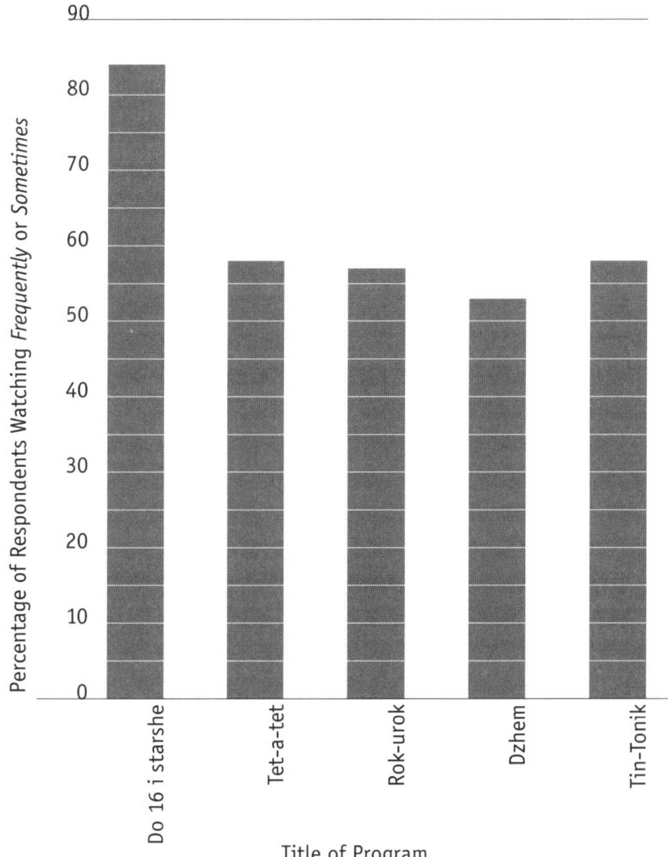

Diagram 2.2 **Youth programs watched by young people**
(Samara and Ul'ianovsk, November 1997)

ming was confirmed by a separate nation-wide survey of youth conducted in 1997, which found that the most popular programs among youth were foreign films and music and entertainment programs, followed by Russian films, information programs, and sports programs (RNISiNP 1998, 50). It also reflected the experience of Western societies (Oswell 1998).

A Touch of Gloss: A Makeover for Russian Youth Magazines

The press, including newspapers, magazines, and specifically youth-oriented press media, was the single most important source of information about the West for young people; 69 percent of those surveyed in Samara and Ul'ianovsk cited the press as a source of information for them. The importance of the press rose as the age of respondents increased; in the 18–20 and 21–25 age groups almost 10 percent more respondents in each group cited the press as a source of information. Respondents in Ul'ianovsk were also more likely than those in Samara (a difference of over 10 percent) to cite the press as an information source, a fact probably attributable to the relative poverty of alternative sources in the smaller city.

In the Soviet period there were a number of magazines especially for young people: *Studencheskii meridian*, *Rovesnik*, *Molodaia gvardiia*, *Smena*, *Vokrug sveta*, *Iunii naturalist*, and others. The end of the state monopoly, however, led to the collapse of existing publishing houses and the emergence of new publishing houses and organizations independent of the state.

The first stage in the post-perestroika magazine boom was characterized by the appearance on the youth market of a large number of "yellow" (pornographic and semi-pornographic) publications with a blatantly sensationalist content and marginal cultural status. The second stage saw the emergence of Russian versions of international publications. In addition to translated texts, lifted directly from Western sources, these publications also included Western material specially adapted for Russia's youth and original pieces. Most magazines which appeared during this period, however, were publications for "new Russians," whose categorization as "youth," even when they were objectively "young," is problematic. By the end of the 1990s youth publishing had entered a new phase, one marked by the gradual displacement of openly pornographic and sensational publications, the emergence of magazines targeted at very rich youth, a growth in popularity of publications with a "subcultural" and underground slant targeted at specific audiences, and the spread of fanzines (amateur magazines produced by fans of a particular cultural or musical trend).

Western publishers have been quick to move into the Russian market, producing Russian versions of Western "glossies" such as *Cosmopolitan*, *Playboy*, and *Marie Claire*. At the time of research a significant section of this magazine market had been captured by the *Burda Moden* trading and publishing company, which publishes a range of women's magazines (*Woman, Liza*, *Nastia*, and *Priiatnogo appetita*), family magazines (*Moi prekrasnii sad*, *Moi uiutnii dom*, *Otdokhni! Moi mir*, and *Vot tak!*), and youth magazines (*COOL!* and *Cool Girl*).

Independent Media handled the Russian publications of a range of well-known Western magazines such as *Cosmopolitan*, *Harper's Bazaar*, *Marie Claire* (women's magazines devoted to fashion, beauty and health), *Playboy*, and *Men's Health*. The publishing company *Argumenty i fakty* also produced a number of youth and women's publications, including *AiF. Liubov*, *AiF. Ia Molodoi*, *AiF. Zdorov'e*, *AiF. Dochki-materi*, *AiF. Umnik*, *AiF. Semeinii sovet*, and men's magazines such as *Kul't Lichnostei* (about celebrities) and *Draiv* (a car magazine), as well as *Yes!* (for teenage girls).

Diagram 2.3 **Youth magazines read by young people**
(Samara and Ul'ianovsk, November 1997)

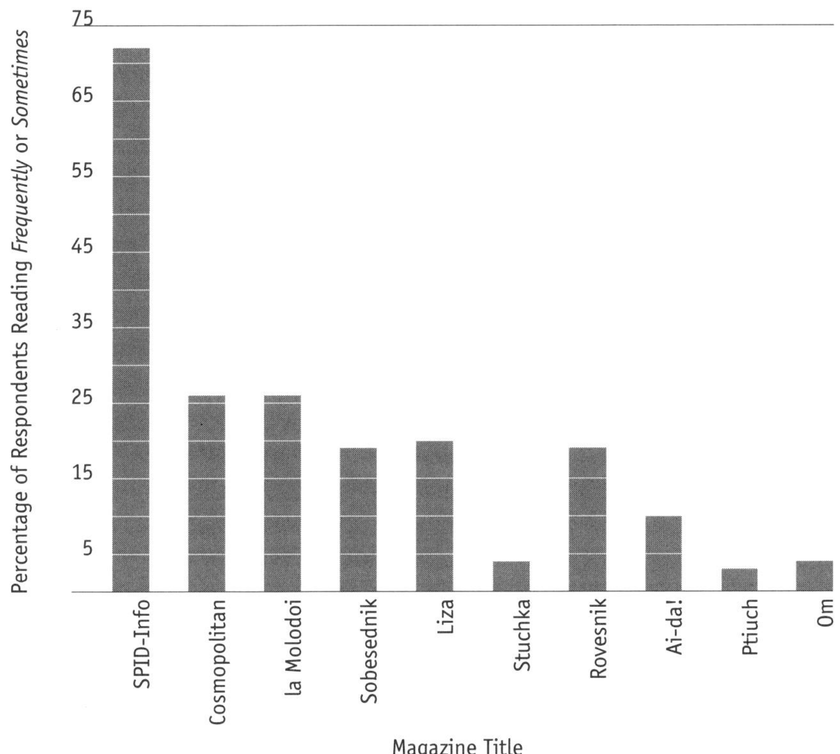

Specialty magazines for young people and teenagers, originally adopting the format and style of Western magazines, first appeared in 1995. One of the largest youth publishers was *Rovesnik*, which produced four magazines for teenagers and young people: *Rovesnik*, *Shtuchka*, *Vse zvezdy*, and *16*.

According to the survey conducted in Ul'ianovsk and Samara, the magazine most widely read by young people in November 1997 was *Spid-Info*—24 percent of those surveyed read it "often" and 48 percent read it "sometimes" (see Diagram 2.3). *Cosmopolitan* was also popular (26 percent of respondents read it "often" or "sometimes"), especially among women (39 percent of women read it "often" or "sometimes" compared with 14 percent of men). *Ia Molodoi*—an offshoot of *AiF* with a newspaper format—was read with similar frequency to *Cosmopolitan*, although its readership was spread almost evenly across young men and women. *Ia Molodoi* was the only mass newspaper in Samara and Ul'ianovsk to be directly targeted at young people, and it addressed young people in more serious and less primitive tones than the youth magazine *COOL!*, but in less sophisticated format than the quality youth magazines *Ptiuch* and *OM*. *Sobesednik* was similar in its choice of subject matter and style to *Spid-Info*, and was also popular among young people, occupying fifth place in terms of readership (19 percent of the sample read it "often" or "sometimes"). In fact *Liza*, was slightly more popular (20 percent read it "often" or "sometimes"), but primarily among women (34 percent of women read it compared to 6 percent of men). *Shtuchka*, a *Rovesnik* magazine, targeted at girls from sixteen to eighteen years old, was much less popular (4 percent read this magazine).

Ptiuch and *OM* magazines were not widely known in the provinces; at the time of the survey, only 4 percent of young people read *OM* "often" or "sometimes" and just 3 percent read *Ptiuch*. This low level of readership is probably explained by the fact that the magazines targeted a rather narrow group and wider readership was inhibited by the complexity of the text and layout. Nevertheless those respondents who frequented clubs or were fans of electronic music did read these magazines.

In general, and in no small part because of the success of Russian magazine publishing, young Russians are voracious readers. Despite being firmly lodged in the digital electronic age, reading remains the third most popular form of spending time among young Russians (RNISiNP 1998, 49).

Ivan Goes to Hollywood: Film and Video

Film and video were the next most important sources of information for young people after reading. The survey in Samara and Ul'ianovsk revealed an enormous diversity of film viewing; more than a thousand different "favorite" films were named by the respondents in the survey.[10] This made it difficult to establish any clear preferences among youth—in any case favorite films quickly changed and those cited in 1997 will have been largely replaced with the latest Hollywood sensations. The data did allow a number of tentative conclusions, however.

The results of the survey confirmed those of sociological research conducted in 1995 in Moscow, which suggested that school pupils watched much the same types of films as adults did, that is primarily action films (*boeviki*), historical adventure films, science fiction movies, and "erotic" films (Rondeli 1995;[11] Zlokazova 1996, 88). The Samara and Ul'ianovsk survey also revealed that "action films" (including those of the thriller, sci-fi, and melodrama subgenres) were the most popular films among young people. Almost all were American in origin, and the two most popular in November 1997 were *Terminator* starring Arnold Schwarzenegger[12] and Bruce Willis's *Die Hard* films. The popularity of foreign films continued a trend from the late Soviet period; among the ten most attended movies in 1984, two were foreign. Given that at the time only 25–30 of the 250–300 films on release annually were foreign, this suggested that the average popularity of a Western film was at least twice that of a Soviet film (Shlapentokh 1989, 147).

The 1990s saw a sharp fall in the number of Russian films shown in movie theaters. Research from 1994 suggested that 74 percent of the rolling repertoire of movie theaters was taken up by American films and for the age group 15–18, only one in seven movie attendances was for a Russian film, while 59 percent were for American ones (Zlokazova 1996, 88). The Samara and Ul'ianovsk survey also revealed the dominance of American films in young people's preferences. However, Russian, and Soviet, comedies remained popular among young people, and one Russian film *The Peculiarities of National Hunting* (A. Vasiliev, 1995) was almost as frequently cited as a "favorite" film as the American action films just mentioned.

The wide range of films cited as "favorites" in the Samara and Ul'ianovsk survey suggests that film watching occurred primarily in the home, on video, rather than at movie theaters. This was borne out by other research revealing a general decline in the number of moviegoers in Russia. In 1991 around 20–30 percent of the population went to the movies, by 1994 this had fallen to 7–12 percent (Zlokazova 1996, 86). Among the reasons respondents gave for the decline in the popularity of the movies were high prices, high crime levels, and the hope that the film would be shown on cable or national television. However, this general decline had led to a rejuvenation of the movie audience; in 1996 it was estimated that 80 percent of audiences were under thirty years old and that around 50 percent of young respondents went to the movies between one and three times per month (ibid.).

Indeed, in the second half of the 1990s, the situation of the movies had improved somewhat. In the large cities there had been a growth in popularity of so-called specialist theaters offering a much wider choice of films. Old theaters had been refurbished and new ones opened. However, high ticket prices remained an important factor holding back the stream of moviegoers, and in the provinces there were still only a small number of theaters with a very limited repertoire. American action films continued to dominate, therefore, and high-grossing Hollywood films, featuring Hollywood stars such as Leonardo Di Caprio, had become the new "favorites."

The Reinvention of Radio

McLuhan asserted that the content of each cultural epoch was dominated by a communication technology particularly suited to the development of the consciousness of the age (McLuhan 1964). In tribal society the dominant means of communication was speech—making it the "society of the ear." In Russia, the rapid increase in popularity of various types of radio stations at the end of the 1990s, however, suggested the beginning of a new "age of the ear."

The radio boom in Russia took hold only after the representative survey in Samara and Ul'ianovsk had been conducted, and so its extent was not fully captured in the empirical data. Of all the media, in Russia it was radio that had most successfully exploited the growth in demand for mediated communication. In effect radio had come to act as an accessible and simplified version of the Internet, where one's personal space could be hooked into the public space without detriment to the direct identity of the person. The centrality of the voice in the medium of radio allowed individuals to play with identity, to create and perceive not what existed, but what was desired. It is not surprising, therefore, that radio DJs had become cult figures equivalent to pop stars. In particular interactive radio projects—when two or more strangers came into contact on air—appeared to have had great success in capturing youth audiences.

The growth in popularity of the station Russkoe radio had been particularly rapid and astonishing.[13] Russkoe radio played on an emergent new patriotic feeling among young people in its feature *Russkie gvozdi*, which had begun as a program devoted to Soviet songs of the 1950s and 1960s. The program also ridiculed current pop "hits" by scrutinizing their lyrics. Following its radio success, its presenter, Nikolai Fomenko, began hosting a television show during which the audience and a well-known guest group would, together, compose a new "hit." A similar appeal to a base Russian nostalgia and patriotism had been made successfully in the show *Starie pesni o glavnom*, which consisted of remixes of Soviet songs of the 1950s through 1970s by young singers and, in the public service advertising campaign "Russkii proekt" in 1996. Most recently, a highly popular documentary-soap series on television (*Ulitsy razbitykh fonarei*) by the Russkoe video film company had successfully sought to repair the public image of Russia's criminal investigation department and other law enforcement bodies.

A peculiar feature of Russkoe radio broadcasts, however, was the exploitation of anti-American feeling, ridiculing, for example, American self-confidence and self-absorption. For example, in one program, referring to a poll conducted among Americans on the outstanding figures of the twentieth century, it was claimed that Americans believed that the United States was the leading nation, and that the greatest events in the twentieth century were related solely to American history. The radio station enthusiastically joined in the condemnation of NATO's operation in former Yugoslavia, and the cult figure of Russkoe radio, Nikolai Fomenko, was the original source of the one-liner most readily associated with this difficult period in relations between Russia and the West: "Russian missiles and American airplanes were made for each other."[14]

Advertising: Russians Just Don't Buy It

In the former USSR, foreign (American and European) advertising played a minor role. The most active presence was that of advertising organizations from the former socialist countries of Eastern Europe, reflected in regular advertisements in the press, luminous advertisements on the roofs of buildings, traditional seminars, presentations, fairs, and exhibitions. Vneshtorgreklama, a department of the foreign trade ministry of the USSR, held a monopoly in this field and acted as the main partner of foreign advertising agencies in the country.

In the early 1990s a number of leading foreign advertising specialists and heads of advertising agencies spent some time in Russia. It was in this period that the number of joint-venture advertising agencies began to increase dramatically. The first Russian partners to form joint advertising agencies were large government structures or departments, which had experience in foreign economic activity, advertising, or publishing, such as Soiuztorgreklama, Vneshtorgizdat, Vneshtorgreklama, Promstroibank SSSR, and APN. Joint-venture enterprises created in the early 1990s shared a common fate, however. After a few years the Russian share was quietly bought out by the Western corporations (Young & Rubicam, Ogilvie & Mather, BBDO, and others). During this period these companies, together with a number of other major world advertisers (DMB, Dentsu, Publicitas, Saatchi & Saatchi, McCann Erickson, Grey Advertising, InterEspaces, Carat, Jeronimo, BLD) gradually conquered the Russian market, taking responsibility for advertising for Procter & Gamble, Philip Morris, General Motors, and a number of other large producers of food and other mass demand products that filled the shelves of Russian shops (Cherniakhovskii 1994, 47). The huge growth in advertising activity in all areas and branches of the economy in 1992–94 was a product not so much of rapid market growth, however, but the result of entrepreneurs seeing advertising as "a unique opportunity to make money out of nothing" (Rozhkov 1994, 9). During this period, hundreds of new advertising companies sprang up in Russia.

The "virtual" nature of the market was exposed from 1995 when the advertising market suffered its first collapse. During the last quarter of 1994, for example, the television advertising market was estimated to be worth approximately U.S.$180–200 million, but in the first quarter of 1995 this estimate had fallen to U.S.$100–110 million. One reason for this would appear to be the dramatic fall in production and circulating capital, both of which hit new lows at the beginning of 1995. This decline in the market was accompanied by the first attempts to regulate the advertising market in Russia by the state. On July 19, 1995 a federal law on advertising was adopted, and in the same year, the Public Advertising Council (Obshchestvennii Sovet po reklame) was created. One of the functions of the latter body was to monitor the extent to which advertising campaigns conducted by firms conformed to societal "norms." The public was further "protected" from advertising by a presidential decree, signed on February 17, 1995, "On guaranteeing the rights and welfare of citizens in the light of the spread of advertising"; and in Moscow, a local decree from the mayor required companies and products to be advertised using Cyrillic rather than Latin letters. Although at first this resulted in the English words, and company and product names, simply being written in Cyrillic type, a subsequent law on the compulsory duplication of the text in Russian on all imported goods ensured that slogans and names were properly cited in Russian.[15]

Beginning in 1996, Russian regional advertising expanded significantly as both foreign and Russian companies increased their interest in developing regional markets, and the first conference for regional advertising agencies took place in September 1996 at the International Trade Center in Moscow. The expansion of the advertising market in 1996–97 was significantly facilitated by the stormy pre-election and election shows of 1996–97; an estimated 26 percent of the money spent on advertising in 1996 was political (V. Evstaf'ev 1998). The fees charged for conducting election campaigns were extremely high: from between U.S.$25–50,000 for election to a regional legislative assembly to U.S.$100–140 million for a presidential campaign (ibid.). By the beginning of 1998, Russia's advertising market was the eighth-largest in Europe, even if per capita spending on advertising remained low.[16]

Advertising as a medium is of particular interest to the study presented in this book, since it is both a *new* information medium to Russia and because, unlike the other media discussed above, in its emergent form it was essentially "Western." Prior to the financial crisis of August 17, 1998, for example, 90 percent of television advertising was Western-produced.[17] After the crisis the situation shifted in favor of Russian advertisers, since as many Western advertisers fled the Russian market; and in September 1988, market leadership in television advertising in Russia was assumed by the Russian corporation *Dovgan'*. The overall impact of the August 1998 crisis, however, was the serious contraction of the Russian advertising market.

One of the main hypotheses at the beginning of the research undertaken for this book was that both the novelty and Western nature of advertising would make it a highly attractive medium to young people, and that advertising—particularly Western advertising—would act as a powerful tool for relaying images of the West and as a mechanism for the inclusion of youth into the global market environment. From the initial representative survey conducted in Samara and Ul'ianovsk, indeed it was found that young people were exposed to a good deal of advertising. However, advertising was considered less important than many other media (newspapers, magazines, television, video) as an information source (see Diagram 2.1). Moreover, extensive focus groups revealed that young people were highly skeptical of, indeed irritated by, current advertising. This confirmed findings elsewhere suggesting that former Soviet citizens showed higher rates of skepticism with regard to advertising than other nationals. A study of forty countries showed that only 9 percent of former Soviet Union residents believed advertising to produce good information and that only 10 percent thought it respected the intelligence of consumers, compared to global averages of 38 percent and 30 percent respectively (Richard 1995). This was partially the fault of both crude advertising by inexperienced Russian companies and poorly adapted Western advertising; in the late 1990s there had been significant improvements on both these fronts. A survey of 149 employees of advertising and PR agencies, information agencies, and social organizations published in 1998, for example, showed that 76 percent of involved professionals considered the professional standard of Russian advertising to have improved ("U reklamy tozhe est' reiting" 1998).[18] Nevertheless, the high levels of awareness of the constructed nature of images and messages in advertising meant that it was treated as a source of information not so much about "the West" as about "how the West would like to be seen."

Virtual Information Spaces: The Internet et al.

Use of the Internet in Russia has grown rapidly in recent years. Over the period of this research (1996–99) the number of Internet users in Russia quadrupled, and estimates at the end of the decade suggested that between 1.1 percent and 3.7 percent of the population used the Internet (Harter 2000, 8). Internet usage in Russia remained low in comparison to leading European countries, however; Internet penetration in Finland, Norway, and Sweden was around 30 percent of the population (ibid.). Social survey data suggested that young people (18–24 year olds) in Russia constituted 44 percent—the largest single group—of the most active Internet users.[19] Russians under thirty-five constituted over three-quarters (76 percent) of this core user group. The representative survey in Ul'ianovsk and Samara revealed that around 6 percent of young people used the web as a source of information, although this percentage would undoubtedly have been higher had Moscow been included. In Moscow, Internet cafes were already beginning to appear in 1998; although in January 1998 (when fieldwork in Moscow was conducted) advertising for these cafes had appeared before they had actually opened.

At the time of empirical research—1997–98—actual Internet usage among respondents was low; only cultural producers (such as DJs and those involved in musical performance) mentioned the Internet at all. Since then, there has been a rapid expansion of web sites providing information and chat rooms,[20] and there has been a growing—although sometimes poorly maintained—number of sites related to specific types of music, including Russian rock, rave, club life, pop, and folk music.[21] Western-based sites also provided information on developments on Russian music scenes and information on tours and performances.[22] Some Russian sites recreated the *tusovka* feeling; a Samara-based "doom gothic" site, for example, included a "family album" of photos of the *tusovka* who had generated the site.[23]

Other "virtual" forms of communication—not dependent on access to home computers or Internet cafes—developed alongside the Internet. One vivid example was the *Morning Jam* program on a trendy Moscow radio station (106.8) which invited its listeners to page the program's presenters; the messages were read out on air. A regular group of young listeners began paging and became known as the "Jammers" and formed their own virtual youth cultural group (*tusovka*), with its own nicknames. The Jammers began to meet up and subsequently outlived the program that had inspired them. Rayport Rabodzeenko describes a similar phenomenon surrounding the magazine *Soroka* (Magpie), based in St. Petersburg. The magazine had begun as the "personal pages" section of an advertising and classifieds circular that began publication in 1991. The magazine used a specific format of 200 characters in the form of a "coupon," and young people, often using pseudonyms to enhance the intrigue, filled out these coupons as a means of exchanging messages and jokes. Because of the particular format required, they simultaneously engaged in a unique literary form (Rayport Rabodzeenko 1998, 336). By 1994, "section 801" had become so popular that its publishers sanctioned its takeover of the whole space of the original *Soroka*. From the autumn of 1993, physical gatherings began to take place at an established site for hanging out in the city and, later, developed into an initiative to set up a youth center (337). Thus, although young people enjoyed the opportunities provided by these "virtual" forms of interaction to "remake" their identities and develop new "selves," the desire to turn "virtual" into "real" communications appeared to prevail.

Molding the Youth Cultural Space: Producers' Perspectives

The landscape of the new media space of the 1990s was not shaped by young people alone. Professionals working in the new Russian information space envisaged their relationship with their youth audiences in distinctive ways and sought to mold the media after this image. The material presented in the next section is drawn from expert interviews conducted with professionals working in the press, television, film, and advertising industries whose roles were specifically related to a youth audience or market, and is used to analyze how producers sought to lead their market.[24]

"Good Taste": The New Ideology?

In Soviet times, the media followed the "party line" quite strictly. Magazine, television, and radio editors were part of the *nomenklatura*; they were carefully selected and approved by the regional party committee. In the post-Soviet period, publishers, editors, and journalists were suddenly given the freedom to determine which events to describe and how to describe them; but at the same time, the financial backers of media enterprises emerged as new interested parties in the framing of editorial priorities.

Not surprisingly, all the experts interviewed insisted that they currently enjoyed total freedom and independence in creating their editorial portfolios, and even more so in their selection of preferred themes and values. They emphasized that Soviet "re-education" agendas were long gone (Igor' Rozhkov) and that ideological criteria had been replaced by artistic concerns: "*OM* magazine is a creative [*avtorskii*] project; it contains no ideology, no politics. The creator [*avtor*] is me. At the root of any creative project there is emotion, and emotion is a fleeting, fragmentary, unrepeatable and unpredictable thing . . . [magazines such as] *The Economist*, or *Ovoshchevodstvo* [Vegetable Farming] may need to gear themselves to their readership. What we do is art" (Igor' Grigor'ev).

Despite the worthy declarations, however, a real tension was apparent between the need to provide a commercially viable product and to maintain a trendy youth audience that would be alienated by material that was either too banal and "poppy" (*popsovii*) or too elite and bohemian.

It is traditionally held that the promotion of pop in a publication is evidence of the editorial team's lack of taste, excessive commercialism, and intention to focus on a very average audience. Thus, during interviews, media professionals sought to emphasize their cultural discernment; becoming too pop-oriented might lose one credibility with a key section of the youth audience.[25] On the other hand, most youth publications and television and radio programs remained commercially viable because of their commitment to mass popular culture: "I think that in the 1990s this [promoting pop] is the only possible way for anyone to survive—not just us. It doesn't matter . . . whether we like it aesthetically or not. The Spice Girls or Blestiashchie are just as much of a phenomenon as Nick Cave, and so for us they are just as interesting" (Anzor Kankulov).

The so-called quality publications (*elitnie izdaniia*)[26] were less focused on broad tastes and took as their starting point the ideas, norms, values, and cultural images of distinct sets of youth (such as clubbers, bikers, heavy metal fans, etc.), promoting ideas that would be recognized by "their own [*svoi*]" people. However, an equal tension was apparent in interviewees' statements with regard to "alternative" or "bohemian" culture. Editors sought to emphasize the accessibility of their publications:

We do not target the "golden," "progressive" youth, who are more interested in club-type things. (Igor' Chernyshkov)

Ours is the most accessible youth publication. Our magazine can be bought—and is bought—in the most remote regions. Ia-molodoi is a cheap, mass-circulation youth publication. (Igor' Rozhkov)

Thus editors trod a fine line between avoiding "bohemian" language and style, which might deter a wide audience, and retaining those "alternative" elements essential for maintaining "non-pop" status. They squared this circle by arguing that they provided a non-bohemian magazine about bohemian life, thus opening up a bohemian world to "ordinary" people (Anzor Kankulov).

The peculiar resolution of the irreconcilable demands of art and commerce elaborated by the media professionals interviewed is interesting. On the one hand, they referred to their intrinsic knowledge of their readership or audience, their tastes and preferences (Igor' Chernyshkov): "Our typical reader is a young man of twenty-five who dresses in a certain style, who listens to a certain type of Western music, who watches certain films and reacts to them in a certain way.[27] He finds certain names irritating because they contradict his lifestyle, his understanding, and his ideas" (Anzor Kankulov).

On the other hand, editors categorically ascribed their own tastes to everybody, thereby supplanting the youth audience and its tastes with their own: "If we ever do write about popular figures—people everyone is talking about—then we choose those who we think are worth it. We don't write about NANA, Vlad Stashevksii, Masha Rasputina, or Filipp Kirkorov,[28] because for all their popularity I think they are banal" (Igor' Rozhkov).

The stark reality that the youth media were inevitably consumer-led, therefore, did not prevent editors pursuing their own cultural policies. The counterdemands of youth cultural credibility meant that an aesthetics-led approach, if successfully implemented, could be effective as a sort of niche-marketing.[29] Thus cultural producers stressed not the size of the readership, but its quality (composition). The following statement from the editor of *OM* reads almost as a manifesto of this new ideology:

Taste tends toward entropy, that is, it always averages out. And the more you try to correspond to it, the more you become average yourself. And you end up with an average mass. But things that produce an unusual reaction are always clearly more successful. If you give people not something that they want and can express in their own words, but something that they didn't even suspect existed, they like it, but they can't express it themselves, because if they could they would be famous themselves. . . . We try to do what will be popular in, say, six months' time, to do what is obvious to us, because we have more information, we're at the center of things and so on. I am quite convinced that in our country, in every city, big or small, there are always some people—maybe not many, but some people—listening to Oasis while everyone else listens to Ruki vverkh . . . we work for Moscow, for them. For these people are the cultural cream. They form a positive community, people who are trying to do something culturally. Our position now is that our circulation is in fact not as large as that of our competitors, but our influence is no less great. Influencing people does not depend on the circulation; we're not desperate just to sell more copies. (Anzor Kankulov)

Cultural Content: The West as "Norm"

Cultural producers recognized a fundamental shift in the post-Soviet information space. Interviewees no longer perceived a need from their audience for background cultural information about "who is who," what was fashionable, what people were listening to and reading. Young people, they felt, were informed, and many Western names and cult figures were well established in young people's cultural repertoire. Thus media producers could focus on the "normal" work of journalists in covering current events, new trends, and new faces (Igor' Grigor'ev). The colossal influence on youth audiences of the latest TV channels (MTV for example) and easier access to Internet sites were also understood to have accelerated the process of integrating mass audiences into the global contexts of youth cultures. This "horizontalization" of relations had led to a more mosaic-like character of contemporary youth tastes and cultures. Idols were quickly replaced, and often existed alongside each other; and the arrival of one new cult figure did not require the displacement of another. For media producers this suggested a new generation that had "fewer mentors and idols . . . more choices but fewer desires" (Petr Oleinikov).

Russian media producers themselves were already well integrated into the global information network. At the beginning of the new publishing boom, it was generally accepted that Russian magazines were copies of Western ones,[30] and Western sources were often directly reproduced. By the end of the 1990s, Russian information agencies had become networked into global information centers and their databases, and individual magazines had established direct contacts. As elsewhere, editors' priorities were to obtain information first; an exclusive for Russia was the goal, even if this meant buying information from Western sources (Igor' Grigor'ev).

The West and Western culture exerted a direct influence, not just on the formation of taste preferences among youth audiences, but also on the content and means of delivery of the information targeted at them. Expert interviewees had a rather idealized image of the West as a site of total democracy, freedom, and stability; in other words everything that was missing from Russia. The Western way of life was perceived as a kind of "norm": "The West means striving for freedom and independence, the opportunity to live freely and independently and achieve one's goals. Basically I find it difficult to draw a distinction between the image of the West and the image of normal human existence" (Aleksandr Kachalov).

The main thematic trends in youth publications were music, film, and fashion. However, while America was seen to be the "benchmark" for film (Igor' Grigor'ev), Britain was considered to be the authority in the field of music (Igor' Chernyshkov). Moreover, some publications focused generally on America, while others were centered on British youth cultural trends, in a more or less conscious editorial stance: "American culture . . . I don't know, maybe it's because we are in Europe, we have a different view on most things. American culture is somehow removed from us. It is aggressive, mass-oriented, self-satisfied. And it is enclosed. It is very difficult to break into it from outside. . . . It was just natural for us to focus on Britain. But not on France or Germany—no way" (Anzor Kankulov).

There was a contradiction in the assessment of American and British influences. On the one hand, all the experts—in unison with the survey respondents—recognized Britain (and particularly London) as the center of youth culture, although America was accorded unquestioned priority in film, despite a certain element of skepticism and cynicism about a Hollywood tendency toward simplifying and idealizing life. Moreover, despite the perceived decadence of British culture, it was British rather than American culture that continued to be seen as embodying the highest level of quality and sincerity: "British culture, in my opinion, is the core of European civilization. They have achieved a position whereby their youth culture is the quintessence of contemporary culture as a whole. And a typical person from Britain embodies those qualities which you look at and think—that's modern, that's exactly how things are now. A sort of simplicity of approach. An absence of snobbery" (Evgenii Lungin).

Despite the focus on Western values, Western democracy, and Western culture, which was used according to the editor-in-chief of *Rovesnik* magazine "consciously" to "show Russian reality in the light of Western values, ideals, and experience" (Igor' Chernyshkov), media producers were concerned to provide "measured" information about the West (Igor' Rozhkov). Thus expert interviewees were rather critical in their assessment of the development of the Russian version of the global MTV project, saying that it was far removed from the best examples of American, European, and Asian MTV: "There, MTV somehow unites young people. There are festivals, concerts. MTV here is just a series of videos, and the presenters are inept in the way they talk to the musicians. It's just meaningless waffle" (Evgenii Lungin).

For one Russian television producer, this indicated a deeper problem with the whole concept of a music video channel: "MTV provides nothing of interest. This is also a Western idea. Everything is based on money. All for the sake of money. . . . Some rapper releases a record somewhere in America, the company pays MTV some money, and they have to play this nonsense a certain number of times. So that it sells. A video is like an advertisement for the artist" (Petr Oleinikov).

When asked to predict MTV Russia's potential for development, interviewees spoke of its short-term nature, saying that if the Russian version of this global product did not produce quality programming, then it would not survive. It should be noted that at the end of the 1990s, MTV still could not be received in provincial cities such as Ul'ianovsk, and for young people in these regions, it was experienced only via the various clips and gimmicks that were copied from it and used as inserts in other channels' programs.

Thus media producers did not consider everything from the West to be suited to, or likely to be successful in, Russia,[31] and this made media producers feel a significant responsibility. What came out of this new and fertile Russian media market very much depended on what was put in: "Our society, unlike Western society, is monopolar. There are as yet no points of reference, or clearly defined taboos, in the legislative and moral sense. In fact, the territory itself isn't even defined, let alone the taboos. Everything is so ill-defined that people are just left to their own devices" (Evgenii Lungin).

This lack of definition rendered the future of all new media uncertain. The future of the Russian "glossy" magazines formed the subject of discussion by the editors of *OM* and *Ptiuch* themselves—Anzor Kankulov and Igor' Shulinskii—in an edition of *Ptiuch* at the beginning of the 2000 (*Ptiuch* 2000). The rather pessimistic conclusions were that they would become the hostages of global markets. If the Russian economy managed to sustain them at all, they would be forced to follow a perceived global trend (stemming from American and British magazines) toward "pop" and "simplicity."

Advertising: The Western Invasion

As in the press and television, in advertising also, the first years of rapid development were characterized by the domination of large Western companies. During those first few years there was a widely held belief that Western experience in the field would be extremely useful for Russia. The growth of consumer culture in Russia, alongside "universal" psychological laws of perception and interpretation, suggested that established advertising strategies could be used effectively in Russia.[32] Indeed, at that time advertising was perceived to be a possible means of facilitating Russia's incorporation into the international community.

A decade of development in Russian advertising, however, had shown that establishing brands was fraught with unique difficulties that were unlikely to be anticipated by analyzing other developing markets. At one level, this was a result of the very rapid entry of Western advertisers into Russia's fledgling market, which meant that consumers were offered patronizing, condescending, superficial, and often inappropriate advertising messages (Madden 1996, 9). The concern with "brand awareness" together with the financial benefits of employing global advertising strategies, moreover, often led Western advertisers to ignore or downplay potential peculiarities of the Russian market and supply Russia directly with advertising that had not been adapted at all. As early as 1993–95 several pieces of research were conducted into the specific nature of Russia's advertising and consumer market (Omel'chenko 1993; Grinchenko Wells 1994). By 1996, Western companies themselves were talking of the need to adapt their advertising to the specific features of the Russian market. Thus although the size and potential of the Russian market originally attracted Western companies, the realization that marketing and advertising campaigns would require huge expenditure deterred many firms.

Other companies, however, developed a range of new product marketing and advertising strategies to address the problem. Knorr, for example, launched a new product—a potato pancake—using a Russian recipe.[33] McVities (an English cookie company) opted not to produce special packaging to sell their product in Russia but rather to design packaging for the international market, with a simple product name that was easy to remember for non-English speakers, and ingredients that translated easily into several languages, including Russian. To promote the product, they produced a special television video about McVities cookies with some input from a Russian advertising agency.

By the end of the 1990s, local staff were being recruited with more regularity to work in large advertising companies in Russia, which facilitated Russian input into advertising strategies. Moreover, in the Russian regions—where Western clients did not figure and thus global images and messages were not promoted—there was evidence of the emergence of a distinctive Russian advertising approach characterized by creativity, a social slant, and the frequent use of sex and sexuality to attract the audience (Iurii Grymov).

No assumptions should be made about Russian advertisers producing more appropriate advertising, however; the Russian advertising sphere remained afflicted by structural as well as cultural problems. Professionals working in advertising who were interviewed pointed to the fact that the development of any national advertising practice required a stable cultural and ethical context. In other words a sufficiently long period of stability was required in order for basic values to be formed and adopted by significant communities that could then serve as the basis for the development of the so-called big ideas of advertising companies. Such "big ideas," it was suggested, could only emerge where there was a significant degree of personal and familial welfare and security allowing individuals and families to orient themselves toward self-development and self-improvement. Russian advertising, however, operated in an environment in which only a small section of the population was secure and relatively well off. Thus advertising in Russia worked primarily for very small market sectors whose primary need was actually little more than to create a certain image and maintain status. This heightened the volatility of consumer choice and reinforced the uncertainty of the Russian market in general. As the executive creative director of ARTAMS agency in Moscow put it: "Everything is unstable and rickety, and unstudied. Russia lacks a moral and ethical direction that can be accepted or rejected and flouted. Most Russian people have nothing to go by. . . . Everything is so mixed up in this country today that it is almost impossible to guess how the end user is going to react to an advertisement without doing research" (Viacheslav Cherniakhovskii).

This provides one explanation for the discrepancy between the growing quality of advertising products and the partial decline in the real advertising market.

Global Advertising Images and the Youth Audience

Global advertising is based on the belief that certain products and brands can assume global significance. Coca Cola, for example, is advertised not as an American product, but as something that unites cultures throughout the world; global advertising campaigns thus employ a uniform set of meanings, common to the whole world (Leslie 1995, 414).

In some cases, expert interviewees confirmed that advertisements indeed required no adaptation for the Russian market (Oleg Stukalov). The globality of an advertisement's appeal, it was generally agreed, depended upon its target audience. Thus the creative director of a Novosibirsk based advertising agency stated that "if I am making a commercial for women who buy washing powder, I never permit myself to include any words written in English or have the action take place somewhere other than Russia" (Aleksandr Filiurin).

In contrast, advertising professionals in Russia confirmed the common opinion that youth audiences were more receptive to global images in advertising:

There is no difference in how Russian and American youth relate to things (including advertising). There is a difference between old people and young people. But for young people there are no borders and in this sense everything that is filmed for Western youth may be entirely suitable for Russian youth too. Young people everywhere are thinking about the same problems. Plus we now have the opportunity to think about them with access to the same things as the American who is thinking about them—the same pictures, films, and magazines. The culture is a little different, of course, but for young people it is still very close. (Aleksandr Shevelevich)

Many experts saw the MTV-style delivery of material in the form of video clips, gimmicks, humor, and constant action to lie at the core of successful marketing to young people and thus lifted ideas directly from MTV in their own advertisements for young people, as indicated by the head of an Ul'ianovsk based advertising agency: "Perhaps things don't need as much adaptation for young people—they are the same everywhere . . . the same roller skates . . . MTV style—rapid switching between frames, and a fast-moving camera. Almost the entire world watches MTV, and is party to the same culture" (Oleg Stukalov).

Russian advertising professionals saw young people as essentially more mobile and adaptable to new ideas and as "more receptive to an unadapted advertisement created purely from Western material" (Aleksandr Filiurin). Although differences among youth, especially with regard to social stratification, or rather spending power, were recognized (Vladimir Zabavskii), in general terms, young people were perceived to use advertisements quite differently from adults. Advertisements often did not achieve their primary purpose of encouraging young people to buy things. However, elements of advertising—phrases, ideas, rhymes, and jingles—were reproduced within youth cultural groups and thus became culturally entrenched: "Our people are very malleable, particularly young people. Children run around shouting advertising slogans at each other" (Igor' Rozhkov).

At the heart of global receptivity among youth, according to advertising professionals, was young people's adoration of all things Western: "Unfortunately, if you show our young people today an advertisement that uses the American flag or folk tales, and one using Russian ones, they will choose the former. That's the situation today. Young people know that Americans live better and that everything that comes from America is better. They will show a preference for American goods" (Aleksandr Shevelevich).

This preference was perceived to be "natural" by the interviewee above, although others considered it at least partially a result of advertising itself, which deliberately developed and promoted the American way of life, American symbols, culture, and ideology (Igor' Rozhkov).

It would be wrong to exaggerate the reality of young people's "global" orientation, however. The research conducted for this book suggests that young people did not relate at all to some global images, seeing in them no more than a pretty picture of life "over there." For example, despite the large-scale promotion of Merinda and Seven-Up, and Fanta and Sprite,[34] most young people preferred the original Pepsi and Coke to their "colorful" brothers and sisters. An analysis of these advertisements makes it clear that while all the advertising campaigns for these products had drawn on "global" elements of youth experience, some appeared to "speak" to Russian youth and others did not. In this context the glossy, youthful campaigns for Sprite using the slogan "Image is nothing, thirst is everything. Don't go dry" ("Imidzh—nichto, zhazhda—vse. Ne dai sebe zasokhnut") and for Merinda, employing the slogan "Life is good when you don't rush your drink" ("Zhizn' khorosha, kogda p'esh ne spesha") proved relatively ineffective compared to Pepsi's simple advertising slogan "Buy and win" ("Pokupai i vyigrivai"). Whereas the latter exploited a genuinely common love of football, the former centered on Western-style youth cultures (Sprite) or a very "foreign" image to Russian youth of young people sitting quietly enjoying a long soft drink in a bar.

Although these differences were subtle, they were increasingly recognized by advertisers as they emerged from the long love-affair with global advertising and increasingly implanted into transnational, Western-style advertising distinctive national characteristics. In this way they retained the benefits of brand awareness without assuming the globality of images.[35]

Some advertisers went further still, seeing national images as highly successful in the promotion of products, even among young people (Igor' Krylov). Two expert interviewees cited the example of advertising produced in the style of Eralash,[36] whose familiarity allowed the advertisement to be viewed as more than "an ad" (Igor' Krylov; Aleksandr Filiurin). "National" images were defined as images reflecting everyday realities and experiences in Russia, and while their effectiveness was generally interpreted positively, their use, for example, in advertising Western products was viewed as problematic (Oleg Stukalov). This conformed to a wider trend in Russian advertising toward the use of images appealing to feelings of national pride. This strategy was particularly evident in a range of domestically produced dairy products such as the "From granny's cupboard" series launched by the Lianozovskii dairy, featuring a friendly "babushka," or the series bearing the name of Ivan Poddubnii—a well-known figure from Russian history—who, the advertisements claimed, was sharing the secret of his strength. Other parts of the food industry had revived the use of animals, a practice common in Russian advertising at the beginning of the twentieth century.

Other campaigns had been less successful in exploiting national images, however. The campaign for the "Country cottage" ("Domik v derevne") series employed another *babushka* figure, but one that bore little relation to a Russian granny, being well-groomed, dressed in a white pinafore, and wearing little round glasses, which, in Russia, had only ever been worn by the intelligentsia at the turn of the century. The attempt by the fastfood chain "Russian Bistro" to adopt a character from Russian history—"the genial fellow in the shako"[37]—was also sharply criticized in *Reklama* magazine for both its inauthentic look and its poor image, in comparison to its main rival, McDonald's.

Thus, at the end of the 1990s the attempt to generate a national Russian advertising space had been only partially successful. Although the instantaneously obvious difference between Western and Russian advertisements had been confined to the past, Western advertising continued to enjoy a greater depth of technical experience (Aleksandr Kachalov; Evgenii Lungin). On the other hand, Russian advertisers had a distinct advantage in appreciating those elements of Western advertising that did not speak to Russian audiences, such as the use of shock tactics or extreme human suffering to capture attention,[38] black humor, images of American affluence or extremely "arty" advertisements. At the end of the 1990s, Russian advertising remained only emergent, however. The leading role was still played by Western advertising agencies. Regional advertising in Russia was less bound by external forces in creative decision-making, but was highly constrained financially. The difficulty in establishing a cultural base for Russian advertising was directly related to the absence of a firm ethical context supported by the basic values of the middle class. Adapting Western or "global" images to Russian conditions also continued to impact negatively on the effectiveness of advertising in the domestic information space. This was a result of both the superficial understanding of Russian culture among Western advertising "experts" and the weak "resistance" of Russian advertising professionals, who were constrained by both material factors (leading Western advertising agencies remained the major employers) and the paucity of data on advertising audiences in Russia that might have lent weight to their arguments. Thus television commercials in Russia continued to be adapted by foreign specialists, who emphasized brand awareness and cost-cutting in their advertising strategies, making the end product always more "global" than "local."

Conclusion

It is axiomatic to state that young people are *influenced* by the media. What has been argued in this chapter is that it is not the "influence" of the media on youth so much as the *interaction* between youth and the media that raises interesting questions for contemporary sociological research.

In Russia this mutual engagement has been manifest in attempts by message producers to attract young audiences, not only by keeping pace with the latest technologies, but by harnessing elements of contemporary youth lifestyles. Young people have responded not only by engaging with media intermediaries in acts of style "consumption" but also by employing them in various style games. In the late 1990s, pure, "subcultural" styles were becoming a thing of the past; stylistic movements, genre features, and "subcultural" styles (*prikidy*) had all intermingled and been redefined within a youth cultural practice increasingly exposed to market forces. The commercial sphere had appropriated symbols of youth as a sort of unique brand packaging. At the same time youth cultures avoided those cultural places that had been developed by business, choosing rather to take temporary possession of new places. For this reason, the youth media chose to "mediate" the relationship between global information and local youth cultural practice primarily through the juxtaposition of "underground" ("alternative," "bohemian") and "mass" ("pop culture") trends.

The study of the interaction between youth cultures and agents of the information space thus required not only market research, that is the analysis of cultural preferences and popularity ratings of various cultural "products," but also research into youth cultural spaces, both real and virtual. These spaces had emerged as the increasingly interactive nature of new media replaced traditional forms of contact between an information source and its user with cultural contact between consumers via media channels with their own distinctive texts, aesthetics, and language. Young people, who have experienced a deficit of public (socially significant) dialogue, appeared particularly drawn to media forms in which public and private had been interwoven in new forms. Thanks to interactive radio programs (and the Internet), the night space had become a youth space in which both communicative and physical interaction became virtual. Direct and indirect interaction did not merely complement each other in these practices, they intermingled to such an extent that the personal cultural space incorporated itself into the public, communicative space and vice versa.

3 Talking Global?

Images of the West in the Youth Media

Moya Flynn and Elena Starkova

The previous chapter charted the changing information space inhabited by Russian youth and suggested that new media producers often took Western culture and approaches as their standard or norm. This chapter looks more closely at the discourses of the West produced in the Russian youth media of the late 1990s. It provides a detailed analysis of the thematic context—music, fashion, film, video, television, youth culture—in which specific images of the West were located. It also considers how these discourses shaped what was understood to constitute territorially, and culturally, "the West." The chapter asks whether or not there is a single discursive West and how such a West, or "Wests," relates to Russia.

The analysis of images of the West presented focuses primarily on the medium of Russian youth magazines whose content was analyzed over the period 1996–98;[1] analysis of other media such as youth television[2] or advertising[3] is referred to where it provides interesting comparisons or contrasts.[4] Youth magazines provided images of the West mainly through the discussion of youth culture, music, film, and style. The youth world they created in this way was largely inclusive; a global youth cultural space was presented, of which Russia was a part. However, when concrete cultural phenomena, social values, and characteristics of specific countries were discussed, a greater sense of difference and distance was encountered and the relationship between Russia and the West appeared more problematic. The West emerged as a complex, multifaceted concept, whose meaning fluctuated across the magazines depending upon the context in which it was being represented.

Constructing a Global Youth Culture: Themes and Sites

As noted in the two previous chapters, young people in Russia were considered by discourse makers to be peculiarly "open" to global messages. The supposed global orientation of young people was used, in particular, by advertisers who employed "global images" in youth advertising—32 percent of the television advertising studied used "global" images[5]—and conversely, used images of youth to represent globality. The degree to which global spaces were constructed in Russian youth magazines depended upon both the type of magazine and the subject matter under discussion. The analysis that follows is thus structured around key thematic strands of the magazines—music, style, and film and television—and draws out key differences between mainstream and alternative magazines.

Music

Music was the staple diet of youth magazines, although publications such as *Spid-Info* and *Sobesednik* devoted less space to the discussion of music than exclusively youth-oriented magazines.[6] Individual magazines had different musical foci: *Rovesnik* concentrated on rock music; *OM* and *Ptiuch* provided a more analytic discussion of alternative, electronic music; and *COOL!* discussed pop music and the best-known, usually Western, rock groups. In all the magazines, however, the West—in particular America and Britain—featured prominently and the relative position of Russia in relation to "global" music scenes was discussed.

It was the electronic music and dance scene that appeared as the most "global" music scene. Magazines—primarily *OM* and *Ptiuch*—constructed a global space of electronic music and dance culture that transcended national borders; "a world musical universe" (*OM*, November 1997, 62) understood as a space of free access and interchange between different global sites (including Russia). The American scene, for example, appeared in *OM* and *Ptiuch* primarily via reference to the main centers of music production: Detroit was famous for "Detroit techno"; Chicago—for "club Chicago house" and jazz; and New York was the home of house music.[7]

This does not mean that national and regional specifics were not recognized, however. Indeed, the music discourse across the different publications was often constructed around a comparison of the American and

British music scenes (and culture as a whole); in the case of *OM* and *Ptiuch* magazines, America and Britain represented the two "poles" of Western music culture.

The American music industry was considered to be the largest and most unpredictable (*Ia Molodoi*) and to be traditionally closed to English musicians (*Rovesnik*). Recently, it was suggested, this cultural embargo had been breached by the British group Prodigy whose success in America was equated to the "export of a cultural revolution" (*Aida*, September 1997, 34). The success of Prodigy was attributed by the trendier magazines such as *Ptiuch* to the unusual accessibility of the group's music. This fitted the wider differentiation made between the *commercial* nature of American music and the *creative* aspect of the British music scene. In earlier issues of *Ptiuch*, America was often characterized as "conservative" and "culturally behind" in terms of new music production, although this was redressed in later issues. Music genres in America were considered to be socially rooted: house originated in the gay scene; hip hop in the black community; soul was the "consciousness" of the African-American population. In *Ptiuch* and *Rovesnik*, even individual American musicians appeared as representatives of social movements; Madonna, for example, was not just a highly successful singer, but also a model of new feminism and single motherhood.

Despite the acknowledged commercial dominance of America on the music scene, the discussion of music in the youth media was centered on Britain. London was frequently identified as a world center of music culture and "a mecca for any musician starting out" (*Shtuchka*, 1998, no. 5, 29). The representation of the British music scene in the 1990s stressed the passion and enthusiasm for dance culture and the club scene. *Typical* British music styles discussed were trip-hop, indie-rock, punk rock, jungle, and speed garage.[8] The magazine *OM* provided the most focused information on British music (and indeed British culture in general), including detailed, and often theoretical, discussions of British music, musicians, producers, and labels. *OM*, and to a lesser extent *Ptiuch* and *Rovesnik*, took a wider angle, discussing the music and club scenes outside London, including the development of drum and bass in Bristol and the Manchester dance scene.[9]

Other European countries were discussed mainly in relation to new electronic music. The magazine *OM* depicted France as rediscovering its own space on the international music scene, following the dominance of Anglo-American music, through the development of electronic music and a vibrant club scene in Paris. Germany was presented as the "homeland" of electronic music (thanks to the group Kraftwerk) and as the best place to record techno music (*OM* and *Ptiuch*). Holland was discussed largely in relation to the significance of gabber as an indigenous electronic style.[10]

Global musical influence and exchange was portrayed as moving almost exclusively from West to East, and the West thus featured prominently in all discussion of music in youth magazines. Although magazines aimed at more general audiences provided only individual references to certain musicians and groups, *OM*, *Ptiuch*, and *Rovesnik* provided information about Western music labels, and their relative popularity, and details of music awards.

In the sphere of club and electronic culture, the West was a source of musical influence in the most direct way; Russian DJs traveled to Europe and America to procure records (even though shops with direct supplies from the West had opened in Russia). More important was the wider influence of specific Western musical styles on the developing scene in Russia. In *Ptiuch*, and to a lesser extent *OM*, key events in the development of Russian variants of Western scenes such as techno and hard-core events,[11] break beat festivals, and raves were described in detail. The tone of such articles was inclusive; the events illustrated Russia's inclusion in global music scenes, and the quality of events was described in positive terms and often evidenced by the participation of Western DJs and musicians. The tone of inclusion was enhanced by the special attention paid to describing provincial Russian centers of electronic music. *Ptiuch*, for example, noted the popularity of techno in the Volga cities of Izhevsk and Votkinsk, that the center of hip hop culture was Saratov, and that goa trance[12] was popular in Altai territory. The newly independent state of Moldova, it was suggested, had a particular propensity toward hard core. In the latter two cases a connection was made between the popularity of the music and the specifics of the region—goa trance, it was claimed, had similarities to the thirteenth-century traditional music of Altai territory, and hard core to the traditional music of Moldova. Thus, although the West was considered to be the home of electronic music and to set current standards of production, nonetheless, Russia was placed very much within, not on the periphery, of a scene itself still developing.

Western influence on Russia was also experienced, according to the magazines, through "imitation," that is, the reproduction of the musical style, image, and behavior of Western musicians and groups. In many of the publications Britpop was said to be reproduced in the Russian context through such bands as Mumii Troll'[13] and Splin, although the main debate was about the rapid reproduction of Western "boy" and "girl" bands. There were frequent references to the iconic status of groups such as the Spice Girls, who, it was claimed, represented to Russian teenage girls an enviable independence and stylishness (*Sobesednik* 1997, no. 35, 15). The message of the Spice Girls, and other girl bands, was interpreted as feminist and, in the hope of distancing Russian variants from this label, Russian girl bands, despite their direct imitation of clothes, musical style, and image, were described as "feminine" rather than "feminist" and less aggressive than their Western counterparts.

The American and British electronic scenes were discussed extensively, but not accepted without criticism or evaluation. Rather, magazines such as *OM* and *Ptiuch* distinguished between commercial pop and electronic music, criticizing and rejecting the former. This was seen primarily on the pages of such magazines in the arrogant dismissal of "mediocre" young (Russian) people who "listen to pop" and who were contrasted to young people who were "progressive" in their taste and cultural consumption. However, the commercialization of music was portrayed also as an inevitability driven by the West as evidenced by reflections on the way in which both techno and rap had exchanged an earlier underground status for a mainstream and commercial existence. The distinction between commercial and alternative music was even more prevalent in magazines discussing rock music.[14] *Rovesnik*, for example, distinguished between "real" and "commercial" rock, giving space only to that which, it considered, fell within the former category. In this way *Rovesnik*, although placing Russian rock culture within a wider world music culture, constructed distinct scenes and focused almost exclusively on Western rock "there."[15] Rock music was presented as being produced in the West (primarily Britain and America) and subsequently received by Russia, the latter being firmly situated on the cultural periphery.

In the sphere of commercial rock and pop the boundary between commercial and alternative music was less meaningful, and thus magazines such as *Spid Info*, *Sobesednik*, *Ia Molodoi*, *Aida*, and *COOL!* engaged less readily in such debates. However, youth music programs on television[16] did address the issue at length, primarily through the medium of interviews conducted with Russian pop musicians. These discussions, arising from questions from young people in the audience as well as from the presenter, suggested Russian pop was divided into "traditional" and "commercial" variants and that Western influence was negative and commercializing.

The influence of Russian music on the West was portrayed as insignificant. Russian musicians—especially pop musicians—were represented as being unsuccessful in their attempts to win over the Western public despite the fact that they frequently recorded tracks and made video clips in the West. Although more than 60 percent of the play list on MTV Russia was Western in origin, MTV had never shown Russian bands performing abroad (Henderson 1999). The situation was a bit more equitable on the electronic music and club scenes, however. *Ptiuch* provided information about events it organized with the participation of leading Western performers in Moscow, and about "*Ptiuch*" evenings abroad (in Austria and Britain for example), which had brought Russian DJs to the attention of the West.[17] On the whole, however, the influence of the

Russian domestic music industry on the American and European scenes was considered to be marginal.

Style and Fashion

The West dominated the discussion of fashion—designer, couture, and mass-produced, high street fashion—in Russian youth magazines; Russia appeared in the fashion discourse almost exclusively as a site of consumption.

While this statement held true across the range of magazines studied, each had its own slant. *OM*, *Ptiuch*, *Shtuchka*, and *Cosmopolitan* provided the most detailed discussions of style and fashion trends. While *Cosmopolitan* focused on consumption of clothes, cosmetics, and beauty products, however, *OM* and *Ptiuch* regarded "style" as indicative of (youth) cultural status. The latter magazines thus constructed a similar division to that in music between "mass" and "elite" (focusing on designer and club wear) styles.[18] However, *OM* and *Ptiuch* were also the most globally inclusive and created the impression that the most recent Western styles were accessible to and evident among the trendiest sections of the Russian population. This distinction reflected the different audiences of the magazines; whereas the more popular mainstream magazines addressed a mass audience "taking" fashion ideas from the West, the more alternative publications placed Russia within this global fashion space providing in-depth information about, and thus giving access to, the latest designer and club wear. Nonetheless, Russia remained a passive recipient, not an active participant, in the global fashion scene.

Western designer or couture fashion was sited in Europe, primarily France, Britain, and Italy. In many of the publications Paris was considered the "center of world fashion" (*Ia Molodoi*, June 1998, 14), while London was portrayed as the home of modern youth design thanks to the new wave of young designers such as Alexander McQueen. British fashion was thus portrayed as radical and extreme, crossing gender boundaries with a readiness to mix elements from different cultures. As such it was represented as the "new" center of global fashion (*OM*, January 1998, 76; *Ptiuch* 1998, no. 4, 109). Belgium was also mentioned as a hub of "cosmopolitan" designers able to incorporate influences and elements from around the world. Germany was portrayed as producing good new fashion and providing cheap, mass-produced clothing.

European creativity and elitism was contrasted to American practicality and production for the masses. America was portrayed as the home of simple, practical, standardized, "democratic" clothing. "Jeans" and the "T-shirt" were constructed as symbols of Anglo-American civilization, which had spread throughout the world, and as representative of a Western, democratic dress style previously absent from Russia. Representations of American fashion focused on its mass, consumer quality, whereas European fashion was depicted as creative but elitist.

European fashion (mainly French and Italian) was accessed via boutiques and through dealers in Russia's main cities, especially Moscow. Indeed Moscow's fashion week, which attracted both well-known foreign and Russian designers, was frequently mentioned. The advertising for Western clothes, shoes, accessories, beauty products, and clothing outlets carried by youth magazines was also an important site of information about fashion. In *OM*, *Ptiuch*, and *Cosmopolitan* such advertising was primarily for expensive, Western designer clothes and accessories available only in Western shops in Russia or Russian shops selling Western designer wear (predominantly in Moscow or other large Russian cities). Across all the journals, 67 percent of all advertising for clothing and accessories was for Western items, compared to only 15 percent for Russian clothing and accessories. In *Ptiuch* the imbalance was particularly stark; 88 percent of advertising was for Western clothing and accessories compared to just 6 percent for Russian products. In *COOL!* the mass German fashion enterprise Burda was advertised by the depiction of models wearing Burda fashions and accompanying advice on how to look, rather than information about where the clothes could be bought.

Accessibility was broadened through the growing popularity of second-hand clothing.[19] The idea of "second hand" was mainly discussed in *OM*, *Ptiuch*, and *Ia Molodoi*. In *OM* and *Ptiuch* second-hand clothing was placed within the context of alternative culture and was represented as a statement; to purchase second-hand clothes was "exclusive," whereas buying new, modern clothing was often "banal." *Ia Molodoi* presented the possibility of buying such clothes but not in any context of alternative culture. *Ptiuch* also provided information about flea markets in London and Germany.

Fashion "authority" clearly resided in the West, and the latter was influencing how young people in Russia looked. Teenage fashion was presented as increasingly globally homogenous and emanating from European girls, who were the authority on high street youth fashion (*Shtuchka* 1997, no. 10, 29). Specific styles popular at the time of the research—such as "military style" and "unisex"—were attributed directly to the transfer of Western styles. Western feminism was perceived as having given Western women the right to decide how to live and how to look, and the influence of this was now being seen in Russia. However, young Russian women were still represented as wanting smart, stylish, and expensive clothes, a fact partially explained by the exaggerated desire for good quality designer clothes, which had been completely unattainable during the late Soviet period.

Wider gender discourses on fashion largely reflected the particular direction of the magazine in question. The mainstream magazines concentrated on fashion for women and adopted a traditional approach. The alternative magazines, however, actively attempted to counter this traditional view. *OM* and *Ptiuch* paid significant attention to unisex styles and discussed the latest designs of top Western alternative or extravagant designers, such as Alexander McQueen and John Paul Gautier. *OM*, which was geared toward a primarily male audience, portrayed a fashion space where gender divisions were becoming increasingly immaterial as male and female styles combined with, and drew on, each other.

Nevertheless, although it was widely held that fashion "authority" resided in the West, it was recognized that market dominance was held by "low-quality, mass-produced" clothing imported from Turkey and Poland. This was attributed to the absence of any established fashion industry in Russia, rather than a lack of talented designers. However, any Russian influence on the world fashion scene was limited to one or two individual designers; in general Russian fashion designers were portrayed as "adopting" Western experience and technology. The same was true of the cosmetic and beauty industries; it was Western "experts" and their opinion, which were presented as the authority for the Russian consumer.[20]

Film and Television

While discussion of fashion was dominated by reference to Europe, America dominated discussion of film and television. Hollywood was identified as the main producer of Western films and constituted the dominant image of Western film, particularly among the more popular, mainstream magazines; Hollywood images featured strongly in advertisements for American products, for example. The magazines *OM* and *Ptiuch* paid attention to both American and European independent and alternative film, however.

Much attention in the discussion of Hollywood was devoted to the institution itself. Hollywood was portrayed as symbolic of the American dream according to which anyone could succeed as a film star. Hollywood productions were said to range from portraying traditional American values and beliefs (the "happy end," optimism, and family values) to violent, unprincipled antiheroes. According to *Ptiuch* magazine, such films satisfied demand among both Western and Russian audiences for the combination of "politics and sex." Thus the influence of Hollywood was acknowledged to be global and the frequent discussion of the private lives of its "stars," from Julia Roberts and Michael Douglas to Winona Ryder and Milla Jovovich, was characterized by a familiarity of tone.

While the space devoted to Hollywood reflected the high level of interest in, and consumption of, its products, both Hollywood the institution and Hollywood productions were subjected to frequent criticism. Hollywood was called a "factory of dreams" and an "assembly line" (*OM* December 1997, 105). *OM* and *Ptiuch* magazines criticized Hollywood products for being commercial and for aiming to satisfy mass demand rather than being driven by artistic criteria. These magazines devoted substantial space to independent American film studios and to the productions of "alternative directors" such as Gus van Sant and Quentin Tarantino. They also made a clear distinction between American independent film—described as being artistic, creative, and the provider of "alternative heroes" (from minority communities)—and Hollywood. Hollywood and American film production was compared unfavorably to that originating in Europe, both in content and reception. *Rovesnik* suggested that Hollywood's success was based upon technical superiority and an ability to constantly recreate the history of the twentieth century. The absence of creative ideas in Hollywood, it was suggested, was filled by drawing on other cultures—namely European—and "originality" in recent film was attributed to France, Britain, the Czech Republic, Finland, and Holland (*Rovesnik*). British film, in particular, was portrayed as creative, progressive, and alternative, qualities embodied, at the time the research was conducted, in the cult film *Trainspotting* and the actor Ewan McGregor (*OM*, *Ptiuch*).

The magazines generally considered films to be premiered and released in Russia without delay. This was certainly true for Moscow, from where they went out to regional theaters. Moreover, the market for pirate videocassettes was highly developed, which meant that films just premiered in the West were often available for home viewing in Russia. However, *OM* and *Ptiuch* highlighted the fact that "interesting" films on video (rather than mass-produced pirate videos of mainstream films) appeared much later in Russia because of their relative unprofitability. With regard to alternative, independent film *OM* and *Ptiuch* were dismissive of the understanding and reception these films received from the "wider" Russian public, acknowledging only limited popularity among a "narrow" elite.

Substantial space in the magazines was devoted to the influence and distribution of American films and television programs via Russian domestic television channels.[21] It was largely assumed that young people had access to "global" youth programs and music channels, and most attention was paid to MTV and the German channel VIVA-2.[22] The West was identified as having influenced the production methods and presentation formats of domestic Russian television. Presenters, it was suggested, had been "Americanized" and on certain Russian youth channels (such as disk-*kanal*)[23] compared not unfavorably with Western European and American presenters on MTV. New Russian youth music programs—such as *Rok Urok* and *Dzhem*—illustrated this process; *Rok Urok* adopted a Western-style "talk show" format, while the presenter of *Dzhem* fashioned a self-consciously American style.

America was the main source of production of movies and dominated images of the West received via film and television. The youth magazines devoted substantial space to film and television, and the worlds they presented appeared familiar and close to Russian youth. However, this sense of inclusion did not preclude significant criticism of both the medium itself and of the images of America, and the West, received through it.

Youth Cultural Scenes: Insiders and Outsiders

The different audiences to which the different magazines spoke were evident from the youth cultural scenes that emerge from their pages. The more mainstream magazines and youth television programs oriented themselves toward what they perceived to be "normal" youth. *COOL!* was addressed to a wide, predominantly teenage, audience and combined information about commercial pop music and stars with an ongoing exchange with its readership on teenage issues and problems. *Ia Molodoi* also addressed a broad youth audience, although with a wider age range than *COOL!* raising topics of general interest (music, film) but not in any specific or detailed manner. Although the journal attempted to correspond with its youth audience in terms of its language and humor, it inhabited a generalized youth cultural world. Thus, although the magazine expressed an awareness of various youth groups and styles, it took an outsider's view on them; specific youth cultural groups were not identified as part of the magazine's readership. *Rovesnik* was predominantly a music publication and aimed mainly at a young male audience (reflected in its focus on rock music and the frequency of articles on topics such as preparing for fatherhood and professional training). *Shtuchka* provided information and advice to a teenage female audience. *Rovesnik* and *Shtuchka* had a high frequency of directly translated articles written by Western authors, which were used to illustrate difference rather than commonality across the youth scene. Although *Aida* was published as a youth magazine, the style of discussion and the nature of its journalism distanced it from youth; its target audience was "traditional" Russian youth. In all of these magazines, information was provided about the place and time of origin of particular youth cultural groups and the social environments in which they had arisen. However, these were almost always short individual references with little linkage between them. "Subcultural" youth was thus constructed as an "other" located outside the intended magazine readership.

"Alternative" youth magazines—such as *OM* and *Ptiuch*—provided more historical and contemporary cultural information about youth scenes worldwide, and a broad range of youth groups found a home on the magazines' pages. *OM* provided detailed information about different youth cultures and was aimed at "elite" youth—the alternative, wealthy youth of the capital. The magazine's vision of the youth world was set in the context of alternative culture and presented an image of a highly stratified youth world described in global terms and including Russian youth. *Ptiuch* focused specifically on dance and club culture and electronic music at global, national, and local levels. The magazine provided information to the reader about raves, dance events, and clubs not only in Russia but in a number of European cities (Zurich, Berlin, Paris, London), providing in-depth descriptions of the music, style, and "public" one might encounter. In this way, the magazine facilitated its readers' participation in a global space of club and rave culture and discussed the developing scenes in Russia and Eastern Europe in the same way as the "Western" club scene. *Ptiuch* was aimed at young people engaged in club and dance culture and was valued not only by active participants in the vibrant scenes of Russia's largest cities, but also those in the regions who used it as an important source of information about the latest trends, music, and albums.[24] *Ptiuch* presented an image of a global club culture, disrupted only by the "local" Russian problem of the *byki*, that is clubgoers with money but little taste and a source of constant irritation to "real" Russian clubbers (see Chapter 5).

A number of contemporary global youth cultural groupings appeared regularly on the pages of *OM* and *Ptiuch*. These included "Generation X," the term coined by Douglas Coupland in 1991 to distinguish a post-baby boomer generation (those born in the late 1960s and early 1970s) characterized by social disengagement. The Generation X phenomenon became closely linked to the development of grunge on the American West Coast in the early 1990s, which quickly became popular around the world. "Yuppies" too, although essentially a Western phenomenon, were said to be increasingly apparent in Russia as Western economic influence and values of ambition, success, professionalism, and materialism were extended to Russia. Cyberspace provided another site for the development of global youth cultures. The Internet was described as an important site for cultural exchange for members of youth scenes with a global membership (one example given in *Ptiuch* concerned hip hop culture).

In this context, the discussion of rave culture was particularly illustrative of the relationship between different magazines and specific youth cultural scenes. Rave featured in both mass and "alternative" magazines but in very different ways. In mass publications individual articles on rave addressed the question of what rave was and what its significance might be for contemporary youth; they attempted to understand it from the outside. The more conservative magazines even expressed traditional Soviet concerns about the negative impacts of Western youth cultures; in this case that "acid and rave will turn the younger generation into morons" (*Aida*, March 1998, 50). *OM* and *Ptiuch* in contrast, saw their readership as part of the rave scene; rave was familiar and not addressed as an issue outside everyday life.

The language used in the magazines also reflected their positioning in relation to an identified "global youth culture." *OM* and *Ptiuch*, which sought to include their readerships in a wider global youth culture, used English words, phrases, and expressions widely,[25] predominantly in the sphere of music but also in articles related to issues of sexuality and gender, fashion, and the media. Although the other magazines did use some English words and expressions, they did so to a lesser extent, and predominantly in the sphere of music. The magazines' usage of English phrases and words might be classified as follows: *Ptiuch* and *OM*—very high usage; *Rovesnik (Shtuchka), Ia Molodoi*—moderate usage; *Spid-Info*, *Sobesednik*, *Cosmopolitan*, *Aida*, *COOL!*—little usage.[26]

In the magazines where use of English words was low, the actual "type" of usage was similar. The highest number of foreign words related to music and different musical tendencies, for example, *pop*, *rok*, *pank*, *di-dzhei*, *di-dzheistvovat'*, *di-dzheiskii*, *rok-n-roll*, *reiv*, *reiver*, "rave."[27] Adjectives using an English language root—such as *di-dzheiskii*, *superpopuliarnii*, and *rok-n-rol'nii*—were often declined according to Russian grammatical rules. English words were borrowed extensively also in discussions of show business, business, fashion, and politics. In *Cosmo* the employment of English words and expressions reflected the dominant themes of the magazine. English words were most frequently employed in the contexts of fashion and appearance, work, career, and business. These magazines rarely rendered words into Latin type and never mixed Latin and Cyrillic types.

The quantity of English words in *Rovesnik* and *Ia Molodoi* was much greater. In *Rovesnik* the concentration on music was reflected in the employment of a wide range of musical terms. The most frequent were those connected to rock music, for example, *rok*, *rok-n-roll*, *rok-muzika*. Other borrowed terms referred to different music genres, including a large number referring to the rave scene and electronic music, and to music production. Latin type was used in reference to types of music—for example "grunge," "punk," "thrash," "heavy," "hardcore fan"—however, in general, Latin type was used much less often than Cyrillic. The other main contexts where English words were used were the mass media, sport and leisure, and youth cultural movements and groups.

In *Ia Molodoi*, English was used in a broad range of contexts, including business, youth cultures, sexuality, gender, and sport. *Ia Molodoi* reflected the tendency, which was seen in *Rovesnik* and in the more alternative publications of *OM* and *Ptiuch*, to use English words and expressions in the context of the Internet and computers, for example, *interfeiz*, *sait*, *noitbuk*. Russian and English were also mixed as in *namba raz* (number of times) or "Super *nuzhno*" (very necessary). Latin type was generally used only for random expressions—for example, *gud-bai, sorri, yu finisht, ful kontakt, o'kei*—on most occasions Cyrillic type was preferred,

OM and *Ptiuch* magazines showed a more complex and more conscious use of English language expressions. In *OM* the majority of English words were in a music context and mainly related to electronic music, for example, *tekno*, *minimal tekno*, *khaus*, *progressiv-khaus*, *khardkor*, *embient*, *trip-khop*. *Reiv*, and other derivatives of this word, were widespread, for example, *reiv-muzika*, *reiv-klub*, *reiv-kultura*, *reiv-odezhda* (rave-clothing), *reiv*-party, *reiverskii*, *reiver*. Borrowed words littered discussions of club culture, for example, *chil-aut* (chill-out), *klubnii saund* (club sound), *flaeri* (fliers). The single most frequently used word was *di-dzhei*, and this word also had the greatest number of derivatives, including *di-dzeiskii*, *di-dzheistvo*, *di-dzeiremiks*. English was also used extensively in the discussion of music production.

Language was used in the journal to distinguish between types of alternative music and their scenes and mainstream styles of music and culture—*alternativnii*, *andergraund*, and *andergraundnost'* versus *meinstrimnii* and *meinstrim*. English words were used to a greater extent than in other publications to talk about gender and sexuality. Terms employed in this context included *boi-gerl frend*, *macho-agressiia* (machismo), *gei*, *lesbiianki*, *transvestit*. In discussions of drug culture and fashion and style, a large number of borrowed English words were found. This was true also of discussion of the Internet and computers where words were as frequently written in Latin type as Cyrillic. Despite the greater use of Latin type in this magazine, the majority of English words nevertheless appeared in Cyrillic. Although it was difficult to quantify the overall extent of English language borrowing in *OM*, the use of English words was a normal part of the text flow in the publication.

The use of English words and expressions was most widespread and complex in the magazine *Ptiuch*. The majority of borrowed words related to electronic music and dance and club culture. The quantity and variety of words was greater than in *OM*, as was the more varied use of either Latin or Cyrillic type. Some examples included *tekno*, "techno," *tekno-stsena*, *khaus-muzika*, "acid house," *dzhangl*, "jungle," *dzhangl stsena*, "hardcore," "trance," "ambient," *dab*, "drum and bass," *dram-end-bas*, "rave," *reiv*, *reiv-dvizhenie* (rave movement), *chil-aut*, and *flaer*. Words that related to the production of music and the music industry in general were also widespread—*remiks*, *miksovat'*, *sempler*, *semplirovanie*, and *demo-zapis'* (demo-tape). As in *OM*, the complexity and freedom in the way the words and expressions were employed demonstrated the way the music discourse was constructed in the magazine and the assumption by the publication that its audience could also "use" this language freely.

A significant number of English-language borrowings in *Ptiuch* related to computers, the Internet, and cyber culture: "on line," "cyber," "cyber space," "Internet," *khakeri*, *kiberprostranstvo* (cyberspace), "email'*ii*," "on line *chatov*." Two other contexts where English was frequently employed was sexuality and gender—*gei*, *lesbiiskii*, *lesbiianki*, *uniseks*, *androginnii-androginost'*—and drugs and drug use—*drag diler, ekstazi*, "recreational drug," ecstasy.

Although the use of Cyrillic type still dominated, in *Ptiuch* Latin type was used more than in any other magazine. Cases of Russian and English words being used sequentially were also in evidence, for example: *nastoiashchii* entertainment ("real entertainment"), mainstream *kul'tur* (of mainstream cultures), straight *liudei* ("of straight people"), *teper' tekno eto*—big thing ("now techno is the big thing").

Alternative magazines assumed that English language use presented no barriers to their readers; indeed in both *OM* and *Ptiuch*, English words and expressions were frequently found on the readers' letters page. The vocabulary used in *OM* and *Ptiuch* demonstrated both the more alternative discourse found in these two publications and the assumptions the magazines made about their readerships. In the other magazines, the familiarity of the readership with the language of global youth culture was not assumed.

Individual publications worked within very different constructions of the youth scene. Non-youth specific magazines (*Cosmopolitan*, *Spid-Info*, *Sobesednik*) did not appear to recognize a youth scene, prioritizing articles on medicine, politics, and economics over those related to youth cultural phenomena. For youth magazines like *Rovesnik*, *Shtuchka*, and *Ia Molodoi* the youth scene existed but was largely undifferentiated but for a few peripheral subcultural groups, which were "other" and predominantly "Western." For alternative magazines such as *OM* and *Ptiuch*, however, the youth scene was extremely culturally diverse, and the magazines worked to include the reader into the exciting global youth scene they themselves inhabited.

Rerooting "the Global": Putting "the West" Back In

Images of the West were not confined to the common ground of youth cultural concerns—music, fashion, film, and youth culture—however. When more holistic portraits of the West—and in particular America, Britain, and Europe—were constructed, the emergent discourse of the West appeared both more distant and more critical.

America: From Apple Pie to Litigious Pets

In the majority of magazines (*Rovesnik*, *Shtuchka*, *Spid-Info*, *Sobesednik*, *Ia Molodoi*, *Aida*) America was the primary and dominant reference point in the West. However, in the alternative magazines—*OM* and *Ptiuch*—although America remained the major reference point, it was presented in opposition to Europe, and often in a negative light.

There were clear differences in how America was positioned in each of the magazines. *OM* and *Ptiuch* did not present any single view of America; representations fluctuated depending upon the issue under discussion.

However, in general, the discourse was more negative than positive and often superior in tone. Thus *Ptiuch* described America as "stupid America" (*Ptiuch* 1996, no. 9, 26) and Americans as "paunchy Americans" (*Ptiuch*, 1996, spring, no. 1).[28] *Rovesnik* echoed this negative stance, although less overtly, since its articles were more descriptive and less evaluative in nature. In *Cosmopolitan*[29] America was frequently held up as the "authority" or "standard" although not inherently the ideal. *Sobesednik* addressed a wide range of aspects of American life, and the discourse was predominantly neutral, although in certain spheres (such as technological development) America was compared very favorably with other countries (including Russia). In *Spid-Info*, the West was almost synonymous with America. The general tone of its writing was neutral, and the majority of articles related to medical research. *Aida* made little direct reference to America; its representation of the country was limited to random facts mainly associated with aspects of Hollywood.

The magazines reinvented America through discussion and critique of characteristics traditionally associated with American society: the importance of work, family, money, success; the rights of the consumer; a belief in the law and the protection of individual rights; and the promotion of healthy lifestyles. The result was an ambiguous and contradictory view of America incorporating negative, positive, and neutral evaluations. The discussion below takes up the main themes of this debate.

American society was universally presented as focused around work, career, making money, and individual success (*Rovesnik*, *Cosmopolitan*, *Ia Molodoi*). This, it was suggested, reflected the strong influence of the Protestant work ethic and puritan values but left little room for genuine emotion, experience, or enjoyment and made society intolerant of failure (*OM*, *Ptiuch*). Mass commercialization and the importance of money had increased the "power of the consumer," but this had led to a degeneration, even absence, of culture (*Ptiuch*). The excesses of wealth and consumerism were illustrated through descriptions of the "absurdities" of the "life of the rich" in America, where bodyguards were essential, huge amounts of money were spent on medicine for pets, and dogs had nannies (*Spid-Info*). Protestantism and puritanical values were reflected also in representations of the American family, which was considered to be another pillar of American society as illusory as American apple pie (*OM*, *Ptiuch*).[30] The high rate of divorce, for example, was used to challenge the image of the happy American family (*Spid-Info*).

Traditionally, the West had been positively associated with respect for the law and the protection of the rights of the individual, and this was reflected in Russian youth magazines, most specifically with regard to the protection of women's rights in the home and at work (*Spid-Info*) and the "toleration" of ethnic and sexual minorities (*OM*). However, there was also discussion of legislation and censorship, much of which was critical, suggesting that measures taken were often extreme, yet ineffective. Examples cited included the closure of clubs in New York because of drug use, attempts to censor rap lyrics (*OM*), the prohibition of smoking in cafes and restaurants in New York (*Rovesnik*), and film censorship (*Sobesednik*). The banning of the clip of the British group Prodigy on American television and the new production of *Lolita* in America (*Rovesnik* 1998, no. 3, 23), for example, were declared to be evidence of "terrible political correctness" (*Rovesnik* 1998, no. 5, 1). Political correctness in general was criticized (*OM*) but especially in relation to what was considered to be the extreme protection of women's rights in the work place (*Sobesednik*).[31] If "political correctness" was the expression of public bodies having taken the law to extremes, then this was matched by individuals' own litigious practice. America was presented as a society where individuals went to court to make compensation claims against plastic surgeons (*OM*), and where pets could bring charges against other pets (*Sobesednik*). This signified the prioritization of the protection of "consumer rights" over all others and, as such, as the ultimate victory of consumerism (*Cosmopolitan*).

Another dominant image of American society—prevalent especially in magazine advertising—was its association with healthy lifestyles. The youth magazines reflected the importance of healthiness and obsession with fitness, sport, and dieting in American society. At the same time, they contrasted these espoused values with the actual health, appearance, and behavior of individuals. References were made to widespread drug use, alcoholism, and excessive eating patterns in American society in general, and among American youth, who, it was suggested, only thought about a healthy way of life after they had turned fifty (*Rovesnik*, *Sobesednik*, *Ia Molodoi*). The concern with personal health, it was suggested, had turned medical research into big business (*Spid-Info*, *Cosmopolitan*).

The critical undertones of the discussion of America in Russian youth magazines—especially the "alternative" magazines *OM* and *Ptiuch*—brought their narratives in line with the academic discourse outlined in Chapter 1. Both discourses presented America as false and illusory. Freedom, for example, appeared as a quintessential characteristic of America—especially in advertising media where images of the Wild West, open highways, the desert, and infinite space were "all-American." This relationship with freedom was presented as imaginary, however, since, in reality, American society was characterized by the rise of conservatism, cynicism, religious fanaticism, and monotheism, which threatened even the "little" freedom that did exist (*Ptiuch*). This echoes Evstaf'ev's argument that while American culture appears outwardly tolerant—since it allows for cultural and religious diversity—in practice the "freedom" being offered is only that of being free from "national sympathies and aversions and essentially free of one's roots and historical identity" (D. Evstaf'ev 1998). Moreover, and more tendentiously, he argues that tough anticrime programs, attempts to control everyday life (the banning of smoking and targeting of obesity), and the drive toward the creation of a "politically correct lexicon" represents a gradual move toward a "fascist" society (ibid.). The magazines did not go so far, but were concerned to deconstruct "traditional" images of America and the American dream. The fierce protection of women's rights, for example, was contrasted with the presence of the commercial use of sexuality through, for example, striptease clubs (*Spid-Info*, *Ia Molodoi*). The image of a well-to-do and wholesome society was undermined with descriptions of "other" tendencies in American society: rising crime, dangerous religious sects (*Rovesnik*); serial killings, drug scandals, the marginalization of increasingly large sections of society (*Ptiuch*); growing incidences of mass suicide, some orchestrated via the Internet (*OM*); and tendencies among youth toward anorexia and smoking at ever younger ages (*Rovesnik*).[32]

The image of America was not unremittingly negative; magazines identified pockets of "acceptable" America. The cities of New York, Chicago, and Detroit, for example, were seen as the saviors of modern America, through their contribution to music and dance culture. New York was still seen as energetic and artistic and as a capital of the world and the home of new clubs and music where tradition and change existed side by side (*Ptiuch*). Interestingly, however, the city earned this accolade through its rejection of American-ness and emergence as a thoroughly "global" city (*OM*). The greatest criticism was reserved for the "real," provincial America (often equated with the conservative Midwest) where life was "gray and boring" (*Rovesnik* 1996, no. 7, 2).

America appeared in different guises on the pages of Russian youth magazines. In a cultural context America was seen as having much to offer the world, particularly with regard to alternative music and independent film, since these media were, themselves, critical of contemporary American society (*OM*).[33] When the discussion moved to American values, lifestyle, and societal norms, then the discourse was more critical. The struggle to preserve values central to American society (freedom, rights of the individual, tolerance) were portrayed as having descended into oppressive forms of "political correctness," while society at large was suffering a crisis of faith, doubt in traditional values, and the descent into the measurement of success in purely material terms (D. Evstaf'ev 1998).

Britain: Cultural Innovation Meets Cultural Conservatism

Images of Britain in Russian youth magazines were quantitatively and qualitatively different from those of America. Britain was discussed almost exclusively in relation to its cultural life. Images of Britain were often specifically linked to key cultural sites (London and Scotland), to a perceived "new" British culture, and to a wider set of characteristics and traditions associated with Britain. Because the discussion of Britain remained at the cultural level, and only rarely moved into any broader discussion of British society and values, a less critical discourse of Britain emerged than of America. The "alternative" magazines, *OM* and *Ptiuch*, were, in fact, noticeably pro-British. Both magazines represented Britain through music, fashion, style, and art as innovative, new, and exciting and, in stark contrast to their discussion of America, made little reference to any national social characteristics. In *Rovesnik*, *Shtuchka*, and *Aida* images of Britain were constructed against the background of dominant images of America and tended toward more stereotypical images and symbols.[34]

Positive representations of contemporary Britain primarily focused on London, which was frequently compared favorably to New York. *Ptiuch*, for example, compared the club scene of London, where the clubs were full of people out to enjoy themselves, to that in New York, where, it was claimed, the public was only intent upon getting home.[35] In contrast to the relationship between New York and America, London was considered to be a *real* British city, which preserved its history and tradition but, at the same time, was able to cultivate vibrant youth, music, club, and fashion cultures (*OM*). London was presented as international and multicultural; a city where one could buy and see anything and meet anyone and everyone (*Ptiuch*). Significantly, London was also considered to be a city of youth; it was the home of youth fashion design and consumption and provided a haven of cheap, trendy, and alternative clothes markets. The only dissenting voice was found in the magazine *Ia Molodoi*, where London appeared as a "dark, hectic, and invariably boring city" which stood in sharp contrast to the rest of "beautiful, quiet, pleasant England" (*Ia Molodoi*, June 1998, 2).

Scotland's centrality in images of Britain was probably attributable to the success of the cult film *Trainspotting* (and to a lesser extent *Brave Heart*), which was discussed extensively in the magazines (especially *OM*, *Ptiuch*, *Rovesnik*).[36] *Trainspotting* provided a screen upon which other images of Scotland were projected, such as that of happy Scottish clubbers who liked to "go mad" but "in style" (*Ptiuch* 1996, spring, 1). Scotland and England were distinguished clearly from each other, and the people of Scotland were represented as proud of their distinctive heritage. Similarities were drawn between Scottish and Russian life. In particular, images of a monotonous, unsatisfying, provincial Scottish life—where people got up, went to work, and drank beer—were seen as reflecting life in provincial Russia (*Rovesnik*).

"New British culture" described contemporary British art, music, fashion, and film, which, it was claimed, were inspired by cynicism, narcissism, a death-wish (*OM*), and a drive toward cultural innovation and leadership (*Ptiuch*). This culture attracted empathy, especially in contrast to American culture and was considered to be relatively uncommercialized (*OM*, *Ptiuch*). Symbols of this culture came from alternative, commercial, and traditional cultural realms and included Irvine Welsh, author of *Trainspotting* (*OM*), the fashion designer Alexander McQueen, the Spice Girls (*Ptiuch*, *Ia Molodoi*), and Princess Diana (*Ia Molodoi*).[37] Britpop was also identified as a uniquely British phenomenon (*Ptiuch*), which had succeeded in generating interest primarily via its "local" forms (Mumii Troll', Splin). At the popular level a cultural trend toward "laddism" (defined as antifeminism, anti-political correctness, and a liking for girls, beer, and football) was identified as characteristic of contemporary British society (*OM*, *Rovesnik*), alongside the more traditional association of Britain with football hooliganism (*OM*).

Other traditional images that continued to hold sway included the association of Britain with the monarchy (and all its conservatism and tradition) albeit mainly communicated through images of Princess Diana (*OM*, *Rovesnik*). Another British institution that remained firmly fixed in the readers' minds was the British pub (*Aida*). British politeness and prudishness remained axiomatic (*Aida*, *Ptiuch*), although the British were seen nevertheless to be less "closed" than other Europeans (French and Germans) and to remain open to foreign influences while retaining a secure sense of "what is best" (*Ptiuch*). Thus, while America was presented as trying (in vain) to preserve its traditional values, in Britain the move away from such traditions was interpreted positively (*Rovesnik*). *Rovesnik* was the only magazine to devote any attention to problems within British society through discussion of social tension arising from clashes between the government and marginal groups in society; the widening gap between the rich and poor; and the rise in the number of suicides among British university students.[38]

For "alternative magazines," *OM* and *Ptiuch*, Britain was a key point of reference in the West and was represented largely in relation to its alternative cultural life. In the mainstream youth publications, although Britain was discussed more often than other European countries, it was much less prominent than images of America and appeared largely through stereotypical and traditional images of Britain. While Britain was an important element of images of the West in Russian youth magazines, unlike America, it could, on its own, never represent the West completely.

Representations of Europe: A Tale of Sausages and Beer . . .

Any overall image of Europe, as a homogenous unit with common features and characteristics, was hard to identify. In the mainstream magazines, Europe was in evidence only through a series of "snap shots" of individual countries, often as places for tourism (especially with regard to Southern Europe). In *OM* and *Ptiuch* fragments of European culture were gleaned through reference to specific music and youth cultural scenes in a number of countries.

The European countries featured most regularly were Britain, France, Germany, and Holland. In the alternative magazines they appeared in relation usually to developments in specific cultural forms or descriptions of particular scenes in individual cities. In the mainstream magazines, portraits of individual countries relied on stereotypical images of national characteristics. Thus France was noted for recent developments in electronic music and film, in the alternative magazines, whereas in the mainstream magazines the French were considered to be "stylish" and to have good taste (an image widely used in advertising) and French men were praised for their "elegant" dress, behavior, and attitude to women (*Sobesednik* 1998, no. 14, 18). Likewise, the alternative magazines focused on key cities in Germany such as Berlin, noted for its peculiar fusion of Western and Eastern European culture (*Ptiuch* 1997, no. 7–8, 47), while mainstream magazines referred to German predilections for "cleanliness," "order," and "efficiency" (*Rovesnik*), and at a more material level "sausages and beer" (*Aida*, November 1997, 21). Holland was reduced to a country of "tulips and cheese" (*Spid-Info* 1997, no. 12, 11) in the mainstream magazines, while in the alternative magazines the country was portrayed as a liberal, successful, and harmonious society (*OM*) whose culture was embodied in Amsterdam as "a place of pilgrimage for the most progressive, stylish, and lively youth in Europe" (*OM*, October 1997, 69).

Thus while *OM* and *Ptiuch* introduced individual European cities in terms of their (youth) cultural scenes and in a way which suggested commonality and included Russia in a wider vision of Europe, mainstream magazines relayed stereotypical "national" images that purported to represent deep-seated national differences.

The East: "Global" Easts and "Local" Easts

The space devoted to discussion of "the East" was insignificant in comparison to that given to the West (America and Europe) (see Diagram 3.1).[39] An analysis of the general orientation of articles across the magazines showed that only 1 percent of articles related to the East, compared to 27 percent relating to the West, and 27 percent to Russia. In the spheres of music and fashion, the number of articles relating to the West increased; 48 percent of articles on music and 39 percent of those on fashion were related to the West. In these two areas, Russian oriented articles accounted for 38 percent and 18 percent respectively. There were no articles on Eastern music in any of the magazines, and only 3 percent of fashion articles were related to the East.[40]

Diagram 3.1 **Space devoted to *the West* in youth magazines**

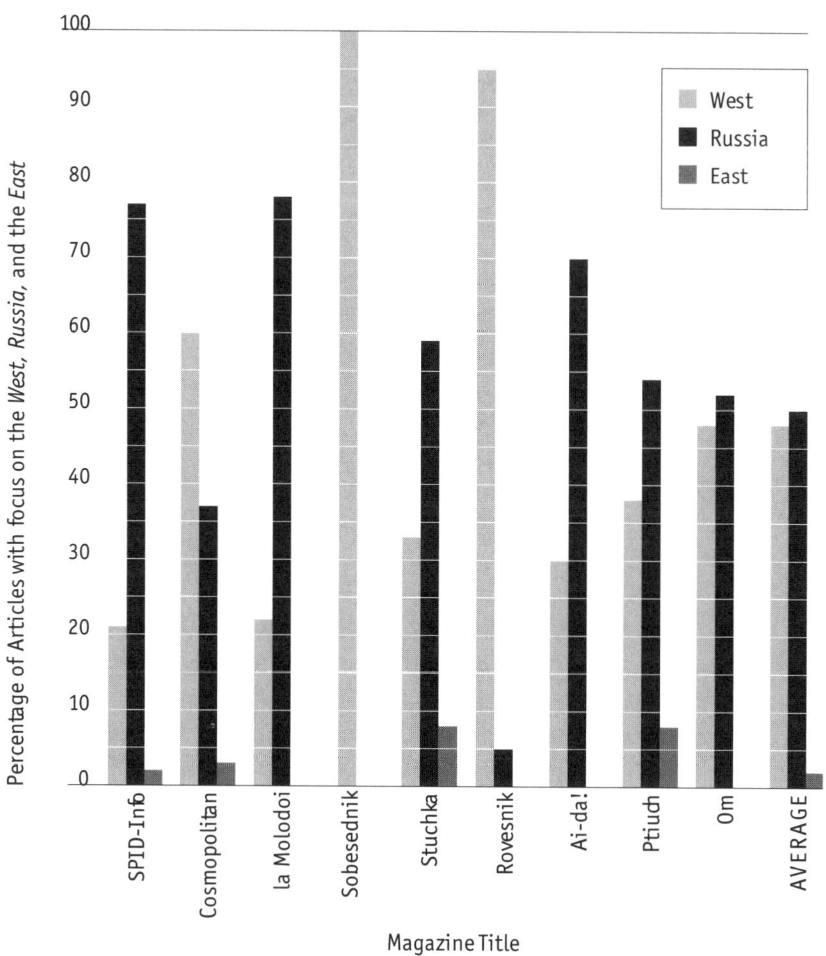

The way in which the East was represented in youth magazines, moreover, reflected their discourses of the West. Thus, in *OM* and *Ptiuch*, global similarities were emphasized over local specifics, and Russia was presented as receiving cultural influences, via processes of globalization, from both the West and the East. "The East" in this context was a "global East" represented by Japan and Hong Kong. The "global East" was perceived as generating a "new" culture, different from the West, but from within a common, global cultural space. In the more mainstream youth magazines "the East" was constructed as a "local East." The "local East" was represented as different from, indeed in opposition to, the West and

Russia, through an emphasis on national specifics, traditional characteristics, and stereotypes. "The East" in these magazines referred to Japan but also China and Korea.

Japan was the main reference point in the East across all the magazines and had two faces. Key images of Japan, particularly in *OM* and *Ptiuch*, came through the channel of contemporary culture—art, fashion, and electronic music—where Japan was considered to be making a meaningful global contribution (*OM*, January 1998, 64). The other representation of Japan was as a "high-tech" country of the twenty-first century. Japan was portrayed as a country producing and distributing high-tech goods on global markets and as able to provide a modern lifestyle (high-tech equipment in homes, modern transport systems, futuristic leisure parks, video and computer games) for its population (*Ptiuch*). This was the dominant image of Japan also in advertising. Mainstream magazines, whose discussion focused on the distribution of Japanese products to Russia and the West, also considered Japan to be technologically advanced and to have significant economic influence globally. Hong Kong was constructed in a similar way, as representative of the twenty-first century with expensive (European) cars and an advanced transport system.[41] The mainstream publications also referred to national, traditional, and often stereotypical characteristics of the Japanese nation and people—as polite, wise, hard-working, sensitive to nature but lacking individualism (*Rovesnik*, *Cosmopolitan*, *Ia Molodoi*).

Representations of China either referred to the continued existence of Communist rule (*OM*, *Ptiuch*, *Aida*), to the rich history and culture of the country, or to current Western economic activity there. Chinese culture was contrasted with that of the West; the deep, humanitarian philosophy of the East was seen to be in conflict with the pragmatic and exclusive philosophy of the West (*Rovesnik*). Admiration was expressed for the tradition of passing on knowledge from one generation to the next, a tradition considered to have been lost in Europe (*Cosmopolitan*). Contemporary China was portrayed as being exploited by international conglomerates, which used cheap Chinese labor with no regard for workers' rights (*Rovesnik*).

Images of Russia: "The West" or "Not the West"?

Russia contained pockets of the West within its borders. Moscow and, less frequently, St. Petersburg were depicted as Western, European, international or global cities, quite distinct from the rest of Russia. Moscow was the window to the West, and the place where both the economic and cultural influence of the latter was felt; Moscow was the site of new Western restaurants, cafes, and boutiques, and it was the destination for Western art and fashion exhibitions, Western musicians and bands (*OM*, *Ptiuch*).

Thus, Moscow was constructed as an international cultural or economic space, included in the global environment, rather than as the national capital of Russia.

While the West had thus infiltrated Russia, the magazines gave little indication of how Russia impacted on the West. *Ptiuch* criticized Russian film for presenting an image of Russia to the world as a country of "idiots, extreme cold, and crime" (*Ptiuch* 1997, no. 5, 61), although its own representations of contemporary Russia concentrated on associations of Russia with the mafia, killings, and uncontrolled capitalism (*Ptiuch*, *OM*). The arrival of individual Russian artists, DJs, and other cultural producers in the West were noted (*OM*, *Ptiuch*), as was the popularity of Russian ballet in Europe and America. The latter was attributed to the fact that while ballet in the West had become business, Russian ballet drew on the Russian national character, remained driven by art rather than commerce, and maintained its superiority over Western dance (*Cosmopolitan*). This fitted a broader image of Russia as a space where, due to the lesser importance of money and individualism, things no longer possible in the West could be achieved (an opinion attributed to European musicians and artists) (*Ptiuch*). In this way, Russia was seen as representative of an earlier, "better" version of Europe, a former existence that European onlookers sought to regain through their interaction with contemporary Russia. This dual image of Russia as both a traditional cultural space depicted by Russian weddings, nature (*priroda*), Russian churches, history, and fairy tales and as a "New Russia," represented by symbols of "New Russians," image, and wealth, also emerged in television advertising.[42]

Reconstructing a Single West: Drugs, Sex, and Values

It should be clear from the foregoing discussion that the Soviet discourse of a single West, and one synonymous with America, had been shattered. However, in some specific areas of discussion in youth magazines "the West" was considered as a homogenous entity. This single West emerged where the cultural practice and values of "the West" were compared and contrasted to those of Russia, or where the influence of the former upon the latter was the main focus of debate.

Representations of Western Drug Culture

When drug use was discussed in youth magazines "the West" was considered to have a common experience that contrasted that of Russia. Indeed drug use was discussed largely within a Western context—through descriptions of the situation "there"—and little direct reference to the situation existing in Russia was made. Although different attitudes within the West were identified, nonetheless Russia was considered to be significantly different. Drug use was portrayed as a "normal" part of Western culture, past and present (*OM*, *Ia Molodoi*, *Rovesnik*). Tolerant attitudes toward drugs, open discussion of the issue (which in Russia was often taboo), and the use of drugs for recreation and relaxation were also characteristic of the West according to some of the magazines (*Ptiuch*, *OM*, *Rovesnik*). The discussion of the present drugs situation in Europe and America combined representations of the centrality of recreational drugs to the club and dance scene (*OM*, *Ptiuch*); the use of cannabis for recreational and medical purposes and campaigns for legalization (*Ptiuch*, *Rovesnik*, *OM*); and references to the dangers of drug use, including the HIV threat and the "culture of fear" surrounding drug usage (*OM*, *Ptiuch*, *Rovesnik*).

Individual magazines largely evaded any clear stance on drugs; the only magazine with a persistently negative attitude toward drugs was *COOL!* which made its position clear in editorial messages and in attitudes expressed toward drug use among musicians. *Rovesnik* primarily presented the issue through articles—predominantly "scare stories"—written by Western (English or American) authors about drug use in the West. *Ptiuch*, and to a lesser extent *OM*, promoted an image of the West as the "authority" and primary source of information about the range of views on drugs. *Ptiuch*, in particular, described in detail what and how drugs were used within Western youth culture and suggested that if recreational drug use had been "normalized" in the West, then Russia, as part of this global youth cultural space, could, and should, adopt the same attitude. This was, perhaps, a direct enactment of the advice it gave in one issue; the "etiquette" of drug use was such, the magazine claimed, that if someone offered you a smoke you should *never* refuse (*Ptiuch* 1996, no. 9, 32).

Sexuality and Gender

Russia was considered to be "behind" the West in terms of the development of sexual relations and attitudes to sexuality, a fact largely attributed to the absence of the "sexual revolution" of the 1960s in Russia (*OM*).[43] Two distinct approaches to the theme of sexuality were evident in youth magazines, however. *OM* and *Ptiuch* devoted considerable space to discussions of sexuality; and although the information was often explicit, it was aimed at a narrow, "alternative" section of youth and often placed the discussion of sexuality (and gender) within wider discussions of youth culture (style, music, and film). *Sobesednik*, *Spid-Info*, and *Rovesnik*, which addressed more mainstream readerships, referred primarily to heterosexual behavior and were more critical of "alternative" sexualities. Although in *Spid-Info* and *Sobesednik* the material was often clearly designed to shock its mass readership, discussions of sexuality were frequently placed within the context of health and medical research.

Despite the recognition of difference, the alternative magazines considered sexuality to be an intrinsic part of a wider youth cultural practice, which Russia was increasingly adopting. *OM* and *Ptiuch* thus considered homosexuality, androgyny, bisexualism, sado-masochism, and transvestism as rich sources for contemporary Western art, film, style, and music. The global sex industry was also considered to be one of the foundation stones of cultural globalization.

For the mainstream publications, however, the "difference" between the West and Russia in terms of sexuality was not in the process of being overcome. In *Rovesnik* the discourse was exclusively heterosexual—often framed as instructing correct sexual practice—and contained elements of sexism. In *Spid-Info* and *Sobesednik* most of the discussion of sexuality and sexual practices referred to research that was being carried out in Europe and America, both with regard to medical issues and sexual practice. Russia was also seen as being exploited by the West, as the provider of "sexual services" through East-West prostitution and the pornography industry (*Sobesednik*). Indeed a rare example of the cultural influence of Russia on the West appeared in relation to the production of pornographic films; because the film industry in Russia was relatively unregulated, such films, it was said, were produced in Russia and then exported to the Western European market (*Sobesednik*).

Representations of gender were made through constructions of "typical" Western men and women. These constructs were contrasted to the "typical" Russian man or woman and their relative positions within society discussed. Significantly more space was devoted to the discussion of Western and Russian women than men (with the exception of *OM* magazine). Most of the magazines employed stereotypical images and emphasized the difference between Russia and the West. Western women were represented through images of strength, power, beauty, and independence, often employing examples such as the Spice Girls or "alternative" Hollywood actresses, such as Uma Thurman, Milla Jovovich, or Winona Ryder, who presented a new image of independence and androgyny, rather than displaying the traditional Hollywood characteristics of femininity and beauty (*OM*, *Ptiuch*). Polls revealing perceptions of the "most attractive" men and women in the world (*Spid-Info*) or the results of research conducted in America and Europe that revealed key characteristics of contemporary Western women (*Rovesnik*, *Cosmopolitan*, *Sobesednik*, *Spid-Info*) were also used to explore these themes. Russian women were the major source of imagery for constructing the Russian "other"; they were presented as beautiful, but shy, and lacking initiative (*Rovesnik*), not "wanting" feminism (*Cosmopolitan*), and dependent upon men (*Sobesdenik*). Socially too, Russian women were presented as sexual objects for Russian and, increasingly, Western men to enjoy.[44] Representations of Eastern women (from Japan and Thailand) fell into a similar mold.

OM magazine focused its gender images on men. Famous British personalities—Jarvis Cocker from Pulp, or the actor Ewan McGregor—were used to depict the "new Western man." The only other representations of Western men were provided again through evidence from "research" and constructed stereotypical pictures of typical French, Italian, and British men, often in relation to their "romantic" characteristics (*Rovesnik*, *Cosmopolitan*, *Sobesednik*).

Economic Exchange and Influence

The West was seen as a single entity when it was portrayed as an agent of economic influence upon Russia (*Sobesednik*, *Spid-Info*, *Ia Molodoi*, *Cosmopolitan*). This influence was seen in the opening of Western and Western-style shops, salons, and restaurants (mainly in the capital), in the activity of large Western companies, the creation of joint enterprises, the impact of Western advertising campaigns, and the increased use of Western technology and products.

In some magazines this process was used to indicate less the difference between Russia and the West than the inclusion of cities such as Moscow into "the West." Such economic interaction, however, revealed differences in business practice and work culture. In the business world relationships in Russian firms were said to be warmer (*bolee dushevnie*) although less polite, than in the West (*Cosmopolitan*). In the West, it was claimed, people went to work to "work," in Russia they went to make friends (*Rovesnik*).

Economic and cultural influence was seen to be increasingly inter woven. Thus Western companies were said to have engaged in cultural activities—such as Coca-Cola's sponsorship of Russian students (*Sobesednik*) or Proctor and Gamble's investment in the Russian youth press (*Ia Molodoi*)—in order to gain commercial advantage. The only examples of Russian encroachments into Western markets, however, involved exploitative practices: the export of pornographic material from Russia to Europe, the increase in both Russian female and male prostitution in Europe, and the use of Russia's children's homes by Western adoption services (*Sobesednik*, *Spid-Info*).[45]

Western Values: Just Say "No"

Perhaps most significantly, a unified "West" was portrayed when the discussion moved from the description of lifestyles to the ascription of values. There was a widespread recognition that life in the West was materially more prosperous, comfortable, and peaceful, and that in the West the individual was protected by the state and by effective legislation (*OM*, *Cosmopolitan*, *Sobesednik*). However, recognition of the material benefits of the West was tempered by rather different attitudes toward Western values. Thus, while the West appeared as the "standard" to which one should aspire in many spheres of life, Western values were, on the contrary, represented as alien (*OM*). Western societies were portrayed as being governed by rationality, selfishness, individualism, superficiality, materialism, hypocrisy, and coldness. These values inversely reflected "Russian" values of emotionalism, generosity, collectivism, genuineness, spirituality, sincerity, and friendliness (*OM*, *Sobesednik*, *Ptiuch*).

Conclusion

The image of "the West" on the pages of Russian youth magazines was a collage consisting of often diverse and contradictory representations of different "Wests." The nature of the discourse varied depending upon the orientation of the magazine and the subject matter addressed. In discussions of youth culture, music, fashion, and media, the discourse tended to be global and inclusive; Russia was seen as participant and as recipient, producer, and critic. This discourse emanated primarily from the magazines *OM* and *Ptiuch*, however, while in the other magazines Russia was portrayed as a recipient of Western influence in these spheres. In discussions of values, traditions and characteristics of society the discourse was one of difference and was consciously critical. No single meaning, therefore, was attached to the West; a multitude of messages were received and required considerable reworking by young people to create sustainable images of the West.

4 Through Their Own Eyes

Young People's Images of "the West"

Elena Omel'chenko and Moya Flynn

> It was Lesha who suggested that young people liked the Western way of life more than the Russian [way of life]. That is probably what society in general thinks. . . . Personally I see things completely differently. It is those people who are about thirty to fifty [years old] who are more inclined to idealize that [Western] way of life, it is they who want to live in the West more, because for youth now our life is already not that different from the West. But for those aged thirty to fifty America, in particular, seems an impossible thing to achieve.
>
> —195, Samara[1]

Images of "the West" presented in the Russian youth media, and described in the preceding chapter, were an important, but not the only, source of images of the West for young people. Alongside impressions cultivated by the Russian mass media—as they formulated "new" discourses about Western life—or by Western films, commercials, music videos, and news broadcasts on global and international networks, there were three additional channels from which young people in Russia drew their images and stereotypes of the West.[2] These sources were stereotypical notions of "abroad," "them," and "their" morals and "their" ways of living, which held sway in Soviet (and prerevolutionary Russian) society;[3] interpretations of respondents' own experience of travel to the West; their personal impressions of interaction with foreigners or the tales recounted by friends who had been "over there"; and other information-rich environments such as family and school. Messages received via these channels were not always mutually reinforcing. Contradictions between images of the West emanating from the media and those that had been "inherited" were commonplace. This "inheritance" was transmitted, not only through the school system,[4] but also via the family and, in the case of the latter, not only from parents but also grandparents.

inherited knowledge

This chapter explores the range of images of the West held by young people as articulated during interviews and focus groups in the cities of Samara, Ul'ianovsk, and Moscow and in response to a representative, questionnaire-based survey among young people in Samara and Ul'ianovsk.[5] It reconstructs a picture of the Western world as a whole as well as of the individual countries that respondents most readily associated with "the West." Although the chapter essentially describes the images articulated by young people, it does not suggest that they receive and absorb such images in unmodified form. The images of the West articulated were multilayered and could take a single immutable form (be stereotypes) or be compound constructs. Almost every individual's personal narrative of the West could be unpacked to reveal its historical roots; analogies with ideological constructs of the Soviet period; new ideas, arising from the *perestroika* period and from open access to information and culture; and radical ideas, which were highly critical of any stereotypical image of the West as a whole, individual Western countries, or Western people. In the course of mapping the range of images, therefore, the authors have been concerned to indicate how images of the West are reworked and reconstituted as they are filtered through layers of individual psychological makeup, own and others' experience, and changing cultural reference points. As this process is charted, it becomes clear that young Russians were acutely aware of the constructed nature of media images. Moreover, the critical faculty of young people was sharpened by the social context of information gathering and processing, that is the filtering of media messages through the critical lens of family, teachers, and peer group.

Locating "the West": A Lesson in Virtual Geography

At the most basic level the West was defined as Western Europe and North America, as is evident from Table 4.1, based on responses to a closed question in the survey conducted in Samara and Ul'ianovsk.[6]

Table 4.1
Which of these regions or countries would you class as belonging to the West?

Region or country	*Yes*	*No*
Western Europe	92%	5%
North America	80%	15%
Eastern Europe	32%	50%
The Baltic States	4%	92%
Russia	5%[a]	84%

[a] *Interviews and focus groups suggested that this 5 percent consisted of those respondents who equated Moscow and other large capital cities with the West and for whom youth culture was the main element in a shared identity between Russia and the West.*

In-depth interviews and focus groups with young people revealed a much more complex picture. For young Russians "the West" in general was a set of historically and culturally constructed "virtual" spaces, whose cultural, symbolic, consumer, and value contours reached across and beyond physical geographical territories. For many respondents, America, Europe, and England appeared to represent the West in general,[7] but the virtual nature of "the West" was confirmed by the fact that respondents also located it in Japan, Moscow, and even Ekaterinburg.

The West as America

> When I talk about the West, I think specifically about America.
>
> —53, Moscow

When talking about the West as a whole, the respondents' most clearly defined images were those associating it with America. Moreover, the respondents were keen to emphasize that this association was commonplace: "When people talk about the West, they mean America, American music, American films" (1, Ul'ianovsk).

This association is not unique to Russians; while Europe may still lay claim to being the "centre of the Old World," nonetheless "all myths of modernity are American" (Baudrillard 1988, 81). But America also represents the "decay" of modernity; and thus it was when the West was directly equated with America, that images of the West were infused with the greatest negativity.

The West as Europe

Europe was most frequently associated with England (used often as a synonym for the United Kingdom), France, Scotland, Germany, and Italy. The prominence of England in images of Europe was explained by the dominance of English among the foreign languages that were taught in Russian schools and by the fact that most youth cultural messages (MTV, film and video products, compact discs, and the Internet) were received in the medium of English language. It was also related to the perceived "special role" of Britain in leading youth cultural trends.

In the process of equating the West with Western Europe, respondents were emphasizing two important "others." The first was America: "civilized," "cultured" Western Europe was contrasted to what was described as an American "lack of culture." The second was Eastern Europe, which although being "like the West," remained outside its borders because of its socialist heritage (235, Samara). Thus "the West" was associated with Western Europe where the latter was imagined as a compact, localized area in which life, shopping, and leisure pursuits were made simple.

The West as the Capital (Moscow)

Respondents, especially in Ul'ianovsk, frequently associated the West with Moscow, since Moscow was the most tangible example of Western life. Moscow—and for Ul'ianovsk respondents sometimes St. Petersburg, Ekaterinburg, and Samara as well—was no longer part of Russia, but belonged to "the West."

"Young people in the West do not differ from those in Moscow, only from provincial [young people]." (1, Ul'ianovsk)

"Moscow is the same as London." (41, Ul'ianovsk)

The notion of shared identity was based on images of the life and culture of young people from the capital promoted especially by magazines, television programs, and music videos. While in the provinces Moscow was perceived as a cultural mecca (especially with regard to the club scene), provincial young people were envisaged by Muscovites as inhabiting a cultural wilderness where "nothing progressive could ever happen" (53, Moscow). Thus young people from the capital might also see themselves as belonging to the center and, in this sense, to the West.

The West as "Not the East"

When compared to Western Europe, Russia was viewed as both territorially and culturally closer to the East; but when compared to the East, Russia became associated with the West. "The East is much further away for us, the East is not at all clear to us. The West—we can discuss it. . . . It is even easy sometimes to communicate with the West, but the East?" (51, Moscow).

The "obscurity" of the East, its dissimilarity from "us," the cultural distance between Russia and "the East," were central to constructing this opposition. Youth culture was frequently referred to as a source of evidence of affinity with the West. In the opinion of one respondent from Ul'ianovsk, for example: "Nothing fashionable or youthful comes out of the East, and young people there are hemmed in by strict rules of behavior . . . but in Russia, like in the West, things are completely different" (38, Ul'ianovsk).

In youth cultural terms negative images of the East were epitomized by Indian films, which were compared unfavorably to Western films (19, Ul'ianovsk; 37, Ul'ianovsk; 206, Samara): "Indian ones [films] are rubbish. Everyone likes the American ones better" (9, Ul'ianovsk).

Eastern forms of Western music and styles were also either dismissed or ridiculed (39, Ul'ianovsk; 54, Moscow): "I know that in Japan there is a group that plays punk rock, punk rock in Japanese, it is ridiculous. I have heard it once or twice. I laughed hard. . . . We are probably nearer to the West than the East. . . . The East is completely different" (39, Ul'ianovsk).

At a more fundamental level, Eastern societies were associated with work, Western ones with leisure and space for cultural creativity:

19, Ul'ianovsk: *What is there in the East? Japan, Vietnam, what is there? There is nothing there. People work there. . . . Well in Vietnam there are also a lot of military, there is fighting. . . . Korea, there they also all work. Take Korea, Mongolia, Japan, they are all working . . . China as well . . .*

Interviewer: *Don't people work in the West?*

19, Ul'ianovsk: *No, they work, but there [the West], you see, people think about their leisure, about how they spend their time, but in Japan, from early childhood, they are taught just to work . . . but Europe is considered a kind of gathering point for musicians. . . . Musicians concentrate in those countries where the politics provides an opportunity to be creative.*

The only positive reception to Eastern cultural forms was encountered in relation to Eastern martial arts. The arts of kung fu and Taekwando, for example, were considered to lend a philosophical and spiritual dimension to Western boxing or wrestling, which were only physical sports (187, Samara; 209, Samara; 238, Samara).

There was thus an apparent contradiction in young people's identities. As "Russians" they saw themselves as living in a unique country, being neither East nor West. As young people, however, they perceived themselves to be closer to the West. How this apparent contradiction was negotiated in the formation of youthful identities is explored further in the second half of the chapter.

The West as "Over There," "Abroad"

Although the majority of respondents did differentiate between components of "the West," in some respondents' narratives there remained a composite image of "abroad" (*zagranitsei*) consisting of an indivisible and unified "West":

I can't ever work out which cities and which countries they have there. It's just abroad and that's all. (193, Samara)[8]

Of course, the West is a single [united] culture . . . for us it is a single culture. They are not greatly divided among themselves. (231, Samara)

This image referred back to the Soviet stereotype that posited "abroad" as that which is "over there" (*tam*), where "they" live and where "everything is different." The term "abroad" was used specifically to refer to the West, therefore, and hardly ever with regard to the East.[9] The term was usually spoken in a negative and disparaging tone evoking past notions of the "stupefying influence" (*durnoe vliianie*) of "degenerate capitalism" or present criticism of the fact that "the West will not help Russia."

The West as Where Everything Is "the Very Best"

When talking about the West in general, concrete geographical references sometimes disappeared altogether, leaving only a loose and normative notion of the West defined primarily by the quality of life perceived to exist there. There were two key signifiers in this image: the West as the developed (*razvitii*) world; and the West as having the "very best" of everything.

When describing the West as "developed," respondents envisaged it as something indivisible, identical, and homogenous and imbued it with great symbolic value; the West symbolized superior progress, a marker of "quality," "the very best" that was available. "The West is a highly *developed* [respondent's emphasis] country" (37, Ul'ianovsk); "Everything there is the very best, highly polished, of the best quality and the latest fashion" (216, Samara).

The West was in this way associated with flourishing enterprise and the "future," since Russia was perceived to be following in the West's footsteps as it moved toward a market economy. At the same time, however, development in a "Western" sense was perceived by respondents to be a consumption-led, materialistic form of development not automatically accompanied by spiritual development. On the contrary Western style development was often associated with spiritual degradation (illustrated by the high level of crime and cheapness of life). The significance of this complex image is explored in greater detail in Chapter 8.

Life in the West: The Party Turns Sour

Standards of living and "life in general" were considered to be superior in the West; in comparison, living in Russia was considered to be little more than survival. The positive aspects of this "easy life" were associated primarily with the rule of law based on the individual's awareness of his or her own rights: "They have it in their blood, all this lawfulness, this idea of playing by the rules. We can still only dream about laws that they have had for ages" (95, Ul'ianovsk).

The confidence of people in the West in "their rights" (162, Ul'ianovsk) was perceived to create a carefree and easy environment,[10] imagined as colorful, bustling city life: "Cities there are so noisy and full of life, with bright lights and lots of people all sort of bustling around" (13 Ul'ianovsk).

An abundance of all imaginable pleasures turned even daily life in the West into a never-ending party. However, being free of worries was not equated by respondents with being genuinely "free," and this very abundance of pleasures was thought to numb people's ability to appreciate happiness, familiarity to breed boredom, and the absence of problems to make people less satisfied with what they had. Having indulged themselves so much with the good life, they were forced to "invent risk" to challenge themselves.

An example of this—repeated by many respondents—was the belief that, despite the poor provision for leisure and entertainment in Russia, Russian people knew how to have a good time. In contrast "partying" in the West was described as boring and festivity as essentially superficial: "We are the only ones with such an inborn sense of fun" (131, Samara).

Western People: They Are "Different"

Descriptions of the "adult" world of the West were highly critical, especially in relation to what respondents felt were Western people's attitudes to Russia and Russians.

The majority of responses demonstrated stereotypical notions of Western people as endowed with a peculiar set of qualities by which they could be distinguished instantly from Russian people.[11] Western people were imagined to be calm and composed and free of the angst, complexes, and aggression described as characteristic of Russian people (63, Moscow). However, this calm—which was a product of the abundance and stability of life in the West—went hand in hand with Western people's coldness, lack of genuine spirituality, and extreme individualism. Sincere feelings and warm relations were considered totally uncharacteristic of Western people:[12] "There is no time for such feelings there" (141, Ul'ianovsk); "Friendship and close relations are more reserved in the West" (194, Samara).[13]

Generosity, when shown by Western people, was also considered to be tinged with material considerations: "They may share with you expensive things which they have loads of anyway, but the stuff they want, they keep for themselves" (67, Moscow).

In contrast to Westerners' fixation with themselves, Russian people were characterized as having a strong sense of collectivism and community: "Everything here is always shared, people are always trying to come together, we celebrate all our holidays together, and everyone tries to pull together all of the time" (161, Ul'ianovsk).

An example of this, cited repeatedly, was that Westerners had no proper sense of neighborliness, often not even knowing their nearest neighbors. This reflected a deeper rupture between, on the one hand, a perception that Western people were highly cultured and well brought up but, on the other hand, that there was no depth or sincerity to this superficial politeness.

Another key element of Western social interaction was said to be the obsession with "image" (*imidzh*) (in Russian a term used primarily in this negative sense). This was evident in claims that Westerners could always be picked out of a crowd because of their particular manner of dress. At a more profound level, respondents claimed that there was "a certain Western type," "a Western type of face," or "a Western facial expression," although these remained vaguely defined.

Westerners on Russia: A Country of Bears and Degenerates

The attitudes of people from the West toward Russia and Russian people occupied an important place in Russian images of the West. As Ronald Hingley puts it, "It is not understanding of, it is *recognition* by, the West that Russians crave" (Hingley 1977, 121) and, as a rule, find wanting. Respondents were particularly offended by what they perceived to be a failure—attributed especially to Americans—to recognize ethnic differences among the people of Russia, considering them all "just Russians" (187, Samara). Ignorance about the history and culture of Russia was at least partially attributed to the Western media "which spouts any old rubbish about people in Russia" (213, Samara). Thus respondents believed that Westerners continued to hold outdated stereotypes of Russia as an uncivilized country of "Russian bears, degenerates, and so on and so forth" (215, Samara).

Such stereotypes were also interpreted as a result of Western introspection and arrogance, however. Once again, it was Americans who were accorded the harshest criticism: "They [Americans] think that their people are always number one and that they are better and superior everywhere they go. Even in relation to us, they just can't imagine that you could find any kind of intellect in such houses and such tumble-down apartments as ours. And as far as a wealth of material culture goes, well they think that they are way above everyone else already" (95, Ul'ianovsk).

Russian national identity, it was felt, was very much understated; and this practice was contrasted, in particular, to what was interpreted as American national "self-advertising," of which the most common symbol was the ubiquitous American flag.

Westerners in Love: Gender Differences and Gender Relations in the West

Differences in gender relations in the West and Russia were discussed in a number of interviews and extensively in focus groups,[14] although generally speaking these were issues which young women discussed with greater enthusiasm than young men. Romantic and sexual relations in the West were characterized as more fun, carefree, and happy than in Russia: "Romance is more fun there. When it comes to loving, people go out and have fun, they are really happy. It seems to me that all this is in fact much more characteristic of Western people" (270, Moscow, male).

In contrast in Russia, it was suggested, everyday worries could not be put aside even for people in love and there was a tragic dimension to "true love": "We are more inclined to a kind of love which is, well, I don't know, more tragic. . . . Russia is inclined to tragedy . . . a search for that special unspoken something" (192, Samara, female).[15]

Respondents also perceived Western people to be less bound by moral and social norms. Such norms were largely seen as a legacy of "Soviet upbringing" and often viewed rather negatively:

In this sense, of course, the West is ahead of us. While we still have these limits on our behavior, these restraining bonds, in the West people are becoming more and more uninhibited. . . . Here, in Russia . . . if a girl is approached by more than one guy, she won't talk to them, she'll either just cut them dead or just walk off. (194, Samara, male)

It's all dead easy for them, they have no inhibitions, while here in Russia there are just loads of people who are scared even to go up to someone and get to know them. (258, Samara, female)

However, some respondents considered this "freer" attitude to reduce relationships to a rather crude level. In general terms male and female respondents agreed that the main obstacle to the pursuit of romantic relations in Russia was strict social norms about what constituted "correct and dignified courting," although they also recognized the emergence of a new generation of young people in Russia "whose values are closer to American values" (265, Moscow, male),[16] among whom "relations between the sexes [are] based on these relatively loose principles" (266, Moscow, male).

Responses to specific commercials revealed perceptions among young Russians of Western people as less inclined to see women as "the weaker sex." The prompts for this discussion were a Harley Davidson commercial featuring a young woman riding a motorbike herself (as opposed to being on the back of "her man's") and a commercial for Wash and Go in which a girl flagged down a car for a lift. Interestingly it was the young women respondents who were "outraged" by the failure of the men to assume their proper role:

Here it is more acceptable, if a girl is walking with a guy, that he will be the one to flag down the car. (110, Samara, female)[17]

Perhaps such relations are also possible here, but the guy would definitely help the girl onto the motorcycle. (124, Samara, female)[18]

Young male respondents, however, argued against the passive role of women, especially in seeking first contacts with the opposite sex: "Why is it unacceptable for a girl to go after a guy here? Why do we think that it always has to be the guy running after the girl? Aren't guys human beings too?" (167, Samara, male).[19]

Although such attitudes may well reflect a specific period in young men's lives when they feel under considerable pressure from the responsibility for taking the initiative in romantic relationships, they undoubtedly contributed to the shaping of gender relations among young Russians.

Western Women Through Russian Eyes

Just how do young Russians imagine Western women and Western men? The survey conducted among young people in Ul'ianovsk and Samara revealed the following portrait of a typical Western woman:

- independent, lacking inhibitions or complexes, free (530 references);[20]
- attractive appearance (505 references);
- business-like (360 references);
- having a carefree approach to life and good material circumstances (120 references);
- original, having good communication skills and personal qualities (85 references);
- pragmatic (75 references).

Less frequently Western women were characterized as housewives, wives, and mothers (50 references) or as having traditional female qualities such as "tenderness" (50 references), or in terms of their relations with men (80 references). These stereotypes were confirmed in in-depth interviews and focus groups during which Western women were portrayed as people who prioritized their work and career development; more concerned (than Russian women) with themselves, their originality, and their appearance than with their family; and less concerned (than Russian women) about what men thought of them.

In thinking through these images, respondents clearly saw the most important difference between Western women and Russian women as being that women in the West were not oriented toward starting a family ("getting" a husband and having children) as the absolute purpose in life, which must be achieved as early as possible. What is more, this orientation was perceived to be absent both from women's own consciousness and from the attitudes of those around them: men, their parents, and their friends. In Russia, in contrast, respondents felt that public opinion and constant reminders to girls about their "natural" destiny had made this the only path open to them, and the condition of perpetual waiting to find

"the right man" made Russian girls more serious and more burdened with worries than their Western counterparts, denying them many of the pleasures of youth.

In contrast to Western women, Russian women were portrayed as more beautiful and "less aggressive in their appearance" (178, Samara, female),[21] more inclined toward and better able to apply make-up, and more gentle and more feminine, reflecting "a kind of post-Soviet modesty" (101, Ul'ianovsk, female).[22] Thus, although Western women were repeatedly referred to as "attractive," their outward appearance was considered to be artificial. Among Russian women, only "New Russian girls" were seen to be "close" to Western women. Such young women were described as insincere, focused on material things and seeking a beautiful and carefree life.

Western Men Through Russian Eyes

Survey data allowed the construction of the following portrait of Western men:

- business-like and professional (547 references);
- wise, well-mannered, and cultured (353 references);
- attractive (324 references);
- independent and free (287 references);
- materially well-off (235 references);
- good communication skills (235 references);
- pragmatic (140 references).

In-depth interviews revealed that respondents were less eager to pass judgment on men than on women and their statements were reticent and, on the whole, stereotypical. The clearest image to emerge was that Western men were smart and well turned out. They were also described as more self-confident than Russian men.

Thus a common picture of Western women and men emerged as having business-like qualities,[23] being attractive in appearance, independent, prosperous in a material sense, pragmatic, clever, well educated, and cultured. In describing the qualities of Western women and men, however, young people compared them not with each other, but with *Russian* women and *Russian* men respectively. The qualities cited, therefore, often referred to qualities perceived as lacking in Russian men and women (independence and freedom from complexes among women, manners and smartness in men). Interesting also was the relative lack of reference, when talking about men, to their relations with other people (men as fathers, husbands, and sons); the fact that references in the survey to men as "manful" and "strong willed" (45 references) outnumbered those to men as "family men" (43 references) would suggest that the "new Western man" had not yet reached provincial Russia even as an image, let alone a reality.

Young People in the West: Born Free

When young people in Russia talked about their Western contemporaries as opposed to "Westerners" in general, they revealed a degree of identification otherwise absent. At the most fundamental level this was apparent from *how* young people talked about Western youth, that is, they drew on situations taken from their own experience in attempting to understand or explain the lives of young people in the West, rather than referring to more abstract stereotypes.

It would, however, be wrong to take at face value claims that "young people are the same everywhere" so often stated by respondents. Interview analysis suggested rather that there were at least two different versions of "sameness" as perceived by respondents.

The first reproduced a relatively old stereotype that a certain section of Russian youth, because of its material wealth and cultural capital, was able to enjoy the same kind of life as Western youth. In the past this was the so-called golden youth (*zolotaia molodezh'*) living in Moscow but, at the end of the 1990s, this group was larger and more heterogeneous. It included "new Russians," the children of "new Russians," young people from the creative professions and bohemian counterculture (young actors and artists, show business types), and models and other "professionals" (computer specialists, employees of banks and joint enterprises). One respondent from Ul'ianovsk described the kind of people perceived as similar to Western youth thus: "Young people from both Russia and the West can behave that way in terms of music and style of dress. That is to say rich young people here can behave like that" (96, Ul'ianovsk).[24]

This approach effectively defined well-off and professional youth as "Western" and therefore "not ours," recreating, paradoxically, a Russia isolated from the wider world.

In contrast, those young people adopting the second version of shared identity opened up possible points of connection and communication with young people across the globe. This second version of shared identity posited young people, regardless of their country of origin, as being divided by lifestyle choices, in particular their primary orientation toward education, career or creative activity, or lack of such. Thus statements that "young people are the same everywhere" (189, Samara) were qualified; the same kinds of young people existed everywhere, that is, clever and stupid ones, well brought up ones and poorly brought up ones, people who liked to stay in and listen to music and those who preferred a "street life." In short, both in Russia and abroad, there were people who had a goal in life, and there were young people "who don't give a damn about how they live their lives" (101, Ul'ianovsk). This version of shared identity appeared to be more carefully and consciously formulated and avoided a vision of young people in the West as a homogenous mass.

What's the Point in Being Free If You Don't Know How to Party?

When discussing likeness and differences between Western and Russian youth more concretely, it emerged that Westerners were seen to have two distinct advantages over their Russian peers: freedom; and material opportunities. Young people in the West were perceived to be free, unfettered, and unplagued by outsiders who taught them to behave "properly": "They are so free that they can stand up, sing a song, dance, right where they are, or sit on the grass or in the street, right in the middle of the road, they can do whatever they want" (253, Ul'ianovsk).

They were "free" from interference from both the police and from members of the public, who might laugh at someone just for being different. "They [the Western public] can even say, 'It's okay, don't you worry about it! We don't mind what you wear' . . . and so on. They just don't pay any attention to things like that" (90, Ul'ianovsk).

The notion of young people's freedom was closely linked in respondents' perceptions to an image of the West as a realm of universal plenty. Young Westerners were considered to have access to easy money, which allowed them, for example, to dress much better than young people in Russia. This, together with the absence of taboos or prohibitions with regard to dress or behavior, was viewed as lying at the root of their freedom from inhibitions and anxieties. Young people in the West were imagined as wearing clothes that were looser, more comfortable, and free from status symbols, since they had no need to prove their affluence.[25] Structural constraints on Russians—lack of money and "closed borders"—also restricted their opportunities to travel. In contrast young Westerners were perceived as having much greater opportunity to travel and "see the world" (206, Samara; 209, Samara).

Freedom also meant freedom from social norms. In particular it was noted that young people in the West were not so strictly obliged to observe social rules and predetermined gender roles: "Girls don't have to get married between the ages of seventeen and twenty there. They are more full of the joys of life there at twenty-five or even thirty-five" (247, Ul'ianovsk).

A third characteristic of Western youth—their rational and balanced approach to life—was evaluated more ambivalently. The perception that young people in the West had their lives planned out to the minutest detail was interpreted positively where it was combined with images of stability, calm, and an absence of anxiety in relation to the future. At the same time such pre-programming of life was seen as contradicting the essential nature of youth itself—which was a time of absolute freedom.

The most intriguing discussion of sameness and difference concerned the art of "partying." On the one hand, the fact that Western young people "hang out" was seen as something they had in common with their Russian peers: "Young people there drink and everything just the same as here, they are no different" (39, Ul'ianovsk).

The better material situation of Western young people was even perceived as facilitating their ability to party, since, unlike Russian young people, who occupied doorways and yards, Western youth had places to go where they could all hang out as a group (29, Ul'ianovsk). However, for many young people the way in which young people in the West hung out indicated much that was different between them as indicated in one respondent's image of Western parties that was articulated after viewing the film *Kids*:[26] "So everyone comes over to your house and they all go off somewhere, and start doing something or other, which nobody can make any sense of. A load of weird looking, dodgy-looking types arrive. Guys, I mean. The girls are wandering about, drinking, chatting, and amidst all this there is a feeling that it is all quite chaotic and there is no obvious reason why everyone came in the first place" (4, Ul'ianovsk).

Other respondents also noted that "parties in the West are boring events" (13, Ul'ianovsk)[27] "In the West, young people generally stay in their houses, they somehow hang out together there and they don't drink strong alcohol. . . . It's not that great in the West. It's boring" (38, Ul'ianovsk).

In particular there was concern at the lack of preparation for "parties" shown by Western young people; respondents found such a nonchalant attitude to guests inappropriate.[28] The crucial difference, however, concerned not the "event" (the party) but the process; respondents contrasted the dull events of the Western "party" to the grand scale of drinking and eating engaged in by Russians and, more importantly still, the opportunity provided for openly expressing your sentiments, talking honestly, and revealing your innermost self to one another.

Despite the broad identification of Russian young people with their Western counterparts, there remained a sense among respondents that in talking to their Western contemporaries they would be inhibited by the fact that they remained self-conscious (bound by social norms) and not completely equal. In this sense the "macho" references, especially to Westerners' inability to drink in the same way as young Russians might be interpreted as a defense mechanism; a necessary "something" that young Russians could do better.

Blinded by, or Playing with, Stereotypes? Disentangling "the West"

A handful of respondents suggested that the West was essentially undifferentiated (39, Ul'ianovsk; 38, Ul'ianovsk; 231, Samara), but the vast majority made clear distinctions between Europe and America and had specifically focused images of America, England, France, and Germany.[29]

America: A "Nation" Without a "Culture"

Images of America were either immediate associations, which were quickly produced and generally positively responded to ("Harley Davidson," "Hollywood," "California," "sun," "freedom," "the FBI," "Pepsi-Cola," "the American constitution," "New York," "American style," and "the American dream"), or more considered and critical references to American lifestyles, values, and culture.[30]

The positive images were generally shaped by media representations in music videos, advertisements, music, and films; and their frequency and familiarity made them comfortable. Such images were so familiar that America became a sort of "second homeland" for many across the globe (Roniger 1995, 264). While this is perhaps not surprising, the degree of consciousness of the power of global communications to make "other" appear "familiar" is more so. This is how one fifteen-year-old school student—who had never traveled to the West—explained why the West was associated primarily with America: "That's because of the films, that's why its nearer, we are just swamped with films produced in America" (232, Samara).

Apparently bold, bright and uncritical images of America were thus less a product of Russian youth's naïveté about the West than of a recognition that such images were "symbols" that did not necessarily reflect reality.

One of the most immediate, positive images associated with America was that of "freedom":

The spirit of freedom. For some reason I always associate freedom with America. (64, Moscow)

America embodies freedom and equality. People's lives there are like a fairy tale. Life is good there, everyone is happy and there are no poor people, everything has a happy ending. (19, Ul'ianovsk)

Positive statements were also frequently related to American stability and freedom from the constant upheavals and cataclysms that peppered life in Russia (62, Moscow). However, freedom was complexly understood, and respondents were keenly aware of the employment of "freedom" as a symbol of and by America: "They shout it out on every street corner, that they are all free. . . . That is why they have such fluid and flexible legal codes and laws and why even the statute book upholds and embodies this sense of freedom. That is to say they try to personify that freedom themselves, to be its embodiment" (68, Moscow).

The association of freedom with America was transmitted via images of its natural environment, which was imagined as a country, like Russia, of vast open spaces, natural diversity, and never-ending highways. As one respondent, in response to the Harley Davidson after-shave commercial, put it: "The landscape is 100 percent American, people, motorcycles, sunset, sunrise, everything" (72, Moscow).

However, the type of freedom experienced in the two countries was perceived as very different, and the American style of freedom was no longer as attractive as it once had been: "Five years ago, when freedom was in fashion here, we thought of it as some kind of forbidden fruit. We thought that it would be great, my God, everyone was in such a rush then, the spirit of freedom, now nobody is interested in that freedom" (114, Samara).

Consciousness of the constructed nature of the American dream—and concern that other Russians were taken in by it—was particularly strong among those who had traveled to America themselves. The respondent below, who had spent three weeks in Los Angeles on an exchange visit when he was sixteen years old, noted: "They [Americans] would look at us in pure amazement if they knew that we thought of America like that. If they knew that America had blown itself up into a big soap bubble, which we sit and admire as it emerges from Hollywood . . . as though it represented a faithful picture of America. It is a great delusion" (187, Samara).

Evidence that, in fact, many young people were already questioning the image of America as all that is modern, clean, bright, and new was to be found in directly contradictory statements: "I think it is very dirty in New York" (42, Moscow); "For me America is associated with such a lot of dirt" (224, Samara).

The "dirt" referred to here is spiritual or moral rather than physical in nature, and this reassessment was a product not only of increasing travel to the West by young people but also a consequence of the arrival of low-grade American movies in Russia.[31] Exposure to a constant stream of Hollywood "B" movies had seriously undermined former perceptions of the West as having "the best" to offer, at least in cultural terms. In particular there was a strong awareness of the continued existence of racist attitudes (5, Ul'ianovsk; 6, Ul'ianovsk), "white" supremacy and discrimination against "non-white" Americans (56, Moscow):[32]

In America, for example, if you go into a certain district and for example Negroes [negry] *are there, there are like two races there, the black and the white. If you go, for example into a certain district, you can be killed if you are white. . . . That does not happen here. Among youth that doesn't happen either. Here Russians* [rossiiane] *are inter-ethnic, that is there are different nationalities, but in America even though they tried to get rid of it, nevertheless there is a difference between Negroes and whites. (6, Ul'ianovsk)*

The most immediate cultural reference for this image were the numerous "gangland" films that portray the deep divides in American cities. However, discussion of the injustices of slavery in America go back to the 1820s and 1830s when they provided the intelligentsia with the opportunity to indirectly criticize Russian serfdom, and racism remained a dominant theme in Russian writing on America throughout the Soviet period (Peters Hasty and Fusso 1988, 8).

Indeed, any sense of "community" was absent from respondents' images of America. Respondents believed that true, meaningful friendship simply did not exist in America:

All their relations are like that. "Oh, great," and you're instant friends for life, just like that. But anything more and its "Oh no, sorry that's your own problem." (52, Moscow)

Nobody there is really genuinely or deeply interested in how you are. They ask each other all the time: "How are you?" "How's things?" but it is not the done thing to answer, "Not great actually." They do not visit each other's houses and cannot ask their neighbors for salt or bread, often they do not even know who their neighbors are. (224, Samara)

Another persistent, but negative, stereotype among young Russians, and especially among those who had had direct contact with Westerners, was that Western people (and Americans in particular) had a lower level of general education:[33]

The general intellectual level of the masses is lower there. (52, Moscow)

They [Americans] are impenetrably stupid, well it's some kind of underdevelopment really, there is no depth to them, they are superficial somehow. They may have a really high degree of knowledge but it is all superficial. (59, Moscow)

This lack of education was said to be evident in their ignorance and uncultured behavior: "People there walk around the Salvador Dali museum with absolutely no restraint, they are quite happy to clamber around on the statues for a photograph, and they eat potato chips and so on wherever they are. It would never enter my head to do such things" (57, Moscow).

Respondents imagined Americans as permanent tourists, surfing world culture with an air of disdain, confident that nothing of any real significance existed anywhere outside America (1, Ul'ianovsk). This discourse echoes European stereotypes of the commercial materialism, social fragmentation, lack of culture, and sheer artificiality of the American experience dating back to the early nineteenth century (Ellwood 2000, 28).

The poverty, or even absence, of culture in America was often linked to the constitution of the "nation" itself: "American culture . . . is one big jumble [*kasha*], there everything has been mixed up: all religions, all tendencies [*napravleniia*], one has merged into another. And that is where the many sects come from because everything has been . . . mixed up. . . . I would not live in America even though people say now that America and Russia are very similar" (224, Samara). The intimation that the formation of the American nation had left it "rootless" and thus "cultureless" was spelled out even more clearly by the following respondents:

All the riffraff from all around the world suddenly just came together in one place and just look what came out of it! (56, Moscow)

The Americans don't have a nation as such. . . . It is a dirty nation that has no roots. (19, Ul'ianovsk)

Although Russia, not to mention the former Soviet Union, was deeply multiethnic, Russians considered themselves only to be guilty of not paying enough attention to their roots; they were not "rootless." This distinction appeared to be founded in the differentiation respondents made between a "false" nation of immigrants and the peculiar national culture that had emerged in Russia out of the sharing of a single space by different peoples over centuries.

America was perceived to be able to assert itself in the world arena and export its values and cultural products around the world, not because of its superior cultural status as a nation, therefore, but because of its ability to inculcate a strong sense of patriotism among its citizens and because of its sheer power as a state:

America is the strongest power in the world. We are not the only ones being Americanized by America. (56, Moscow)

America is the strongest state and therefore it is able to impose its music, films, and politics on others. (13, Ul'ianovsk).

Despite the apparent success, power and buoyancy of American society, its "rootlessness" was perceived by young Russians to be the source of its inevitable demise: "It [America] reminds you of the *Titanic*, which is sailing along and sailing along but then there is so much lawlessness and such high crime rates that in the end there will come a moment of reckoning when the whole thing will go down" (224, Samara).

America Versus Europe: Appearance Isn't Everything

Where Europe was talked about as a single entity, it was often in contrast to the perceived "other" of America. America won the competition with Europe when it came to excitement and openness to new acquaintance:

It [Europe] is boring, especially in Belgium. I just couldn't talk to them at all. I was supposed to stay there for a month but after two weeks I simply left. I had had enough. (60, Moscow)

English people are fundamentally different from Americans. They never smile. (52, Moscow)

Significantly America was seen positively in those aspects in which it was perceived to be "like Russia," that is as a "young" nation of unlimited possibilities, and in contrast to a weary and ossified Europe (Peters Hasty and Fusso 1988, 8–9). One example of this was the perceived absence in America of deep divisions of social class or caste that were considered to bind European society and culture: "The main difference is the lack in America of castes, the lack of caste thinking. Any two people will talk to each other happily" (51, Moscow).

However, for others the perception that "Americans always have a smile on their face, which you can't wash off . . . even if you are talking about something sad" (52, Moscow) indicated a belief that American beauty, harmony, and friendliness was superficial only. In this sense, as Baudrillard notes, the smile expressed not happiness or emotion but emptiness and indifference (Baudrillard 1988, 34). Thus, although Americans were praised for being less reserved than Europeans (especially the English), Europeans were nonetheless seen as expressing their emotions more naturally; in contrast Americans were perceived as demonstrative, melodramatic, and unnatural when they tried to be emotional (232, Samara). This was apparent in the following metaphoric comparison of European and American cities: "The difference is that Europeans don't try to show off outward beauty to the same degree. That is to say, in Europe there are hardly any of those tall buildings, made of glass. . . . In addition, Europeans have a certain inner harmony. That is to say that, well, outer beauty and inner beauty of the soul . . . exist in more or less equal proportions and so it is as though a certain compromise has been achieved" (195, Samara).

Europeans were imagined to be more civilized and more cultured than Americans and to dress in a more "acceptable" manner: "There is something civilized about them. If they wear a T-shirt then it fits and if it's a shirt or a jacket then it comes down to the waist as it should, in a civilized fashion" (163, Ul'ianovsk).

Indeed, several respondents were of the opinion that, on the whole, people led more modest lives in Europe than in America (40, Ul'ianovsk).

With regard to young people, no major differences between American and European youth emerged. However, respondents did note that the superficiality of education noted above was characteristic of America and not Europe. It was also suggested that American young people had a great degree of freedom and independence (234, Samara),[34] and that they were less disciplined and more pretentious than Europeans (224, Samara).

America was perceived to be more aggressive than Europe. This related both to American society—with its high crime rate—but also to external relations: "America is not so tranquil as England, because there is a high crime rate there" (207, Samara); "For me, Europe is not aggressive at all, while America might be" (233, Samara).

Perceptions of America's intentions toward Russia were not without their ambiguities, however. A representative survey conducted by the Russian Independent Institute for Social and National Problems among young people (aged 17 to 26) at the end of 1997,[35] revealed that young people viewed America as both an extremely friendly state to Russia (14 percent considered it a friendly state, second only to Belarus) but also the state most hostile toward Russia (17 percent of youth) (RNISiNP 1998, 40).[36]

When characterizing the connection between America and Europe, respondents thus spoke of Europeans' "struggle" against "Americanism" (50, Moscow) and the imposing character of the American way of life: "Even in Europe [as well as Russia] nothing is done just like that, without interference from America" (13, Ul'ianovsk).

England: A Country of Extremes

The only other country to receive specific and sustained discussion in interviews and focus groups was England.[37] Interestingly, a commonly expressed opinion was that London, and Britain in general, represented a kind of elite Europe (50, Moscow), and spending time in England was seen as far more meaningful than spending time in Berlin for example, or even in Paris. In some way, English cultural phenomena were endowed with significance that was more than national, which was indeed international or global, as shown by the global resonance of groups such as the Beatles or Pink Floyd (51, Moscow). In general, images of England and English people were divided between those describing a very conservative, history and culture-laden society and those related to youth cultural nonconformity.

Stereotypes of England repeated by respondents suggested that England was a country saturated with the cultural history of its past. Concepts such as "Old mother England," "Good old England," and "the misty Albion" remained relatively attractive and positive, since they suggested a concern to preserve the past (something which respondents often criticized

Russians themselves for failing to do). "They [the English] all walk everywhere, guard their castles; even their taxis are old. They respect and value old things and all kinds of art" (241, Samara). While the ethnic diversity of America was generally interpreted negatively (a "kasha"), British diversity was viewed rather more ambivalently. This may result, on the one hand from a lack of clarity about the relationship between different national groups within the United Kingdom. England was often paired with Scotland rather than with Ireland or Wales, while the concept of Great Britain was hardly referred to at all. Indeed, tartan was even considered to be a symbol of *England* (100, Ul'ianovsk).[38]

London, however, was seen to consist not only of "historically" British peoples but also of recent immigrants ("foreigners"), and this was used to explain some of the characteristics of the English: "Maybe it is because there are so many foreigners in England. In London they probably make up about 50 percent of the population" (52, Moscow).

In particular, it was suggested that this might explain why the English were stand-offish, more fastidious, faithful to tradition, and conservative; they wanted to "close themselves off" from foreigners. "They are totally preoccupied with themselves. They don't engage in close contact with others. When I was in England, I got to know Jewish, Irish, Scottish, and American people but not English people" (52, Moscow).

Other stereotypes, which were supported by experience, included the obsession and aggression of the English with regard to football (56, Moscow) and the impenetrable nature of the English sense of humor (19, Ul'ianovsk).

The image of London was also diversely presented. Although England was often described as the "coolest" place in relation to youth culture and fashion, provincial respondents in particular also imagined London as a very conservative city. The image of London as the capital of youth culture was widely articulated by those who had spent time in London or whose friends had done so. English young people had "the coolest and most interesting parties" (54, Moscow), were highly "progressive" and cultured (38, Ul'ianovsk), and were recognized as the authority on all new tendencies and trends; "English young people always get to know about things earlier. For some reason, over there they are the trendsetters" (11, Ul'ianovsk).

Germany was the other European country referred to relatively frequently, primarily in the context of specific events (such as the Berlin "Love Parade") or youth cultural trends (for example, breakdancing, snowboarding, skinheads), which were perceived to be particularly developed there. At the more general level, images of Germany were stereotypically of a "strict" (234, Samara) and "clean" (19, Ul'ianovsk) country whose people were "practical" and "efficient" (19, Ul'ianovsk).

Conclusion

It has been suggested in this chapter that young people did not absorb images from the media about the West in any direct or unreflective way. Not only did young people draw their images of the West from other sources than the media—school, family, friends, own experiences—but images, regardless of their original source, were subjected to these interpretative filters as they were processed by individuals and located within whole worldviews. The result was the continued existence of stereotypical images of the West, but also a growing number of images, a greater complexity of those images and increasingly complex interpretation of them.

Images of the West continued to be dominated by images of the United States, and America remained the most significant point of reference against which "one's own" could be identified and separated from "others." The explanation of why images of America were most frequently articulated by respondents (especially those from provincial areas) to describe their notions of the West lay, according to respondents, in the abundance of cultural products—movies, videos, popular music—from America. American films, portraying positive images of "the American dream" and of "America the great power," were still the most common basis upon which images of the West (America) were formed. America also continued to hold the greatest attraction for young Russians. A representative survey of Russian youth conducted in 1997 found that of those young people stating they would like to go abroad, the preferred country of destination was America: 21.4 percent stated America compared with 12.6 percent preferring Germany, 9.5 percent England, and 8.8 percent France (RNISiNP 1998, 42).[39]

At the same time, the most negative narratives of the West were also those associated with America. America was thus that which was most loved by Russian youth—for it signified an authentic culture of "space, speed, cinema, technology" (Baudrillard 1988, 100)—and that which was most hated, since it appeared banal, vulgar, and most importantly, rootless. This love-hate relationship, Baudrillard argues, arises from America's location as "the anti-utopia of . . . the neutralization of values, of the death of culture" (Baudrillard 1988, 97). Thus perceptions of similarities based on images of both Russia and America as "new powers" with "noble savage" roots, and in opposition to the old and tired European powers, coexisted with a vision of America and Russia as polar opposites.

While the "love-hate" relationship with America might be considered to be a legacy from the past, young Russians appeared to exist in *global* spaces to a much greater extent than their parents' generation. This was evident from the fact that young people interpreted images of youth and youth culture in the West in a more positive light than those of Western people in general or the West as a whole. It was also shown in respondents' imagined solidarity with those young people in the West who adopted similar lifestyles, listened to similar music, and had shared values, tastes, and leisure activities. It was in this respect that young people appeared to be making a break from a past tendency to see the West only as a reference point for self-appreciation (Hingley 1977, 121) and to seek rather to understand others' experience through their own.

Russian young people, however, were in no way a new and Westernized generation unrecognizable to their parents. The use of the West as an "arbiter of ultimate reality" (Hingley 1977, 122)—to inversely reflect all that was positive, and negative, about Russia—is deeply embedded in Russia's past. Equally, young Russians were not uniquely globally isolated and thus defensive with regard to their own "difference." Many of the criticisms leveled at the West (and in particular at America) can be found among Western European and other youth. Indeed, Ellwood argues that the French "hold the United States up as a mirror to look, in fact, at themselves" (Ellwood 2000, 27) in a parallel argument to the one set out in this chapter.

Perhaps most importantly, exploring young people's images of the West has suggested that, far from being "dazzled" by the new and bright images of the West, young people in Russia were highly conscious of the way in which images were mobilized for specific purposes. Thus the use of Western settings for video clips of Russian singers or groups were not seen as disrupting *Russian* meanings but as legitimate in so far as they served specific purposes (by creating a particular ambience, reaching out to a particular audience, or allowing the creation of a "fantasy world" or beautiful image). While a predisposition toward a critical attitude to the media might be borne of past image manipulation in the political realm, current distrust was associated with the world of commerce. Many respondents regarded the simplistic nature of new images—advertisements in particular—as additional proof of the fact that they did not reflect reality. They had been deliberately created (by ideologues of show business, the commercial industry, and the American government) in order to promote "the American idea" in a more effective manner and to offer visual evidence of the superiority of the American way of life over the Russian.[40] One respondent even suspected that the Russian government might be deliberately promoting an abundance of Western images in order to focus people's minds on that which the country was trying to achieve (191, Samara).

Despite the continued reproduction of a range of stereotypical images of the West and Western people, therefore, young Russians revealed a well-developed critical faculty with regard to media images of the West. This media literacy gave young people the confidence to interact with Western cultural messages and forms on their own terms. It is the outcome of this engagement—in concrete cultural practices—which is discussed in the subsequent chapters.

5 "Progressives" and "Normals"
Strategies for Glocal Living

Hilary Pilkington (with Elena Starkova)

> Globalization . . . can be grasped in the small and concrete, in the spatially particular, in one's own life, in cultural symbols that all bear the signature of the "glocal."
>
> —Beck 2000, 49

The first part of the book has been concerned with tracing the flow of Western commodities and cultural forms that increasingly shape the cultural world of Russian youth. Young people themselves have appeared as sophisticated and critical readers of these texts, but have been portrayed, nevertheless, primarily as "local" receivers of "global" cultural products and images.[1] The second part of the book turns its attention to the everyday cultural engagements of young people with global cultural commodities and forms. In the course of the next four chapters, the book explores how young people in their communicative, stylistic, and musical practice differentially employ the global and local. It is in these daily, concrete, and often mundane practices, it is suggested, that young people define distinctive "strategies" for contemporary "glocal" living.

The current chapter is intended primarily to introduce readers to a number of youth cultural scenes in urban Russia at the end of the 1990s.[2] The manifest diversity and fluidity of these scenes (see Diagrams 5.1–5.3) necessitates a return to a number of theoretical questions that lace the book, however. The first of these concerns how to assess the impact on Russian youth cultural practice of the opening up to the West. This question is addressed not by quantifying the "Western" cultural consumption of young people, but by exploring their cultural practice as a series of local engagements with global cultural forms. By tracing lines of continuity and rupture between the scenes of the late Soviet and post-Soviet period, the chapter asks whether the distinctive Russian youth cultural scene of the late 1980s has survived the torrent of contemporary global cultural flows.

More importantly, however, this chapter is specifically concerned with locating the spectrum of microsocial formations of youth in the social and cultural fabric of Russia at the end of the twentieth century. Earlier suggestions that glocalization is an inherently stratifying process (see Chapter 1) are given empirical weight in this part of the book. The "radically unequal" impacts of globalization that result in some becoming fully "global" while others remain fixed in their "locality" (Bauman 1998a, 2) are explored as they are manifest in the stratification of the contemporary youth scene. Young people's microgroups are socially located in this chapter. Their specific communicative, musical, and stylistic practices are detailed in Chapters 6 and 7. In Chapter 8 the question of how best to conceptualize the outcome of global-local cultural engagements is addressed directly, with particular attention to the relevance of theories of "cultural hybridization."

In the process of mapping microgroups formed by young people, it became apparent that the broad trends of the Russian youth cultural scene confirmed many of the findings of recent studies of youth cultural practice in late modern, Western societies that have led to calls for the development of a "post-subcultural" approach to youth. The third strand of analysis in this chapter thus relates to how the study of "peripheral" youth cultural scenes might inform emergent "post-subcultural" theories.[3] In particular, it is argued here that a new approach should build on subcultural theory's concern to socially embed youth cultural practice, but enact this through empirical studies of cultural practices across the *whole* youth scene. Although current "post-subcultural" critiques evidence the growing "de-differentiation of the subcultural-conventional divide" (Muggleton 2000, 52), by confining their empirical study to those traditionally inhabiting the subcultural side of that binary, they reinvest primary significance in stylistic practice (albeit increasingly supplemented by attention to musical taste). In mapping the Russian youth scene at the end of the 1990s, the authors have been concerned to present young people's "subcultural" and "conventional" identities from vantage points on both sides of its border; a border, it is argued which although frequently transgressed, remains clearly discernible.

Remapping the Scene: The Rebirth of "Subculture"?

Diagrams 5.1–5.3 reconstruct the youth cultural scenes in 1997–98 of three cities:[4] Moscow, Russia's political and economic capital; Samara, a major and relatively economically buoyant city on the Volga river; and Ul'ianovsk, a smaller city in the middle Volga region with a reputation for political and sociocultural conservatism.[5] The maps were constructed on the basis of qualitative data gathered between autumn 1997 and spring 1998 and are inherently subjective,[6] since they reflect young people's own narratives of their location on the scenes.[7]

Remapping the youth cultural scene is a dangerous exercise, since the very act of "naming" microgroups of youth focuses attention on difference, antagonism, closure, and separation. This lends credence to a reading of the maps as evidence that the collapse of the intrusive Soviet state, and the "flowering" of market relations, has allowed Russian young people to "fix" identities to discrete subcultural styles in a way previously prohibited by the peculiarly state-saturated nature of the "dominant culture" in Soviet Russia.[8] The appeal of such a reading lies in its apparent confirmation of the evidence of subcultural practice among Russian youth. Fran Markowitz, for example, suggests that for young Russians "each sound goes with a look, an attitude, and a relationship to society. Identification with a particular musical group or genre thus provides a way to cement ties to a real or imagined collective" (Markowitz 2000, 132). Such a reading also neatly fits commonsense notions of Russia's "one step behind" pattern of modernization; just when researchers of youth culture in the West are debating what comes *after* "subculture," in Russia the term is being posthumously rehabilitated, presumably reflecting new consumer opportunities for youth in Russia equivalent to those in post-World War II societies in the West.

Although recognizing these temptations, the authors' preferred reading of these maps is not as a series of negotiations with the "dominant culture," but as strategies for managing glocal lives employed by young people primarily to differentiate themselves from a local "other." The current interest in the concept of subculture in relation to Russian youth, it is suggested, is not a theoretical response to "objective" social and cultural processes, but reflects a desire among social scientists to reengage with theoretical concepts previously dismissed primarily for ideological reasons.

"Subculture" in Soviet Russia was perceived by Soviet sociologists to be an ideological, not a theoretical, category and discursively constructed as relevant only to capitalist societies.[9] Concepts of both "sub-" and "counterculture" were ritually critiqued by Soviet sociologists as "bourgeois" because they suggested conflict between *generations* was replacing class struggle as the motor of history and thereby distracting youth from their *true* revolutionary interests. Moreover, their focus on the cultural sphere was criticized for promoting the illusion that economically rooted class antagonisms could be overcome through cultural practice, that is, by changing manner, style, or clothes (Davydov 1977; Ikonnikova 1974, 1976; Khudaverdian 1977, 1986; Kurbanova 1985, 1986). Paradoxically, therefore, Soviet sociologists criticized the work of the CCCS (despite its neo-Marxist origins) and, in their concern to show Soviet society to be free of generational conflict, adopted a structural-functionalist approach to youth culture, which emphasized the role of youth cultural practice in the successful *socialization* of young people and rejected any possibility of rupture between generations (Pilkington 1994, 74–78).

It was in the mid-1980s that cultural theorists began to reappropriate the notion of "subculture" in application to Soviet society (see Kuchmaeva 1987, Matveeva 1987, and Orlova 1987),[10] although the first empirical work on Soviet youth subcultures was undertaken by social psychologists at the end of the perestroika period (Fel'dshtein and Radzikhovskii 1988; Shchepanskaia 1991). Sociological literature on the theory of subculture remained absent, however. Even when, in the mid 1980s, youth groupings acting outside formal institutions became more visible and more widespread, the Western neo-Marxist concern with "dominant" and "resistant" cultural practice was eschewed. Instead of being referred to as "subcultures," alternative youth groups became dubbed "informals" (*neformaly*), thereby locating their participants within "nonofficial spheres of society and in a horizontal rather than vertical relationship with the dominant culture.[11] Empirically, these subcultural youth formations were analyzed through mechanistically constructed classifications of "positive," "neutral," and "negative" "informal" groups (Sundiev 1987, 1989; Levanov and Levicheva 1988; Levanov, Levicheva, and Rubanova 1989; Plaksii 1988; Gromov and Kuzin 1990).[12]

Just as "authentic subcultures" in the West have been shaped, if not created, by interactions with the media and academia (Redhead 1990, 25; Thornton 1995, 162), so too the *neformaly* were a product of the formal structures of Soviet society (the CPSU, the *Komsomol*, and their media). However, the *neformaly* label was quickly adopted by those on the youth cultural scene and by the late 1980s had acquired a degree of authenticity. The term signified, however, only a positioning in relation to dominant social and political institutions; *neformaly* were those who sought expression outside official state structures (the *Komsomol*, the CPSU). Consequently the collapse of those structures and the radical reconfiguration of the formal, state sphere in Russia during the 1990s rendered *neformaly* identity no longer meaningful, even to those who had previously self-identified with it: "There is no such notion of *neformaly* nowadays. The concept of *neformaly* could exist when 'the formals' [*formalisty*] existed, in particular the Central Committee of the VLKSM [All-Union Leninist Communist Union of Youth, or *Komsomol*] and so on" (a former punk, 231, Samara).

Just as postwar subcultures in the West were romanticized by a generation of academics with 1960s political agendas, so too the Russian *neformaly* have taken on an academic half-life as harbingers of democracy.

The collapse of Soviet-style regimes across Eastern Europe led "informal" practices, not only to be recognized as a widespread feature of state socialist societies, but also to be interpreted as central to bringing about regime change in them. Wallace and Kovatcheva, for example, suggest that youth cultural groups' "non-conformist expression of style became an act of defiance" which "challenged the regime by undermining the very basis of its functioning—authoritarian power and conformity" (Wallace and Kovatcheva 1998, 170, 177). "Informal groups" were considered to be "the embryo of civil society" (Hosking 1988) and youth cultural practice to be the site upon which youth were "trained" for the transition to postsocialist and postmodern society (Ule 1998, 174).

For other scholars, however, the designification of the notion of *neformaly* has suggested the need to reject the term as an inauthentic and politically overdetermined concept and look for a more authentic *cultural* formation with a pre-glasnost' and post-glasnost' existence. In such readings of the late and post-Soviet scene the *tusovka* has been posited as the core of "alternative" cultural practice and envisaged not as *resistant* to state power but a means of *escaping* from, or ignoring, it (Yurchak 1999, 84).[13] For Yurchak, it was the aesthetics of *steb* that was central to *tusovka* culture in the late Soviet period,[14] whereas for Rayport Rabodzeenko *tusovki* first and foremost "generated alternative social spaces" (an "elsewhere") to counteract "a profound sense of alienation" (Rayport Rabodzeenko 1998, 540–48). For both these writers, though, a marked continuity of youth cultural practice between the socialist and postsocialist periods is explained by the nonpolitical, that is, *creative cultural*, character of *tusovki* (Rabodzeenko 1998, 56).

While theorists in the West[15] have sought a more culturally rooted and "authentic" category for the analysis of youth cultural practice in Russia, paradoxically, the response of Russian sociologists to the designification of the term *neformaly* has been to explore the possibility of rehabilitating the Western concept of youth "subculture." In the late 1990s, the first three sociological texts on Russian youth subcultures were published (Omel'chenko 2000; Kostiusheva 1999; Islamshina et al. 1997).[16] The late entrance of Russian sociology to the debate on subculture has meant that it has avoided the class reductionism of earlier Western theories of youth subculture. In these texts, subcultures are interpreted as the constituent parts of late modern society in its "disintegrative" state, and subcultural affiliation is portrayed as a lifestyle choice (Sokolov 1999; Godina 1999, 51) rather than class destiny.[17] Sokolov's argument that subcultures should be studied in terms of what is being chosen by its members rather than what is "resisted" through subcultural affiliation (Sokolov 1999, 19) combines a traditional Soviet approach (emphasizing continuity rather than conflict between generations) to youth culture with a post-resistance model of youth subculture.[18] Thus, in line with emergent post-subcultural approaches in the West (Thornton 1995; Redhead 1997; Hetherington 1998; Muggleton 2000; Bennett 1999b), first attempts to map the post-Soviet youth cultural scene by Russian sociologists recognize, as one of its characteristics, the erasing of borders, and frequent movement, between subcultural groups (Islamshina et al. 1997, 54).

Such "subcultural" diversity, fluidity, and slippage was found to be characteristic of the Russian youth scene, as illustrated in Diagrams 5.1–5.3 by the representation of microgroups within overlapping spheres. Empirical studies in the West suggest that this increased fluidity is indicative of more profound trends in late modern consumer-based societies toward "unstable and shifting cultural affiliations" (Bennett 1999b, 605), which have led to the emergence of "postmodern subcultures." These, Muggleton suggests, differ from postwar subcultures in that they display a limited perception of themselves in collective terms, a transient attachment to any one style—and thus a weakened sense of the boundaries between different subcultures—and a failure to recognize divides between the subcultural and the conventional (Muggleton 2000, 52–53).[19]

The analysis of the Russian scene carried out by the authors confirmed the significant fluidity between different style affiliations in the subcultural section of the youth scene (those parts of the youth scene inhabited by the *neformaly* and *tusovki*, see Diagrams 5.1–5.3). However, these fleeting subcultural affiliations were revealed to be housed within broader and deeper youth cultural strategies referred to, following young people's self-identifications, as "progressive" and "normal."[20] In contrast to "postmodern subcultures," these youth cultural strategies were not bought at the "supermarket of style" (Polhemus 1997, 150) but carved out of the social cleavages of Soviet modernity. Moreover, these strategies had clear boundaries, which, although frequently transgressed, were meaningful for not only subcultural (progressive) but also mainstream (normal) youth. In the analysis that follows, readers are introduced to a range of young people engaged in microgroups falling within one or other of these youth cultural strategies. In the concluding part of the chapter, the reasoning behind the delineation of such strategies is explained and a broad typologization of their constitutive elements is set out.

Progressives: Reaching Out, Moving On

The passing of the *neformaly* reflected the fact that youthful identities at the end of the 1990s in Russia were no longer defined against a single other—formal state structures—but were multifocal. The cultural space of the *neformaly* became inhabited by young people with a wide range of style affiliations but who shared a progressive youth cultural practice drawing on a core set of *tusovka* meanings and practices. Post-Soviet *tusovka* practice did not seek primarily to resist or even evade the state but, as Yurchak notes, involved "a creative appropriation of cultural symbols through market and nonmarket techniques from state-run cultural spheres, from the official post-Soviet market and from diverse subcultures and black markets that escape official control" (Yurchak 1999, 78). If Soviet *neformaly* had been wholly defined by their relationship to the state, in contrast post-Soviet *tusovki* had multiple reference points and sites of interaction: the West, consumption, creative activity, commerce and the media, and very importantly, other youthful identities. The constellation of individual *tusovki*, their degree of separation, independent coherency, and self-confidence to stand outside the *neformaly* label, however, varied significantly across the three city-based scenes studied.

Sheltering Diversity: Ul'ianovsk's Subcultural Cocktail

In defiance of the logic of post-subculturalism in Western societies, it was the relatively undeveloped subcultural scene in Ul'ianovsk that displayed the least division by style affiliation. Although at the end of the 1990s, it was possible to locate individual, style-based *tusovki* in central cafes and on central squares in Ul'ianovsk, the range of styles and movements evident in other cities remained conspicuously absent (see Diagram 5.1). There was rather a single, central *tusovka* composed of hippies, punks, heavy metal fans, and rock musicians who retained a collective identity as *neformaly.*

Subcultural fluidity had been fostered in Ul'ianovsk by the traditional sharing of two main city center sites for hanging out: Lenin Square, referred to simply as "the square" (*ploshchad'*), and the tennis courts (*korty*). The Lenin Square *tusovka* included a wide range of style and music-based *tusovki* such as Depeche Mode fans (*depesha*), skateboarders (*skeitera*), rappers (*repera*), punks (*panki*), and hippies (*khippy*) (254, Ul'ianovsk). Rock fans and music lovers in general (*rokery, metallisty*, and *melomany*) might hang out there, or outside the House of Culture "Chkalov." The movement of the *tusovka* scene increasingly off the streets and into central cafes and bars, as the commercial service sector developed in the city, was reflected in new meeting points in the "lower bar" in the Lenin Memorial Center, in the "top cafe" of the Trade Unions building, and sometimes, in the Chkalov club (33, Ul'ianovsk).

On the fringes of the *neformaly* scene in Ul'ianovsk, were those young people who attached an ideological motif to their practice, such as skinheads (*skinkhedy, britogolovie*), punks (*panki*), and anarchists (*anarkhisty*), although the number of young people engaged in these groups in Ul'ianovsk was so small that there was disagreement among respondents over whether there were any skinheads in the city at all.[21] Also partially overlapping the *neformaly* were the "romantics"; this is a term employed

Diagram 5.1 **Mapping the youth scene in Ul'ianovsk, September-October 1997**

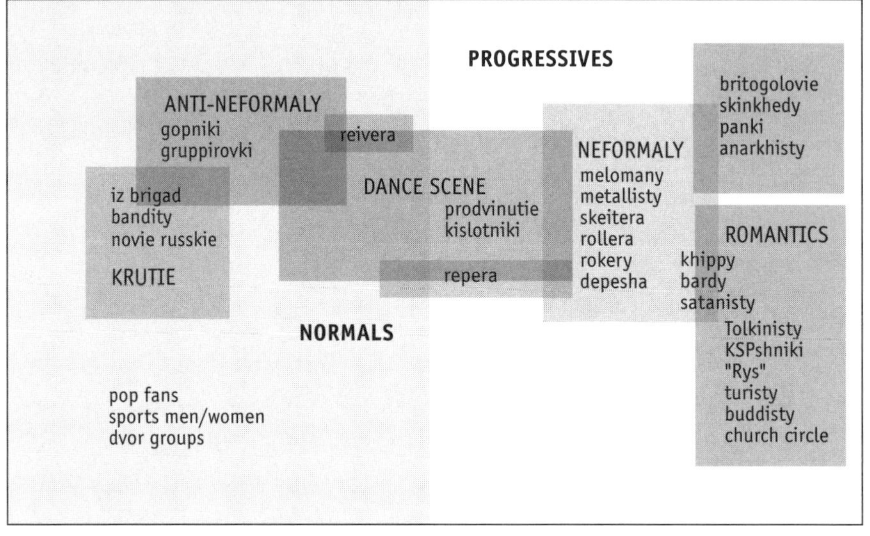

by the authors[22] rather than the respondents to indicate diverse groups of young people interested in historical periods and events, spiritual and religious aspects of life, folk traditions, folklore, and nature.[23] The life strategies of such young people positioned them close to the *neformaly*, although the activities in which they participated were often more institutionally organized. The role-play movement (*dvizhenie rolevikh igr*)—also referred to as the "games tusovka" (*igrovaia tusovka*)—included groups such as the Indianists (*Indeanisty*), Dungeons and Dragons (*DnD*) enthusiasts, the chivalry movement (*Klub rytsarskogo dvizheniia*), and the Tolkienists (*Tolkinisty*).[24] Although the role-play movement clearly overlapped with other *tusovki*, and in terms of its practices at games (gatherings in the forest, drinking, campfires, communal singing) and membership it was close to the *turisty*, it also took a highly organized and ritualized form (Fig. 1).[25] The movement had emerged in Ul'ianovsk in 1991—when *The Hobbit* and *The Lord of the Rings* trilogy began to appear widely in Russian translation—although it would seem that other cities saw the movement develop earlier, reportedly from around 1987 in St. Petersburg (Rayport Rabod-zeenko 1998, 400). While fantasy movements—associated in the West with science fiction, technology, and cyberspace—might appear to sit uneasily within the spiritually oriented "romantics," the Tolkienists were a vivid example of the "indigenization" of global cultural movements (Islamshina et al. 1997). The Tolkienist interviewed in Ul'ianovsk referred to the games as a "purely Russian phenomenon"

Fig. 1 *Tolkinisty* in Moscow. Preparations for the annual Hobbit Games included making costumes and material artifacts and was a skilled and time-consuming affair. Photo by Alexandr Tiagny-Riadno, March 2001.

(1, Ul'ianovsk), having its origins not only in groups of Tolkien fans but also drawing inspiration and membership from the Krapivin club of the 1970s,[26] the *turisty*, and the bard and folk movement. The "Russianness" of the movement was enhanced in Ul'ianovsk as a result of its association with the club "Rys'," from whose members many Tolkienists had learned the skills of Russian medieval battle (*slavianogoretskaia bor'ba* and *kulachnaia bor'ba*), which were central to the performance of the Tolkien games.

"Subcultural" fluidity—epitomized by the retention of *neformaly* identity—characterized youth cultural scenes in smaller provincial cities, such as Ul'ianovsk. It reflected, however, not a self-confident cultural diversity among youth in the city, but a protective shield for a range of city center *tusovki* against their traditional cultural enemy, the *gopniki*.[27] This was because, the *tusovka*—central to Moscow and St. Petersburg "informal" communication—was never the dominant mode of interaction in cities like Ul'ianovsk, which conformed rather to the Volga model of territorial gang formation (Salagaev 1997; Pilkington 1994, 141–60; Omel'chenko 1996). This cultural context explained the relatively weak formation of style distinction, which was interpreted by *neformaly* as a sign of the scene's immature (pre-subcultural rather than post-subcultural) state. This was expressed by the following respondent's description of the intermingling of punk and hippie styles in the city: "It's a complete medley, a total cocktail [of styles]. . . . A punk goes by . . . [with] completely crazy eyes . . . [but] *fen'ki*[28] up to his elbows, a complete cocktail" (253, Ul'ianovsk).

This "cocktail" was not celebrated as postmodern style surfing, however, but regretted. At worst the openness and fluidity of the scene was perceived to threaten individual *tusovki*; role-play events, for example, had suffered from the disruptive interest of *satanisty* ("Satanists," or "occultists"),[29] *turisty*, and "new Russians" (who commissioned games for their entertainment). At best, it was interpreted as evidence of the "inauthenticity" of locally fashioned *tusovki*: "I don't know if you can call us hippies, but [we are] people with hippie ideas . . . freedom, which manifests itself first of all in the freedom of movement" (11, Ul'ianovsk).

Thus, out of necessity rather than choice, *neformaly* on the Ul'ianovsk scene described themselves as sharing not a distinct subcultural style but rather a peculiar approach to life: "[*Neformaly*] are those who look to the future, to the future to come . . . to change our Ul'ianovsk somehow with regard to young people. That is, we . . . try to approach things a bit differently [*nestandartno*] from the rest" (33, Ul'ianovsk). Other definitions of *neformaly* as "independent" (29, Ul'ianovsk) and "different from normal [*obychnie*] youth" (3, Ul'ianovsk) by respondents confirmed the dominance of "attitude" as opposed to style in "alternative" identities (Muggleton 2000, 125). However, in this instance the glossing over of differences between individual style affiliations was not explained by the weakening of collective identities, but rather by the imperative to differentiate, and protect, themselves from an implied, hostile "other" in the form of the majority of conventional, "normal" youth dominated by *gopnik* attitudes.

Defending the Right to Rock: Neformaly in Samara

In Samara, a larger but nonetheless provincial Volga city, individual *tusovki* were distinct, although they identified themselves primarily by musical taste as opposed to subcultural style: "The division is by musical genre. . . . The majority of young people in Samara are clearly divided according to musical trends. I mainly talk to [those who listen to] hard rock, *metallisty*" (207, Samara).

The content of *neformaly* identity in Samara consisted primarily in the expression of a preference for rock as opposed to electronic dance music, since the latter was sufficiently developed to constitute a real threat to the former. Thus, in contrast to the Ul'ianovsk scene, which remained essentially bifurcated between alternative and mainstream youth, the scene in Samara had three established poles: *neformaly*, the dance or club scene, and anti-*neformaly*.

Diagram 5.2 **Mapping the youth scene in Samara, April 1998**

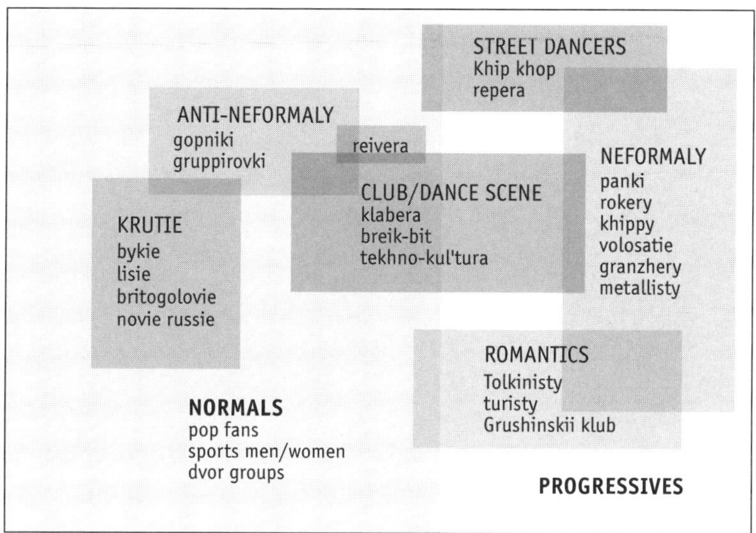

The importance of locality to specific scene development was evident in Samara from the centrality of bard music to the activities of the "romantics." The pivotal role of the club Rys' in Ul'ianovsk was played in Samara by the Grushinskii klub. This was explained by the fact that Samara is the home of the Grushinskii festival and widely considered to be the birthplace of the *KSP* (folk) movement.[30] The festival is the largest and best established open-air music festival in Russia and attracts around 100,000 people with interests in a wide range of rock and folk music.[31] The setting of the festival—requiring a long trek across fields to reach the site—and the participation by many festival participants in a ritual kayak trek after the festival has finished suggest what for many is an inextricable connection between the bard and ramblers' movements (*turisty*) (Fig. 2). Despite the organized structure underpinning the bard movement in Samara,[32] its members referred to the club as a *tusovka*, and they were recognized as such by the *neformaly*.[33]

"Alternative" identities on the Samara scene of 1998 were undergoing extensive reconfiguration in 1998. The threat of the *gopniki* was on the decline, a trend discussed in greater detail later in the chapter. This had allowed *neformaly* to abandon the label as a collective defense mechanism and refine their affiliations according to musical taste. However, at the same time a threat had emerged from within, in the form of the new urban dance scene, which competed with the old *neformaly* for "alternative" youth identities. The resulting renegotiation of space and affiliation within

Fig. 2 Grushinskii festival, Mastriuskovskie lakes, Samara region. The festival takes its name from Valerii Grushin, a student of the Samara (then Kuibyshev) Aviation Institute who drowned in 1967 while trying to save children whose kayak had overturned in the Uda river. Photo by Alexandr Tiagny-Riadno, Summer 1998.

the alternative scene meant that Samara respondents showed a greater sensitivity to distinctions between subcultures than did young people in Ul'ianovsk, although the intergroup tensions characteristic of the Moscow scene were not yet apparent.

The Tusovka Grows Up and Leaves Home: Moscow "Neformaly"

In Moscow, individual *tusovki* were well established and led independent existences outside the extended family of *neformaly* (Fig. 3). This reflected the relative inactivity of anti-*neformaly* in the city and the displacement of the conflict between *neformaly* and anti-*neformaly* onto tension between individual *tusovki*. Each individual *tusovka* would require extensive ethnographic work if we are to gain a truly valid picture of the youth scene in Moscow, and the representation depicted in Diagram 5.3 only scratches the surface. Three elements of the Moscow scene might be highlighted, nonetheless, to illuminate differences from the provincial youth cultural maps (see Diagram 5.3).

First, there was a more highly developed skinhead scene in Moscow consisting of: football fans (who often modeled themselves on English fans); more politicized young "nationalists"; and *tusovka* style *skinkhedy*. There has been insufficient ethnographic work to date to precisely conceptualize

Fig. 3 Hippie on the Arbat in Moscow attending a concert of Ania Gerasimova, of the "Umki" movement. Photo by Oleg Belikov, Summer 1998.

the relationship of these three elements to one another and thus they have been depicted in Diagram 5.3 simply as interlinked. Research outside Russia has suggested that contemporary skinheads had come a long way from the localized, working-class subcultures of resistance of the 1970s; skinheadism has become closely interwoven with national and global youth cultural scenes and virtual spaces created by new information technologies (Willems 1995; Ware and Back 2001). At the beginning of the 1990s, the skinhead movement in Moscow was small and dominated by "football fan" and "*tusovka*" skins (Pilkington 1996a). At the end of the decade, journalistic reports confirmed that skins continued to gather at the *Gorbushka* record market—a traditional hangout of *neformaly* especially in the mid-1980s—where they purchased their "neo-Nazi chic" (Caryl 1998). However, Tarasov has suggested that in the course of the 1990s, what he refers to as "the new fascist youth subculture" (Tarasov 2000b, 39) developed rapidly and extended its social base considerably; by summer 1998, he estimated that there were between 700 and 2000 skinheads in Moscow (Tarasov 2000a, 47).[34] Encouraged by displays of sanctioned "racism"[35]

Diagram 5.3 **Mapping the youth scene in Moscow, January 1998**

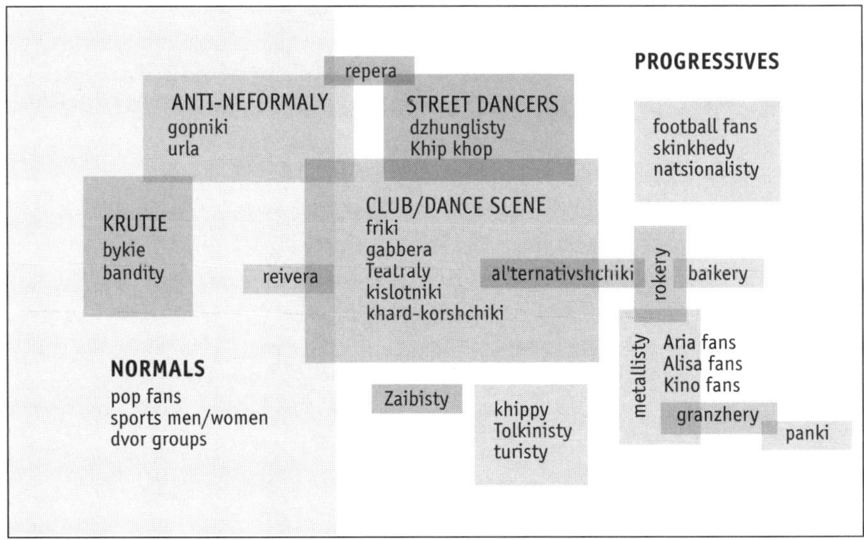

and a "politics of silence" about skinhead activity, he argues, young people from peripheral and disadvantaged parts of the major cities of Russia have taken out their frustration and envy of the new Russians against ethnic minorities and foreigners (Tarasov 2000a, 50; 2000b, 49).[36] Not only were skins locally rooted, however, they were also translocally connected: they adorned themselves and their gear with the Confederate flag, listened to "Oi" music, were in regular contact with neofascist groups in other countries, and had their own web sites.

A second group not encountered (although reportedly existing) in the provinces were the ZAiBI (*Za anonimnoe i besplatnoe isskustvo*, "Supporters of anonymous and free [of charge] art"). This group was committed to developing the "primordial creative impulse" and thus emphasized the practice of artistic creativity rather than its "results," which, they argued, should be neither authored nor owned (Fig. 4). This *tusovka* was unusual in combining a high level of resourcing—it had its own publications as well as access to premises in central Moscow where there was a wide range of recording equipment—with a determination to avoid the institutionalization of its activity. Members resisted even any imputed sense of collectivity:[37] "If you hear something from us, it is a personal opinion, not as a *zaibist*, just as a social being living on this earth. . . . You could say that our whole collective is revolutionary, anarchistic, anti-Nazi. But that is a coincidence" (49, Moscow).

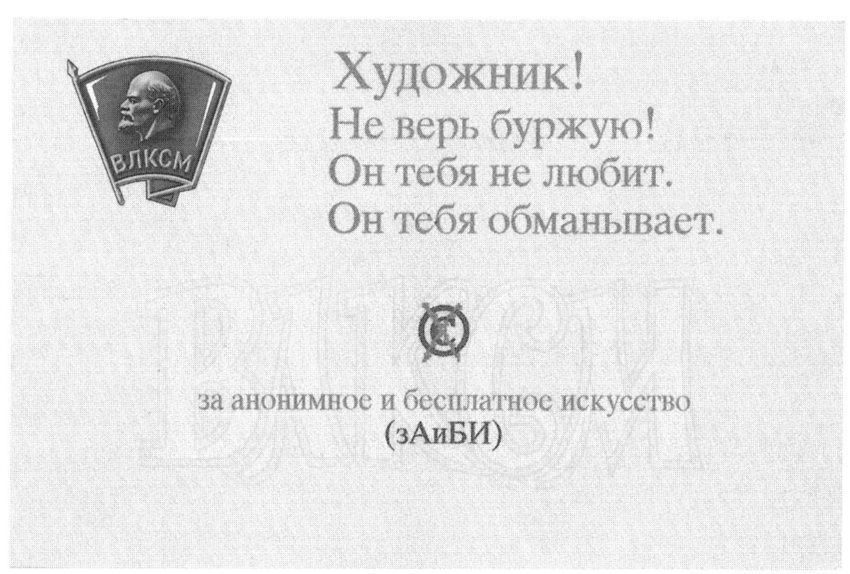

Fig. 4 The ironic invocation of Soviet symbolica was typical of the cultural practice of the ZAiBI ("For anonymous and free art") movement.

The self-consciously postmodern identity of the *zaibisty* was demonstrated when one of this group was encountered by chance at a gig of the band Distemper (29 January 1998, Petroclub). Although the respondent described the gig as an "antifascist" concert, the audience included around twenty skins, whose collective identity had been reinforced in the ritual display of aggression in the metro station where they had gathered before the gig.

Finally, Moscow displayed an emergent *tusovka* of "alternatives" (*al'ternativshchiki*) who were defined by their interest in music that straddled the boundary between dance music and alternative rock (exemplified at the time of empirical work by the Russian group Mumii Troll' and by Britpop bands such as Oasis). Although such groups were popular in other cities among both neformaly and those into the dance scene, only in Moscow could we identify a group that listened to this music primarily.

The more complex scene in Moscow inevitably generated greater internal differentiation. The most obvious example of this was the common reference to specific band fans (Alisa, Kino, and Aria fans, for example) within the broader grouping of *metallisty* (see Diagram 5.3). Within large *tusovki*, modes of differentiation and distinction emerged also around hierarchies of age (*stariki* and *pionery*), or "coolness" (indicating individuals who were distinguished by their knowledge, style, and intellect). What was most striking about the Moscow scene in the late 1990s, however, was the decline in hierarchical divisions based on age and coolness that so characterized the *neformaly* in the 1980s. This, it is argued below, reflected both the impact of the new urban dance scene and the expansion of informational access in Russia such that direct "connections" with "the West" no longer wholly defined one's ability to be "in the know."

Club and Dance Scenes: The "Progressives"

It was from the club and dance scene that "progressive" identity hailed; dance scene members described themselves as progressives (237, Samara) or those who listened to "progressive music" (54, Moscow; 60, Moscow). These were terms used widely by scene-leading youth cultural magazines (see Chapter 3) but had been adopted by those on Russia's club and dance scenes. Although the term "progressive" served to clearly differentiate those on the dance scene from "the mass" of "mainstream" youth, it was extended to a wide range of "alternative" youth in an act of inclusivity designed to contrast the perceived particularist practice of older style-based *tusovki*. This was articulated by a clubber from Samara thus: "*Progressivy*, they are all the same, even the *neformaly* by the way are *progressivy*—they are all the same thing" (215, Samara). The celebration of diversity and temporary transcendence of traditional bonds of community (based on class, ethnicity, gender, status) has been widely observed on club scenes in the West (McRobbie 1994; Thornton 1995, 15; Malbon 1998, 273–77). In Russia it was reflected in the rejection of sectarian divisions based on musical allegiances perceived to prevail among *neformaly*, and their replacement by a more fluid sense of commonality (237, Samara). The criteria for this, according to one fifteen-year-old clubber from Samara, was not dressing, or even dancing, well but simply being "sociable, kind, and gentle" (214, Samara). However, in contrast to the emphasis in the West on the bodily and tactile essence of this community (Malbon 1998), Russian clubbers related their corporeal movement to a wider sense of social and cultural movement, or more specifically "progress": "The common interest is that we want to move on, we don't want to stay in one place. We want to be developing all the time, there should be no regression. . . . It is movement alone which unites us" (253, Ul'ianovsk).

Despite the proclaimed openness and lack of hierarchy on the dance scene, internal divisions were apparent. These were most developed in Moscow,[38] where clubs, as in the West, catered to a range of musical tastes and scenes.[39] These ranged from clubs that played expensive, but mainstream, progressive house[40] mixed with pop (Utopia, Metelitsa), designer, and trendy (Titanik, Master) to lesser known youth-oriented clubs (Plasma, Luch, Les) where the music—jungle,[41] drum and bass,[42] gabber,[43] hardcore,[44] and trance[45]—was frequently harder and newer (Fig. 5). Young

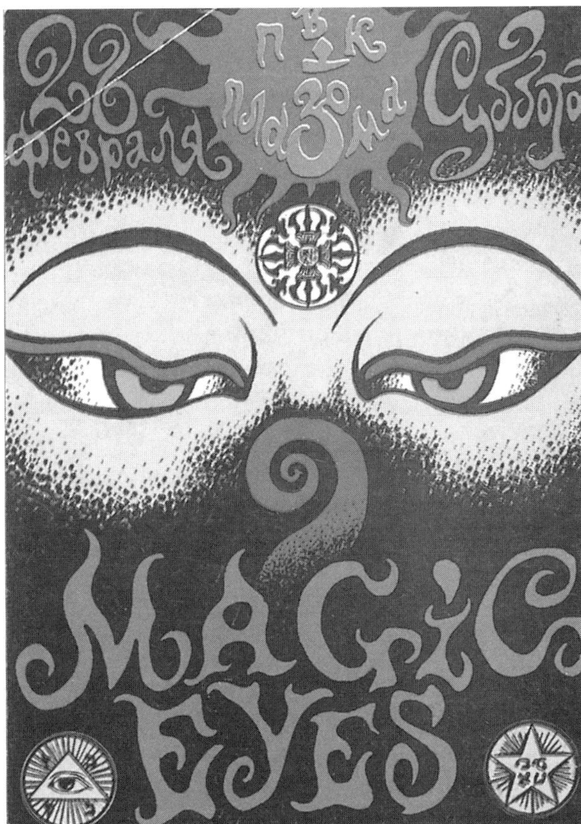

Fig. 5 A flier for the Plasma club. Moscow, February 1998.

people used these clubs—especially in the early evening (until eleven P.M.)—to put on their own particular sets, make their names as DJs and promoters, and give their particular *tusovki* a base. Moscow clubs also accommodated a vibrant "alternative" scene[46] as well as gay and Western expatriate[47] scenes.

Video was increasingly becoming central to the Moscow club experience, and new clubs such as Virus had VJs working alongside the club DJs. Flier and face control systems were well established,[48] and many clubs were free or had minimal entrance charges unless a special event was scheduled. From a provincial perspective this indicated the maturity of the Moscow scene. However, the financial crisis of August 1998 had had a tangible impact on the club scene in the city, slowing its growth, and leading new clubs to focus on the more profitable business of casinos or broader entertainment complexes. Indeed the first signs of decline in Moscow club culture appeared in the summer of 1999 when Moscow DJs were reported to be increasingly traveling abroad, and the dance scene was reported as becoming divided between clubs for uncritical "consumers" and restricted membership clubs for DJs and musicians.[49] The stratification of the club scene in Moscow has since become institutionalized through the widespread restriction of access through club membership systems.

The wide choice of venues facilitated the division of the club and dance scene in Moscow according to specific music preference. Subdivisions of the dance scene identified by Moscow respondents included jungle (*dzhunglisty*), hard-core (*khardkorshchiki*), and gabber (*gabbera*) (see Diagram 5.3),[50] although in some instances affiliations were bound up with a specific club rather than a particular subgenre of music: "Those who listen to trance do not call themselves anything. They just say 'I listen to trance'. . . they are not called 'trancers' or anything. They used to be known as . . . the *lesnie* because those who listened to trance used to hang out at Les" (54, Moscow).

That old *tusovka* practices die hard was evident from the existence of the *teatraly*; a group of clubbers defined by the fact that they hung out at Teatral'naia metro station—a traditional *tusovka* site in central Moscow. The significance of such central meeting points, however, had become more pragmatic. While "access" was always a key element of *tusovka* practice, the flier system and new profession of "promotion" had made this a much more formal aspect of *tusovka* gatherings, as indicated by the following member of the *teatraly* in Moscow: "Of those who hang out on Teatral'naia, every second person is a DJ, and every third person is a promoter . . . and every second [*sic*] person is a dancer. . . . So we can get free entrance, practically anywhere" (54, Moscow).

In Samara the club and dance scene had developed rapidly since the first clubs opened in spring 1996. In April 1998 there were two youth-oriented clubs—Aladdin and Tornado—which charged an entrance fee from $1 to a maximum of around $5,[51] when a DJ from Moscow or St. Petersburg was playing the club (Fig. 6).[52] There were four expensive central clubs for new Russians with money (Mankheten, Dzhungli, Ekvator, and the latest addition, Aisberg), which charged $10–15 for entrance on weekends. These clubs also staged live gigs, however, which attracted young people, and on cheaper midweek nights, a youth crowd gathered at Dzhungli. Samara also had a number of peripheral clubs drawing specific crowds such as the hip hop club Sandra and the suburban Panter. Local "houses of culture" across the city held discos at weekends, some of which referred to themselves as "clubs."[53]

Clubbers in Samara were not subdivided as in Moscow and identified largely as "progressives" (*progressivy* or *prodvinutie*). However, clubbers also identified more specifically as *klabera*, that is people for whom the clubs were their second home, their way of life.[54]

In Ul'ianovsk it was hard to talk of a "club" scene as such, although in autumn 1997 there were around twenty DJs in the city who divided up

Fig. 6 A flier for the Tornado club. Samara, April 1998.

work in the six clubs or discos (Sensatsiia, DK Chkalova, KT Pioner, U Ivanoff, Pilot, and Sev Klub)[55] and developed their own "alternative" projects (often referred to as "parties" or *vecherinki*) on specific nights at these venues. In autumn 1997, a leading DJ in the city estimated that between forty and sixty young people attended such *vecherinki* regularly, although sales of tapes and disks suggested many more people were listening to dance music but not getting out to clubs (Bliumfel'd 1997).

The failure of a club culture to develop in Ul'ianovsk[56]—despite the wide popularity of rave music—might be explained by three local factors: the physical environment of the dance scene; the political and economic climate of the city; and the prevailing sociocultural atmosphere. The buildings housing the dance scene in Ul'ianovsk were old "houses of culture" or "youth palaces," constructed to Soviet dimensions and more suited to their daytime use (such as children's ballet classes) than their weekend, evening use as discos.[57] Consequently, there were no "chill-out" rooms, and bar areas were limited and often uncomfortable. The large halls meant minimal interaction with the DJ, too much space to "lose yourself" in any "mass of

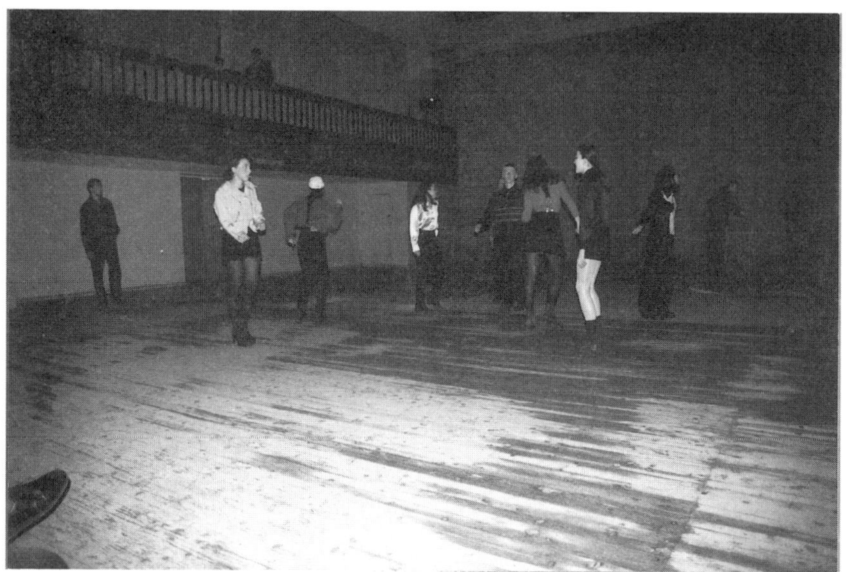

Fig. 7 "Giving oneself up to the crowd" was not an option in the Sensatsiia disco. Ul'ianovsk, October 1997. Photo by members of "Region."

bodies," and no sense of the emotional charge of sharing a limited space with others, which was central to clubbing elsewhere (Malbon 1998, 273). A self-awareness (selfconsciousness) in dance practice resulted, reinforced by the ubiquitous mirrors, toward which dancers gravitated to check out their movements (Fig. 7). The less commercial clubs in Samara shared some of these problems; Tornado was housed in a refurbished movie theater and Aladdin was situated within a larger "House of Culture" (DK Zvezda). Nevertheless both of the Samara clubs had been refurbished and had exclusive use as clubs.

In Ul'ianovsk there was significant resistance on the part of the local administration to private enterprise, which made it difficult to gain the permission necessary to open clubs. In addition a plethora of local administrative "norms" meant that discos closed at eleven P.M. and teenagers under sixteen were not allowed on the street after nine, unless accompanied by an adult. Extreme conservatism in economic reform and a highly paternalistic social policy in Ul'ianovsk had minimized the income differentiation and social stratification in the city. This had given rise to a general perception that clubs and discos were frequented primarily by racketeers (*bandity*) spending ill-gotten gains, rather than "young people like us."

Despite these obstacles, those involved in the dance scene in Ul'ianovsk identified themselves in a broadly similar way to those in Moscow and Samara as "progressives." There was also some evidence to suggest that the Ul'ianovsk dance scene might be becoming less isolated as local DJs began to network more effectively with those from other regional centers and the city's commercial sector proved increasingly able to support cultural life through sponsorship of events and media publications.[58]

Since it is "clubbing" that has formed the empirical basis for much post-subcultural theorizing in the West, it is worth considering briefly whether the meanings attached to clubbing have traveled to Russia as well as the music itself.

It is clear from the exposition above that the Russian club scene reflected back the inclusivity, "classlessness," fluidity, and diversity that have been said to characterize dance scenes (or at least members' perceptions of them) in the West. As there, "subcultural" identities among Russian clubbers were not created through any exclusive style, and the sheer physical pleasure of dancing was central to the attraction of clubbing. A notable absence in Russian clubbers' narratives of the club experience, however, was "the crowd," or rather the pleasure of "losing oneself" in the crowd, that Malbon so convincingly argues lies at the center of the communality of clubbing on the London scene. The sensation of (temporarily) ceding one's body to the crowd, the music, and the atmosphere, or more precisely, of fluctuating between belonging to the crowd and "differentiation" from it (Malbon 1999, 185–87) is, indeed, hard to imagine within the physical constraints of the provincial Russian club scene. The "intense sensual experience" of London clubbers (Malbon 1998, 271) was replaced in Russian clubbers' narratives by comfort and domesticity—the club was "a second home." The significance of communality in clubbing experiences was also undoubtedly restricted by the arrival in Russia of new styles of urban dance music in their post-rave form. Members of the scene did not bring with them any inherited sense of community or euphoria from early rave scene. Moreover, this meant that the movement arrived in its post-Ecstasy form; and because of the prohibitive cost of the drug in Russia (see Chapter 6), it has stayed that way.

So what do clubs mean to Russian clubbers? In the West, clubbing has provided a spatial shelter from the speed-driven postmodern city characterized by a deficit of meaningful social interaction. The "disindividualizing" aspects of the postmodern age—the submerging of the individual in a vast whole—are represented in "the valuing of space through the image, the body, and territory" (Maffesoli 1996, 138). Clubs are simply sites of postmodern tribal gatherings in which the place is everything, the individual nothing; a space in which "egocentric" cultures are, albeit temporarily, displaced by "lococentric" cultures (Maffesoli 1996, 138;[59] Malbon 1999, 183). The modern urban space inhabited by young Russians was experienced quite differently, however; and the meanings of clubbing were not easily transported.

In Russia—at least outside the two capital cities—modern city living was not characterized by speed, intensity, organization, and punctuality so much as disorganization, negotiation, dysfunctionality, and dust. While many people, nevertheless, shared with Western citydwellers a desire for greater social interaction, this was not expressed in enjoyment of mass rituals (spectator sports, shopping centers, festivals, political events), since these were associated with thoroughly disembodied, public displays of unity with little intrinsic meaning. The "crowd" in the urban Russian context was not a temporary euphoric gathering, but a constant and hostile presence—pushing you on, or off, the bus or tram, jostling you in a queue, shouting slogans at a rally, its tactility was oppressive and uninvited, and the prospect of giving one's individual sense of identity up to it associated with totalitarian oppression rather than communitarian liberation.

For Russian clubbers, therefore, refuge from the city was not sought in disindividualizing, tribal gatherings but in a post-*tusovka* grouping that fused people and place in an embodied communication facilitating individual "progression." At the macrolevel this different relationship between clubber and crowd is suggestive of a peculiar (that is non-Western) relationship between individualization and modernization; in Russia individualization occurred through public penitential practices (rather than the private confessional practices characterizing Western Christian societies) and in the context of mutual surveillance among peers (Kharkhordin 1999). Late modern society in Russia, therefore, is not saturated with individualism, and indeed, the spatial and temporal proximity of territorially rooted and "gang" based youth cultural practices acted as a constant reminder to clubbers of the constraining cultural force of "the mass." Thus, at the microlevel, the different relationship between clubber and crowd on the Russian scene reflected the fact that while the music to which the clubbing crowd danced was "global," clubbing was culturally enacted within a reconfigured set of local *tusovka* practices. This form of "emotional community" (Maffesoli 1996, 9–30) might indeed transcend individualism, for it was constituted in an embodied communication of a particular set of people in a particular place. The significance attached to that communication by clubbers themselves, however, was embedded in a firmly modern notion of individual "progression" where progress was defined as movement away and distinction from, not identification with and submergence in, "the mass."

"Normals": Being Ordinary

The naming practice of "progressive" youth means they dominate the youth cultural maps presented in Diagrams 5.1–5.3; in fact in all three cities of this study, "progressives" constituted a minority of the youth scenes. The majority of young people are located in the left half of the maps; they hung out around their place of residence or with school or college friends, listened to music, and took part in some kind of organized sports, musical, or other leisure activity. These people generally referred to themselves as "normal" or "ordinary" (*obychnie*) youth (Fig. 8). This did not signify cultural inactivity—they might be pop fans, participate in sporting or other organized leisure activities, or have a well-established group of friends with whom they hung out in the courtyard of their housing block (*dvor*) or around the school or college building. It was not a narrowness of activity or identity that distinguished normal youth from their progressive counterparts, therefore, rather it was their lack of profession of a music or style-based identity.[60] Indeed labeling in this way was consciously rejected by normal youth: "I think it is stupid to judge a person by what he listens to. . . . I consider all these names ['subcultural' divisions] to . . . reduce a person to a minimum, they humiliate him" (187, Samara).

The majority of ordinary kids were conscious of their difference from, but were largely indifferent to, those they saw as having subcultural affiliations. However, where *dvor* groups articulated particular hostility toward subcultural groups, they might be considered to be *gopniki* (233). This was a term not of self-identification, but one applied by *neformaly* or *progressivy* who defined the *gopnik* not in individual terms, but as a vodka-swilling, semicriminalized, gray mass of people (215, Samara; 11, Ul'ianovsk), who picked fights for the most trivial of reasons, usually on grounds of appearance (hair or clothes) (208, Samara; 164, Samara; 32, Ul'ianovsk; 34, Ul'ianovsk; 35, Ul'ianovsk; 36, Ul'ianovsk) or because they did not like the way somebody else "stood out" (37, Ul'ianovsk). Since the *gopniki* were defined as "group" beings, they were most often referred to in the plural as *gopa* or *gopata*, or as *ulichnie* (street kids) or *byki*.[61] Sometimes synonyms referring to lack of, or rural, culture were employed, such as *sel'chane* or *sel'skie* (villagers) (237, Samara), *krest'iane* (peasants) (251, Samara), or *urla*[62] (peripheral louts) (52, Moscow). The bearers of this culture were defined as people who went to discos in cheap sports clothes, shot heroin (237, Samara), and were "stupid," "mediocre people" (251, Samara; 252, Samara), who dressed uniformly and had no manners (11, Ul'ianovsk).

In attempting to give structure to the amorphous youth cultural scene, however, it is important not to follow *tusovka* respondents' lead in labeling all those outside the progressive scene as *gopniki*. Within the normals there were at least two distinct groups of young people: those ordinary kids who hung out in *dvor* groups or were engaged in more or less organized leisure activities, and anti-*neformaly*. Both of these broad groups positioned themselves on the youth scene in conscious opposition to the *neformaly*. However, ordinary kids (*obychnie*) related to a generalized

Fig. 8 "Normal" lads hanging out in a communal kitchen. Ul'ianovsk, October 1997. Photo by Hilary Pilkington.

notion of *neformaly*, seeing them as an incomprehensible phenomenon with dubious morality (18, Ul'ianovsk; 236, Samara) but not as personally threatening to their cultural space. Anti-*neformaly*, in contrast, articulated not only a common rejection of neformaly "norms," but also a positive sense of the qualities of "normal" (*normal'nie*) people (3, Ul'ianovsk).

This difference was reflected in how the two groups talked about their own "normality." Whereas *dvor*-based groups referred to themselves as "ordinary" (*obychnie*) kids, *anti-neformaly* used the normatively loaded term *normal'nie* indicating their belief that they represented the "moral majority" and that their aggression toward the *neformaly* was carried out in the interests of this "majority."

Although at the end of the 1990s, the anti-*neformaly* continued to articulate hostility toward *neformaly* and progressives, the extent and nature of actual conflict between progressives and normals varied significantly between cities and had generally declined since the 1980s. At that time there had been two distinct *gopnik* practices: "beating each other up"[63] and "humiliating *neformaly*."[64] At the end of the 1990s, the practice of "humiliating" *neformaly* was reported primarily from Ul'ianovsk (13, Ul'ianovsk; 12, Ul'ianovsk) and usually arose in the form of physical provocations or challenges directed toward those identified as "other" by virtue of their physical appearance or manner. In Moscow, and to some extent Samara, however, *gopniki* no longer made their presence felt in the way they had in the late 1980s and early 1990s (52, Moscow; 56, Moscow; 57, Moscow). Some *gopniki* had been incorporated into more widely accessible forms of popular youth culture (such as rave),[65] but their gradual demise was largely attributable to more effective policing and the new economic climate, which had refocused *gopnik* gangs (*gruppirovki*) away from traditional *dvor*-against-*dvor* fighting and toward organized crime (Salagaev 1995; Omel'chenko 1996, 222–26). Marketization had freed up the space previously inhabited by the black marketeers; and in this semilegal economic sphere, the *gopniki* matured into new figures on the youth cultural scene: *bandity* (racketeers), and those *iz brigad* (see Diagrams 5.1–5.3).[66] In colloquial talk these strata were often referred to generically as *krutie*, defined by one respondent thus: "*Krutie* are people who have money, have power, that is, have influence on things . . . because of their strength and their money" (33, Ul'ianovsk).

Ironically, the progression of *gopniki* into more serious crime (protection rackets, drug pushing) had made the city streets relatively safer: active gang affiliation was mentioned rarely, and *dvor*-against-*dvor* fighting appeared confined to those under sixteen. Moreover, the widespread use of drugs, as opposed to vodka, at usual sites of conflict such as discos, it was claimed, had reduced levels of intergroup aggression (222, Samara).

Those on the progressive scene felt culturally, if not physically, threatened by a second group among the normals, the new Russians. Antipathies toward the new Russians were generated not solely because they were rich, but because they tended to boast about their money and spent it conspicuously (210, Samara).[67] New Russians were primarily associated with quantity rather than quality of consumption (see Oushakine 2000b), and in particular with flashy cars and gold jewelry. They commanded little respect or trust, however; indeed material wealth was considered to be antipathetic to moral wealth:

There is a saying in Russian that "a full person does not understand the hungry." . . . All my friends are hungry. . . . I just wouldn't feel comfortable with a person who considered me a failure. . . . All the people with whom I mix know my system of values. [They know] that I value above all, and they value above all, normal human relations and having a brain, having a cultured brain. Among the children of new Russians, the final word in culture is "tamagochi."[68] *(231, Samara)*

Despite the mutual disdain between progressives and new Russians, actual conflict between them was rare, since the cultural spaces they inhabited rarely overlapped.

The "subcultural-conventional" divide intrinsic to subcultural identities was not only alive and well among progressives, therefore. The majority of normal young people, whether antagonistically oriented toward progressives or indifferent to them, articulated a clear recognition of that divide and consciously adopted a conventional positioning. Whether "new rich" or "*dvor* poor," above all these young people were, by design, "ordinary."

Defending Territories and Crossing Borders: Revisiting Rap and Rave

In all three cities studied, the youth cultural scene appeared in young people's narratives as divided between progressives and normals. This did not mean the territories on either side of this symbolic line consisted of loyal and homogenous subcultural armies, however. As noted above, there were at least two quite distinct groups within the normal sector of the map, and in practice this territory housed individuals all of whom expressed their "ordinariness" in different ways. Among the progressives, moreover, despite clubbers' magnanimous inclusion of the *neformaly* as progressives, those on the club scene displayed a patronizing attitude toward them,[69] since leaving "behind" such *tusovki* was often central to their own narratives of "progression" (250, Ul'ianovsk; 253, Ul'ianovsk). However, the "defensive" role of *neformaly* identity in the provinces, meant that (physical) conflicts within or between *tusovki* were a feature primarily of Moscow youth cultural practice,[70] and actual conflicts between clubbers and *neformaly* were not expressions of institutionalized intergroup conflict but a result of individual acts of aggression (241, Samara). Even the border between progressives and normals cannot be represented as more than a perforated boundary fence; it was frequently crossed and increasingly infrequently defended. Studying those border disputes that did arise, however, is a useful way of exploring the tensions within "progressive" and "normal" strategies.

The defense of territory was essentially part of normal as opposed to progressive identity. Only one progressive group—the rappers—retained its concern with marking out and defending its own physical and cultural territory. There were two objects of rappers' aggression. The first were skinheads—who were in general the most isolated and reviled group within the progressives—since skinheadism was directly associated with fascism and considered morally abhorrent (227, Samara) and intrinsically "anti-Slav" (63, Moscow). For rappers, their own sense of affinity with African-Americans via hip hop culture[71] gave the conflict a very personal meaning. As a former rapper from Samara put it: "If you put a skinhead next to me it would be North against South, plus against minus, [we have a] completely different concept of life. They hate black people [*negry*] and I love black people [*negry*], I respect them because . . . all music came from the blacks [*chernie*], any music, jazz, blues, reggae, hip hop, soul, the best kinds of music have been done by black people [*chernie*]" (227, Samara).

Conflict arising from skinhead activities in the provincial cities was sporadic, since it was generated not by local skins, but by skins in the city "on tour" from other parts of the country (34, Ul'ianovsk; 35, Ul'ianovsk; 36, Ul'ianovsk). In Samara, one respondent claimed that the Klu Klux Klan had opened a branch in the city, and its members had beaten a rapper to death (241, Samara), but this story remained uncorroborated. In Moscow, however, there was widespread talk of mutual aggression on the part of rappers and skins, who were described as the "two great armies of Moscow youth" (Caryl 1998).

While skinheads were the ideological enemy, a more mundane territorial conflict was waged by rappers against "ravers." "Ravers" (*reivera, reivery*)[72] denotes the large group of "ordinary" young people who listened and danced to electronic dance music, but who were not part of the "progressive" club scene. These young people were referred to as "ravers" by *tusovka* respondents, although since naming was, in itself, a *tusovka* practice, it was a label rejected by those implicated: "*Reivery*, there aren't any *reivery*, [just] normal guys, *gopniki*, from the brigades, they listen to rave" (3, Ul'ianovsk).

Because it was a not a term of self-identification, *reivera* was a very slippery concept (Fig. 9). It was used in Samara and Ul'ianovsk sometimes as a synonym for *klabera* or *kislotniki*[73] but also specifically to denote normal rave listeners.[74] In Moscow—where peripheral youth identified themselves almost in equal numbers as "rappers" or "ravers," their territorial battle was revealed in the graffiti war in every outlying district of the city (Figs. 9–11). When transposed to the city center, however, the war of words was transformed into something more serious. In the summer of 1997, for example, a centrally based group of rappers came into conflict with the *teatral'nie*. The following version of the conflict was recounted by a member of the latter *tusovka*: "The rappers had been gathering on Pushkin Square for years but suddenly decided to tell the ravers to clear off their meeting place at *Teatral'naia*. . . . And the rappers came to *Teatral'naia* and beat up three guys, took [their] club fliers off them, that is 'turned them over' [obuli] as we say" (54, Moscow).

This conflict, ostensibly over central city space, was temporarily resolved following a return invasion of the rappers' meeting place by the *teatral'nie*, after which it was agreed that each *tusovka* would stay where they had always been and leave the other alone. However, in November of that year the rappers again began to appear at *Teatral'naia* and "take stuff off" the kids there. This practice—known as *obut'*—has a long cultural history and is only very partially explained as an act of symbolic dispossession of artifacts related to an opposing subcultural trend (Pilkington 1994, 258). One seventeen-year-old Moscow rapper—who was encountered and interviewed in a Manezh shopping center cafe as he was trying to sell a

Fig. 9 Mainstream youth dancing at the Chkalov House of Culture. Ul'ianovsk, October 1997. Photo by Elena Omel'chenko.

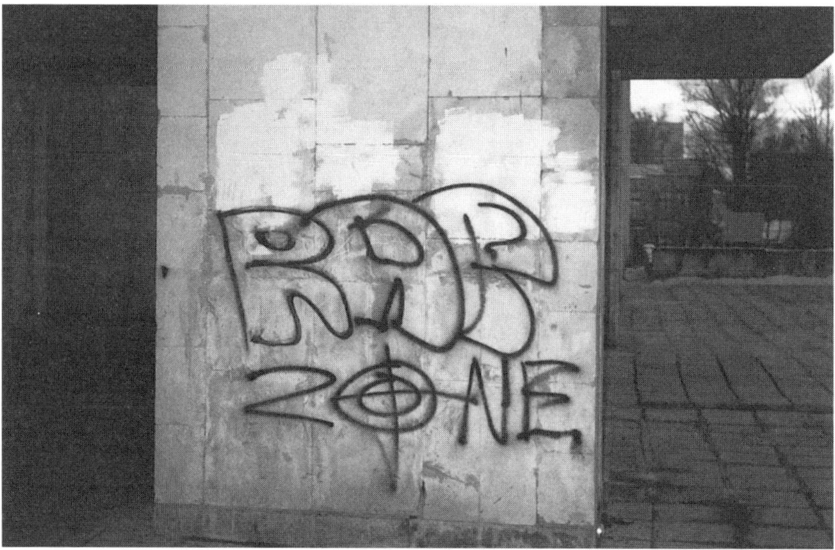

Fig. 10 Graffiti on the walls of the Palace of Youth. Moscow, January 1998. Photo by Hilary Pilkington.

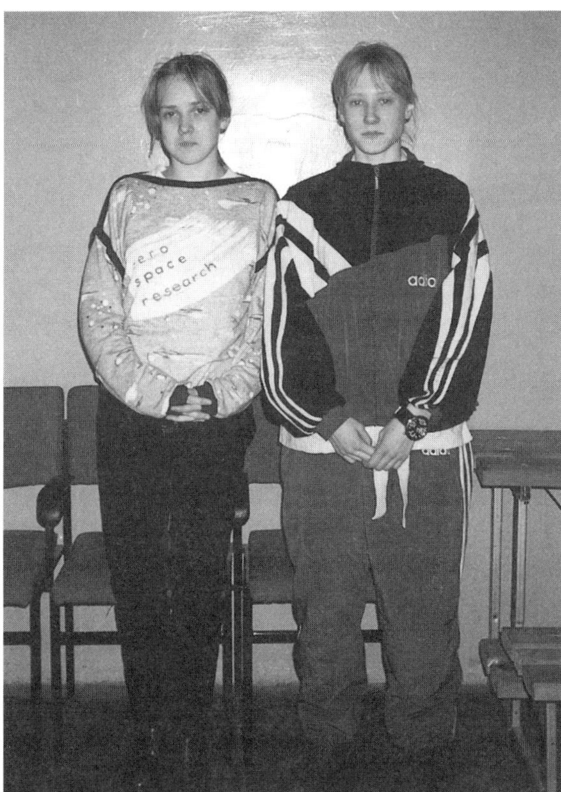

Fig. 11 Girls from an outlying district of Moscow who engaged at a competitive level in sport (judo) but also self-identified as "ravers." Moscow, January 1998. Photo by Hilary Pilkington.

personal stereo he had taken off another teenager—noted that he engaged in the practice in order, quite simply, to make money (61, Moscow). There was also a certain amount of opportunism in seeking to "put down" those perceived to be "weaker,"[75] as is evident from another rapper's account of the motivation for picking on the ravers: "I don't understand this unisex style. . . . A man should look like a man. . . . They [ravers] can't stand up for themselves, I don't like that either. . . . I went up to their crowd [on Pushkin Square] . . . and ripped them off for a stereo and some money. Why didn't they jump me? . . . I just don't understand them" (63, Moscow).

The aggressively male street positioning of the rappers—absent from most progressive identities but intrinsic to *gopnik* practice—was evidence of the transparent borders between youth strategies. In its most progressive form, rap was culturally located among a range of musical and dance movements rooted in hip hop culture, and reflecting many of the performative characteristics of the 1970s New York scene,[76] referred to as "street dance" in Diagrams 5.2 and 5.3. At this end of the spectrum, rap was integrated into the wider club and dance scenes, and movement in and out of rap to trance and jungle and back to rap was common (54, Moscow):

"There is usually just one [*tusovka*], there is no strict division, like, you are rap, I am break beat, mainly we are all together. Even those who listen to rap are beginning to listen to house. . . . You have to dance to something at discos. . . . For those who listen to electronic music and rock, metal, there is a division, but [not] among rappers" (228, Samara).

At the same time the origins of hip hop culture as a culture *of* the street but *above* the street (that is, above gang rivalry) was attractive to many young Russians who had grown up in peripheral city districts still pervaded by territorial, *gopnik* strategies. Local experience and one's attachment to and status in a local group were central to hip hop culture—as reflected in the importance of neighborhood crews or posses (Rose 1994, 34–35). For young Russians rap thus provided a localist strategy, closeness to the street, and "tough" masculinity alongside an "alternative" interest in music and style.

Rappers and ravers are depicted in Diagrams 5.1–5.3 as straddling the border between normal and progressive strategies. The fact that both movements had progressive and normal manifestations provides evidence of the porosity of the border between these cultural strategies. More importantly, it suggests that young people may appropriate cultural forms—such as rap and rave—as vehicles for crossing the border between normal and "progressive" identities.

Conclusion

This chapter has suggested that youth cultural scenes in Russia at the end of the 1990s were characterized by great diversity and fluidity, although at the same time, young people continued to recognize a significant division between "alternative" ("progressive") and "conventional" ("normal") youth. In the course of exploring the different microgroups active on these scenes, the authors have sought to explain them neither as class-reflective subcultural styles, nor as fleeting, consumer-based affinities. At the risk of appearing to attribute too much agency and self-consciousness to youth cultural affiliation, progressive and normal identifications have been presented rather as "strategies," which draw not only on style and musical taste, but on a wide range of life positions. Their adoption, while influenced by the social cleavages of the past (socioeconomic, spatial, gender, ethnic, and sexual differences), equally importantly reflects a pathway for negotiating the present and a means of envisaging the future. In the concluding section of this chapter, the distinctive elements of progressive and normal strategies are identified (see Table 5.1), while their concrete manifestation in youth cultural practice is detailed in Chapters 6 and 7.

Young people adopting a progressive strategy had their roots in the old Russian *tusovki* (subcultural groupings). This was evident in their desire to create individual styles rather than "follow fashion" and in their

Table 5.1
Progressive and normal strategies for "glocal" living

	Progressives	Normals
Horizons	Outward looking Translocal orientation Pulled toward the "center" Claimed city center space	Inward looking Locally rooted and territorially demarcated Used city space diffusely
Sociation	Multiple circles of friends and acquaintances Celebrated diversity of their social circle *Tusovka* was main site of sociability	Single, stable crowd of friends and acquaintances Friends drawn from place of study or residence (dvor)
Individual and society	Focused on the individual Emphasized lifestyle choice Drug and alcohol use viewed as personal choice Rejected rigid notions of gender and gender roles	Focused on the group Referred to *group* norms concerning use of drugs or alcohol Employed traditional notions of gender identity and displayed hostility to gender-bending
Music and style practice	Allegiance to particular music Cultural capital attributed to musical knowledge and preference Used clothes and attributes to create individual styles	Music did not hold cultural capital Music used as background to other peer group activities Hostile to standing out through style Preferred current fashion

profession of allegiance to particular types of music (especially rock, electronic dance, and bard music). More importantly, since allegiances were generally temporally constrained, progressives acquired cultural capital via the distinction between "authentic" and commercial ("pop") music, and they *used* music in cultural practice in such a way as to align themselves as information-seeking, outward looking, "progressive" young people. Thus progressives tended to have more links with, and access to, Western cultural experience and products and consciously identified themselves as outward (Westward)-looking, forward-moving individuals. In concrete terms, for example, they considered themselves to have a more Western, "relaxed" approach to gender and gender roles (although in practice they retained a conservatism regarding sexuality). The breadth to the horizons of young progressives—their ability to travel and see beyond the locality—was clearly reflected in their pull toward the center. They disparaged "provincialism" and claimed city center space for their cultural practice (*tusovki*), which increasingly took place in clubs, cafes, and bars rather than on the city streets, parks, and metro stations as was the case in the late Soviet period. These *tusovki* were the main site of their social activity, although progressives had multiple circles of friends and acquaintances and were proud of the diversity of people with whom they mixed. Moreover, these microgroups were first and foremost constituted of *individuals*; progressives emphasized lifestyle choice and prioritized personal choice over group norms in making decisions, for example, about the use of drugs and alcohol.

Progressive strategy was articulated, even named, by those who adopted it. The majority of young people, however, labeled neither themselves, nor others, in such distinct ways. These young people have been described as adopting a normal strategy. While this term has the disadvantage of incorporating two quite distinct groups—ordinary kids and anti-*neformaly*—it does at least follow their own terminology and avoids resorting to their negative identification as "non-tusovka" youth. In part, at least, normal strategy did in fact hinge on a rejection of *tusovka* practice. This was most evident in the reluctance, even hostility, expressed by young normals to "standing out" through style and to "gender-bending." Thus a preference for current fashion and a dislike of unisex clothing and long hair reflected, not only a set of style tastes, but also an aversion to what they perceived to be the nontraditional gender norms of alternative youth. Although normals expressed musical tastes, they used music neither as cultural capital, nor as an end in itself, but as a background to other peer-group activities, especially meeting members of the opposite sex or drinking with members of the same sex. Thus normals rejected the division or labeling of young people according to subcultural style and socialized rather with a single, stable crowd with whom they studied, or from their place of residence (*dvor*). Although the gang structure of these groups common in the later 1980s and early 1990s, had largely disappeared, nevertheless, the group had an existence over and above its constituent members. Normals, for example, referred to *group* norms—rather than personal choice—concerning the use of drugs or alcohol. Perhaps most importantly, and in sharp contrast to progressives, normal youth located its cultural practice locally, around home (*dvor*) or place of study, rather than centrally. They used city space therefore diffusely through practices of "going out" (*gul'iat'*) and hanging out in the *dvor* or entrance way (*pod"ezd*), which gave the impression of being in control of one's territory. In fact, however, this practice reflected a narrowness of horizons and a localized and inward-looking strategy for negotiating the present.

6 The Dark Side of the Moon?
Global and Local Horizons

Hilary Pilkington

> Globalization and localization may be two sides of the same coin, but the two sections of the world's population live on different sides and see only one of the sides—rather as people on earth see only one side of the moon. Some have the planet as their residence, while others are chained to the spot.
>
> —Beck 2000, 55

The "world-wide restratification" accompanying the dual processes of globalization and localization results, according to Bauman, in "free choice" for some, yet "despair born of a prospectless existence" for others (Bauman 1998a, 70). In this chapter, the encounters of young Russians with processes of "glocalization" are explored at the microlevel through the people, places, and activities that constituted young people's daily cultural practice. It will be suggested that the identifications of young people as progressives and normals, outlined in the previous chapter, reflected the degree to which their view of "the moon" was restricted by their more or less "global" horizons, but at the same time constituted distinctive strategies of drawing upon global and local resources to create lives with prospects.

How did Russia—having inherited Soviet global superpower status —end up on that side of the planet lying in the shadow of globalization? Although Russia retains pretensions to a place in the sun (see Chapter 1), its experience of globalization—as the flip side, not of a successful, "high modernity," but of the collapse of Soviet-type modernity—has made the consequences of globalization particularly difficult to manage. The collectivist, paternalist, and statist nature of the Soviet variant of modernity, for example, has meant that the ensuing trends toward individualization within late modern society have taken particularly extreme forms. While the freedom for individual choice in post-Soviet Russia clearly has its deeper origins in the gradual weakening of traditional and early modern bonds of family and class, it has been *experienced* as a sudden political and economic "liberation" that brought with it previously unimagined spheres of individual responsibility. At the same time, the "risks" of late modern society have been felt acutely in Russia, since the reflexive quality of modernity in post-Soviet Russia is rooted in the high-cost, low-yield version of Soviet modernity (Arnason 1993; Sakwa 1996, 357–60; Castells 1998, 9–25). Moreover, Russia's recent encounters with globalization—in particular, the coincidence of the emergence of Russia into global financial markets with the financial crashes of the 1990s—have intensified concerns about the potentially destabilizing implications of global modernities.

For youth the uncertainties of the global, postindustrial labor market have been intensified in Russia, at the national level, by a decline in investment in education and training and, at the local level, by the continued importance of personal and social networks in recruitment into the most lucrative employment positions. The collapse of state-embedded social organizations structuring and managing young people's careers, leisure time, moral welfare, and upbringing has transformed the experience of living in Russia overnight from one of being tied to a chronically stable state to being "unleashed" into a critically unstable society. The past decade has witnessed also the extensive privatization or redeployment of youth leisure facilities in the context of little cultural compensation; the domestic consumer industry has been slow to develop—making consumer products largely imported and expensive—while weak flows of private and public capital have meant that few "alternative" youth leisure spaces have emerged. Even in the United Kingdom—where one might think the consequences of late modernity could be relatively easily managed—it has been suggested that the current diversification and individualization of style, leisure, and consumption is, in fact, indicative of a new set of constraints on, and even facilitates the marginalization of, some (especially unemployed) young people (Furlong and Cartmel 1997, 54–63). In the Russian context, not only do young people confront newly inaccessible leisure spaces (private clubs and gyms, casinos and hotel movie theaters), but previously accessible ones (municipal movie theaters, opera and ballet houses, summer holiday camps) have been turned into commercial, retail spaces or have ceased to operate altogether.

This chapter explores contemporary urban youth cultural practice in Russia as strategies for negotiating this social environment. At the broadest level, this has manifested itself in a leisure practice focused around "getting together" with peers rather than on any specific activity or social space. This is evident from Diagram 6.1, which indicates the main sites of leisure for young people (aged 15–25) in Samara and Ul'ianovsk in 1997. The data from the representative survey conducted in these cities showed that young people most frequently spent leisure time with friends (or indeed family) at home, on the street, in the countryside, or in the yard (*dvor*). Interestingly, the survey revealed remarkably little difference between sites and forms of leisure in the two cities, despite the significantly better leisure infrastructure of Samara.[1] That young people have generated local, cultural responses in the form of affective microgroups (Maffesoli 1996, 97)[2] to help negotiate the increased uncertainty of life trajectories and the individualization of the "risk" associated with the combined impacts of globalizing processes and the move into late modernity is not surprising.[3] Tricia Rose, for example, links the emergence of hip hop culture, with its microgroupings of neighborhood "crews," to the economic and social restructuring of urban America following the first impacts of globalization (Rose 1994, 27). But what did young people *do* in Russia when they "got together" and what meanings were attached to their gatherings?

At the end of the century, localized microgroupings of young people in the West are closely connected to the formation of consumer-based lifestyles (Maffesoli 1996, 97; Chaney 2001; Bennett 2000, 27). In post-Soviet, provincial Russia, however, the notion of a lifestyle constructed through consumer choices is difficult to maintain. Consumption is still less based on choice than on availability, a condition described by Bauman as "the anti-value of consumer society" (Bauman 1998b, 58). Moreover, in the absence of post-Soviet cultural production, engagements with Western cultural commodities remain central to young people's real, and imaginary, consumption; and as Oushakine argues, their vocabulary of consumption has become stunted and characterized by markers of quantity rather than quality (Oushakine 2000b).

In the absence of distinctive consumption patterns as markers of lifestyle "tribes," what is it that consolidates the microgroups of young people described in Chapter 5? In this chapter, it will be suggested that for young Russians such groups were formed and maintained by specific practices of communication (*obshchenie*). The centrality of communication to the formation of microgroups is not ignored by Western theorists; Maffesoli, for example, suggests that microgroups emerge "as a result of a feeling of belonging, as a function of a specific ethic and within the framework of a communications network" (Maffesoli 1996, 139). The example of Russian youth cultural practice, however, suggests that "communication" is not only a structural precondition for the coming and being together of young people, but is a set of verbal and embodied practices constitutive of the group. When "communication" breaks down, either

Diagram 6.1 **How, and where, do young people spend their time?**

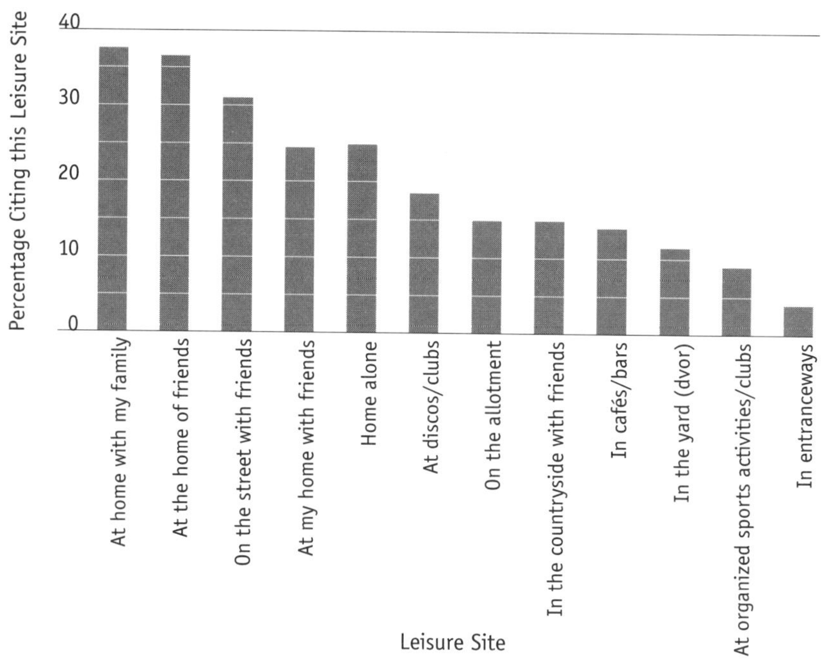

because trust or commitment is lost, or because individuals seek new forms of communication through different styles, types of music, sports, stimulants, etc., the group is redefined and reconstituted, or disbands. It is these communicative practices that, in post-Soviet Russia, constituted the substance of the "affectual" quality that Maffesoli ascribes to neotribal formations (Maffesoli 1996, 6).

"Progressive" Communication: An Information Pipeline

> Communication [*obshchenie*] is the air, which the brain breathes. When I am getting fresh information, I am swimming somehow. If all the information taps were turned off, I would drown. . . . The flow of information is the most valuable thing. It is the main thing in communication.
>
> —231, Samara

Progressives were characterized above all not by their interest in a particular musical genre or their adoption of a specific "subcultural style," but by a distinctive mode of interaction with society in general and their peers in particular. Central to this interaction was a mode of communication rooted in Russian *tusovka* life of the 1980s and early 1990s (Pilkington 1994; Rayport Rabodzeenko 1998). Shared musical, dance, style, or interest preference might have constituted the explicit purpose for getting together, but in fact acted as a setting for the kind of intimate communication central to the creation of the meanings and symbols of *tusovka* life.

Post-*tusovka* (progressive) identity remained rooted in an embodied communication,[4] in which "play" and "spontaneity" continued to be important elements. The point of meetings on the square in Ul'ianovsk in 1997, for example, was described as to "get together" and "have a laugh" (*prikalyvaemsia*) (21, Ul'ianovsk; 241, Samara). Yet, the tusovka also created an environment of intimacy; each tusovka generated "its own pleasures [*kaif*], own music, own jokes [*prikoly*], which others don't understand" (227, Samara).

The wider media and information environment with which tusovki of the late 1990s engaged, however, had changed beyond all recognition from the 1980s. This was reflected in post-*tusovka* youth's communicative practice, which was characterized by increasingly broad horizons and openness to new—global, national, and local—flows of information. Moreover, as suggested in the words of the former punk from Samara quoted earlier (231, Samara), a determination to harness new informational flows for self-development was clearly detectable within progressive strategy. The primacy of attitude over style (Muggleton 2000, 125) in post-*tusovka* life was articulated starkly by a nineteen-year-old clubber from Ul'ianovsk defining the progressive outlook: "We want to move somewhere further, we don't want to stay in one place, we want to develop all the time, no regression should exist . . . only movement unites us. . . . Whether you like Soviet pop or drum and bass, is not important" (250, Ul'ianovsk).

Progressive young people were thus characterized by their tendency to look outward, to maintain broad horizons, and to seek new information and cultural stimuli. It might be tempting to draw parallels between the desire for information among progressives in Russia and, the information fetishism of another Eastern youth cultural formation, the *otaku*.[5] In contrast to the *otaku,* however, for Russian progressives scouring the information load of late modernity was not an end in itself, but the means to communication; the information fed the communicative practice, not vice versa. Moreover, new information and stimuli were sought not through virtual but through real communication via a cultural practice rooted in the reconfigured *tusovka* (Fig. 12). Unlike the *otaku*, who spoke without context, for progressives the *tusovka* provided a vital social context for communication. It facilitated communication with people who were more knowledgeable, more traveled, and who held more cultural capital than oneself. Respondents defined the *tusovka*, thus, as a constantly changing group of people who provided stimulation and access to a wider world of "interesting" people (56, Moscow; 54, Moscow; 253, Ul'ianovsk). The *tusovka* allowed individuals to accumulate their own cultural capital by

Fig. 12 "Hanging out" *tusovka* style. Ul'ianovsk, September 1997. Photo by Hilary Pilkington.

employing connections within the *tusovka* to access cultural events (using the flier and guest-list systems) and gradually move closer to the coolest people on the scene (254, Ul'ianovsk).

While progressives were far from Russia's version of the socially inept stay-at-homes of Japan's *otaku*-generation (Greenfeld 1993, 1), they were nevertheless prone to a sense of insecurity. The constantly changing, progressing nature of the *tusovka* meant that there was always a danger of being left stranded in a *tusovka* from which others had already moved on (21, Ul'ianovsk). Thus, although the *tusovka* provided constant new stimuli, and acted as the focus of interpersonal communication, it was also experienced as something ephemeral:

I have close friends whom I can ring up at 1 am and say "I need . . ." and they will come. And I have a social circle [krug obshcheniia], lets say a tusovka, in which I revolve. . . They are not friends but really good acquaintances, they are all dear to me, in principle I love them all, but they are not my friends . . . [close friends are . . .] simply like-souls [rodstvo dush], I can feel that they want to give me something and I can give them everything within me, it is a uniting, a kind of coming together even . . . but the tusovka is . . . a collection of diverse people with different characters, with different life principles, philosophies and so on . . . they are people alien to me . . . with whom you can have a drink, find out about the gossip and what is new and chat with them. Friends are those with whom you talk intimately at night, who calm your soul. (253, Ul'ianovsk)

Progressive respondents frequently differentiated in this way between "real friends" and *tusovki*. Friends were people to whom you could talk about everyday problems (homework, relations at home, parents) and who understood and advised (53, Moscow). More importantly still, they were people you had known for a long time and whose friendship had been "tested" (231, Samara; 222, Samara).

Progressives tended, therefore, to have multiple circles of friends and acquaintances (*krug, kompaniia*) and to express pride in the diversity of people with whom they mixed, since this was perceived to reflect their ability to manage multiple identities in a complex cultural world (23, Ul'ianovsk; 24, Ul'ianovsk).[6] At the same time, they retained a small number of really close, or "best," friends in whom identity was rooted although rarely "represented." Although far from a typical example, in one case the friendship of two young women (aged fifteen and sixteen) in Samara had led them to fuse identities, creating a single being, with a shared name (formed from the initials of each of them), with her own world. This world acted as a (virtual) site of cultural practice, where the two friends retreated from their wider group of acquaintances (associated with the hippie and rock music scene) to develop "at their own pace" (232, Samara; 233, Samara).[7]

"Normal" Communication and Friendship: Strength in Depth

In sharp contrast to the progressives, in their communicative practice normals valued most highly not new information, diverse people, and a sense of perpetual motion, but the security generated by a stable, territorially rooted friendship network. Normals did not revolve in constantly changing *tusovki*, but formed friendships based on their place of study, residence, or leisure activity. Such young people inhabited concentric circles of best friends; small groups of friends (*kompaniia*) based on the home[8] or *dvor*, study, or leisure activity; and finally a wider group of acquaintances with whom they might "go out" (*guliat'*). The latter group was the least stable; it often expanded in the process of "going out," as new acquaintances were encountered and incorporated. However, the practice of guliat' provided a set of norms to govern this process. In contrast to progressives, normal respondents spontaneously referred to spending time, both at home and out, with partners (216, Samara; 236, Samara; 19, Ul'ianovsk).

Those respondents who expressed a hostile attitude to progressives, themselves mostly from Ul'ianovsk, tended to inhabit only the widest of these concentric circles, having large groups of friends and acquaintances —ranging from half a dozen to two dozen people—based either on the *dvor* or place of study. Since such respondents were exclusively male, their friendship groups were described as gatherings of "the guys": "friends . . . classmates and friends generally . . . peers . . . we are the closest friends . . . we just hang out with the guys [*s bratvoi*], you might say . . . it is a large group [*kompaniia*], about twenty people" (9, Ul'ianovsk; 10, Ul'ianovsk) (Fig. 13).

In contrast to *tusovka* youth, who managed multiple identities as a matter of pride, a particular feature of this kind of normal strategy was to bring different friends together in "one's own gang" (*svoi*). This process was described by two young men who had become friends during training for kick-boxing, whereafter one of the friends had introduced and integrated the other into his *dvor*-based group (2, Ul'ianovsk; 3, Ul'ianovsk). Another respondent proclaimed "for me everyone is *svoi*" (30, Ul'ianovsk) in a symbolic appropriation of others perceived to be "like him."[9] This practice generated a sense of security and control especially, as in the case of the above respondent, young people from the periphery were seeking space for their own leisure (for example, in city center discos) on others' territory.

The predominantly macho character of such friendship groups should not conceal their significance for personal development. One respondent, in particular, noted how the group atmosphere that had developed during kung fu training sessions had generated important life-long friendships, which had continued even when these friends had given up training: "We have a very close bond now. . . . It is hard to explain but it is not simply a friendship but a connection on a higher plane, which kind of unites us" (187, Samara).

However, whereas progressives described their interaction with one another as purposeful—as a frenzied "exchange of information"—normals perceived their communication as "time-out." Normals described their communication as "chat" (217, Samara) and said they liked to "recall funny moments from life . . . talk about all kinds of things, films, gossip" (236, Samara). The following description, by two teenage guys from Ul'ianovsk, of the way they passed time in the group was indicative: "We sit on the bench, sit and smoke, talk about life, with the girls . . . now the circus has come we will go to the circus . . . we go to the disco . . . have fun, smoke dope" (10, Ul'ianovsk).

In contrast to the *tusovki*, who often met up in the city center, normal respondents tended to meet in each other's apartments or on benches in the *dvor* (5, Ul'ianovsk; 6, Ul'ianovsk; 15, Ul'ianovsk; 29 Ul'ianovsk). The focus of the get-together might be listening to music or watching a video: "We sit, talk. Then we go out. We go to their house, to my house. We play cards, listen to the tape recorder. I don't know we do something or other. Cook something, organize something, a kind of party. Nothing in particular happens as a rule" (28, Ul'ianovsk).

Fig. 13 "The lads" hanging out at their favorite bench close to the school they all attended. Ul'ianovsk, October 1998. Photo by Hilary Pilkington.

Even if the chat was preceded by a visit to the theater, the play was discussed only to ascertain whether or not it had been enjoyed (187, Samara). This is not to suggest that the communication among normal respondents was not meaningful. Indeed some respondents differentiated "meaningful communication," described as "something closer, more serious" (235, Samara), from "relaxing" communication of the kind which might be experienced while talking or dancing at a disco (234, Samara). Everyday communication ("who has done what?") was thus distinguished from more intimate talk (*po dusham*), which was done in twos or threes.

Thus while progressives—through their information-seeking practices—symbolically marked out a global communicative space, normals had a locally demarcated communicative practice in which friendships provided a depth of security measured by its potential for defensive mobilization. As we saw in Chapter 5, these different strategies held the potential for conflict as young people of both types sought to enact their communicative practice in urban public spaces.

Journeys to the Center of the City: Negotiating Public Space

The negotiation of public space in the city was central to both progressive and normal youth cultural strategies. This reflected less the attractions of the youth leisure infrastructure offered by the city—with the exception of Moscow—than the constraints on domestic space that had made the street and the yard (*dvor*) important youth sites (see Diagram 6.1). Thornton cites the relative lack of personal space within the home for young British people as potentially explaining the significance of clubbing within British youth culture. Comparing the scene to America, she argues, the greater access of American youth to domestic personal space (private rooms, phones, and Internet access) and to cars as an extension of that space (Thornton 1995, 16–17) reduced the importance of claiming their own public spaces. At the time of the current study, young people in Russia would not have dreamed of owning their own car, no respondents displayed a mobile phone (these were negatively associated with "new Russians"), and a good proportion of young people would not have their own rooms at home. These domestic constraints meant that both progressive and normal youth spent much of their time in public spaces of the city. The kind of spaces they inhabited, and the way they used them, reflected their quite different cultural strategies, however.

Progressives: Cool People in Cool Places

Intrinsic to progressive strategy was the claiming of space in the city center, where "interesting" people could "hang out" (*tusovat'sia*) away from the "gray masses" of the periphery who sought to impose their own conformity on them. Even when they themselves lived there, progressives viewed peripheral (suburban) space as culturally alien territory controlled by the *gopniki*: "I live beyond the Sviaga, in a district of our city where people who work at the factories and so on live. I don't know one person there. I go straight home from the bus stop as fast as I can without looking around" (251, Ul'ianovsk).

Tusovki have always claimed central city space to meet; in the 1980s such places were usually a square, park, or metro station. The actual place was not necessarily significant—often nobody could remember why the group actually met there—what was important was the knowledge that your crowd would be there and that the site was away from the strictures of both formal sites of leisure such as clubs run by the *Komsomol*, school, theaters, and movie houses and the oppressive conformity of the *gopniki*. In the 1990s, however, the availability of old municipal buildings for use for commercial leisure together with the collapse in participation among

Fig. 14 Punks at a concert given by the Red Hot Chili Peppers. Moscow, Summer 1999. Photo by Oleg Belikov.

youth in formal leisure activities have allowed young people to colonize new city spaces.

Rock and other *tusovki* continued nevertheless to meet in parks and city squares (see Chapter 5), and in the larger cities at gigs (*seishny*) and concert venues (Fig. 14): "I meet with friends at various *tusovki* where various groups are playing, it is interesting to watch. Together it is more fun, also to play, to mess around. . .and there are often *tusovki*, around the [Dom Kul'tury] Zvezda, in the main out of town park, at concerts in the Zvezda, in the Dom Kul'tury Sovremennik" (206, Samara).

Increasingly, however, provincial *tusovki* used cafes as *tusovka* sites and looked forward to the development of the kind of live venues for rock music already mushrooming in Moscow and St. Petersburg (21, Ul'ianovsk).

Hip hop, breakbeat, and rap *tusovki* were located somewhere between neformaly and clubbers in terms of sites of *tusovki*. Specific hip hop nights or clubs even in the provinces had made hip hoppers more comfortable in club environments than rock fans. The centrality of "the street" to their particular culture, however, meant that they simultaneously continued old *tusovka* practices of "having a laugh" on the city's streets:

*[We]. . . hang out on the street. We gather, call the crew [*chuvaki*], suit up [*prikidyvaemsia*]. . . virtually every day we get together, go somewhere, we roam around the 15th [district]. We take a tape recorder with us, switch on rap. Sometimes we climb up somewhere. In the winter we had a laugh [*prikol'nulis'*] in some quarter. We rolled a barrel to the corner of a block of flats, threw in paper, lit it, and warmed up like they show the blacks [*negry*] warming themselves in the films. (241, Samara)*

The centrality of dance to these groups allowed them to colonize previously official sites of youth leisure. In Ul'ianovsk a small rap *tusovka* took over an aerobics class at the Pioneers palace, effectively turning it into a dance club (254, Ul'ianovsk), while a breakdance group had persuaded the director of a Samara school to let them use the premises for their club (228, Samara). The "romantics" also made use of official leisure sites, either taking part in organized clubs such as the Grushinskii klub housed in the Dom Kul'tura "Zvezda" in Samara, or organizing their own activities there. A medieval singing ensemble linked to the Tolkienists met and practiced in the Trades Unions building in central Ul'ianovsk, which was home also to Rys' and a successful breakdancing club (Fig. 15). The potential danger of moving into official sites, however, was loss of control over the activities ending in the collapse of the group as one former member of *SKUT*[10] explained: "*SKUT* went downhill. At the start the teachers were from the street and their technique was better. But . . . they started to pick those with higher education, they don't dance street dances well, and the level of teaching deteriorated" (228, Samara).

Retaining a connection to the street was important to progressive identity. Rollerbladers, skaters, and skateboarders, for example, used official skating parks and venues where they offered specific advantages (especially the provision of equipment to develop skating and jumping techniques), but it remained important to feel that you could "skate everywhere it is possible to skate" (53, Moscow) (Fig. 16). The "romantics" also tried to get out of the city, into the countryside; in the summer months they would go out on treks (*pokhody*) for up to a month at a time, and in the winter would ski, walk, and camp out in the forest on weekends (51, Moscow; 56, Moscow).

The relocation of *tusovki* from city parks, squares, and streets into commercially oriented and controlled spaces has been led by the club *tusovki*, although in Moscow traditional metro station *tusovki* (such as Teatral'naia) had been retained as a useful meeting point for people from across, and beyond, the city, before the final destination was decided on (54, Moscow). In Samara, where most clubbers frequented only two or

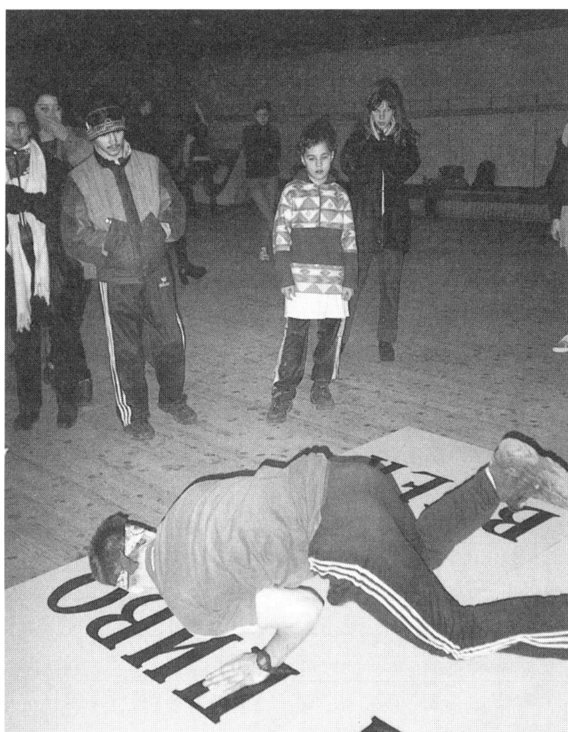

Fig.15 Breakdancers training at a club in Ul'ianovsk. Photo by Moya Flynn, October 1997.

three nearby clubs on a regular basis, young people usually met up in the club itself without prior arrangement (230, Samara; 215, Samara; 237, Samara; 250, Ul'ianovsk; 253, Ul'ianovsk). Young clubbers even created sites for their own *tusovka* by organizing parties, usually in the early part of the night (to eleven P.M.) when the club would otherwise be empty (60, Moscow).

The club scene was fluid and constantly changing. Clubs opened and closed rapidly as money appeared and then ran out, and conflicts with the local authorities or police (primarily in relation to drug use) arose. Club *tusovki*—unlike *tusovki* of the 1980s—were thus not always the same people in the same place, rather particular clubs became the focal points of certain *tusovki* for a specific period of time. Some clubs—those considered to be for "uncles with big bellies"—were not used at all, or only on specific nights when there were special student prices and sets. Specific *tusovki* also formed at particular clubs on nights when certain DJs were playing. However, "favorite" clubs that housed regular *tusovki* sites did not necessarily reflect any subcultural affinity, but earned their place in clubbers' affections more complexly. Thus one hip hop fan chose to hang out at a techno/house/trance club (the Aladdin) rather than at another club which organized regular hip hop nights because he considered his "circle of communi-

Fig. 16 Roller skaters. Moscow, March 2001. Photo by Alexandr Tiagny-Riadno.

cation" to be at the former (225, Samara). The popularity of the Aladdin in spring 1998 was explained by its particular vibe:

It is the most youth-oriented club, the wildest [otviaznii], *the most* tusovochnii, *that is you feel really at ease in it and we feel good in it, just nice. (213, Samara)*

The best DJs in the city play there, really . . . it is just great. (214, Samara)

The difference in this kind of use of clubs from that of "people with money," who often visited a number of clubs in a single night, was self-evident. However, progressives were beginning to feel a deficit of *tusovka* in their club lives and were turning toward more *tusovka*-friendly environments such as house or dacha parties:

*Many people are bored of going to clubs already because . . . virtually all the parties are the same, they can give them beautiful names, do some beautiful fliers, but there is nothing worthwhile there. Something good comes up maybe once every two months. And so many now prefer to go to a club, hang out there, listen to music, and then a group of friends [*kompaniia] *goes off to someone's house or dacha to continue the party, because they bring music with them. (54, Moscow)*

This was an emergent feature not only of Moscow club culture, but also provincial club life (251, Ul'ianovsk; 252, Ul'ianovsk).

The marked decline in conflict between groups of youth on the streets of Russia's cities over the last decade might suggest that the emergence of clubs, cafes, and other commercial leisure venues has helped reduce conflicts between youth by filtering potentially antagonistic sections of youth into lifestyle-specific venues. Although this argument works well for venue-rich Moscow, in the provincial cities of research the division of city space was more complex. In Samara young people distinguished between clubs for "youth" and clubs for "the jackets" (*pidzhachki*) (227, Samara). The latter type were commercial clubs despised by clubbers and used only on specific youth nights when a different kind of music was being played and entrance tickets cost only a tenth, or less, of the usual price. The "youth clubs" in contrast, were unattractive to the new rich because they did not suit their "serious" image (227, Samara). While this kept the "new Russians" at a distance, other normal young people sometimes ventured into the trendier youth clubs; the youth club Tornado in Samara, for example, was used on Mondays by local youth from the surrounding blocks of flats much to the distaste of the regular clubbers there (213, Samara; 214, Samara). However, as a rule, this practice of mutual avoidance appeared largely effective; only one case of serious conflict within a club was recounted. This occurred in Samara where the venue at the Institute of Communications, renowned as a meeting place for heavy metal fans, was closed because of fights provoked by *gopnik* incursions (232, Samara; 233, Samara).

Although marketization had brought a plethora of new commercial leisure spaces, young people continued to feel restricted in their use of urban space. The reasons they cited for this were: interference by the authorities and police; the impact of the market on access to leisure; and young people's own sense of what constituted safe and unsafe places for them to be. In the 1980s hostile encounters with police or municipal authorities were regular events for *tusovka* youth; indeed these encounters were part of *neformaly* identity (Pilkington 1994). Although at the end of the 1990s, such conflicts were rarer, nevertheless, rollerbladers in Moscow found themselves frequently "moved on" by police and barred entry from the more upscale shops in the city center. A sixteen-year-old clubber from Moscow also recounted an incident when her *tusovka* had been declared to be an "unsanctioned meeting" and cleared off a central city square by the police, who arrested a number of the group (54, Moscow).[11] (Fig. 17.) Access to premises also continued to be an issue. A group of young people actively engaged in generating youth leisure and creative ventures in

Fig. 17 Bikers enjoyed particular attention from the police, since traffic regulations provided a convenient site of intervention. Moscow, March 2001. Photo by Alexandr Tiagny-Riadno.

Ul'ianovsk had been repeatedly frustrated in their attempts to persuade the city authorities to give them access to a dilapidated building that they had intended to restore and make operable themselves. A group of break-dancers in Samara had struggled also to find premises for their dance group—an experience that had made them acutely aware of the lack of fit between discourse and policy on youth at the local level: "We went to various schools, everywhere, but were told 'no, you can't.' It is strange. They say 'teenagers mean drugs,' 'they have nothing to do,' 'they sit around entrance ways.' But when you ask to be given a hall in which to train, it is 'no you can't.' It is very strange" (228, Samara).

Clashes with the authorities sometimes ensued from conscious challenges raised by young people to the control of city space. The above respondent noted the pleasure his group took in making "gray" and "black" city sites "their own" by covering them with graffiti drawings (228, Samara). The most spectacular of these challenges were those generated by the ZAiBI, who organized "actions," "happenings," or "events" around Moscow during which an abandoned industrial site or municipal building would be located and used for spontaneous musical performances, or painted or drawn upon (46, Moscow; 50, Moscow). Such events were both creative and confrontational as suggested by the fact that they were sometimes referred to by respondents from this group as "terrorist acts."

More common sources of restriction to the use of public space were a result of the commercialization of leisure facilities or the fears of young people themselves. High entrance prices kept young people out of many clubs and always out of the bar areas; young people not drinking or eating were often asked to vacate seats in these parts of the club. The commercial viability of clubs was dependent on the "new Russians" and *byki*, who inhabited precisely this club space, and many of the legendary clubs in the cities of study (the Hermitage in Moscow, for example, and the Koleso in Samara) had closed down for financial reasons, despite their huge popularity among young people.[12] The paradoxical closure of successful venues left young people confused, frustrated, and skeptical, as indicated by the following sixteen-year-old skater from Moscow, describing how a new skate park at the Olimpiskii stadium went from being a huge success to closure within days:

[On the opening day the entrance fee was an affordable 10,000 *rubles]... by the third day the cost had gone up to* 30,000 *rubles, but still there were a lot of people coming. On the fourth day, they charged for the ramp and for the trampolines separately,* 30,000 *rubles for the pipes,* 10,000 *rubles for the trampolines, and* 60,000 *rubles for the ramp ... on the first day [after that] there was a maximum of ten people. On the next day there was nobody at all. They closed it straight away. Maybe the aim was to close it.* (53, Moscow)

Possibly the greatest restriction to the use of public space by progressive youth, however, arose from their own sense of where it was safe and unsafe to be. Progressives inhabited city environments in which they had pockets of safety—*tusovka* sites, specific clubs and venues, and home—but in order to reach these they had to travel through threatening urban spaces. In particular many progressive young people found the courtyard (*dvor*) a threatening environment, from which they had required protection as they grew up (224, Samara). Clubbers often contrasted the safety of the club upon arrival;[13] with the frightening experience of traveling to it through the city: "The first time I went on my own, I was simply forced to flag down a car, because on the tram ... it is just a nightmare. I arrived and shouted 'Yes, Yes!' [in English]. I had got to Aladdin in one piece, unharmed. I knew that I would go in and definitely meet people I knew" (213, Samara).

For progressives in Ul'ianovsk, even one's own tusovka site, in this case the Chkalov club was avoided on Saturday and Sunday nights when it was dominated by normal youth (254, Ul'ianovsk). There was also a gender dimension to urban safety; while young men described places where they might be challenged by other (*gopnik*) youth on the streets or in their clubs as "unsafe", young women were more concerned about using public transport and being "on their own."

The claiming of central city space remained central to reconfigured *tusovka* practice. It marked a symbolic distancing of oneself from the regressive forces of the periphery and reflected a deeply embedded sense of spatial hierarchy that envisaged Moscow as the most cultured, informed, happening, progressive place and provincial cities and towns as restrictive, cut-off, uncultured, and conservative. The use of formerly state-owned municipal properties for commercial leisure had opened up new leisure and entertainment opportunities for young people, but had also brought new constraints upon access and new challenges in negotiating the use of city center space with other groups of youth.

Normals: Going Out, But Going Nowhere

In contrast to the centrally based and increasingly commercially sited leisure spaces of progressive youth, normals maintained an unfocused ritual of "going out" (*guliat'*) in their free time at weekends and in the evenings. This activity was sited mainly around the place of residence; young people sat on benches in the yard (*dvor*), smoked, and talked. When the weather became cold, the group might move inside to an entranceway (*pod"ezd*) or, even better, someone's flat. An entranceway might sometimes be preferred, however, since it provided a private space for "best friends" to talk away from the thin walls of parents' flats (44, Moscow). Where a particularly private—and warm—space was needed (often because alcohol or drug use was involved) young people might occupy a local cellar (podval) (42, Moscow; 43, Moscow).

For normal youth, the practice of *guliat'* provided the communicative space that the progressives located in the *tusovka*. This space was used to "chat, resolve . . . problems" (240, Samara), and might involve playing cards or singing along to a guitar.[14] *Guliat'* was embarked on usually with one or two close friends, a partner (19, Ul'ianovsk), or a sibling (7, Ul'ianovsk), but the group usually grew as friends and acquaintances were encountered along the way. The fact that *guliat'* was a facilitator to communication rather than the purpose of activity itself was indicated by the fact that reference to it was frequently prefaced by the phrase "doing nothing." This is how one seventeen-year-old respondent described what she did in the evenings and weekends: "[We do] nothing. We walk [*guliaem*] . . . sit with friends . . . on the street" (27, Ul'ianovsk).

The significance of this "doing nothing" was evident from the preparation that preceded it, however: "In the evening we usually go out about six, we walk [*guliaem*] . . . mainly the two of us, but we may arrange a meeting with the girls, [then] the guys show up, we have a laugh, have fun [*guliaem*] . . . We also go out [*guliaem*] at the weekend . . . in the morning we catch up on sleep . . . by the time you have got yourself together, put your make up on it's about two o'clock, lunch time. Then [we] go out [*guliaem*]" (7, Ul'ianovsk).

The growing commercial development of Russian cities has increasingly attracted normal youth into the center of the city to *guliat'*. This was particularly true of Moscow youth who went into the center to "go round the shops, see what is being traded" (42, Moscow; 43, Moscow) but was increasingly the case in Samara as well, where, it was said, everything was concentrated in the city center (236, Samara). Shifting the site of *guliat'* has changed the activity itself, however. Two Ul'ianovsk teenagers noted that a trip to center required "money" and "girls" (9, Ul'ianovsk; 10, Ul'ianovsk).

For this reason such activity—often focused on a trip to a city center disco—was generally confined to the weekends (usually Saturday nights).[15] For some young people, traveling to the center was unproblematic (7, Ul'ianovsk) and offered the excitement of broadening one's circle of acquaintance (especially of the opposite sex). But others were nervous, especially of returning home when most public transport had stopped (234, Samara). In contrast to the progressives, who were not afraid to arrive at a club alone, for normals going to a disco was a group affair. This was partially due to a fear of being "uncomfortable" on your own (234, Samara). Knowing those you were with also increased the sense of personal safety: "You know that, God forbid, if anything were to happen to you, you can name them all, you can say where they come from and so on. You can relax and not think what time it is, that you need to go home otherwise there will be no public transport. To go by car is quite frightening now, at least for me. I can't go on my own, I am afraid. Even if I have money, I always prefer to go by public transport. I never get into a car on my own" (236, Samara).

Those respondents who expressed fear about crossing the city at night were female. For young men, it was not the journey, but rather the disco itself that presented a threatening, even "dangerous" (5, Ul'ianovsk; 6, Ul'ianovsk) atmosphere.[16]

The word *guliat'* has a number of meanings in everyday Russian speech. One of the commonest—"to party" or "to have fun"—was described at greater length in Chapter 4, and almost always suggested the involvement of alcohol or drugs. When talking about their cultural practices, some normals, used the term *guliat'* in this way (9, Ul'ianovsk; 19, Ul'ianovsk).[17] Other normal respondents used the term interchangeably with that of *lazit'*, although the latter implied aggressive movement between yards (*dvor*) or blocks, beating up members of other *dvor* groups (238, Samara; 25, Ul'ianovsk; 26, Ul'ianovsk). The majority of normal respondents, however, used *guliat'* to signify a central part of their cultural practice as distinct from "going out" (*idti v gosti*) where this implied visiting each other's houses. *Gul'iat'* provided the space for communication central to peer activity and, symbolically, gave young people the "keys to the city." Since they roamed freely, rather than claiming specific city-center "homes," normals were much less likely to articulate a sense of exclusion from, or restriction to, their use of public space than progressive youth. While, as Furlong and Cartmel note, the apparent ability of these young people to engage in new leisure and consumption experiences only falsely obscures the social divisions which mediate that experience (Furlong and Cartmel 1997, 64), their localist cultural strategy, with its temporary relocations of the group on a "night out," successfully managed these divisions.

Negotiating the Risk Society (with a Little Help from Our Friends and Families)

The increasing impetus for young people to manage individually both the challenges of getting an education, starting careers, and establishing intimate relationships and the "risks" associated with drug use and unprotected sex meant that the leisure times and spaces described above had to be carved out of wider, often pressing, lives. These lives only occasionally involved global interactions; mostly they focused on local, everyday negotiations of time, money, and space. While the very real pressures upon young people should not be underestimated, the narratives of respondents alert us to the fact that many young people's lives—even in late modern society—remained deeply embedded in families and households. Those home environments—the view from those windows—moreover, were central to whether young people envisaged their own lives and futures as framed by global horizons or local boundaries.

Progressive Lifestyles and Normal Lives

For progressive young people the *tusovka* often became all-absorbing, at least for a certain period of their lives. Nevertheless *tusovka* practice did not itself constitute a virtual or parallel world; it had to be trimmed and shaped to fit around other life activities centered at school, college or university, work, and home.

Home and domestic duties appeared in young people's narratives remarkably rarely, probably because most college and university students continued to live with their parents.[18] Although one might expect living at home to inhibit progressive lifestyles, in general, parents appeared in young people's narratives as remarkably tolerant, understanding, and enlightened, prepared even to listen to "rap, house [and] break beat" with their teenage children (230, Samara). Members of club *tusovki* had the greatest problems because of the hours they kept, and two students noted how they had, at first, told their parents that they were staying over at friends rather than admit they were at clubs.[19] Their lifestyle remained difficult to manage: "At first I just wanted to sleep but now we are used to it. . . . I don't [go clubbing] every night because of study. I don't get enough sleep at all. Whenever I am home I just sleep. I come home from school, then sleep, then do my homework, sleep again, and then go to work" (214, Samara).

The vast majority of respondents (over 80 percent) in the qualitative element of the study were still full-time students, and the difficulties of balancing study and nightlife followed progressives into higher education: "I study at the Samara Pedagogical University and studies take up probably half of my time . . . about 10 percent goes on homework and the rest I devote to clubs . . . you can do anything in a club, even study, if necessary, and during exams [study] mainly goes on there . . . of course I get criticized for not studying and spending all my time there" (237, Samara). Many respondents exploited the new commercial opportunities in the leisure sphere to generate an income, or supplementary income, working as DJs, club promoters, dancers, or trainers (60, Moscow; 228, Samara; 229, Samara; 230, Samara; 215, Samara; 218, Samara; 219, Samara; 227, Samara) (Fig. 18). For some these activities constituted a possible future profession, although they expressed concern that the structural obstacles to opening one's own business (especially local authority resistance and organized crime payments) would prove prohibitive (227, Samara).

In comparison with progressives, normal young people complained more frequently of a lack of free time, which, they said, was consumed primarily by homework, study, and preparing for exams. Other necessary priorities included "catching up on sleep" (234, Samara; 7, Ul'ianovsk; 8, Ul'ianovsk) and getting ready to go out (7, Ul'ianovsk; 8, Ul'ianovsk), although domestic work (helping at home or at the dacha at weekends) and part-time employment were also mentioned (28, Ul'ianovsk; 13, Ul'ian-ovsk).

One reason why normal respondents were more likely to complain of having little free time was that their leisure activities were often more structured (taking place at specific and regular times) than was the case for progressive youth. In particular, sport played a significant role in the lives of normal youth. Many respondents "trained" three or more times a week in sports such as judo, kung fu, figure skating, shaping, gymnastics, weightlifting, and kick boxing. Training took place often in the early evening, leaving little time at home for anything other than eating, doing homework, and going to bed. Such respondents, especially the younger ones, who saw "training" as an obligation rather than a leisure activity, were most likely to say that they had little or no free time (44, Moscow; 187, Samara).

For some respondents, the organized training session acted as a means of providing access to a wider group of "one's own" people (*svoi*), from across the city: "Most of my friends are those with whom I have done

Fig. 18 Breakdancers who worked at Tornado club. Samara, April 1998. Photo by Hilary Pilkington.

sport at some time and we really like to get together. . . . I go to training sessions like to a club. It is my club" (187, Samara).

Two young women engaged in a skating and performance group noted that they spent time with the group outside training, going out to the countryside in the summer and celebrating birthdays and main holidays with them (211, Samara; 212, Samara), while one fifteen-year-old still kept in touch with friends made playing in a city basketball team, even though her studies had forced here to give up actually playing (218, Samara).

Sport was not only a way to make friends, however; it was also a means to attain physical fitness and even "spiritual growth." Most respondents were engaged not in competitive team-based sports, but sports that focused on personal development. Forms of martial arts remained very popular among young men,[20] for example. Although such sports had an acknowledged street use—if applied in the form of self-defense (3, Ul'ianovsk)—those who continued in the sport were described as people who wanted "to achieve something in life" over and above being able to defend

Fig. 19 Kung fu training session. Samara, April 1998. Photo by Moya Flynn.

themselves (2, Ul'ianovsk): "The main thing is personal feeling, personal condition, being in control of your body, having body and mind as a single unit. That is very important" (187, Samara).

This respondent viewed kung fu as a philosophy or "a whole system"; indeed it was precisely the spiritual side of the sport that had made it more attractive than others (such as boxing and judo) in which he had been involved previously (Fig. 19). While it is tempting to read the interest in kung fu and kick boxing among normal youth as an indication of a tendency to look "East"—rather than "West"—in fact kung fu has become a global cultural form with distinct local meanings. In Russia these meanings were multiple and undergoing reconfiguration. Although martial arts have their origins in the East, they were popularized through Hollywood movies and lent authenticity during the Soviet period by their prohibition. In the post-Soviet period they have been reauthenticated through reference to their combination of *spiritual* and physical training, but many "alternative" young people have been attracted away from martial arts to traditional Russian combative arts (*slavianogoretskaia bor'ba* and *kulachnaia bor'ba*), which have enjoyed a revival.

For normals sport also played an important role in negotiating the boundaries between childhood and adulthood by facilitating their move into positions of authority. This process was closely connected with an evolving relationship with the trainer. The two respondents engaged in kung fu described relations with their trainer as "comradely" (209,

Samara), which they saw as reflected in the fact that the respondents were no longer asked to pay for their own training sessions and had been entrusted to train some of the younger members themselves. A young woman who had developed a close relationship with her trainer at a shaping class had been offered training and employment after four years of attending the class (216, Samara). For another, this taste of the adult world had already led to her decision to base her future professional life around her sporting activity (211, Samara).[21] Although, as a rule, revelations about the "hidden" side of Soviet sporting triumphs in the post-Soviet media had led many young people to treat the prospect of professional sporting careers with skepticism, for some individuals success in sport had led to otherwise impossible opportunities to travel abroad (187, Samara).[22]

Whereas in the past, *tusovki* were associated with young people dropping out of officially approved forms of leisure, progressives of the 1990s participated widely in sport, physical exercise, and other club-based activities; all but two progressive respondents were engaged in some kind of sporting activity (including football, volleyball, cycling, hiking, boxing, acrobatics, athletics, bodybuilding, aerobics and "shaping," skiing, roller skating, and swimming). However, the role sport played in the lives of progressives was different from that of other youth. Virtually none engaged in sport competitively; they participated rather for a feeling of "self-satisfaction" or to lift their mood (206, Samara) and were not prepared to make the "sacrifices" necessary to do sport professionally (164, Samara; 208, Samara).

While a lack of competitiveness characterized all progressive engagements with sport, it was particularly characteristic of young women. With the exception of volleyball, the sports in which young women participated were individual rather than team activities. Moreover, even the physical demands of dance were written into progressive female identities as something engaged in for enjoyment and which did not require training or physical preparation. In sharp contrast, dancing was often described by male respondents in sporting terms; they articulated a conscious desire to master acrobatic dance moves and an enjoyment of the respect apportioned from others who saw them perform (228, Samara; 229, Samara; 230, Samara).

Does Body Conscious Mean Health Conscious? Alcohol and Drugs in Young Lives

This new attitude to physical exercise suggests that leading a "healthy way of life" was no longer a phrase uttered with disdain by those with *tusovka* identities; being "alternative" was compatible with making healthy choices. Indeed such choices were necessitated by the increasingly risk-laden environment young people inhabited.

One set of risks that young people negotiated on a regular basis were those related to drug use. Social survey data suggest that around 8 percent of Russian youth periodically use drugs, 1 percent use drugs regularly, and a further 15 percent have tried drugs (Popov and Kondrat'eva 1998, 65). Regional level surveys, however, show much higher usage, and one conducted in Ul'ianovsk at the end of 1998 suggested that 14 percent of school students and 32 percent of sixth-form students (*starsheklassniki*) had used drugs (Omel'chenko 1999b, 12). Among young people hanging out on the streets of St. Petersburg, it was estimated that 90 percent used drugs sometimes, and that 4 percent were dependent on drugs (Shul'gina 1996). The drug-saturated environment that young people negotiated has made abstinence from drug use, therefore, an increasingly conscious position (Shiner and Newburn 1999, 155).

Talk, awareness, and use of drugs is much more common among progressive youth in the late 1990s than it was among *tusovka* youth of the 1980s. Among the progressive respondents involved in this study, only one talked at any length about his own current habit, which, at the time, centered on Ketamine[23] and cheap, CIS produced, hash, used to make hash "milk" and "snickers"[24] because it was not of high enough quality to smoke (59, Moscow). However, many other respondents talked about past or current experimentation with drugs by themselves or within their circle of acquaintances. One respondent recounted how one of the former members of his band had died of a drug overdose and how a second former member was now a drug addict who had so damaged himself mentally that he no longer left the confines of his flat (231, Samara).[25]

On the club scene, synthetic "energizing" drugs were most popular, although those used widely in the West, such as Ecstasy,[26] were only rarely encountered because of their high cost. Paradoxically, therefore, Ecstasy on the Russian club scene was considered a drug of the "old" (that is, the rich) rather than the young (251, Ul'ianovsk). The cheaper alternatives were to inhale heroin (237, Samara),[27] to use antidepressants and tranquilizers, primarily Librium or Temazepam (37, Ul'ianovsk; 39, Ul'ianovsk), or "homemade" pills (*kolesa*).[28] The last were particularly unpredictable in their effects: "One of my good acquaintances downed a lot of pills, which had been made in some chemistry labs here in the Medical Institute . . . the students do it. . . . Nobody could talk to him for about five days because he couldn't utter a word afterwards. . . . When he came round and found that a week had gone by, he was extremely surprised" (231, Samara).

Many clubbers, however, preferred to drink vodka, or the increasingly fashionable tequila, to induce the energy "rush" they sought (237, Samara).

Among rock *tusovki*, the smoking of cannabis (known as *plastik, plastilin, or anasha*) was common (208, Samara; 164, Samara), as well as the use of pills and harder drugs (59, Moscow). Alcohol consumption was routine.

There was no common view on drugs and alcohol and their role in progressive lifestyles among respondents. On the contrary, these young people treated alcohol and drug use as a matter of individual choice: "Drinking, like drug use, all depends on your mood" (237, Samara).

The state's role was considered to be one of provision of medical supervision to facilitate individual choice, rather than to usurp it through prohibitive legislation (231, Samara). This need not imply any moral relativity or indeed indifference to the use of drugs, however. A complex set of differentiations and personal and group choices were discussed and a complicated value matrix emerged. One element of this was a common distinction drawn by young people between "drug users" and "drug addicts" (Omel'chenko 1999b, 50). Although this differentiating practice is found among youth in many other countries, it is especially notable in Russia, since in the media and in medical and criminal discourse the term *narkoman* is generally applied both to people with drug addictions and to any individual taking an illegal drug. The disentangling of these categories by young people indicated that drug use in itself was not considered to be indicative of a "bad person"; one fifteen-year-old respondent described a group of rappers she knew as "warm [*dushevnie*] people" (218, Samara), despite their drug use. Drug addicts, on the other hand, were perceived to have adopted antisocial behavioral characteristics, such as "always asking for money" and stealing (164, Samara; 208, Samara).

Progressives differentiated, not only between drug users and drug addicts, but also between drug users "now" and "in the future." Thus choices about drug use were not made once and for all, but repeatedly and might elicit different responses at different moments in life: "Drugs predominate . . . in the sphere of youth but with time this will disappear and, of course, with age because it is a kind of fashion, it is a kind of culture . . . when a person is thirty he is thinking seriously about starting a family, he may even have a family . . . but when you are studying, it is easier to take drugs" (237, Samara).

Moreover, although progressive young people considered drug use a personal issue, they saw their choices as having social impacts, especially on family and friends, and awareness of this had persuaded individuals to give up drug use (228, Samara). The *tusovka*—and more importantly, its form of communication—might also be threatened by excessive use of drugs as in the case of the rock *tusovka* described below: "It was a good crowd [kompaniia] . . . it split up in principle because drug addicts appeared. . . . Now we see each other rarely. . . . Part of our crowd . . . have themselves already begun to get into drugs. . . . They have become different. Of course we sometimes maintain contact, to be polite we say hello . . . so we keep contact but don't particularly communicate [*obshchaemsia*]" (208, Samara).

In contrast, where drug use was not an addiction and friendship, or *tusovka* life, retained its primacy over the drug taking within it, the *tusovka* survived. One student respondent from Ul'ianovsk noted how individuals from the *tusovka* (who used the respondent's flat as a common hangout) did not use drugs there out of a concern to protect him from both the police and his neighbors (11, Ul'ianovsk). The choice to abstain from drug use, indeed, was readily mobilized within *tusovka* identity via the claim that it was the activity, the *obshchenie* itself, which gave the "high" (*kaif*) rather than any artificial substance (33, Ul'ianovsk, 39, Ul'ianovsk): "I, for example don't smoke and try not to have alcoholic drinks on principle. The joy in my life I get from knowing what to be happy about. I know that I am a happy person and I have my own thing, I don't have to get drunk in order to get a *kaif*" (33, Ul'ianovsk).

On the basis of currently available data from Russia, it is almost impossible to draw any firm conclusions about the relationship between different forms of youth cultural practice and levels and types of drug use. The first study to address this found that around 10 percent of school children who said they had tried drugs at least once identified themselves with "club *tusovki*" and another 5 percent identified themselves as *neformaly*. Thirty-three percent of those who had tried drugs, however, identified themselves with either *dvor* groups or gangs (*gruppirovki*) (Omel'chenko 1999b, 47). While this clearly suggests there were more normal drug users than progressive ones, since the former also constituted the vast majority of young urban Russians it does not necessarily indicate a greater propensity toward drug-taking among either normals or progressives.

Among normal youth in the current study, use of alcohol and drugs was common. Drinking was widespread, even among the youngest respondents.[29] A member of one *dvor* group said the group drank (wine and vodka) "only on holidays" which was subsequently defined as "birthdays, teachers' day, *Komsomol* day . . . well every day" (2, Ul'ianovsk). Most respondents recognized the widespread use of drugs among their peers, and the use of dope was so widespread that questions regarding "smoking" required clarification as to what substance was being referred to. The use of *dimidrol* (a prescription tranquilizer) was also reported as being used by acquaintances of two Moscow respondents (42, Moscow; 43, Moscow), although hard drug use was reported only by one normal respondent who had experimented with cocaine (19, Ul'ianovsk).[30]

While this does not facilitate any comparison of levels of alcohol and drug use among progressives and normals, it is possible to suggest on the basis of the current study, that alcohol and drugs were used differently by normals and progressives. Unlike progressive youth—who emphasized that alcohol and drug use was a matter of personal choice—for normals it was viewed as part of whole life strategies and subject to group norms (42,

Moscow; 43, Moscow; 12, Ul'ianovsk). Smoking dope, for example, was a group activity; money was pooled and joints rolled and smoked communally (10, Ul'ianovsk; 9, Ul'ianovsk). While this is common practice with cannabis use, a study of drug use among school age children in Ul'ianovsk showed a tendency for an increasingly broad range of drugs (including heroin, cocaine, and toxic substances) to be used in a group setting (Omel'chenko 1999b, 14). The peculiarly group-based practice of drug use among normals was exemplified, however, by a dispute that had arisen among members of one group of friends over which was better—smoking dope or drinking. The moral high ground was taken by the dope-smokers, since the high from drugs did not "debilitate" in the same way as alcohol inebriation (9, Ul'ianovsk; 10, Ul'ianovsk). This group also used stimulants (*kolesa*), especially for discos, although some members of the group equated their effect to drinking and declared them uninteresting (9, Ul'ianovsk; 10, Ul'ianovsk).

While the group nature of drug use among normals might be interpreted as constituting peer pressure on others to engage in drug use, it also meant that there was strong encouragement *not* to drink or take drugs in those groups where "a correct way of life" was the group norm (12, Ul'ianovsk). One young woman described how her friendship group worked to ensure the exclusion of drug users: "I just don't understand when people say drugs help you forget about your problems. . . . Even if a [drug addict] came in [to our circle] he would quickly leave because there would be nobody to do it [take drugs] with" (236, Samara).

Others also noted that girls in their group did not drink or smoke dope with them, and indicated that they were not expected to do so (9, Ul'ianovsk; 10, Ul'ianovsk). In contrast abstention decisions among young men were reported only as a result of disincentives arising from the punitive approach to drug use in Russia. Two respondents claimed they had given up drug use when their friend had been expelled from his institute after being picked up by the police in possession of hashish (17, Ul'ianovsk; 18, Ul'ianovsk). While a first offense might only lead to inclusion on the juvenile offender register (and thus the requirement to report daily to the police), being caught a second time would have meant a prison sentence (3, Ul'ianovsk).

Gender, Gender Relations, and Sexuality: Progressives in Everything?

The exemption of girls from group norms—and girls' own adoption of the role of moral guardians—was indicative of the traditional approach to gender relations inherent in normal youth cultural strategy. Another aspect of this attitude was a disinclination to discuss gender relations; they were seen, not as "relations," but rather as "essences."[31] In contrast, young people adopting a progressive cultural strategy consciously aligned themselves with what they interpreted to be a "Western" approach to gender, defined by less inhibited relations between young men and young women and the stretching of traditionally rigid gender boundaries.

Showing an awareness of these issues, a number of respondents noted their "unusual" gender preferences in friends: two young women said they generally preferred male company (232, Samara; 233, Samara), and one young man mainly mixed with girls (237, Samara). One male respondent from Samara also had a strikingly non-macho notion of the kinds of qualities young women and young men looked for in their male friends: "Probably the girls would like a nice guy with a good sense of humor, the guys would like a reliable friend, probably happy or, on the contrary, interestingly sad" (206, Samara).

That progressive youth consciously sought a cultural environment in which both sexes were respected was evident from the disgust expressed by two female clubbers at the attitude they sometimes encountered in clubs from older men who went to clubs primarily to pick up girls (213, Samara; 214, Samara). Young women in the role-play movement had mounted an active defense of their right to full participation in the face of a clear gender division of roles within those parts of the movement to which the staging of mock battles and fighting were central. This had become an issue of contention for some female members in the Ul'ianovsk-based *Rys'* club where the main activity was medieval fighting. The club was clearly male dominated; and at games organized by the group, women tended to be spectators to the male fighting (1, Ul'ianovsk), a fact which had led to altercations and difficult relations within the group (1, Ul'ianovsk; 254, Ul'ianovsk). This partially explained the withdrawal of some women from *Rys'* and their closer involvement with the Tolkienists, where there was more space for active involvement. Video footage of the Hobbit Games in 1995 confirmed that while relatively few women were involved in the fighting, they were active in the ceremonial aspects of the games and might carve out specific roles for themselves. In Ul'ianovsk, a medieval singing group had been formed by a group of young women, and this group played out the role of minstrels in the Hobbit games (1, Ul'ianovsk).

On the whole, however, sexism within *tusovki* was denied, and gender imbalances explained as simply "the nature of things." In the case of rap, the absence, or limited participation, of girls was explained by reference to the dangerous nature of involvement with rappers (61, Moscow; 63, Moscow).[32] Among hikers (*turisty*), it was suggested, the equal participation of girls would limit the possibilities of the group as a whole; a student who organized long-distance hikes said the groups he led were usually 70–90 percent male because otherwise the group would be too weak to transport the kayaks (51, Moscow). The apparently nonmacho bard movement was male dominated also; although female bards did exist, it was suggested that they found it more difficult to tell the kind of bawdy stories frequently used in bard music, and thus any increase in the number of women would alter the nature of the genre (224, Samara). Even behind the explanations of apparently unusual gender preferences—why women preferred male company, for example—lay gender stereotypes suggesting that guys were "more straightforward" and didn't "gossip" or "betray" you.

In the sphere of dress and style, both attempts to kick the norm and the persistence of underlying prejudices about essential differences were apparent among progressives. Female clubbers talked positively about choosing to wear loose and comfortable clothing (almost always T-shirts and loose trousers) (213, Samara; 214, Samara), and one male clubber from Samara wore unisex clothing. However, the latter reported receiving critical comments about his sexual orientation as a result of his dress style (237, Samara). Indeed, unisex style was widely disliked even among those close to the club scene such as breakdancers and rappers, who directly linked unisex to effeminacy and homosexuality (230, Samara; 229, Samara; 228, Samara).[33]

Homosexuality itself remained tightly linked to the perception of feminine traits in men and masculine traits in women. Although young progressives in Samara, for example, were increasingly aware of an emergent gay scene in the city, it was characterized as consisting of effeminate boys with dyed hair and "girly" mannerisms who wore "close-fitting clothes" (225, Samara). A gay acquaintance of one group of respondents was caricatured as having feminine traits, such as constantly dyeing and straightening his hair, using face powder, and being domestic. Moreover, his presence was perceived as threatening; it was made a condition of being in the group that he didn't make sexual approaches to its other male participants (215, Samara). Even the failure to demonstrate an aggressive male (hetero)sexuality provoked concern; reluctance to talk to girls was interpreted by one group of friends as grounds for concern that one of their number was gay (215, Samara). Other respondents were even more blunt about their prejudices, describing homosexuals as "wrong in the head" and "deviants from nature," who should be avoided (231, Samara) or suggesting the need to differentiate between "genuine" gays, who "can't help themselves," and those just following trends imported from America (56, Moscow). The non-native origin of homosexuality—and more recently bisexuality (56, Moscow)—was in fact a recurrent theme in young people's sexual discourse (Omel'chenko 1999a).

The material position of the vast majority of young Russians was such that real everyday activities surrounding home, school, college, work, and leisure were more locally framed than was their globally mediated cultural consumption. Even in this, most domestic of spheres, however, young people appeared to inhabit cultural worlds with quite different horizons.

While the pressures to study and earn money constrained leisure activities for both progressives and normals, what free time they had was structured differently. Normals tended to engage in a greater number of organized leisure activities of the Soviet type (sports and clubs, for example) alongside unstructured time-out spent among territorially located peer groups. Progressives, on the other hand, had a greater propensity to combine leisure pursuits with study or part-time work, blurring the distinction between the two and creating the impression of a whole lifestyle. In managing the risks of late modernity, progressives responded with an individually oriented discourse of choice, taking up the challenges of individual responsibility thrown at them. Their broad horizons allowed them to draw on perceived "Western models" of response where—as in the case of negotiating changing gender relations—this was perceived to help. Normals on the other hand continued to refer to group norms in managing new environments and, in the case of questions regarding gender and sexual preference, excluded rather than engaged with the challenges of late modern diversity.

Conclusion

> I have never been further than *Karsunskii* district. Only to the village.
>
> —7, Ul'ianovsk

This sixteen-year-old in Ul'ianovsk, coming to the end of her school career, did not see her future as an infinite horizon opening before her, but as tightly bound within local networks. Her future prospects, she said, were dependent upon where her mother could "get her in." Such limited horizons suggest little sense of inclusion into a global world of information and opportunity. Although this respondent also recognized the existence of some kind of global youth experience ("young people are the same everywhere"), this attitude was not borne of an inclusion into it, but from a lack of knowledge about anything existing outside her own immediate environment. Nothing else could be imagined.

While this is a real, and common, experience among provincial young Russians, this chapter has been concerned not to suggest that Russia has been completely excluded from the "light" of globalization and its youth condemned to "prospectless" existence. The social and economic transformations of the last decade have altered everyday lives in Russia fundamentally, but the global context of youthful negotiations of these structural changes, it has been argued, does not undermine established social stratifications, but reconfigures them according to new, glocal dimensions. Bauman's division between the globalized rich and the localized poor, it has been suggested, is evident not only at a global level, but is repeated at national and local levels. Moreover, it is a social cleavage with a clear reflexive edge; global-local and core-periphery positionings are not only reflected in youth cultural strategies, but awareness of them actually shapes those strategies.

At one level, globalization and the social changes associated with late modernity have broadened the horizons of all young people and equipped them rapidly to move in a multimedia world with remarkable intertextual proficiency. For young people with the social and cultural capital to permit them to claim a space in "the center," these opportunities were mobilized in a progressive cultural strategy framed by broad horizons and characterized by a tendency to look outward and to seek new information and cultural stimuli. Translocal style or music affiliations were often a source of such information and a focus point for their gaze on the global horizon. Given the global domination of Western messages and forms in the youth cultural sphere, looking outward inevitably meant "looking West." However, progressive strategy could not be reduced to a process of "copying" the West or be equated with "Westernism." Indeed, those young people who appeared to be most attuned to Western ways of life were actually most critical of them (see Chapters 7 and 8), as they symbolically claimed a place at "the center."

For those young people whose horizons stretched only as far as their home district, globalization had meant an increasingly narrow focus on locale. Heightened competition for places in higher education, for professional training that might guarantee a "real" salary, and above all, the desire for a degree of social security, meant that young people's lives often focused intensively on study, work, and earning money (legally or illegally). These activities continued to require extensive local networking, and this was the resource upon which normal youth drew in their cultural negotiations of the new environment. Having no pretension to a place "in the center," normal youth used the depth of their local connections to seek to secure themselves a minimal material security that might facilitate global consumption.

7 Reconfiguring "the West"

Style and Music in Russian Youth Cultural Practice

Hilary Pilkington

> *233, Samara*: It is clear what we liked [about Nirvana], it was the overwhelming energy . . . it was so repulsive, but the energy nonetheless grabbed us and dragged us along, it was a struggle in our heads . . . a physical sickness. My temperature would go up and I would have a flood of tears.
> *232, Samara*: It wasn't normal.
> *233, Samara*: . . . and then it more or less calmed down . . . but there were side effects, and we suddenly went into brighter music as it were. Thoughtful texts started to attract us. More Russian of course.
> *232, Samara*: To be more precise, not "more Russian" but "Russian" . . . at last we began to understand. And . . . it turned out that Chizh was very close to us . . . the most important thing for us is to find the text and read the text, it is impossible otherwise.

This is how two young women in Samara explained how they switched allegiances from the American grunge[1] band Nirvana to the Russian rock band Chizh & ko. after being "revolted" by a video of Nirvana in concert. It reflects at the micro level how "the West" has been reconfigured in Russian youth cultural practice over the course of the last decade. At the start of the 1990s, young people of this "alternative" persuasion, Rayport Rabodzeenko suggests, engaged with "the West" primarily through a process of the enactment of exoticism and "mimesis" of a "real culture" felt to be missing in their own society (Rayport Rabodzeenko 1998, 35, 56). At the end of the 1990s, "the West" continued to act as an important reference point in progressive youth cultural identification. However, increasing direct interaction with representatives of, and cultural artifacts from, the West and their experience as "imposition" rather than "forbidden fruit" had caused young people to reposition themselves in relation to this "other"; an "other" that was no longer located in an exotic "elsewhere" but increasingly "here" (to turn Rayport Rabodzeenko's formulation around). The processes of cultural globalization that had brought "the West" to a much broader spectrum of Russian youth, and deeper into the

heart of Russia, had resulted in a progressive (post-*tusovka*) strategy among alternative youth, which sought to reauthenticate (parts of) domestic cultural practice, differentiating its members from an imitative, mainstream other. It was this mainstream (the normals) who were now accused of copying the West, where that "West" was equated with commercial and therefore inauthentic cultural production.

This chapter takes as its empirical terrain elements of popular culture with high global content (Held et al. 1999, 341). It addresses directly the question of how the West and its cultural production signify in young people's stylistic and musical consumption and practice. By considering the musical and stylistic preferences, and more importantly, how music was *used* by both alternative and mainstream youth, it sets the reconfiguration of the West in the context of the social and cultural stratification of the Russian youth scene. It shows how points of access to and modes of engagement with the global were different for progressive and "normal" youth, resulting in multiple local narratives of global cultural forms. These engagements, it is suggested, reflect neither a distinctive Russian imitation of Western forms nor a resistance to global styles and types of music, but indicate how young people draw differentially upon both the global and the local as resources in the construction of progressive or normal lives.

Style and Fashion: Imported Style on Local Bodies

Style was the sphere of cultural consumption and practice in which young Russians were most aware of a deficit of domestic production. This was a mentality inherited from the Soviet period when devotion to Western attire was so great that, in the 1980s and flying in the face of dominant ideology, Soviet factories began to produce clothes bearing Western commercial logos (such as Marlboro or Levi-Strauss) in an attempt to pass them off as Western products (Shlapentokh 1989, 151). For youth of the late 1990s, Russian-produced clothing remained something to be avoided, resulting in a heavy dependence on Western imports. The wearing of Western clothes was explained by the failure of contemporary Russian companies to produce anything other than "the same clothes they produced twenty years ago" (210, Samara), although other respondents claimed that the problem was rooted in a longer-term historic inattention to style in Russia (253, Ul'ianovsk; 250, Ul'ianovsk; 213, Samara). By the late Soviet period, this state of affairs had produced a binary division between those who had access to, and dressed in, imported Western (*firmennaia*) clothes and those with little option but to wear domestically produced clothes. Post-Soviet style practice was more complex, however. The greater availability of non-Russian (although not necessarily Western-made) clothes had dislodged the meaning of *firmennaia*, which had begun to be used to refer to an article of clothing with a recognized designer label rather than Western clothes per se. Although Western designer items were still more likely to be sought after by progressives—especially those on the dance scene[2]—than "normals," nondomestically produced clothes were worn by youth across the scene. This universality belied a fundamental difference in style practice between progressives and normals, however. For progressives, the creation of style was central to both subcultural belonging and to maintaining an individual stance within the group; style allowed one to both fit in and stand out within the group (Muggleton 2000, 67). Normals, in conscious contrast, dressed to avoid standing out while seeking to look fashionable by wearing imported clothes in combinations that conformed to local fashion looks. Thus, paradoxically, it was in the sphere of style that young Russians drew most commonly on the Western or "global," in terms of their material and cultural consumption, yet did so to create highly localized distinctions.

Progressive Style: Dedicated Opponents of Fashion

In common with the findings of recent studies of post-subcultural style in the West, there was little sense of any homologous connection between style and subcultural group formation on the Russian youth scene of the late 1990s. Where young people continued to associate particular groups with certain styles, this was generally in relation to *neformaly* (hippies, punks, bikers, and heavy metal fans) identified with the 1980s. In the representative survey of youth in Samara and Ul'ianovsk, for example, when young people were asked to state their first associations with particular youth groups, it was a particular style of dress which frequently came to mind where "traditional" *neformaly* were concerned, whereas music, behavior, or attitude might be the primary association for new dance scenes (rave, techno, hip hop, rap). Even in the case of older subcultural styles, only one respondent suggested any connection between the style and the values of the group; in this case punk style was said to reflect the punk's recognition "that the world is a huge rubbish tip and all people are disgusting" (232, Samara).[3] For progressives themselves, moreover, the very diversity within their microgroups meant that style allowed a sense of individuality within a selfconsciously nonconformist group look; a practice Muggleton terms "distinctive individuality" (Muggleton 2000, 63).

This self-conscious but relaxed attitude to style was particularly evident among dance music respondents (Fig. 20).[4] A small group within the scene adopted designer club wear, but outside Moscow these people never numbered more than a handful in each city (237, Samara), and no single "club" style was evident (225, Samara). Individuals might create their own "freak" styles,[5] but the majority chose clothes that were, above all, comfortable for dancing (215, Samara; 229, Samara). Dance scene members closer to the hip hop end of the spectrum, for example, generally wore

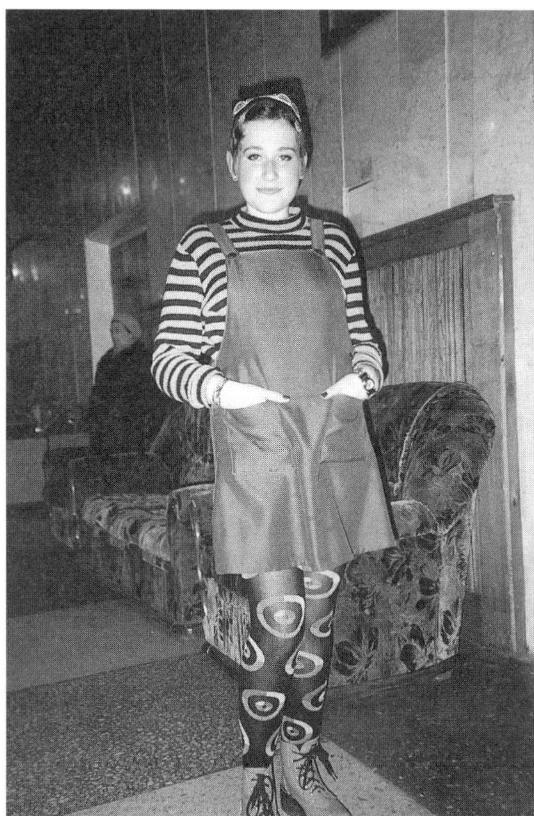

Fig. 20 "Progressive" style at a "Toxic Vibes" night at the Chkalov House of Culture. Ul'ianovsk, November 1997. Photo by Moya Flynn.

oversized jeans, high running shoes or boots, and baggy sweat shirts (242, Samara; 34, Ul'ianovsk; 35, Ul'ianovsk; 36, Ul'ianovsk). This was partially for comfort, and safety, while dancing, although the baggy trousers worn by hip hoppers or break beaters were an important signifier of the distance they had traveled from the "smart" and "shaven" look of the normals.[6] The "trousers round our ankles" look of the Russian hip hop scene also held a degree of self-irony, however, as is evident from the self-caricaturing of Samara hip hoppers illustrated in Figure 21.

Attitudes to style on the dance scene reflected the wider fluidity of the *tusovka* and its relative lack of concern with differentiation from other groups, as expressed by a male respondent on the dance scene in Ul'ianovsk: "I like clothes which create a mood, I like clothes which are accessible to me . . . in which I feel comfortable . . . sometimes I want to create some kind of character for myself . . . [but] I rarely wear things that would place me in a concrete *tusovka*. . . . I just like stylish things" (254, Ul'ianovsk).

Fig. 21 An ironic approach to style; poster on the wall of the hip hop club Sandra. Samara, April 1998. Photo by Hilary Pilkington.

Progressive style practice in general, moreover, was concerned with expressing all sides to an individual's character rather than establishing a secure subcultural self. Respondents were ambivalent about subcultural style conformity. Two Samara dance scene respondents (who generally wore loose-fitting trousers), for example, described how they would occasionally wear a dress and smart shoes to have a bit of fun by "standing in" not "out" (214, Samara; 213, Samara) (Fig. 22). This attitude conformed to a wider progressive lifestyle that sought to maximize experience and opportunity by mixing in diverse crowds, moving between different styles, and experimenting with different "selves." Style practice for progressive youth was thus not primarily about copying Western styles as a way of stating a translocal, subcultural affiliation, but it was about looking "stylish" (*stil'no*) in an individual way as opposed to following fashion: "I have a bad attitude to the word 'fashion' . . . 'fashionable' is a broad word—but 'style' it is a narrow, and individual [thing]" (227, Samara).

Fig. 22 Clubbers in Samara; style was secondary to feeling comfortable. April 1998. Photo by Moya Flynn.

Style was not just stumbled upon but actively sought via a process of experimentation with clothes and hairstyles until one's "own style" was achieved (210, Samara; 1, Ul'ianovsk; 52, Moscow). Indeed, in the Russian provinces, the limited choice of the local "rag markets"[7] set "progressive" youth an ongoing challenge to "stand out."[8] Accessing clothes was an acute problem for provincial respondents. who complained they "wasted" considerable time scouring markets and shops for clothes. They attributed this to their dependence on the "shuttle traders"—importers of clothes, usually from Turkey and Poland—who resupplied the market with the last thing that had sold well rather than leading fashion in a progressive way. Not only was there less choice in the provinces, but clothes were also more expensive, since the shuttle traders added a markup for transportation from Moscow. To avoid this, some respondents traveled to Moscow themselves to buy clothes and footwear (237, Samara), while others placed "orders" with those who could afford to do this (22, Ul'ianovsk). A second, and increasingly popular option, was to buy from second-hand shops where designer gear sent as "humanitarian aid" could be picked up cheaply (213, Samara; 214, Samara). There was a kind of subcultural capital to be gained from finding something really cool for next to nothing: "Generally I think it is *klubno* and funny [*prikol'no*] to go to a second hand and buy a T-shirt for 10,000 rubles.[9] . . . I think it is better to buy clothes in the second hand where I know for sure that they have been brought from Europe rather than spending huge money on some T-shirt . . . when I don't know what the quality is like. . . . I have a lot of friends, a lot of girl friends who dress from second hands now, the choice there is just fantastic" (215, Samara).

Some respondents resorted to the tried and tested Soviet era strategy of raiding grandparents' wardrobes for suitable things to alter (23, Ul'ianovsk), and one respondent suggested that individuals might even engage in shop-lifting.[10]

The creation of style did not only bring individual satisfaction, however; it had a deeply social significance. Style allowed one to "stand out" and thus extricated progressives from what they perceived to be a herd mentality among the majority of provincial youth: "We have a herd mentality here. One sheep sets off and they all follow. [laughter] We don't have any individuality . . . it is only just now that lots of shoes, lots of clothes have appeared, and so individuality has begun to appear . . . before if one guy wore a leather jacket, narrow shoes on a thin sole with pointed toes . . . jeans . . . then all the guys wore them" (215, Samara).

For progressive youth, therefore, as soon as something became fashionable, for example, dyeing one's hair, or piercing one's eyebrow, it had to be abandoned as cheap and nasty (206, Samara; 213, Samara; 214, Samara).

By "standing out" progressives were not distancing themselves from the older generation, therefore, but, first and foremost, from the "mass" of (conventionally dressing) youth. And it was the latter, rather than parents, who gave progressives grief over their particular styles of dress.[11] One fifteen-year-old from Ul'ianovsk, with short-cropped hair, explained why he had abandoned his earlier style: "Now, on the contrary, I don't stand out because literally six months ago, I had a pony tail, my hair was this length [points to shoulders]. . . . I had ripped jeans . . . those same *gopniki* hassled me, spoiled my face a little, and I decided to change, not to stand out. . . . It is harder for a guy to stand out . . . not everyone would touch a girl. . . . I do think it is harder for guys" (37, Ul'ianovsk).

This practice was gender specific; it was young men who were targeted. The very different approach to girls who sought to stand out was confirmed by two female clubbers from Ul'ianovsk who, dressed in bright tops and torn tights with the express intention of shocking the public, found that they were given a wide berth and treated as "insane" rather than being confronted directly (250, Ul'ianovsk; 253, Ul'ianovsk). Hostile reactions to nonconventional style were also locally specific; while such occurrences were reported often by respondents from Ul'ianovsk, they were very unusual events in Moscow.

Normal Style: Smart but Fashionable

For normal respondents style also had a social significance, but it was a mode of collective rather than individual expression. Normals generally sought to dress "fashionably" (42, Moscow; 43, Moscow; 9, Ul'ianovsk; 10, Ul'ianovsk; 5, Ul'ianovsk; 6, Ul'ianovsk), and the "high-street" (chain-store) fashion at the time of interviewing (September 1997–April 1998) was generally considered for girls to be bright colors, platform shoes and shoes with square toes and blunt heels, close-fitting wide-legged trousers or flared jeans, tight tops, and cashmere coats. Synthetic materials were particularly popular. Young men were wearing long thick woolen overcoats, leather raincoats or short, leather pilot's jackets, jeans (usually black), running shoes (Reebok or Adidas), leather shoes with thick soles, sweaters or jackets, and even suits. Short hairstyles were essential for young men.

Two male respondents explained their, and their friends', "fashionable dress" quite explicitly: "We wear jeans . . . black, black jeans . . . any [brand] . . . when we wear sports clothes, we wear running shoes . . . we have jeans and shoes or sports clothes and running shoes . . . if you go outside, then running shoes, track suit trousers, jackets with hoods, a knitted hat if it is cold" (9, Ul'ianovsk; 10, Ul'ianovsk).

Two other male respondents prefaced their equally prescriptive statement with a claim that they did not adhere to any particular style (see Fig. 13): "Some wear sports wear [*sportivnii kostium*], some wear jeans, it differs, we try to dress in a modern way . . . some have Reeboks, some Adidas . . . now mainly they wear black jeans, a leather jacket, then leather footwear" (5, Ul'ianovsk; 6, Ul'ianovsk).

The preference for sportswear among young men (25, Ul'ianovsk; 26, Ul'ianovsk) marked the key distinction between progressive youth—who refused admittance to their clubs to people wearing sports gear—and normal youth. However, normals did not appear to attach any specific meanings to its adoption beyond that that it was a comfortable mode of dress that was exchanged for black jeans and a shirt when going out to a disco (see Fig. 9). However, the term used to talk about sportswear—*sportivnii kostium* (sports suit)—effectively reinstated highly casual dress as "smart and fashionable."

In sharp contrast to progressive youth, normals had no desire to shock via their dress or even to stand out. Indeed quite the opposite effect was sought, as indicated by the following respondents describing their preferred mode of dress:

*[I dress] comfortably, beautifully and preferably so as not to stand out too much . . . long skirts, a cardigan [*kofta*] with a v-neck, well I could wear a dress of course. . . . Jeans? At night when it is cold outside . . . high-heeled shoes. (7, Ul'ianovsk)*

The criteria for clothes is that they are comfortable . . . and that they do not shock me or [other] people. (234, Samara)

We dress like everyone dresses . . . not like hippies dress for example. (27, Ul'ianovsk)

We don't like to stand out . . . so that everyone looks at you. (45, Moscow)

I don't try to stand out. I dress averagely, I don't try to dress as anything. (29, Ul'ianovsk)

Normal respondents also made a clear distinction between everyday wear and dressing up for special occasions such as the theater (187, Samara) or a party (44, Moscow; 45, Moscow) (Fig. 23). The "smartness aspect to normal" dress codes was not defined against "casual" (for example, sports) clothes, however, but in direct opposition to what was perceived to the consciously styled "scruffiness" of progressives (*neformaly*):

They [neformaly] make them [their clothes] themselves. They get a jacket and cut off the arms . . . get a jacket and put holes in it like tramps. (2, Ul'ianovsk)

They cut their jeans . . . their jeans are ripped, like that. (3, Ul'ianovsk)

Some normal respondents expressed a desire for more stylish clothes and explained the poverty of style among normal young people by the limitations of the clothes markets in the provinces and, above all, the limited financial resources of young people (235, Samara; 14, Ul'ianovsk). "Rag markets" were the main source of clothes for normal respondents; for young people in the provinces this meant the central city market while for those in Moscow, markets were situated in outlying parts of the city, as the city center was full of expensive designer shops. Some respondents also bought in shops and trade fairs. Few normal respondents bought clothes outside their city of residence, although one school student from Ul'ianovsk said she bought all her clothes when she went back to her home city of Novosibirsk because it had a better choice and cheaper prices (12, Ul'ianovsk).

Buying locally did not imply buying Russian, however. Normals, like progressives, insisted that young people did not wear anything produced

Fig. 23 Dressing up was important to "normal" youth strategy. Young women at the Chkalov House of Culture, Ul'ianovsk, October 1997. Photo by Hilary Pilkington.

domestically (216, Samara). Imported clothes came mainly from Eastern countries, primarily Turkey, although in Samara the shuttle traders were increasingly importing clothes from Italy and the United Kingdom (235, Samara).

Ul'ianovsk respondents were particularly frustrated by both the narrow range of choices open to them and the "collective" notion of fashion which inhibited "alternatives": "In Moscow couture forms fashion but here in Ul'ianovsk the shuttle traders bring the fashion. . . . Moreover, if something appears and you like it, but others don't, you may not be able to wear it because . . . you are afraid . . . and you abandon it" (15, Ul'ianovsk).

This position among normals was predominantly expressed by young women, since pressure to conform was particularly strong for men. One or two male respondents shared the desire for nonconformity, however, and compared the collective mentality of Ul'ianovsk unfavorably with other provincial cities, such as Tol'iatti (19, Ul'ianovsk; 13, Ul'ianovsk). Individual respondents also rejected current fashion, preferring "classic" styles (218, Samara) or choosing clothes on the basis of quality (44, Moscow), suitability for professional life (235, Samara), comfort, practicality, and convenience (234, Samara, 238, Samara), or "what suits me" (236, Samara) rather than because they were fashionable.

There were some common positions, and frustrations, between normal and progressive youth in relation to fashion and style, therefore. However, important differences in style practice remained between them and were not only financially, but also culturally, determined.[12] Normal strategy was to conform to peer norms about fashion, rather than choosing to "stand out" and "attract comments" from peers (12, Ul'ianovsk). The comments came from those with the most hostile attitudes to "standing out": "The *neformaly* dress as they like. They are different, they have different clothes. For example they buy new jeans and rip these jeans. I don't like that. If you buy jeans, you should wear them normally. For the *neformaly* we don't dress right and they for us" (3, Ul'ianovsk).

The anti-"style" positioning of normals was thus fashioned by that section of normals who were antagonistically oriented toward progressives (*neformaly*). In the context of continued problems of access to a diverse range of affordable fashion items, however, it was maintained by the broad swathe of normals. Moreover, this peer pressure restricted still further the stylistic practice of "alternative" youth, already limited by the specific positioning of provincial Russia in the global-local flow of commodities. Consequently, the bricolage, retro-chic, and "style surfing" commonly encountered in Western stylistic practice (Polhemus 1997) were largely absent from the Russian youth scene of the 1990s. In style more than any other aspect of youth cultural practice, young Russians were self-consciously dependent on Western imports and deeply insecure about their own stylistic engagements.

Music Use: Putting Flesh on the Russian Soul

The insecurity of Russian youth about their own, local interpretations of global style, was not encountered in their musical practice. This is partially explained by the fact that access was less restricted. Since "global" and "Western" music[13] could be heard via the television, radio, and cheaply produced cassette recordings (alongside more expensive compact disk purchases and concert, gig, or club attendances), it did not require the same degree of consumer purchasing power, and thus experimentation was possible. Russian interactions with popular Western and global music, moreover, had a history dating back at least to the early twentieth century (Gorsuch 2000, 120–38), and had produced well-established subgenres such as "Soviet" or "Russian rock" and Russian "pop." The historical presence of these "Russian" forms of global music lent young people knowledge about and confidence in local products absent from their stylistic practice.

Thus, while global musics became mass phenomena in Russia during the 1990s, young people engaged with them actively and differentially, drawing them into their distinctively local progressive and normal cultural strategies. A single type of global music, such as electronic dance music, thus produced multiple local forms—"rave" and "club culture" variants—and through their identification as "clubbers," "alternative" youth designated a particular engagement with global dance music as "authentic" and "ours." Another strategy employed by progressives to counter the increasing accessibility of various types of global music (such as Western pop) to a broad spectrum of young people, was to label them "commercial," and thus "inauthentic." This paved the way for a (partial) reauthentication of types of "local" music, such as Russian rock. Thus while it might have been expected that the outward-looking tendency of progressives would draw them exclusively to Western music and translocal (global) subcultural affiliation, whereas the locally rooted normals would prefer home-grown Russian music, this was far from the case. Rather, progressive youth listened primarily to either new types of dance music or Western and Russian rock music, while normal youth listened mainly to both Russian and Western pop or electronic dance music, but rarely to rock (of any origin).

This pattern has something in common with findings in the West that link musical preference to the social backgrounds of young people; studies from a range of countries in Europe, North America, and Australasia suggest preferences for mainstream pop, heavy metal, and reggae music are found primarily among working-class and lower-middle-class youth, while middle-class youth prefer "alternative," "underground," or "progressive" rock, jazz, folk, and blues (Frith 1983; 205; Shuker 1994, 232). While some of these correlations held true for Russia, there was no direct equation between progressive and middle-class or normal and working-class musical preferences. It was not so much the preferred musical genre that separated progressive from normal youth, but the *use* of that music within a wider cultural practice that expressed not only aesthetic tastes or social roots but also changing attitudes to the West. This is not to suggest young people listened *either* to Russian *or* to Western music—most listened to both—but to confirm Stratton's observation that as music and style move out of their original contexts, they develop their own specific cultural significances, often far removed from any original celebration of American (or Western) consumerism (Stratton 1985, 189). In the discussion that follows, therefore, the mapping of the musical preferences of progressive and normal youth is presented as secondary to attempting to understand the different meanings attached to that music and the cultural practices developed around it.

Musical "Progressions": Rethinking Authenticity and Creativity

Music is central to young lives. In the West research suggests that listening to music is one of the most important leisure pursuits of young people (Frith 1983, 205; Shuker 1994, 230). Data for Russia confirm that young people are more inclined than the older generation to listen to music (27 percent as opposed to 14 percent of the population as a whole "usually spend leisure time" listening to music) and to go to bars, discos, and clubs (11 percent compared to 4 percent of the whole population) (Fond Obshchestvennogo Mneniia 2000).[14] But how does musical taste relate to wider identities?

Progressive youth attached much greater significance to music than did normal youth (see Chapter 5). Although young progressives professed strong musical identifications, however, those affiliations were not routinely with a single kind of music; progressives had at least clustered, and sometimes wide-ranging musical preferences. Nor was musical taste constant; on the contrary, "progression" and development in musical knowledge and taste was valued. This pattern confirmed findings from the West suggesting that the close ("homologous") relationship between musical taste and visual style, at the heart of theories of subcultural identities among youth (Clarke 1976, 179; Jefferson 1973, 10; Willis 1978, 53) had become unhinged in the 1990s (Bennett 1999b, 613). In the discussion below, therefore, it is suggested that "progressive" musical tastes indicated not an exclusive identification with one subcultural style or movement, but rather mobilized notions of musical diversity and knowledge to set up a broader, but equally significant, distinction between "authentic" ("our") and "commercial" ("for the masses") music.

Musical Diversity

Almost all progressives were passionate about their musical preferences, but they saw them neither as exclusive nor fixed.[15] The tendency toward subgenre fragmentation on the urban dance scene, not surprisingly, meant that it was in this genre of music that diversity of taste was most apparent. Progressives routinely talked about a wide range of styles of electronic dance music, including techno, hard techno, light techno, gabber, trance, jungle, hip hop, rap, gangster rap, heavy rap, garage, speed garage, trip hop, ambient, breakbeat, ragga, dub, house, deep house, jazzy house, funk, soul, drum and bass, and hard core.[16] Although dance scene respondents appeared most sensitive to musical differentiation, however, they were least likely to be oriented exclusively to one type of music. As one respondent noted: "There isn't anyone who listens to trance and only trance. You can listen to house as well, you can listen to jungle. I . . . listen to jungle as well as trance" (54, Moscow).

"Rock," in contrast to dance, was employed as a relatively homogenous category, although some respondents classified their musical preferences as art rock, rock and roll, heavy metal, grunge, or punk. Evidence of diverse tastes within rock came at the level of performer rather than subgenre. Thus while each *tusovka* would identify a number of bands as group favorites, individuality within the group was expressed through personal predilections. Such favorites were almost always cited in two categories—"Western," and "Russian"—although most rock fans listened to both. Most frequently preferred Russian bands were the classic groups and performers of Soviet rock such as Mashina Vremeni, Akvarium, Nautilus Pompilius,[17] Alisa, Kino, Voskresen'e, Kalinov Most, and Ianka Diagileva. The newer bands mentioned included Krematorii, Auktsion, Grazhdanskaia Oborona, Chizh & ko., and Agata Kristi, while groups such as Splin and Mumii Troll' were acceptable listening to both dance and rock fans. Favorite Western bands were also largely "classic" groups such as the Beatles, Jethro Tull, Pink Floyd, Nirvana, Sex Pistols, Bon Jovi, Metallica, Scorpions,[18] Jim Morrison, Queen, Led Zeppelin, the Doors, and King Crimson.

Minority interests included ethnic or world music, especially Celtic, Indian, and "eastern" music and meditative and folk music. The recreation of such music electronically on synthesizers for consumption by "new age trendies," however, led to the labeling of such music as "pseudo" (1, Ul'ianovsk). It is, of course, primarily in the latter form that local music is turned into world music for global consumption.[19] In Russia such local music would be Russian folk or bard music (*avtorskaia pesnia*), which was the preferred music of a number of progressive respondents (51, 56, Samara; 220, Samara; 1, Ul'ianovsk.[20] However, since such local Russian music rarely, if ever, made it into world music sections of commercial outlets, it continued to be viewed as "authentic" music. Jazz and classical music were cited among the preferred types of music of two progressive respondents; greater interest in such music might have been expected, given past Russian strengths in avant-garde forms of both styles. One respondent did note, however, a current trend in the clubs to include in sets well-known symphonic music (in pure as opposed to sampled form) (250, Ul'ianovsk).

Exceptions to the presentation of progressive musical taste as eclectic were found primarily in relation to pop music, which featured in progressive youth's talk as an object of derision. Only three progressive respondents admitted to liking even elements of pop (220, Samara; 230, Samara; 223, Samara) despite its popularity among youth in general. The significance of this, as well as some more specific musical dislikes among sections of progressive youth are discussed in the next section.[21]

Musical "Progression"

Progressives emphasized that their musical tastes were fluid, diverse, and open: "I have grown up too much to say I have some concrete musical tastes. I like . . . black music from jazz, to rap, [and] what has emerged out of it; electronic variations on the theme of trip hop, break beat, jungle, drum and bass, gabba, ambient. . . . I really like all kinds of Latin variations. . . . I just like rhythmic music . . . music that puts you in a good mood" (254, Ul'ianovsk).

Thus, while subcultural identities might be important in the "growing up" process, they were not central to progressive strategy. Being progressive reflected rather a personal evolution: "I am sure that in a year's time I will be listening to something else because . . . eighteen months ago, I myself was listening to hard core, but now I talk about it unflatteringly. And a year ago I said that jungle was something terrible. How could you listen to it? Now I even like break beat" (54, Moscow).

This pattern was not exclusive to dance scene youth, or to the capital city. There was evidence of "progression" from rock onto the club scene (251, Ul'ianovsk) and within the rock world. Two respondents from Samara, for example, recited their long history of musical progression from Russian pop, through grunge to the Beatles, Pink Floyd, and finally to Chizh & ko. almost as if they were pursuing a personal research project (232, Samara; 233, Samara). Adherence to a single musical or visual style was neither a key group nor individual value; indeed, conversely, it was an indicator of a failure to engage with the wider world and its new information sources that was central to progressive identities. This does not suggest that there were no constants amid the diversity and progression, however, rather that what remained stable was not the cultural form but a particular practice. As Muggleton notes, what was fixed was not any single subcultural allegiance but the commitment to the ever-changing but genuine expression of self (Muggleton 2000, 96). For Russian progressive youth this "genuine expression of self" was deeply rooted in the notion of the "realness," or authenticity of the music with which they engaged. Thus, their movement through different music and style affiliations was accompanied by an ever-deepening sense of the division between "authentic" ("own") and "commercial" ("other," "mass") music.

Musical Authenticity

Authenticity in terms of musical *production* was defined by progressives as "pure," "unspoiled" (224, Samara), and "independent": " 'Independent' is music that has not enjoyed commercial success and never will" (231, Samara). Authenticity was thus inversely related to commercial success and popularity. In contrast, "nonauthentic" music was defined as "popular," "for the masses," and "commercial": "There is progressive house, which is a bit of a silly music . . . I am not one of those who likes commercial culture. . . . The masses like it . . . it is not quality . . . it is designed for making money quickly. There are many examples of that—Prodigy, Scooter" (225, Samara).

In terms of music *consumption*, authenticity was associated with both being there at the start of a musical trend but also recognizing its real meanings: "When rap had just arrived in Russia [four years ago] we had our own group, we danced rap. We listened, got all the recordings, video cassettes, learned the movements . . . before it was in fashion. . . . Now only the real rappers are left, those who love it. . . . Those who came to rap only because of its extremism, they have gone and only the real ones have remained; those who genuinely value it" (225, Samara).

On the dance scene authenticity was defined by the absence of "the masses," that is the *byki*, and thus clubs where access was gained via invitation or "face control" were rated more highly than those charging high entrance fees: "The worse the place [building], the better the club is considered. . . . That is why the Titanik[22] is not liked. It is said that only *byki* and *lokhi* go to the Titanik because it is so sterile there, all cleaned. The only good thing about the Titanik is that the sound is good . . . going to the [central] clubs like that is below our dignity . . . nobody from the *teatral'naia*[23] would be likely to pay to go there" (54, Moscow).

Each city had its "legendary" clubs, which were looked back upon with great nostalgia. Central to such status was the fact that they were relatively unknown, not advertised, and thus open only to a small crowd.[24] In Samara, *the* legendary club had been Koleso, in Moscow it was Les: "It was a club legend because it was virtually unadvertised . . . the fliers were just drawn by hand. But you just had to be at Les, and virtually nobody paid to get in, only our own crowd [*svoi*] went. I don't know how they made money, probably from drugs. . . . it was an old cafe . . . almost dilapidated, the sanitary arrangements were awful . . . but everyone really liked the atmosphere" (54, Moscow).

Where access was not restricted through knowledges and tusovka practices, then commercialization and the slide into mass or "pop" culture always threatened: "We have a radio station called 106.8 about which everybody knows. A year ago it was prestigious to listen to this radio station. It was considered *our* station. Now the station has become completely poppy [*opopselo*]. They got a new program director who puts on stuff that makes you feel sick, as we say. And so now if you listen to 106.8, you are already seen as . . . [*makes face*]" (54, Moscow).

Mass consumption of a particular kind of music could thus render it nonauthentic; it became, literally, "pop." Although mainstream pop music generally has been more popular among girls than boys and among younger rather than older teenagers (Shuker 1994, 234), progressives avoided the temptation to characterize such tastes in gendered terms. Respondents explained differences in taste rather as one of "mass" tastes versus "other" (alternative) tastes (37, Ul'ianovsk; 13, Ul'ianovsk; 39, Ul'ianovsk; 164 Samara; 208, Samara).[25] The "immaturity" of those listening to commercial music was invoked, however, both as a real description and as a metaphor for "nonprogressive" attitudes. Thus, those who listened to such music were characterized as "teenagers" into "rave" and "basketball" (38, Ul'ianovsk). Among rock fans, a common way of expressing the relationship was to depict nongenuine fans as those into the "attributes" rather than the music. Thus young punks were described as being hooked on drugs and drink rather than music (231, Samara) while some rock fans' connection to the music was said to be only as deep as the band T-shirts on their backs (232, Samara; 233, Samara). This characterization of the "other" suggests the way in which progressives perceived stylistic or musical commitment as being wholly compatible with (subcultural) "progression."

Authenticity and "the West"

The peculiar history of the development of popular music in Russia means that musical preferences and uses inevitably have expressed not only aesthetic tastes or social roots but also changing attitudes to the West. The association of musical and stylistic authenticity with noncommercialism in post-Soviet Russia problematizes the established link between authenticity and "the West." In the immediate postwar period and through the first beginnings of a local rock scene in the Soviet Union, "the West" signified the "authentic" automatically. The West was the source of latest musical recordings, fashion, youth cultural commodities, and information, which were accessed via foreign visits or friends abroad and passed around, accruing ever greater cultural capital until something new arrived on the scene. Given the importance of "being there at the start" noted earlier, young people were also acutely aware of the origins of specific youth cultural movements and often referred to the difficulties of being a "real" hippie, punk, and so on in Soviet or Russian conditions:

I understand that Russia is always comparing itself to the West and there is a sense of having to wait till everything reaches us. . . . Especially in the States, for example. After all they invented the hippies. . . . You can't be a hippie in the same way in Russia as in America . . . for example, in America it is warmer. . . . But here, the winter. . . . how can you be a hippie [in the winter] when you have to rush home before you freeze? . . . For this reason I think that it is hopeless trying to be a real hippie in Russia. (11, Ul'ianovsk)

In the early 1990s concerns about Western authenticity reached their height as people feared that their market naïveté would be exploited by sharp traders selling cheap imitations (in musical recording equipment, tapes, fashion) from China and other Eastern countries. Moreover on new electronic music scenes, the high dependence on technology and club infrastructure meant that the West retained its role in defining the "authentic" as the first generation of nonofficial cultural producers began to travel freely to the West and sought to recreate the music and atmosphere they found in clubs and other venues there (Yurchak 1999).

In many instances, therefore, Western music continued to be considered the "norm," to which Russian music failed to conform. One respondent claimed to have only Western recordings in his collection, since current Russian music was "monotonous" and bearable only as "background" (227, Samara). A more common response to the relative merits of Russian and Western music, however, was the profession of an emotional affinity with Russian music but a critical evaluation of it. Russian music was perceived to be behind that of the West in terms of quality of sound and production and musical professionalism (210, Samara; 11, Ul'ianovsk):

Five years ago we all listened to rock intensively . . . Soviet rock. . . . I am not afraid to say it was not of the best quality. I think that there are only two outstanding groups, Mashina and Akvarium. . . . The rest in my opinion do not stand up to criticism. (51, Moscow)

It [Russian rap] has not quite matured to the level of that played abroad. (63, Moscow)

Among progressive respondents, those who consciously preferred Russian music constituted the minority and consisted primarily of those interested in bard music (51, Moscow; 56, Moscow). Only one respondent expressed a conscious antipathy to Western music (and indeed "everything English language and Western") in general (56, Moscow).

The economic and political reconfiguration of Russia in the 1990s, however, had nonetheless dislodged the "natural" correlation between "authenticity" and the West. The rise in popularity of commercial Russian pop together with the new competition for "alternative" or "progressive" youth identities furnished by the dance music scene, had caused Russian rock musicians, and increasingly their listeners, to begin to redefine the authentic away from, even in opposition to, "the West." In musical production this has been manifest in the affirmation of the importance of poetry in rock and the concomitant deemphasis of the Western prioritization of harmony and rhythm. Even in the early 1990s, Cushman found "an emergent sense of nationalistic pride" among St. Petersburg rock musicians and an increasing interest in experimenting with traditional musical themes and instruments (such as the balalaika and baian) within the rock genre (Cushman 1995, 315). An allegory for this process is provided by Kostya Kinchev's song "Together" ("My vmeste!"), which describes how a Russian rock fan abandons the "authentic," native tongue of rock and roll (English) and discovers Russian rock whose Russian text expresses real Russian experience (Friedman and Weiner 1999, 121).

For consumers of rock music a reauthenticated Russian rock was associated with a romantic image of the poor artist: "I think that people who play here are simply more spiritual, sort of rich simply because they have no recognition. A person without recognition has to focus in on himself, and he develops into an individual who does not need outside approval, who does not have to become a superstar, otherwise he will die" (231, Samara).

This reflects both a tradition of Russian rock—rock music in Soviet Russia could not be commercial, since it was excluded from official economic structures (Cushman 1995, 124)—but also a conscious distinction from highly commercial and manufactured forms of pop and rock sited in, or emanating from, the West. The move away from the consumption of Western cultural forms mirrors a similar process in relation to material goods, which was manifest in a practice centered on scouring shops for rapidly diminishing supplies of domestically produced food products (Humphrey 1995). The fact that Russian rock music was referred to by respondents often as *otechestvennii* (literally "of the fatherland" but used more widely to signify domestically produced commodities or culture) rather than "Russian" (*russkii* or *rossiiskii*) suggests the deep domestication of this subgenre of Western music.

Enacting Musical Tastes: The Significance of Music to Progressive Identities

For rock fans and dance music lovers alike, music was central to their self-definition as information-seeking, outward-looking, "progressive" young people. For some respondents (associated with rock *tusovki*) the music itself could literally act as a source of self-development: "If a person begins to listen to all [different kinds of music] . . . he will acquire a great quantity of knowledge because practically all music has a philosophical dimension, whatever style it is, our rock that is" (32, Ul'ianovsk).

Among rock fans music was bought, swapped, listened to, and then discussed. This practice itself quickly turned music into a commodity: remembering names of groups, having cassettes or compact disks, recalling specific tracks, relating them to subgenres and "eras," were all practices that revealed musical knowledge. In this sense rock *tusovki* were far from groups of "fans" in the traditional sense of the word (that is where the focus of fandom is upon a particular star). Rather, rock *tusovki'* conformed to Shuker's notion of a "serious fan" or aficionado whose involvement in the music is one step removed and semi-intellectual; they collect records and tapes, generate information about genres and artists, read magazines, and go to concerts (Shuker 1994, 239). Indeed this process of emerging from obsessive involvement with a particular group to a wider appreciation of the progression of rock and its local traditions was central to the development of rock *tusovki* (232, Samara; 233, Samara) and was closely connected to their identity as critical consumers. A distinction between mainstream fans and those listeners preferring uncommercialized but critically acclaimed bands has been documented since the 1950s (Shuker 1994, 248); and in the 1990s, such "critical" listeners are able to use the cultural capital accruing from their position to foster assimilation into the dominant social elite (Trondman 1990; cited in Shuker 1994, 25).[26]

Despite the relative inclusivity of the urban dance scene in terms of gender, age, sexuality, and socioeconomic background (and subsequently ethnicity), it remains stratified. In understanding the internal workings of the scene, Thornton draws on Bourdieu's notion of "cultural capital" (knowledge accumulated through upbringing and education which confers social status) to recast "hipness" on the club scene as a form of "subcultural capital" (Thornton 1995, 11), reflected in "being in the know," using the latest slang, and being adept at performing the latest dance styles. Such subcultural capital was important on the Russian dance scene too. Individuals who were knowledgeable about music, or had access to primary sources of information, were talked about with reverence (54, Moscow; 253, Ul'ianovsk; 227, Samara). Those on the scene who had been to clubs in the West or who were able to "read English magazines . . . in English" (253, Ul'ianovsk), even, were accorded respect. Travel to other cities in connection with music or dancing provided knowledge and information and was valued highly (33, Ul'ianovsk). The increasingly wide availability of information, style attributes, and music helped foster the club scene's self-image as open, democratic, and nonexclusive (see Chapter 5). However, even within the dance scene hierarchies were maintained. The junglists, for example, considered themselves to be the ultimate in "cool," while others, such as the hard corers, were described as immature, or even *lokhi*[27] (54, Moscow). Moreover, because dance scene culture was itself defined by "clubbing" rather than "listening to music," new forms of hierarchy and access emerged via control of access to clubs and the use of space within them. Intricacies of style(s), hierarchies of "coolness," and techniques of dancing governed the door and the dance floors of clubs in London according to Malbon (Malbon 1999, 55–60). In Russia exclusivity was maintained by a range of mechanisms from dress codes and "face control" to flier systems:

In my spare time I organize parties in clubs . . . and I do exclusively jungle music. . . . someone . . . does the fliers . . . somebody else does the drawings . . . we distribute them, invite interesting people, people we would like to see at our club. (60, Moscow)

Some clubs of course have face control to keep out people in track suits. (215, Samara)

Face control was clearly a cultural practice rather than a commercial one. In Ul'ianovsk and Samara where face control was only partially in existence, the club *tusovki* were very much in favor of its introduction—as it would exclude the *gopa* with whom otherwise they had to share "their space"—despite the fact that it clearly undermined the notion of a "democratic" dance scene. And, in any case, even without formal controls of access, small groups of especially cool people emerged: "In any *tusovka* a temporary closed, privileged elite, small elite may emerge. . . . there are probably two or three individuals who have similar tastes, some charismatic characteristics who will just . . . have an authority and be able to influence what music people listen to" (254, Ul'ianovsk).

Music was central to progressive cultural strategy; it consumed significant energies and lent a certain subcultural capital to individuals. The way in which music was used by rock and dance *tusovki* varied significantly, however: rock fans *listened* to music, clubbers *danced* to it, and hip hop fans did both. While this difference was not directly linked to patterns of preference for either Western or Russian music, it has significance for understanding the decentering of the West in the process of global-local engagements with music and thus requires a more complex approach to the role of music in progressive identities.

Getting to the Roots of Rock: Text, Meaning, Content, Soul

Rock *tusovki* members primarily *listened* to music. This meant sites of music use were home based and quite often detached from *tusovka* gatherings. One sixteen-year-old respondent who mainly listened to music at home noted: "The first thing I do before even turning on the light is to turn on the radio or put in a cassette" (233, Samara).

Rock *tusovki* respondents from the provinces liked listening to concerts on cassette or watching them on video (210, Samara; 232, Samara; 233, Samara), reflecting their relative lack of access to live music—in contrast to Moscow respondents (56, Moscow). In Samara, rock *tusovki* gathered around live music venues, such as the Zvezda, and at smaller gigs (*seishny*), for example, at the infamous Institute of Communications (208, Samara; 164, Samara). The main complaint in Samara was the lack of small club-style venues for rock performers and the lack of investment into the promotion of Samara's own rock bands without which it was impossible to succeed on the national scene (232, Samara; 233, Samara). This meant local bands played in each other's flats, and young people just starting out on the scene did not hear about such events. One compensation in Samara was that it was home to the annual Grushinskii Festival, which was the largest open-air music festival in Russia and provided unparalleled opportunities for information swapping between *neformaly* from different cities (see Chapter 5).

Rock listeners tended to define their musical preferences in terms of specific bands and their histories. For them tracing the "roots," influences, and origins of music was important and in rating bands, doing something "first" or "original" was the ultimate accolade: [on the Beatles] "I have a huge respect for everything that is unrepeatable. I will never stop respecting the Beatles despite who they were themselves and whatever they did. . . . I even have a huge respect for the Sex Pistols . . . because they started something" (232, Samara).

This echoes the meanings attached to music by Russian rock musicians themselves, for whom serious rock music was above all an aesthetic practice, an art form (Cushman 1995, 98). For some—such as the lead singer of the Ul'ianovsk rock group The Slippers, Lesha Nikolaev—this suggested that DJs were little more than "parasites" living off the musical compositions of others (Bliumfel'd 1997, 6). Members of rock *tusovki* also dismissed dance music and the role of the DJ as "uncreative": "I don't understand music like rap, techno, rave . . . well not that I don't understand it. It just isn't close to me, I don't like it. . . . I prefer a live sound . . . when you do something yourself, create. But that [techno] is all computers" (21, Ul'ianovsk).

Thus, although in general progressives were more likely (than normal youth) to be involved in producing music themselves,[28] those who were involved in mixing as opposed to composing music, and rhythm as opposed to text in electronic music, were often disparaged by rock-based *tusovki*.

It was not only the creative process that was perceived to be missing from electronic dance music, but *meaning*. The deficit of meaning attributed to dance music was rooted in its lack of text. For those listening to Russian folk music (*avtorskaia pesnia*), the significance of the text was axiomatic: "[Bard music] carries with it some meaning, it is not just pop: 'you love me, I love you too, let's get together. . . .' It has something else, it has philosophical texts. That is why the text is important. . . . It contains thoughts, unbelievable sincerity, that is why I talk about texts" (224, Samara).

It is a long established thesis that Russian rock, too, is text based and has a peculiar poetic quality (Cushman 1995, 107). From the musician's perspective the primary purpose of the art of rock was to communicate experience in a poetic way (103). This was something appreciated by members of rock *tusovki*, who envisaged rock music as a process of engagement between performer and listener, the outcome of which, for them, was the comprehension of "meaning" (206, Samara): "I think that music should have a text, and it is best if it is your native language and with some meaning because text without meaning is pointless . . . to understand a text you have to listen carefully . . . you can't, for example, listen to Liube in a street car . . . I would never listen to Soviet rock on a Walkman" (39, Ul'ianovsk). Thus, dance music was criticized for its monotony and constant repetition, which had no power to stimulate thought (210, Samara), and did not require engagement from the listener (57, Moscow). For some, this reduced electronic music to "an eruption of sound" (206, Samara) that was intolerable unless listened to after drinking or taking drugs (56, Moscow; 57, Moscow).[29] For rock and folk *tusovki*, therefore, new electronic music provided stimuli only for the body, not the mind.

Moving On: Dance, Technology, Progress

Respondents on the dance scene did not simply "listen" to a particular music; they felt themselves to be involved in "a whole youth culture" (237, Samara). Thus texts were not central to the meaning of music; as one clubber put it, "If I needed words I could read poems" (253, Ul'ianovsk). Dance music listeners consequently referred less frequently to specific tracks, albums, or even DJs when talking about the music they liked. Central to the culture, rather, was dance: "I like music, I listen to it and dance to it. Even when I was doing rap, I did not know, that this was such and such a group, and that was that song. I like a song, I know it, I can dance to it, I know what the lead in is to the music, what comes when, but for me it is not important what music it is, the song, the group. . . . I like all club music" (230, Samara).

Dance scene *tusovki* members enjoyed themselves most when they just let go, jumped, and threw themselves about (213, Samara; 214, Samara) on the dance floor, letting the music take over:[30] "Break beat is a lively music, you have to move to it, you move simply. You let out all your energy" (230, Samara).

Dancing was not just a bodily function, however; it was situated in a broader cultural practice conforming quite clearly to *tusovka* traditions of "communication" (see Chapter 6).[31] The balance between dancing and *obshchenie* depended on the specifics of the club and one's own mood—often a euphemism for how much the individual was under the influence of drink or drugs (237, Samara)—but was central to "progressive" strategy of differentiating "normal" "dancing" from their own "club culture."

This distinction is best illustrated by clubbers' understandings of the difference between "the club" and "the disco." The club was understood,

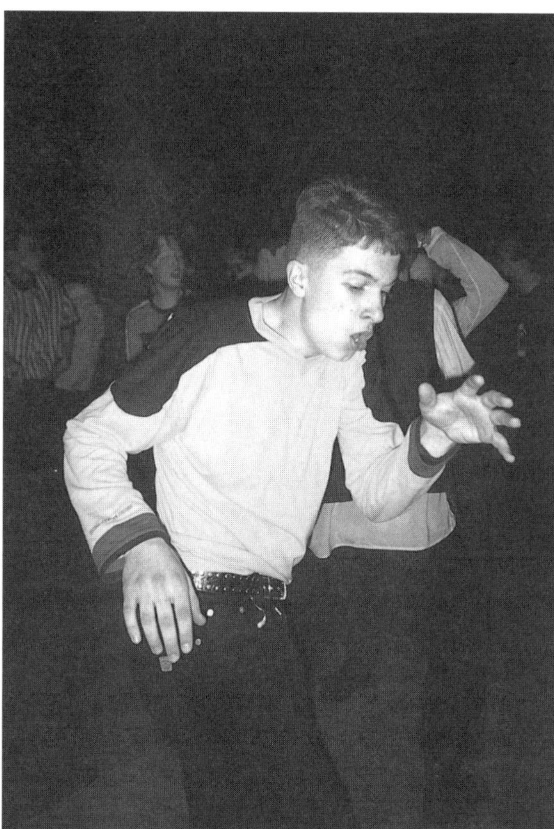

Fig. 24 Dancing at a "Toxic Vibes" night, Chkalov House of Culture. Ul'ianovsk, autumn 1997. Photo by Elena Omel'chenko.

not as a "leisure space," but as a second world—a physical, social, and emotional world in which clubbers could live out alternative existences: "A disco is a little room or huge hall . . . those [who come] have no life there, they just come to dance . . . they call it leisure [*otdykh*]. But . . . when a person is in a club he or she is removed from normal life . . . it becomes a way of life, that is what differentiates a person from someone who just goes to a disco" (237, Samara).

This was made possible partly because of the superior design, lighting, equipment, level of service, security, and refreshment available in clubs (227, Samara); a club was a comfortable place in which it was possible to spend long periods of time. More importantly, however, clubs were social spaces housing their own club *tusovki* (237, Samara): "In a club you have your own *tusovka* . . . that is a certain *tusovka* gathers, people get to know each other, communicate, that is some kind of relations are spun . . . but a disco is a one-off amusement; you come, have fun but don't hang around there afterwards" (215, Samara).

Thus, paradoxically, it was at the discos that dancing was at a premium, since they were generally open for only three or four hours in an evening (213, Samara; 214, Samara). In contrast, the best clubs were places to "relax" in an unthreatening atmosphere (231, Samara), which felt "like going home" (213, Samara; 214, Samara).

The club was also felt to embody a different musical aesthetic. Clubs operated a system of "resident" and "visiting" DJs, each with their own program.[32] For dance scene respondents this had two significances. First, it meant that DJs in clubs did not "put on any old pop" (237, Samara), which ensured the exclusion of the unwelcome "other," that is, youth who did not understand this music. Second, authorship over the set played was accredited to the DJ, since another differentiating feature from a disco was that DJs did not accept requests from the floor: "In a club nobody goes up to request music because the DJ would not put it on, especially not for money" (215, Samara).[33]

The absence of this practice indicated that DJs in clubs did not just respond to mass demand but worked creatively with the best materials they could find: "DJs can do scratch, play with the frequencies, take away the low ones, add high ones, play one track over another . . . [what they do] is creative" (227, Samara).

DJs themselves, at least those from the provincial cities of study, did not pretend to a creative role—the quality of the equipment they worked with, they said, prohibited this.[34] They interpreted their role, rather, as one of creating a general "feel" or atmosphere. It was not so much the individual artist who was important, but the mood created between DJ and dancers, which allowed positive vibes to flow. In contrast, the pop, house, and techno music played at discos, it was said, was "churned out" (*goniaiut*) for the masses.

Although, in contrast to the rock *tusovki*, Russian produced recordings were a rarity on the new dance scene, it would be simplistic to suggest clubbers were simply "imitating" a Western music genre. New dance music itself is not a "Western" music with a single home, but a constantly mutating sound generated from a series of global-local interactions. House music had American roots—in the New York underground disco scene of the early 1970s, and the house and garage scenes that developed out of the Chicago gay clubs of late 1970s (where the first "acid house" appeared). The rave (acid house) scene, however, developed out of European engagements with house music—specifically the encounter of British youth with it in Ibiza clubs and the recreation of that Balearic experience in clubs in Britain from the summer of 1987. The rave scene itself developed over the following two summers as young people traveled to legal, and illegal, open-air and warehouse "parties" across the country (Ingham 1999; Bennett 2000; Thornton 1995; Redhead 1997). Moreover, although the "authentic" rave moment of the new dance scene predated the emergence of the dance scene in Russia, the latter was not solely club based. At the end of the 1990s, there were two annual organized raves, the most important being the Kazantip festival.[35] Kazantip was a three-week-long dance festival held annually in August on a small peninsula on the northeastern coast of Crimea on a site adjacent to the construction site of an unfinished nuclear power station.[36] Local raves were few and far between, since initiatives for open-air events were frequently stymied by the local authorities. However, traditional "summer discos" provided spaces for outdoor dance events; and in Samara, an annual antidrug event held in spring allowed a number of rap and breakdance groups to perform "on the street" (230, Samara).

Rap: It's Not What You Say, It's the Way That You Say It

At the street end of the dance scene spectrum (break beat, rap, hip hop) young people were less concerned with environment than "clubbers"; one respondent stated that he could "dance anywhere . . . as long as I like the music" (230, Samara). In this sense, the use of music within hip hop culture fell between the "listening" and "dancing" uses of rock and club *tusovki* respectively; another example of its "in-between" status noted in Chapter 5. Text was important to rappers, but it was considered more important for that text to produce good rhythm and delivery than for it to be reflective of Russian experience. This was explained by a Russian rapper in the course of justifying his preference for English over Russian-language rap: "I find American [rap] closer [than Russian] because I know English well and understand what they sing. They sing about what they want to. Ours try to fit in with them but it doesn't really work" (241, Samara).

This respondent was the vocalist in his own rap group, for which he composed and performed in Russian. His own preference for non-Russian rap, however, was rooted in a belief that "whites" did not have the "right intonation" to be able to perform rap properly. Although a growing number of rap artists performed in Russian, Russian-language rap did not have the self-awareness, for example, of French rap. France is an interesting comparison precisely because French-language rap's ability to speak to French literary tradition and the traditions of the chanson française (Huq 1999, 136) would seem to provide a model for Russian rap, which also inhabited a space within a national popular music that was highly word and meaning conscious. Indeed, Huq suggests, French language rap—despite its employment of *banlieue* slang—has been heralded as a protector of French-language culture under the onslaught of anglophone production (139). French rap also comes out of the resource-deprived "suburbs" (*banlieues*) of the cities; in this sense French urban space is structured similarly to that in Russia and differently from that in the United States or the United Kingdom where "ghettoes" are located in the inner cities.

The failure of rap to generate the same resonance in Russia as in other European (and non-European) countries is rooted in the problematic transfer of the meanings invested in rap as a music genre. This stems, above all, from the nonracialized character of Russian urban space. While "peripheral" (suburban) youth certainly inhabited infrastructure-impoverished environments, they did not experience that impoverishment as an ethnically rooted segregation and discrimination. Unlike North African youth in France or Turkish youth in Germany, therefore, rap did not express a strategy of resistance to racial discrimination (Bennett 1999a; Huq 1999; Mitchell 1996).

In Russia, rap was situated within a crossover progressive strategy (see Chapter 5), creating a set of tensions within rap culture that has made a distinctively local Russian rap problematic. Rap in Russia remained concerned with "the street" and often attracted suburban (normal) youth. At the same time, its outward-looking orientation and city-center based *tusovki*, took it away from the streets (or "yards") in which its mem-bers' experiences were located. Given this, a local Russian rap form is most likely to be generated from interaction with "gangsta" themes and the obscenities of American rap. These had wide appeal for Russian rappers and spoke to the experiences of some rappers in territorially based, criminally linked gang structures of peripheral areas of Russian cities. However, a preexisting Russian popular music genre related to the criminal subculture—known as *blatnie pesni*—may inhibit such a development.

Despite the fundamental differences in the pleasures of music for dance scene and rock scene members, their relationship to music and the significance of music in their wider cultural practices held much in common. Engagement with music and knowledge about music required an outward-looking and onward-moving attitude to life. In contrast to common perceptions of *tusovka* youth as being "Westernizers," this did not equate to a primary preference for Western (nonlocal) music. It meant rather that significant identity investment took place in engagements with music and a certain degree of status was accorded to knowledge about music and position within music-based *tusovki*. Above all, progressive use of music involved a strong notion of engagement with "authentic" music. The understanding of the "authentic" was undergoing significant reconfiguration in relation to the new cultural and economic environment of post-Soviet Russia but retained as its essence its signification of a noncommercial and non-mass music use.

Music Use in Normal Lives: A Background Beat

Normal youth was precisely the mass to which progressives referred in differentiating their own music use. Despite their engagement with a wide

Fig. 25 Young rappers in Ul'ianovsk. Hip hop culture was a vehicle for crossing the boundary between "normal" and "progressive" strategies. Photo by Moya Flynn, October 1997.

range of global as well as local musics, normal respondents did indeed have different music tastes and different uses of music within their wider cultural practice.

Normal respondents cited as their preferred music only a fraction of the music genres mentioned by progressive youth. Tastes were expressed vaguely and nonexclusively and—in contrast to progressives, who clearly distinguished between electronic dance music and pop—normals liked both rave *and* pop. Normals did not refer to techno or electronic music—as part of a wider dance culture centered on clubbing—but to rave music. "Rave," for normal youth, was a generic term for electronic music, indicating a number of commercial forms of house music released on compilation cassettes and played widely at discos. Those describing rave as their preferred music did not generally distinguish between different kinds of electronic dance music, although the terms "house" (17, Ul'ianovsk; 41, Ul'ianovsk), "trance" (17, Ul'ianovsk; 41 Ul'ianovsk;), and "techno" (5, Ul'ianovsk; 6 Ul'ianovsk) were used on occasion. Some respondents had favorite groups, which might be Western, such as Prodigy and Scooter, or Russian, such as Ruki vverkh. Indeed a remarkable loyalty to the first Russian electronic pop groups was shown; over the whole period of empirical work (September 1997–May 1998), survey, focus group, and interview data showed that the groups Ruki vverkh and Ivanushki Inter-

national retained their strong followings. Western groups of a similar ilk—primarily Scooter and Prodigy but also pop groups like the Backstreet Boys—also remained popular. Unlike "progressive" followers of electronic music, however, normal ravers never referred to favorite DJs or mixes.[37]

Pop music was cited as a preferred music particularly by young women, although—like their progressive counterparts—normal respondents denied any more general gender difference in music tastes.[38] Respondents said they listened to both Russian and Western singers and groups. Favorite Western performers included Abba, Maria Carey, Whitney Houston, Bjork, Sting, Sinead O'Connor, Madonna, George Michael, Back Street Boys, East 17, and the Spice Girls. Favorite Russian singers and groups were Sergei Penkin, Larisa Dolina, Ruki vverkh, Blestiashchie, Strelki, Tat'iana Snezhina, Boris Moiseev, Shura, Ivanushki International, Professor Lebedinskii, Tat'iana Bulanova, and Dima Malikov. Male respondents often also cited rock-pop crossover bands and singers such as Kino, Nautilus Pompilius, DDT, Petliura, and Linda (209, Samara; 10, Ul'ianovsk). There was also a marked generational difference; older respondents tended to cite more traditional *estrada* pop singers, including Alla Pugacheva (209, Samara), while younger ones were more likely to cite the new Western-modeled "boy bands" and "girl bands" (see Chapter 3), such as Ivanushki International, Blestiashchie, and Strelki.

A number of normal respondents mentioned rock as a kind of music to which they listened. The Russian rock groups preferred were almost exclusively Soviet rock bands of the 1980s such as Aria, Kino, Alisa, Nautilus Pompilius, DDT, and Garik Sukachev, although one respondent mentioned Chizh & ko. The Western rock groups and singers mentioned included Metallica, Nirvana, Chris de Burgh, Brian Adams, Elton John, Queen, and the Beatles. Other minority interests included classical music (187, Samara; 234, Samara), *blatnie pesnii* (criminal folk ballads) (240, Samara), and rap (3, Ul'ianovsk).

The existence of rock fans and other minority interests within a mainstream appreciation of pop and rave, suggests that normals, like progressives, had musical tastes that were far from fixed. However, normal respondents did not articulate this diversity as a product of their own evolving or "progressing" tastes. Their catholic tastes were attributed to a relative disinterest in music, rather than being an eclectic mix borne of a wide knowledge of music. Respondents citing an interest in rock, for example, did not necessarily have their own collection of tapes at home (238, Samara). Another noted: "At home I have a tape recorder but I virtually never listen to music, I am indifferent to it. . . . I like it when people with a good voice sing, people who have a good ear, whom it is pleasant to listen to, pleasant music" (236, Samara).

The wide range of tastes found among respondents was thus often the result of an ability to listen to virtually "any music" (44, Moscow; 15, Ul'ianovsk; 16, Ul'ianovsk), a tendency to select music according to mood rather than genre (187, Samara; 5, Ul'ianovsk; 6, Ul'ianovsk) or a lack of time to devote to music-listening (187, Samara). This relative neutrality toward music was reflected in few expressions of absolute dislike of a particular genre of music among normal respondents.

Normal attitudes to music reflected the role of music listening in respondents' whole ways of life; music was a background beat, and no more. Active participation in musical projects was rare among normal respondents; just one said he played in a school-level band (45, Moscow). Even listening to live music or going to hear particular sets by a DJ was not central to music use for "normal" respondents. Two respondents from Moscow who declared their favorite group to be Prodigy, for example, had not attended the free concert performed by the group recently on Red Square. Music was rather purchased mainly in the form of collections of "super hits" produced by local radio stations and sold as cassette tapes, or recorded from the radio to create personal compilations (209, Samara). One young woman from Ul'ianovsk explained how she expanded her own music collection: "Mainly I have cassettes, and tape from the radio. You switch on the radio, if you like it, you tape it. If you don't like it, you don't record it" (7, Ul'ianovsk).

Favorite radio stations and favorite compilation cassettes, it was said, were a particularly good background to completing homework (16, Ul'ianovsk).

Unlike progressive youth, for normals knowledge about music carried little subcultural capital. Respondents often failed to define their own musical preferences in terms of genres or specific groups and, consequently, were not inclined to make critical distinctions between musical genres or between "authentic" and "commercial" variants of a particular genre.[39]

Public Music, Private Music: Western Rave and Russian Pop

For normals, like progressives, the appeal of electronic music lay in its danceability: "I listen to rave, techno, that kind of music. . . . I am not interested in what groups. I am more interested in the music . . . it is a lively music, more lively, danceable" (5, Ul'ianovsk). Moreover, rave allowed young men to dance in a way that fitted their gender identity: "We are sportsmen, we need something fast. . . . you can dance to it, it is good, you work your legs, not like the *neformaly*. . . . And if a person is drunk or high, it is comfortable to dance to this music, to the beats (3, Ul'ianovsk).

The practice of dancing to music, however, was not housed within a wider club culture. Indeed, respondents expressed severe reservations about such clubs, often associating them with drug use (26, Ul'ianovsk;

211, Samara; 236, Samara) and with atmospheres in which no "normal communication" could take place (211, Samara). Thus although some normal respondents went to both clubs and discos (240, Samara), most frequented discos in local Houses of Culture, summer discos in parks, or discos held at schools and colleges often to mark public holidays (218, Samara).

The difference between a club and a disco—from the normal perspective—rested in the control they, as consumers, had over the environment. Discos were perceived to be familiar spaces where local young people were brought together, as described by the following respondent talking about the weekend discos held in her home village: "At home a DJ does the disco. . . . after every song he talks, [has] little chats, makes jokes, and announces greetings, if somebody has a birthday, everyone congratulates him en masse . . . almost all the youth of the village are there . . . more than a hundred" (235, Samara).

While city discos were not quite so "homely," they brought the youth of the local district together and created an atmosphere of ownership through the practice, for example, of requesting favorite tracks that was so despised by progressive youth. The frustration of one respondent at her failure to get her favorite tracks played at a city center disco indicated fears among normal respondents that club practice was increasingly infiltrating "their" discos:

[At the discos they play] . . . pop, both ours and foreign. They rarely put ours on. In the winter it was every other one was foreign, then ours, but by spring it was only foreign . . . it is probably the DJs who are like that. They put on what they like . . . you put in a request, stand there yelling for something to be put on, but it is pointless. He looks at you with empty eyes. From above you can't hear anything. Meanwhile you lose your voice from it, when you come home in the evening, you are hoarse and all for nothing. (7, Ul'ianovsk)

Discos, unlike clubs, required no subscription to a "way of life" or investment in clothes, time, compact disks, or reputation. Discos had none of the lavish furnishings of the clubs; a couple of young women, visiting a new Samara club for the first time, were driven to asking how the (Western style) taps switched on in the toilets. This marked a stark contrast to the *Apix* disco in a peripheral area of the city where there was a fifteen-minute wait for two squat-toilets with no doors to protect users from the eyes of the increasingly impatient line. Such lack of pretension, however, meant that normal respondents felt able to go to the discos "purely to dance" (218, Samara), to "have a laugh" (*prikalivaemsia*) (9, Ul'ianovsk; 10, Ul'ianovsk), "enjoy ourselves" (*razvlekaemsia*) (9, Ul'ianovsk; 10, Ul'ianovsk), and "relax to the music" (14, Ul'ianovsk). Local discos were enjoyed because everyone was known there; they were all *svoi* (7, Ul'ianovsk; 8, Ul'ianovsk) (see Chapter 6). On the other hand, trips to a central disco were important events because they provided the excitement of anticipation of new acquaintances and "opportunities to meet someone" (16, Ul'ianovsk; 15, Ul'ianovsk). The form this took was described by one respondent as a ritual of the girls standing in a circle while the "boys pester us"; if the girls were receptive, acquaintances were made, if they were "in a bad mood," however, they had "no desire to meet anyone" (7, Ul'ianovsk). The chances of such acquaintances lasting were relatively small; it depended largely upon how sober the person had been and whether or not they had telephones at home in order to keep in contact (7, Ul'ianovsk). In reality, this respondent continued, it was often hard enough to remember what they looked like, let alone what their telephone number was.

Evidence that discos were really a backdrop to the serious business of adolescence was even more abundant from male respondents (2, Ul'ianovsk; 3, Ul'ianovsk; 9, Ul'ianovsk; 10, Ul'ianovsk; 240, Samara). Two male respondents talked about guys hanging out at discos, not dancing, with the aim of "picking up" (*tsepliaiut*) girls (2, Ul'ianovsk; 3, Ul'ianovsk), while two others said they themselves danced, but followed this with an self-explanatory "there are a lot of girls—we enjoy ourselves" (9, Ul'ianovsk; 10, Ul'ianovsk). Indeed the highlight of non-club type discos was the "slow dances" that were frequently introduced to break up the set. Unlike progressive youth, normal respondents accepted this aspect of the disco, indeed looked forward to it. This did not of course mean the process always went smoothly. One male respondent bemoaned the kind of "new girls" at discos who refused when you asked them to dance to slow records (240, Samara) while a female respondent described the difficulties of rejecting advances without offending (234, Samara). However, although unwelcome approaches were made, it was not assumed—as among progressive youth—that only "one night stands" could ensue from such acquaintances; people who met in this way could have long relationships or even marry and start a family (234, Samara).

Normal youth thus differed from progressives in that they neither invested, nor reaped, subcultural capital from music. Their sites of leisure often incorporated music, but the music was a backdrop to other forms of peer communication. In much the same way as progressive respondents, however, normals had different moods which found expression through differential music use.

The Uses of Music: Feeding Body and Soul

Normals—like their progressive counterparts—might express a general preference for Russian or Western music, but did not exclusively listen to either; they listened to music regardless of where it originated, providing it was "good" (42, Moscow; 43, Moscow; 218, Moscow).[40] Thus despite clear differences in musical preference, the significance attached to, and pleasures gained from music, between normal and progressive youth (and among the progressives between rock and dance fans), there emerged a common thread in their music practice. Young Russians appeared to engage with global and local music multiply; in different ways, for different purposes. The mechanisms by which such music use was worked into wider youth cultural strategies has been discussed, but underlying these differences lay a shared distinction; young Russians across the scene distinguished between "music for the mind"—or in the Russian cultural context, "for the soul"—and "music for the body."

For members of rock *tusovki*, the soul could only be satisfied by what they considered to be a peculiarly Russian rock poetic:

There is music for the soul and for the body . . . for the soul it is probably Soviet rock, rock from the beginning of the 1980s *and [from the period]* 1989–91. *(39, Ul'ianovsk)*

It [techno] is not music for the soul . . . it doesn't help me, not at all. (206, Samara)

Given Russian rock musicians' understanding of rock music as the art of propagandizing "spirituality and the soul" (Cushman 1995, 99), it is not surprising that rock fans expressed this relationship to rock music. But the same sentiments were expressed by normal respondents who were far removed from the rock *tusovki*: for them it was simply the case that rave, and in some cases Western music more generally, engaged the body, but not the "soul":

[Techno] is completely without soul. Without soul and without meaning. Well maybe there is a meaning but I don't get it at least. (187, Samara)

I don't really like it [techno] . . . the music is almost all the same . . . there is no soul, no meaning in it, it is purely for the feet, to dance. (211, Samara)

Another respondent classified rave as "light music for when you aren't thinking about anything" in contrast to rock music, which was "more for the soul" (40, Ul'ianovsk). The key differentiator, once again, was the presence of "meaningful" texts or words that made Russian music, naturally, "closer": "What do I like? Well first meaning. . . . songs generally contain some kind of meaning . . . it is more interesting when you are listening to music if you understand what they are singing about . . . you can . . . listen to Skid Row and vacuum simultaneously, or read, or do your homework. But listening to Chizh, you can't read or do your homework because you are listening to a song, you are going into the plot, imagining" (13, Ul'ianovsk).

Techno music interrupted such narrative meaning and was contrasted negatively to Russian pop and rock groups such as Ivanushki and Chizh & ko., which had "soulful" songs (236, Samara; 218, Samara). Thus while Russian music was for when one's "soul is singing" (234, Samara), when it came to Western dance music, it was sometimes considered a "blessing" that you could not understand the words (40, Ul'ianovsk).[41]

The distinction between music for "the body" and "music for the soul" was not confined to those whose music preferences lay in the genres of rock and pop; it was made even by those who listened to rave or engaged in dance music culture. "Normal" youth who listened to rave, did so in public or group situations, rather than at home. Dance music, according to one respondent was a "group" thing, for having "fun." At home, he said, he preferred to listen to Russian (*nashi*) criminal folk ballads (*blatnie pesni*) (240, Samara). Another respondent explained that rave and house was listened to "mainly at discos and best of all in cars, in any car it is playing all the time" (9, Ul'ianovsk).

Even progressive dance scene members, for whom dance music was the focus of their *tusovka* admitted to this public/private split: "Of course, we listen to it [trip hop] at home . . . but in general, to be honest, there is one music for the clubs and a completely different one at home" (253, Ul'ianovsk).

Thus when members of dance music *tusovki* took their music home *to listen to*, that music itself changed (229, Samara; 230, Samara; 242, Samara), and despite frequent invectives against "commercial pop," something was found in its texts which reached "to the soul" in a way that even the hippest club sound could not.[42] This is how a sixteen-year-old clubber from Moscow explained the divergent needs of "body" and "soul":

[Club music] on a cassette, it is somehow soulless. I do like to clean up to it, though. I put on some trance or something and it's really good. I used to like doing it to hard core, but then my neighbor would bang [on the wall]. . . . At home I listen to pop . . . it is a simple music. . . . And it has words. That is what is missing in this music [techno], there are no words. But in our *[author's emphasis] pop, there are words which you can listen to. Some sincere [*zadushevnaia*] Ivanushki song, which might reflect what you are thinking about or worrying about right now. Not that I like it, I wouldn't buy the cassette and listen to it for days, but . . . (54, Moscow)*

In this single thought, the above respondent indicated clearly how the global and the local interacted in her music use. Her allegiance to dance music identified her with a "translocal," even "global" cultural trend. However, by identifying with dance music she not so much joined a global "us" but distanced herself from a local "other"; being a clubber marked her out on the local scene as a progressive. However, the local retained the potential to displace the "global"; in a quiet moment at home, it was the usually despised Russian pop of the normals that was able to speak to the everyday concerns of being young, here and right now.

Conclusion

So why, given the apparent resurgence of Russian sensibilities in music production and consumption, was rave considered the most popular music among young Russians at the end of the 1990s? What does this tell us about the relative importance of "the global" and "the local" in Russian youth cultural practice?

The distinction between "soul-ful" Russian forms and materially pleasurable Western ones should be read neither as absolute nor automatic. The appeal of electronic dance musics to young people across the youth scene signified neither a process of Western colonization nor of Russian mimicry. These outcomes were, rather, products of complex and different cultural negotiations.

The formation of progressive identity had required considerable reworking of the relationship between core *tusovka* values of creativity, authenticity, and critique. Increasing exposure to Western commercialized cultural forms and their influences had led progressives increasingly to locate a "creative" and "authentic" voice *here* and to make not Soviet (*sovkovii*) ersatz culture but the commercialism of Western and "new commercial Russian" cultural forms the focus of their critique. In this process, progressives came to see emulation of the West as a "mass" response, while they themselves were distinguished by a more critical approach, which was articulated in a belief that the West was not to be envied (233, Samara).

In contrast normal respondents found it difficult to talk about "the West" or even concrete Western cultural phenomena. Little significance was attached to the origins of artifacts, products, or cultural forms and these were not displayed as symbols of positioning on the youth scene, but acted as the background to the real business of managing everyday life in Russian "conditions." In comparison with progressives, they were relatively indifferent to music and used the medium as a background to other peer activities, rather than valuing its use in and of itself; this led them to be characterized by progressives as mindless consumers of commercial pop and house music. For normal youth, then, the West was also "normal." The West brought with it no inherited "authenticity" arising from its association with "original" manifestations of particular youth cultural forms and movements. Relationships to that West thus required no special reworking.

Although progressives and normals thus drew on "the West" quite differently in the construction of their wider cultural strategies, the pattern of "public" and "private" uses of different musics and the distinction between Russian songs as "meaningful" and Western dance music as music "for feet" found among progressive youth was mirrored in normal music practice. Does this suggest, despite the differences between progressives and normals, some distinctively Russian resistance to global musics constituted in the attribution to Russian music of a greater meaningfulness and soulfulness?

Perhaps. Indeed, this would be an appealing conclusion for globalization pessimists, concerned about its potentially homogenizing tendencies. But it could only ever partially explain young Russians' global-local engagements, for it fails to address perhaps the most pertinent question. Why, given its widely accepted lack of "meaningful texts," was electronic dance music still the most popular music among young Russians at the end of the 1990s?

Intriguingly, the answer to this question was suggested by a (normal) respondent from the Samara region, as she tried to explain the current popularity of rave among Russian youth. Its pleasures, paradoxically, she said, might stem from its potential for detaching or dislocating meaning from music, "probably because . . . our country is in disorder at the moment and [so] there is disorder in people's souls . . . second, they are bored with a specific song [where] the words [and] the music, are somehow determined. A certain set of words, a certain mood. But rave, let's say, you can listen to when you are in a good mood and when you are in a bad mood" (235, Samara).

The attraction to "global" techno, this respondent suggested, was precisely because it represented the mirror image of what Russians valued about their "own" culture. If the value of Russian rock lay in its transmission of the musician's experience in a meaningful, yet poetic, way (Cushman 1995, 103), then electronic dance musics created a "decentered soundscape" detached from any specific musical performance or meaning embedded in text (Ingham 1999, 123). The latter was appreciated for what was missing in the Russian form—the possibility of multiple meanings and experiences. The recognition of this additional reflexive dimension to global-local engagements forces us to return to question of just how young Russians imagine "the West," and its relationship to Russia, in the context of a "globalized" world.

8 Living with the West

Hilary Pilkington and Elena Omel'chenko

> The whole of Russian culture is based on resistance to something. And it is clear that if there is nothing to resist then the culture disintegrates.
>
> —51, Moscow

A recurrent theme in the narratives of young people reconstructed in this book has been the significance of the West as "other" in shaping Russia's sense of self. This chapter directly confronts the question of how Russian culture has responded to processes of globalization. If cultures are increasingly globally rather than nationally constructed, has Russian culture been left bereft of its defining "other"? In order to address this question young people's perceptions of how Russia was positioned in current global flows of cultural exchange were analyzed. In articulating these thoughts, young people explore their own sense of Russia's place in the new global order and present visions of how they imagine "living with" the West in the future.

One-way Traffic on the Global Information Superhighways

Young Russians felt themselves not excluded from, but included in, the global information sphere; only one respondent claimed that Russia was "cut off" from the world and that there was "nowhere to get new information" (215, Samara). That inclusion, however, was experienced as a one-way cultural flow, that is from the West to Russia: "Everything here is from the West. . . . Young people get everything from the West" (38, Ul'ianovsk).

Respondents, regardless of where they were placed on the youth scene (as progressives or normals) perceived music, fashion and, youth cultural movements to originate in the West and, subsequently, to be transported to Russia. Young people, just as the older generation, often described this process as one of imitation:

Rock fans [rokery] . . . *well they try to imitate Americans completely. (187, Samara)*

Everything has come to us from the West. We probably try to copy [pereniat'] *everything from the West. (164, Samara)*

Unlike adults, however, young people were less inclined to suggest that this borrowing had any profound impact on their values and attitudes.[1] The fascination with the West (to the exclusion, for example, of the East) was explained as current fashion and the inevitable consequence of the saturation of the information world with Western cultural forms. In effect, the fact that young people in Russia "know more about [the West]" (206, Samara) was considered to explain their interest in it. Indeed, a greater engagement with the West than the East was neither peculiar to youth, nor to the post-Soviet period (Diligenskii 1996).

Russia was envisaged as embracing all manner of Western cultural forms, and young people generally believed that most youth cultural trends from the West had been accepted among Russian youth. Thus, although specific musical and style forms (for example, reggae, soul, ragga, hard core, and Western boy bands) were described as being less popular than others, young people thought every trend had found its own particular constituency.

In contrast, the general perception among respondents was that virtually nothing traveled in the opposite direction (42, Moscow; 43, Moscow; 238, Samara). Respondents attributed to Russia a real *creative potential*, but imagined the West as better able to transform cultural creativity into something commercially viable (53, Moscow; 187, Samara) through "marketing" (231, Samara). Young Russians perceived current exports from Russia to the West to be natural resources (primarily oil). The only *cultural* exports to be mentioned were the "mafia" and the art of drinking: "[Russia exports] Russian vodka . . . first and foremost! The infectious art of drinking, it is moving across the whole world now. . . . It is an exceptional phenomenon, these big drinking sessions when a great deal is drunk, in amounts horses would drink. This is a phenomenon, I don't see it as negative, just a kind of purely Russian, phenomenon. . . . What could the West take from Russia? I don't know. What have we got?" (51, Moscow).

"West Is Best": Russia Plays "Catch-up"

For some respondents the fact that Russia had "nothing to give" was evidence of its need to "catch up" with the West. This narrative of Russia's relationship with the West conformed to the academic model of "catch-up modernization" (see Chapter 1) in which the West appeared as an example of modernity to which to aspire. Within this narrative, the West signified a higher level of "development" (44, Moscow; 53, Moscow) and "forward progress" (44, Moscow) and was contrasted to the East, which was associated with traditional society and proximity to village life (44, Moscow). The West's higher stage of development was imagined, economically, as a postindustrial society based on leisure (53, Moscow), politically as a state that protected the individual through the rule of law (216, Samara), and culturally as an "energy" able to produce a torrent of new trends and "fascinate and draw in" young people (33, Ul'ianovsk).

In relation to concrete Western cultural products, young people articulating this narrative assumed that "West is best." A common example used to illustrate Western superiority was the comparison between American films produced in Hollywood and the Eastern "Bollywood" equivalent (37, Ul'ianovsk; 9 Ul'ianovsk; 42, Moscow; 43, Moscow).[2] Another was the superiority of Western (designer) clothes and standards of dress (213, Samara; 214, Samara; 216, Samara; 5, Ul'ianovsk; 6, Ul'ianovsk; 27, Ul'ianovsk). Music and musicians from the West were described also as "more professional" (11, Ul'ianovsk; 38, Ul'ianovsk).

Paradoxically, this narrative did not mark a new understanding of Russia following the exposure of the ephemeral nature of Soviet superpower status, but was rooted in popular responses to *Soviet* ideology. As Iurii Levada argues, the mythology of America and the West acted as a kind of reverse reflection of Sovietness, since in the "other" was reflected that which was missing from one's own existence (Levada 1993, 180–82). The acceptance of the "other" as part of the "self" was most obvious among sections of the intelligentsia and youth (Shlapentokh 1989, 142), for whom, like for many elsewhere in the world, America became a symbol of democracy, progress, modernization, consumption, freedom, and pleasure and, as such, became an object of consumption itself (Frith, cited in Brake 1985, 185). Indeed, the isolation of the Soviet Union made the "mythology of America" more tangible than elsewhere, since Western cultural artifacts became cultural capital on the youth scene in the most literal sense. A survey conducted by the sociological journal *Sotsiologicheskie issledovaniia* in conjunction with the newspaper *Literaturnaia gazeta* in

1987 in four large Soviet cities suggested that 58 percent of teenagers viewed obtaining Western goods as one of their "life goals" (Shlapentokh 1989, 142).

The discourse of "catch-up" with the West at the end of the 1990s was more prominent among provincial respondents than those from Moscow and was reinforced by the cultural lag felt in relation to the capital city. For provincial youth a quality product (such as a club) might be described as "like [one] in Moscow" (237, Samara) rather than in the West. In one interview with a group of breakdancers from Ul'ianovsk the cultural chain was summed up thus: "There [the West] everything is developed completely. Here we are ten to fifteen years behind . . . if you look at Moscow, then you can compare it with England, the level is like in Europe, like the West . . . they have good clubs. But if you compare Ul'ianovsk with Europe, well you can't compare . . . they are worlds apart" (34, 35, and 36, Ul'ianovsk).

In order to position the West as "more developed," the respondents had to consider Russia backward or inferior. Drawing their evidence from the youth cultural sphere they knew well, respondents suggested that Russian (and Soviet) rock—with a handful of notable exceptions—simply did not stand up to criticism (51, Moscow; 215, Samara). In some instances the issue was "lag"; the genre, as in the case of rap, was relatively new to Russia (63, Moscow; 215, Samara). In other cases, especially techno music, backwardness was attributed to the country's economic backwardness, which made domestic compact discs unusable but imported ones unaffordable (215, Samara). In other spheres, however, respondents avoided the temptation to apportion blame to "the Soviet past." They were especially critical of the lack of initiative in domestic design and the inability to create a distinctive "Russian look" (213, Samara; 253, Ul'ianovsk), the lack of value attached to their own history and "roots" (187, Samara), and an "uncultured" attitude compared to that of others (29, Ul'ianovsk).

"Cultural Imperialism": One-way Cultural Exchange by Any Other Name

A second group of respondents engaged in the "catch up" discourse quite differently; Russia's need to "catch up" with the West was interpreted not as an economic necessity but rather as a stereotypical rendition of power relations between Russia and the West. In this understanding of East-West cultural exchange, it was suggested that although Russia retained a political "presence" (influence) in the West—because of the size and resource base of the country—culturally Russia remained an absence in the West (52, Moscow; 56, Moscow; 57, Moscow).

This absence was attributed, on the one hand, to experiential factors; people in the West "don't understand" Russian culture (especially film and comedy), since they addressed issues and problems never encountered by Westerners. The same argument was used to explain the failure of Russian (especially Soviet) rock bands to achieve success in the West (210, Samara; 253, Ul'ianovsk). The lack of common cultural ground had been entrenched through Soviet isolation, which was blamed for disrupting normal cultural exchange (63, Moscow; 210, Samara).

On the other hand, however, respondents felt that ignorance among Westerners about Russian culture and stereotypes of Russians as "Ivan the fool," the "Russian bear," or a communist image of policemen on every corner created prejudices about Russian culture, especially youth culture (228, Samara; 215, Samara; 54, Moscow). The preconceptions of Westerners often appeared in superior attitudes: "They [Western DJs] are convinced that it is less developed here, I think. When they come here many say 'Oh, so you have got this too! And it's not at all bad'" (54, Moscow).

As suggested by the example above, respondents often countered what they perceived to be Russia's global cultural peripheralization with narratives of how, once introduced to the real Russian culture, ignorant Westerners changed their attitudes, experiencing the special atmosphere of Russian clubs (54, Moscow) and understanding that Russia was in fact "completely different" from their stereotypes (61, Moscow). One respondent recounted a story of how, when Russian musical compositions had been heard in Paris, at first nobody believed that they were Russian in origin (228, Samara).

Others, however, interpreted current Western superiority as evidence of a deeper "cultural imperialism." Two Moscow respondents described the process thus:

57, Moscow: *There is an Americanization taking place here at the moment . . . foreign language advertising. Foreign goods are everywhere . . . whether we like it or not we are being Americanized. . . .*

Interviewer: *Do you mean Americanized, literally that?*

56, Moscow: *Yes, just that. I think America is the strongest power in the world and is not just Americanizing us but also turning other countries into colonies, quite simply. . . . They try to impose their way of life on the whole world. . . . America it is a huge country, perfect for becoming an empire . . . here there really is an Americanization going on. No other country has such an influence.*

While these respondents were far from "typical" of Russian youth in general, their attitudes were revealing, since they were well-educated and unusually widely acquainted with Westerners and foreign travel. Nor were they alone in their criticism. Respondents from the provinces might not have developed their critique at an abstract level, but they saw, nonetheless, evidence of cultural "invasion," and they interpreted it negatively. Respondents noted that Russia was currently "too influenced by the West" (206, Samara), took "too much" from America (10, Ul'ianovsk), and that "the West . . . still limits, [and] dictates . . ." (235, Samara). This, it was suggested, reduced Russia's independence (10, Ul'ianovsk) and led to cultural homogenization: "Of course I would like Russia to be different from the West. But judging by the way in which the differences are disappearing . . . look even at the signs, how many there are and all in English, why is that necessary? We don't live in England or the United States so I don't think it is necessary. . . . I don't like it" (209, Samara).

The notion of cultural imperialism, moreover, was implicit in the description of the heavy information flow from the West as "all propaganda" (40, Ul'ianovsk) and in the following call to arms to defend European culture by a sixteen-year-old school student from Ul'ianovsk: "America is the strongest state and that is why it foists [on us] music, films, and politics. . . . America is always everywhere. American ships arrive, American planes fly in. That is the current situation, but I don't think they can go on like that for long because it is a puffed-up state" (13, Ul'ianovsk).

The illegitimacy of America's attempt to create a "global hegemony" is evident in this statement in the descriptions of the process as one of "colonization," cultural "imposition," and the reference to military means (planes and ships) by which it is imposed.[3] For this respondent it was clearly the coercive power of the state, not the profound significance of American culture, that had secured the country's place in the world today.

Distorted Reflections: Us and Them in the Hall of Mirrors

Frank Ellis suggests that contemporary reference to "cultural imperialism" by Russians is intellectually unsustainable and a product of "cultural envy and. . . . cultural instability and inferiority" (Ellis 1999, 161). Such a reading of Russian narratives of culture, it is argued here, is too simplistic. In fact, the most common narrative of Russia and the West encountered among respondents was one that envisaged the West not as culturally superior, but culturally *inferior* and, as such, socially undesirable as a model for emulation. This narrative was articulated primarily by respondents from Moscow and Samara and associated the West culturally with commercialism. Western music and films were considered "cheap," "trashy" (209, Samara), and intellectually undemanding (232, Samara; 233, Samara): "I don't like Western music really. . . . I like Russian-speaking [groups] really. I don't know why I have this antipathy to everything English-language and Western, but I only like Soviet films, and I mean *Soviet*. Even our contemporary Russian films are gradually descending to the Western standard, sort of trashy" (56, Moscow).

This was not solely the product of the experience of cultural globalization; Soviet denunciations of American attempts at "ideological expansion" ritually named "bourgeois mass culture" as a key tool in this process (Davydov 1978, 379). The post-Soviet press also indulged in periodic caricaturing of Western culture and its representatives as mindless keyboard operators (Kedrov 1996) or "vitaminized young people" incapable of understanding Russian literature (Kovalenko 1996). In isolated cases, respondents even recited Soviet explanations as to how this ideological expansion was conducted. One student, for example, invoked a common Soviet claim—albeit in the Soviet period used in relation to rock not techno music (Pilkington 1996b, 197–98)—that Western popular music (originating in Afro-American culture) was a tool for undermining European rationality: "It is said that all these rhythms which have come here from America, they have a destructive effect on Europeans. . . . There is a quite an intriguing theory that it is all related to the Africans, that for them it is totally safe. But for us, it affects our consciousness and psyche negatively" (224, Samara).

Another respondent argued that the Iron Curtain had played a positive role, since, without it, Russia would have been "encircled" (by hostile capitalist countries) and unable to embark upon necessary state construction and social modernization (231, Samara). This respondent bemoaned the collapse of the USSR, which he blamed on aspiring politicians' readiness to "take bribes" from Western security agencies, and recalled nostalgically a time when the talk was not of "the West" and "the non-West" but the USSR and "the rest" (231, Samara).

In social terms, while the West may have achieved "modernity" and "constitutional freedom" (51, Moscow), it was perceived to have been at the cost of a meaningful existence: "Western countries remind me of a community of ants because there are very few people left there who really think about what and why things are happening around them" (51, Moscow). In fact this narrative of Russian superiority was more sophisticated than it first appeared. In constructing it, young Russians turned on its head the notion of Russia's "underdevelopment" and thereby created a defensive counternarrative based on evidencing the innate *difference* of Russians. At the core of this counternarrative was a series of "mirror" images whereby the West's positive characteristics represented something which was missing from Russia, while its negative aspects were the inverse of qualities valued by Russians about themselves (see Diagram 8.1).[4]

It is clear that this narrative of the West transposed the dichotomy of the "spiritual versus the material" to the division between "Russia" and "the West." At first this appears illogical; the division between spiritual

Diagram 8.1 **Russia and *the West:* The hall of mirrors**

Russia	**The West**
Emotion	Rationality
Collectivism	Individualism
Directness	Reserve
Warmth	Coldness
Sincerity	Falsity
Depth	Superficiality
Spirituality	Emptiness
Fun	Boring

and material worlds, rooted in Christian thinking, should link rather than divide Russian and Western cultures. However, this division was heavily mobilized in Soviet ideology, especially in the formulation of ideas about upbringing and education of the younger generation. Although consciousness was said to be determined by daily existence (*bytie*), nevertheless, a specific political and ideological consciousness was purposefully *cultivated*. This "Soviet" worldview included the rejection of material wealth in favor of high culture, a disdainful attitude to "consumption," and a cult of individual sacrifice in the name of the collective good. The latter, accompanied by ideals of suffering and self-deprivation, were reinforced by drawing on both Christian and Russian philosophic and literary traditions.

At the end of the 1990s, echoes of this Soviet consciousness peppered young people's talk, but competed with positive associations of the spiritual "comfort" perceived to accompany material prosperity. Seemingly contradictory images of the West emerged in young people's narratives, therefore, as they drew on the dichotomy between material and spiritual values selectively. Material and consumer aspects of Western life were positively evaluated by respondents, since they facilitated an "easy life" characterized by freedom and relaxation. However, paradise in consumer terms, it was felt, was not automatically accompanied by cultural, educational, or spiritual growth (cultural characteristics associated with Russia). Thus, while Western developmental models were appealing materially, it was feared that if Russia were to follow the West in every aspect, it might destroy that which was most precious to it—its *dushevnost'* (soulfulness).

It is difficult to determine to what extent this narrative was a product of conviction, and to what extent it reflected a defense mechanism. Since Russian young people (particularly those from the provinces) believed they would never attain the material wealth and security they perceived to be enjoyed by their Western contemporaries, they might have chosen to declare these things "alien." Regardless of this, however, the predication of this dominant narrative upon perceived *innate* differences between Russians and Westerners is significant, for it implied a conviction that cultural globalization could not lead to cultural homogenization:

It is not possible for people in Russia to be like people in America. . . . I think that the West and Asia . . . are different. There is a different way of thinking and to force Western thinking on a Russian person is impossible. . . . I think that Russia could not become completely like the West, either in politics or economics. It might take something from there, but completely copy it, no. (5 and 6, Ul'ianovsk)

It is characteristic of Russia to copy the West. . . . But that is in the capitals. In the provinces everything has stayed just as it was two or three hundred years ago. The provinces have a life of their own. (1, Ul'ianovsk)

The latter respondent—through her parallel with earlier centuries in Russian history when French had been the dominant culture—reminds the reader once again that Russia is not negotiating cultural globalization for the first time.

Explaining Russia's "Difference": Hybridization or Cultural "Mix and Match"?

There was, of course, a fundamental contradiction between the narrative of Russia and the West that envisaged Russia as "catching up" and that which saw in the West a distorted reflection of the Russian self. If young Russians believed that virtually everything in the West had been adopted in Russia, while nothing Russian traveled in the opposite direction, how could they consider Russia as still fundamentally "different" from the West?

One way of resolving this contradiction was to suggest that although the cultural forms "borrowed" might be Western, when transferred to Russia, they became "indigenized" and infused with Russianness. This process was described by a sixteen-year-old rollerskater from Moscow who argued that young people did not care about the origins of cultural forms or commodities; if they liked it, he claimed, they simply "take it from them, rip it [*sdiraiut*] off them, as they say, and do it . . . for themselves" (53, Moscow). In the process the original "thing" "is changed, it becomes something of its own" (17, Ul'ianovsk; 18, Ul'ianovsk). After all, new musical genres—such as techno—specifically lent themselves to this cultural "reterritorialization" (Lull 1995, 159) as noted by the following Moscow respondent: "It seems to me that all music—even trance—when it is written by our Russians, becomes Russian. They probably bring something of their own to it" (54, Moscow).

The indigenization of Russian rock music is well documented (see Cushman 1995), and a number of well-established youth cultural trends were considered not "Western" but some kind of hybrid or mix. The representative survey of young people conducted in Samara and Ul'ianovsk found that the category "hybrid" was used by 36 percent of the respondents from Samara to describe "heavy metal fans," and by 21 percent of Samara respondents to describe "rap."[5] Before theories of hybridization or creolization are considered confirmed, however, it is worth noting that these figures actually constitute only a minority of youth. Moreover, the category of "hybrid" was never used by more than 1 percent of Ul'ianovsk respondents for any youth style. This finding does not indicate a wider "alienation" from or resistance to "Western" youth cultural trends in Ul'ianovsk (a Slavophile position) but rather a greater tendency to declare such trends to be either "Western" or "Russian." Thus heavy metal fans—who had a long history in Russian youth culture—were considered to represent a "Russian" phenomenon by around a quarter of Ul'ianovsk respondents.

Skepticism about the possibility of fusing Russian and Western cultural forms was articulated in other ways. One respondent, for example, complained that attempts to create a distinctively *Russian* techno always resulted in reducing it to "pop" (because of the Russian proclivity for vocals): "For some reason they concentrate on the vocals, as is typical for Russia . . . but this is meant to be techno-culture, so you have to focus on the music not the vocals, when the vocals go through the whole composition, it is not interesting at all. . . . Even hard core and thrash, they put some Russian roots in there, and it is terrible" (237, Samara).

Other respondents complained that there was "nothing new" in Russian grunge, the only novelty was that "the words are Russian" (232, Samara; 233, Samara), while attempts by Russian rappers to integrate motifs from Russian folktales were considered rather "silly" (254, Ul'ianovsk).

This is not to suggest that theories of hybridization have no value; they have been particularly important in showing how cultural consumption, as well as production, is "a process of active cultural selection and synthesis drawing from the familiar and the new" (Lull 1995, 161). In Russia, however, young people appeared to engage with Western cultural forms in a process of parallel reception rather than synthesis. Thus, Russian folk music and humorous ditties (*chastushki*) existed happily alongside, for example, rap; the latter need not incorporate the former to be meaningful (28, Ul'ianovsk). Rather than seeking to make Western cultural forms "their own," therefore, young Russians differentiated between "global" and "local" cultures and cultural products. Western cultural forms were considered somehow intrinsically "global," while Russian culture remained peculiarly Russian: "Our culture is fundamentally Russian [*rossiiskaia*] but . . . there is a reason why the Beatles spread round the whole world straightaway, it is something all people share [*obshchechelovecheskoe*], not something purely English" (51, Moscow).

What this subtle differentiation suggests is that the nature of the relationship with the West had changed for this generation of Russian youth. The new opportunities for gathering information and for travel meant that young Russians (at least those from the capital cities) no longer felt the need to "catch up" with the West. As people increasingly traveled abroad, everything could be procured almost instantaneously, leaving young Russians "not behind at all" in even the latest dance cultures (60, Moscow). Indeed, some respondents considered Russia to have an advantageous position in that youth cultural trends had been able to draw from both the Western experience and their own culture as they developed, whereas the West had had no earlier experience on which to build (232, Samara; 233, Samara). Moreover, since Russian rock had its roots in Western rock, Russians could understand both Western and Russian versions, whereas, Westerners could not necessarily understand Russian rock (232, Samara; 233, Samara).

To the casual gaze, Russia's capital cities appeared to be dominated by all things Western. The visual impacts of cultural globalization were described by young people, however, as ephemeral (1, Ul'ianovsk) and external (51, Moscow), and as such unable to change the "deep things" inside a person. Far from fundamentally changing Russian culture through the formation of "hybrid" forms as the result of an objective process of one-way cultural exchange, therefore, the Russian cultural space that young people inhabited might be better visualized as a giant "mix and match" counter in which the global and the local existed simultaneously: "Nothing goes anywhere, everything is here and there, it is just that they are found to a greater or lesser extent in different places" (50, Moscow).

Neither East nor West: Retracing Russia's "Unique" Path

The hesitancy of Russian youth in talking about their cultural practices as "hybrid" (*smeshanii*) reflected a much deeper reluctance to see Russia as either a "hybrid" of, or "in-between," East and West. Russia was described by young people rather as a culturally unique entity: "I don't understand why, when people talk about Russia, it has to be either the West or the East. Russia is neither West nor East. It is Russia, it is bigger than the West, and bigger than the East . . . it incorporates [elements of each] but it is completely different" (13, Ul'ianovsk).

A recurrent explanation of this uniqueness was the physical expression of Russia: its huge size (51, Moscow) spanning across Europe and Asia (235, Samara), its climatic conditions engendering a distinctive Russian mentality (207, Samara), and its natural wealth (206, Samara). These peculiarities, together with Russia's historical development, were seen to have given the country its distinctive features. Thus Russia was characterized as "separate" (51, Moscow; 206, Samara; 235, Samara), "peculiar" (207, Samara; 228, Samara), and "unique" (233, Samara) and commonly visualized as a "third point" in a triangle of world civilizations: "Russia is like a third world: the West is one, the East is another, and Russia is a mixture but at the same time something of its own. No, Russia is a third thing . . . we are something peculiar" (235, Samara).

Young Russians had clear ideas about the abstract differences between Russia and the West; they found it more difficult, however, to suggest concrete cultural forms expressing this uniqueness.[6] One respondent mentioned traditional popular music (*estrada*) (209, Samara), another the genre of songs associated with the criminal underworld (*blatnie pesni*) drawn on by singers like Garik Sukachev (240, Samara). Respondents also mentioned the art of singer song writing (*avtorskaia pesnia*) and the bard movement (51, Moscow) as well as writers such as Aksenov, Dovlatov, Erofeev, and Peregin (51, Moscow).[7]

While it is often easier to discern that which is "other" than that which is "self," young Russians did articulate also a conscious concern about the lack of national self-awareness among Russians. When talking of their peers, respondents were critical of the perceived lack of "patriotism" in Russia. They contrasted this state of affairs to that in America, where they saw the American state to be active in inculcating a love for America in its citizens. Respondents believed that positive attitudes toward their country were consciously fostered in Americans from early childhood. This was contrasted to the lack of attention to Russian patriotism in Russia:

There is patriotism, especially among those conditioned in the old way. But not among youth, very little among youth. Even less among those . . . who are sixteen or seventeen years old, they just don't have anything to do with this patriotism. (52, Moscow)

Even in our department there was a guy who said, "I want to go to America, I am prepared to clean lavatories even, if I can live in America." This was very widespread, the desire to leave . . . even if it meant being a nobody, as long as it meant leaving here. (56, Moscow)

Although the mass emigration of Russians to the West anticipated in the early 1990s never materialized, survey data for the end of the decade continued to suggest a specific propensity among youth toward emigration abroad. A survey conducted by the Foundation for Public Opinion in November 1999, for example, indicated that young people (18–35 year olds) were more likely than their elders to desire to "live in the West." Asked whether they had ever had the wish to "live in the West" during the last ten years, 18 percent of all respondents recalled such a wish, compared to 33 percent of 18–35 year olds (Fond Obshchestvennogo Mneniia 1999).[8] More sensitive sociological surveys distinguishing between desire to *travel* and desire to *leave permanently* for abroad found that 10.2 percent of young people (17–26 year olds) said they would like to "leave for abroad forever" compared to 20.7 percent who "do not desire to live abroad" at all. The majority of young people wanted rather to travel abroad temporarily in order to earn money or to take up study or professional training opportunities (55.2 percent) (RNISiNP 1998, 41). This was confirmed by the research conducted by the authors. Respondents talked enthusiastically of traveling abroad as tourists or to study, while stressing that they would always want to return (251, Ul'ianovsk; 252, Ul'ianovsk; 211, Samara; 52, Moscow).

Two respondents had confronted the question of leaving in concrete terms (231, Samara; 187, Samara), and although both had decided to remain in Russia, for one at least it remained a "sore point" (187, Samara). This is not surprising, since flight to the West in Russian culture may be understood as enacting a physical "liberation" but also inducing a sense of guilt and a betrayal of the self-sacrificial element of Russian being (Friedman and Weiner 1999, 124). The latter sentiment was also found among young people's responses to questions about the possibility of leaving for the West, expressed in an irritation at the negative attitude of others to Russia:

Personally I am fine here, I don't want to go anywhere. On the contrary, I don't like that kind of thing. (1, Ul'ianovsk)

I am a Russian [rossiianin], *I was born here and I hope I will die here. (4, Ul'ianovsk)*

Such feelings were rooted not only in "patriotism" but in local identities: "I am just that kind of person. . . . I consider it [Russia] the very best country. I don't disparage the worth of other countries but nevertheless, it [Russia] is the very best. Samara region, where I live, again is the very best [*samaia samaia*]. And Samara city—it is the very best city of all. . . . maybe just because I live here" (235, Samara).

Positive local identities were expressed by the majority of respondents from both Moscow and Samara. Muscovites expressed this identity in both appreciation of the diversity of Moscow and the freedom and opportunities it granted at the individual level, and in its closeness to Europe and world-city status. Together these features made Moscow feel distinct from the rest of (provincial) Russia, almost "like another state" (52, Moscow). Young people in Samara also articulated almost universally positive sentiments toward their home city, seeing it as embodying an almost ideal mix of the prosperity and diversity of a large city and the familiarity and communality of the provinces. In this way respondents turned on its head the implied negative of provincial status: "I . . . would not invest the word 'province' with a negative connotation . . . Samara is a good city *because* [emphasis added] it is a bit provincial" (233, Samara).

In sharp contrast, Ul'ianovsk was almost universally condemned as economically undeveloped, conservative, inhibited, and above all, cut off from the rest of Russia and the world (9, Ul'ianovsk; 3, Ul'ianovsk, 40, Ul'ianovsk; 28, Ul'ianovsk; 29, Ul'ianovsk; 19, Ul'ianovsk): "Ul'ianovsk is a closed zone . . . nobody wants to come here, and few people leave, and those that leave do so for good . . . so there are no new people, there are no new interests, acquaintances, information here at all" (253, Ul'ianovsk).

The contrast between how young people from Samara and those from Ul'ianovsk talked about their home cities indicated that while both perceived those cities to be culturally and economically "behind" Moscow, it was only in Ul'ianovsk that this generated a negative identity with the city. It was not, therefore, being "peripheral" per se that was the problem for young people, but feeling "cut off" from information, interactions, and opportunities associated with the wider world. It was the sense of being "trapped" in the periphery without the means to extract oneself, or to communicate with the outside world which was the issue.

Conclusion

> The East is a subtle [*tonkoe*] thing . . . but Russia, in my opinion, is an even more subtle [*tonkoe*] thing. In my understanding, Russia . . . could fulfill a much more important function than she does at the moment.
>
> —187, Samara

The complex understandings held by young Russians of the global environment within which Russia exists expose the redundant binaries of East versus West, United States and USSR, Slavophiles and Westernizers. Such binaries may retain political capital but cannot adequately house the complex narratives of Russianness being constructed by a new generation of Russians. These narratives were not new in themselves; they drew on images and understandings of Russia's place in the world that young people encountered in the media and in the course of their daily lives at home, school, and work. As such they were rooted in Soviet, and pre-Soviet, cultural stereotypes of Russia and its relationship with the West.

So what, if anything, was new about how young Russians articulated their Russianness in this post-Soviet, and "globalized" world? This study confirmed the findings of both Markowitz and Oushakine suggesting that young people employed the division between "the material" (associated with the West) and "the spiritual," or "soul-ful" (associated with Russia) (Oushakine 2000a, 1004; Markowitz 1999, 1188), as a means of envisaging the new Russia. Oushakine and Markowitz interpret this in the context of post-Soviet development. Thus Oushakine reads the practice as a resort to "elusive, vague and yet utterly stereotypic concepts of 'soul,' 'spirituality,' or 'national character' " when unable to frame or define changes in Russia due to the country's "transitionality" (Oushakine 2000a, 994). In the current study the material-spiritual binary has been understood as a narrative of not only temporal but also spatial "transition," as a means of imagining Russia's unique place in, and contribution to, the post-superpower world.

How did young Russians imagine "living with the West" in this changed global environment? The authors suggest that they continued to use the mirror of "the West" to generate inverse reflections of Russia. The impetus for this had not been lessened, but reinforced for the post-Soviet generation, since the late twentieth century has in general been characterized by what Bauman refers to as a globally determined "local self-differentiation industry" (cited in Beck 2000, 54). The cultural constructs produced by this "self-differentiation industry," though, are acutely sensitive to the subjective positionings of nations within the new global order. In Russia, at the discursive level, globalization had been constructed neither as a consequence of modernity, nor as a vehicle for modernization, but as a transformation of the existing world order that directly threatened Russia's status within it. Moreover, the peculiar importance of the West's attitude to Russia in the formation of Russians' sense of "self" (as described in Chapter 4) reinforced this vulnerability. Respondents thus appeared painfully aware that in the West "the attitude to the country [Russia] and the attitude to the Russian themselves is semiderisory [*polunaplevatel'skoe*]" (235, Samara). This could not but find reflection in reconfigurations of Russianness among the younger generation who approached "living with the West" as a defensive cultural practice.

Conclusion

Hilary Pilkington

> The notion of global cultural synchronization . . . downplays the ambivalence of the globalizing momentum and ignores the local reception of Western culture.
>
> —Pieterse 1995, 53

To understand cultural globalization as a series of processes inducing cultural uniformity and standardization, Pieterse argues, is to tell only part of the globalization story, for it overlooks or downplays its countercurrents: the impact of non-Western cultures on the West; the indigenization of Western elements; the influence non-Western cultures exercise on one another; and the culturally mixed nature of the "Western" culture exported (Pieterse 1995, 53). There has been a growing imperative to expose the flip side of globalization; and as a result, globalization is no longer studied on its own, but always in tandem with processes of *localization*. The result has been the generation of theories of "glocalization" (Robertson 1995), "creolization" (Hannerz 1992), "hybridization" (Hall 1990, 234; Bhabha 1990; Clifford and Marcus 1986), and cultural "reterritorialization" (Lull 1995, 159), which are better equipped to explain real processes of global-local cultural engagement. Perhaps, surprisingly, therefore, these theories have rarely been operationalized in empirical studies; and where they have, they have focused on the study of the " 'hybridization' of top culture—culture at the globalized top" (Bauman 1998a, 3). This book, in contrast, has privileged the empirical; it has focused on exploring the complex local reception of Western culture at the "peripheralized bottom." The book concludes in this vein, by first and foremost outlining the key empirical findings of the research before reflecting upon how such particular case studies can be made to speak to broader theories of "global-local" cultural engagement.

Media, Consumption, Culture: A Taste of "Freedom"?

Cultural globalization has not only brought "cultural revolution" in post-socialist societies, but for some Western theorists "the collapse of the Eastern bloc was also manifestly a *result* [my emphasis] of cultural globalisation" (Beck 2000, 66). Satellite dishes in former East Germany, pulling in ideologies and cultures from outside former communist nations, are described by Lull as a "technology of freedom" (Lull 1995, 125), while for Beck "television advertising . . . changed an environment of shortage and regimentation into a fused promise of consumption and political freedom" (Beck 2000, 66). But have global media and commercial worlds fulfilled their promise? Do the new media engage young people in Russia in a global consumer-based youth culture? And how has access to the global media reshaped their images of the West?

The research conducted for this book confirmed that cultural globalization had opened up new channels of information for young Russians and presented new spaces in which young people could imagine and construct new selves. These selves have been shaped partially in the process of engagement with "global youth cultures" and have involved a reformulation of "self" often experienced as a liberating, creative, and playful process that fits happily within Russian youth cultural (*tusovka*) traditions. New Russian youth media such as the flagship youth magazines *OM* and *Ptiuch* have been central to this process and have revolutionized the portrayal of "the West" to their audiences. By the end of the 1990s, "the West" was no longer presented as the ideological enemy, but discussed through youth culture, music, film, and style in a way that sought to *include* young Russians in a global youth culture. Moreover, Russian youth culture was increasingly written into global youth culture as an active participant; youth magazine editors considered only "around half" of their material to come directly from the West, and only in the field of fashion was local cultural production portrayed as seriously lagging behind the West.

The incorporation of Russian youth into the global market of youth consumption remained partial, however. While "global" cultural commodities and forms were presented in the youth media as "available" to Russian youth for their own enjoyment, discussions of the social contexts of their original production—that is, the social values and norms prevailing in particular countries, or in "the West" in general—situated Russia as *different* from and *outside* the West. Moreover, globally engaged magazines such as *OM* and *Ptiuch* were not widely read outside Moscow; in provincial Russia, young people continued to prefer the non-youth-specific weekly *Spid-Info*. Indeed, in both magazine reading and television viewing, young provincial Russians tended to share "local" tastes with the adult generation rather than "global" interests with young people around the world. In light of this, MTV's international operating maxim "Think globally, act locally" (Hanke 1998, 223) would appear to come unstuck in Russia, where it was those media that had "*thought* locally"—such as national and local radio stations—which had been most successful in attracting new youth audiences. Radio is arguably the most local of all mass media forms and in Russia it was a medium that had undergone dramatic change in recent years, resulting in an extraordinary rise in popularity among youth. This was largely explained by the successful venturing of radio stations into interactive radio, which had generated "virtual" youth communities (*tusovki*) on the night airwaves. Moreover, the particular success of Russkoe radio lay in its self-conscious localism, which allowed some of its DJs to exploit anti-American feelings through the medium of jokes that quickly became common currency among youth.

The example of the success of Russian radio suggested that the media spoke most effectively to young Russians where they were engaged not as consumers but as interlocutors. Young people used media and information sources primarily as sites of cultural, not consumer practice. This was confirmed by the findings of the research with regard to young people and advertising. The empirical research had been designed initially with the expectation that Western advertising would be a primary channel for relaying images of the West. However, although advertising did feature in young people's awareness of engagements with the West, less than one in five provincial respondents surveyed mentioned it as an origin of their images of the West, compared to more than two-thirds of young people who cited the press and television. The fact that Russian consumers were offered patronizing, condescending, superficial, and inappropriate advertising in the early 1990s was partly to blame for this, and such practices have been replaced rapidly by global advertising (at the brand level) adapted specifically for a Russian audience. Nevertheless, it remained in the economic interest of transnational companies to employ global campaigns with relatively little adaptation, especially in youth-targeted advertising, since young people were believed to constitute the most "global" segment of the market. At the end of the 1990s, therefore, young Russians were surprisingly disengaged with Western advertising; it featured rarely in their cultural practice as a focus for promises of either real consumption or political freedom.

Why have young Russians failed to reconstruct themselves as new youthful consumers? In post-Soviet Russia both the economic and cultural terrain have reined in the role of consumer as new social subject. The ongoing collapse of domestic production had created an imbalance in consumption whereby "luxury" items were largely Western imports, unaffordable and increasingly considered to be of dubious quality (Humphrey 1995), while everyday food items of Russian origin were hard to find and often homegrown. In this bizarre recreation of deficit in the post-Soviet period, the logic of advertising was lost and consumer identities rendered problematic. Since most young Russians did not have consuming practices of their own, they identified the subjects of consumption as "new Russians" and imagined its object qualitatively in old Soviet terms (car, apartment, gold, money), but exaggerated it quantitatively to match their perceptions of the size of "new Russian" wallets (Oushakine 2000b). While Oushakine is certainly right to suggest young provincial Russians do not identify as subjects of consumption, it is important to understand this phenomenon as a problem both of *post-Soviet* identification and of core-periphery positioning. Developing a post-Soviet consumer practice has been inhibited by the fact that, at the discursive level, consumption has been only partially released from its past construction as a negative Western characteristic. This has historical precedents of course; flirtations with consumerism in the 1920s, for example, both "helped structure a consumer mentality similar to that of Western Europe and the US" and fueled Bolshevik calls for the need for rational and disciplined forms of recreation and subsequent restriction of the flow of Western cultural commodities (Gorsuch 2000, 131–38). These debates recurred repeatedly in postwar Soviet discourse, which sought to delineate between acceptable consumption of spiritual and leisure artifacts (film, concerts, theater and fashion) born of "rational needs" and "consumerism," which represented a disharmony between material and spiritual demands and which turned people into the "slaves of things" (Pilkington 1996b, 174). Of course, in the post-Soviet period—given its similarities to post–World War II Germany where youth had also been newly released from authoritarian rule—one might have expected consumer freedom to be culturally inscribed as a basic and inalienable right, bringing "spiritual release" in an overpoliticized, overmilitarized society (Poiger 2000, 113). However, the post-Soviet space young people inhabit is not only released from "communist" ideology, but also newly opened to global flows of material and cultural commodities emanating from far beyond "the West" as understood in Soviet times. Globalization has rendered the origins of consumer goods increasingly unknown, destabilizing old markers of Western (*firmennaia*) quality. The retreat to Soviet markers of consumption thus must be understood at least in part as a response to an unnerving experience; the majority of young provincial Russians find themselves constantly in danger of reaching out for a symbol of modernity, but finding they have wrapped themselves in "a product of China." This was poignantly illustrated during a group interview in Samara with a group of folk dancers when one young woman's questions to the author, seeking to elicit concrete advice on which Western products currently on sale in the city were "good quality," caused widespread embarrassment among the rest of the group. The arena of consumption was thus not one that offered the sweet taste of freedom or the enjoyment of hitherto prohibited pleasures. Consuming practice was experienced rather as an almost perpendicular learning curve whose negotiation had been impeded by a chronic mismatch between disposable income and goods available, the rendering of accumulated consumer knowledges redundant by globalization and the need, in public, to dissimulate indifference to "Western," "materialist" emphasis on the value of consumption.

A Russian "Occidentalism"? Continuities and Ruptures in Images of the West

Residues of "communist" ideology evidently continued to shape cultural engagements with the West, but no longer solely defined Russian "occidentalism" (stylization of the West). Determining the substance to Russia's peculiar gaze on the West, through an analysis of the content of images of the West encountered by Russian youth, was central to the research undertaken for this book. That research suggested that "the West" appeared in the post-Soviet media in more diverse and complex ways than it had in the late Soviet past. The West was no longer portrayed as a single entity but emerged as a complex, ambiguous concept, whose meaning fluctuated depending upon the context in which it was being represented. Differentiations between Europe and America, for example, were common, and young people held clear images of a number of European countries (primarily England, Germany, and France) and could compare and contrast Western Europe with Southern Europe. Young people in Russia thus had complex images of the West born of access to a much greater quantity, and increasingly quality, of information. How had this new information revolution impacted on how young people looked to the West in post-Soviet Russia?

Although the requirement for conformity to officially approved values renders sociological data from Soviet Russia unreliable, the findings of Grushin's classic Taganrog public opinion survey published in 1980, might be invoked here simply for illustrative purposes. Only 2 percent of that survey population[1] considered the level of democracy in the United States to be "very high," and the same proportion thought living standards to be "very high" in the United States, France, and the United Kingdom (Shlapentokh 1989, 139). In contrast, the authors' representative survey of provincial youth in Samara and Ul'ianovsk conducted in the autumn of 1997 suggested that the West was associated in young people's minds *pri-*

marily with a high standard of living (71 percent), freedom (79 percent), and individual independence (85 percent). There was also evidence from qualitative data to suggest that young Russians were more inclined to exist in global spaces than their parents' generation. Young people often articulated an imagined solidarity with young people in the West who adopted similar lifestyles and listened to similar music. However, despite the growing differentiation of "the West" among young people, respondents continued to imagine the West primarily through images of America, and the latter were most likely to have a negative content. Less than half of the respondents (48 percent) in the authors' survey, for example, thought the West was characterized by a high cultural level, and America, in particular, appeared in young people's narratives as banal, vulgar, and "rootless."

This pattern of imaginings of America not only revealed continuities from the Soviet past, but also bore similarities to discursive constructions of America in Western Europe and elsewhere. American "shallowness," for example, is a widely held stereotype in France dating back to the early nineteenth century (Ellwood 2000, 28), being attributed to the United States's relative newness and supposed resulting inability to compete cerebrally with the older, established civilizations (Huq 1999, 140). As this suggests, obsessive focus on America and concerns about "Americanization" and its impact on "national culture" have been voiced in many European societies when (upper-class) high-cultural interpretations of "authentic" national cultures have seemed to be threatened by working-class appropriations of American popular culture (Fehrenbach and Poiger 2000, xxvi). Interestingly, the import of American cultural commodities into Japan has been much less controversial than in Western Europe. Fehrenbach and Poiger suggest that this might be because greater Japanese homogeneity has diffused the power of American culture to aid in the articulation of counter-hegemonic race, class, or generational identities (xxviii).

Russia falls between these modes of engagement. On the one hand, in Soviet Russia Western/American cultural influences were highly politicized and constructed as undermining the fundamentals of Soviet society. On the other hand, while far from being a homogenous society, Russia has such a well-constructed myth of "difference" and "uniqueness," that it is able, as in the case of Japan, to diffuse the power of American culture. To understand this, we need to consider less the often stereotypical content of images of the West and America and more the way in which narratives of the West were used by young people to construct narratives of "self" and "other." Building on a well-established Russian tradition, young people used their engagements with images of the West primarily to construct narratives of Russia. Although this practice is shared by other European societies—French debates about America are in a similar way primarily an excuse to reflect upon themselves (Ellwood 2000, 27)—Russia's engagements with America or "the West" differ in that they are conducted as if Russia were outside this cultural orbit. Of respondents in the authors' survey of Ul'ianovsk and Samara, only 5 percent included Russia as part of the "West," while 84 percent specifically excluded Russia.

The mirror to the self in France, or indeed in the United Kingdom, has been used to expose "dangerous," hidden tendencies within. The narratives of young Russians, in contrast, showed how this "mirror" was used to reflect the West's positive characteristics as absences from Russia, and its negative aspects as that which was positive about Russia. As Oushakine notes (and is depicted in Figure 8.1), this practice often results in the recycling of elusive, vague, and stereotypic concepts of "soul," "spirituality," or "national character" without elaborating the content of these notions. (Oushakine 2000a, 995). While even this level of "vagueness" would probably be welcomed by nationalists in many other European countries, where the content of nationhood is invisible to much of the population, the findings of the authors' research suggest that a substance to these notions of "soul" and "spirituality" can be discerned if one moves down from the philosophical plane to the level of concrete cultural practice. These substances are elaborated below and, it will be suggested, Russia's peculiar occidentalism is revealed not in the Japanese practice of domesticating American cultural commodities (Fehrenbach and Poiger 2000, xxviii) but, among the younger generation at least, in a "mix and match" strategy that reflects both a receptiveness to the global alongside a precious guarding of that which is "local" through a carefully constructed narrative of its qualitative difference.

Mimesis? Hybridization? Creolization? Rethinking "the West" in Russian Youth Cultural Practice

The increasing ability of young people to dissociate the West from "all that is good" was evident from the ethnographic research conducted for this book, which remapped the youth scenes of post-Soviet Russia. This remapping exercise privileged young people's narratives of their own positioning on the youth scene. It revealed that distinctions made in the past between "Westernizing" *neformaly* (bikers, hippies, rock fans, rappers) and "neo-Slavophile," *gopnik* youth cultural groups were not only overpoliticized readings of their activity, but based upon divisions which themselves had become less clearly and antagonistically formulated than a decade earlier. The reasons for this have been taken up in the development of two, interlocking arguments.

First, drawing on "post-subcultural" approaches to the study of youth cultural practice in the West, it has been suggested that at end of the 1990s fixed identifications with a single musical genre were rare and style bore no homological relationship to musical preference. Thus within the "alternative" youth space, the maps revealed not a series of discrete style-based subcultures, enjoying a newfound space in which to develop their exclusivity, but interlocking spheres of cultural practice across which young people moved as they made their own "progressions" in the youth cultural world. At the same time, however, awareness of the distinction between progressive ("alternative") youth and the majority of normal ("mainstream") youth remained strong and important to youthful identities. Taking up the challenge presented by post-subcultural approaches to youth, the role this division between "alternative" and "conventional" youth played in shaping identities on both sides of that porous border was explored. Taking this bi-focal stance allowed not only the first mapping of the whole youth cultural scene in Russia, but the placement of musical and stylistic practice within broader life paths. Young people's differential employment of music and style was thus studied within their wider communicative practice, which included patterns of friendship and sociability groups, the location of these microgroups and their employment of urban space, and the relationship between individual choice and group norms in lifestyle decisions.

Developing a fuller picture of youth cultural practice facilitated the development of the second part of the interlocking argument, for it displaced "the West," and its mimesis, as the single significant "other" in Russian youth cultural practice by showing the complex interactions young people had *with each other* as well as with cultural forms and artifacts from the West. Although at the end of the 1990s "the West" continued to act as an important reference point in youth cultural identification, increasing direct interaction with representatives of, and cultural artifacts from, the West and their experience as "imposition" rather than "forbidden fruit" had caused young people to reposition themselves in relation to this "other." The new openness to the West had brought "the West" to a much broader spectrum of Russian youth, and deeper into the "heart" of Russia, as a result of which "alternative" youth had sought to reauthenticate (parts of) domestic cultural practice, as a means of differentiating itself from an imitative, mainstream other. It was this mainstream (the "normals") whom they now accused of "copying the West," where that "West" was equated with commercial and therefore inauthentic cultural production.

This is not to suggest that identities have been inverted and *tusovka* youth have become the new neo-Slavophiles, rather that we can only understand how the West has been rewritten into post-Soviet youth cultural practice by socially reembedding youth cultural practices. The West was not invoked in youth cultural practice as an object of direct affinity or disaffection, rather, specific engagements with "the West" and its working through global-local cultural interactions, in part, shaped the distinctive cultural strategies referred to as progressive and normal. The classification of these strands of practice not as groups but as strategies indicates that they are not only socially located in the past (in the social cleavages of Soviet modernity), but reflect young people's negotiations of the present and imaginings of the future. It suggests that the breadth of young people's horizons—their ability to travel and see beyond the locality—is a key differentiator on the youth scene. Progressive young people were characterized by their tendency to look outward, to maintain broad horizons, and to seek new information and cultural stimuli. They "looked West" in the sense that translocal style or music affiliations (mostly produced in the West) were often a source of such information and a focus point on the global horizon. Paradoxically, however, those young people who appeared to be most attuned to Western ways of life were actually most critical of them.[2] In contrast normal youth located its cultural practice locally, and territorially—around home (*dvor*) or place of study—rather than translocally and symbolically (through style or music). In sharp contrast to the progressives, in their communicative practice normals valued most highly not new information, diverse people, and a sense of perpetual motion, but the security generated by a stable, territorially rooted friendship network. That their horizons were focused narrowly on their personal locale reflected the fact that increasing competition for places in higher education, for professional training that might guarantee a "real" salary, and above all, a modicum of social security required young people to focus intensively on study, work, and earning money—activities which continued to require extensive local networking. Normal young people's horizons then were severely restricted by the bounds of what was realistically possible, producing a cultural strategy that used the depth of their local connections as a means of securing for themselves a minimal material security which might facilitate "global" consumption. Thus progressive and normal youth cultural strategies embodied socially differentiated points of access and modes of engagement with the "global." This produced multiple local narratives of global cultural forms, as evidenced in the different appropriations of electronic dance music by progressive and normal youth. Progressive and normal strategies were also deeply reflexive, however, and the global and the local provided key resources, drawn upon differentially, in imagining and constructing progressive or normal lives.

So what have been the outcomes of Russian youth's engagement with cultural globalization? The argument pursued throughout the book has been that the reflexive nature of that engagement is central to understanding its outcomes. Young Russians were acutely aware of the "core-periphery" model structuring contemporary cultural exchange and understood Russia as being positioned as a "receiver" rather than a "producer" of "global culture." They perceived a one-way cultural exchange with the

West; all major youth cultural trends were believed to have emanated in the West and to have been reproduced in Russia. This reflected not solely a post-Soviet inferiority complex among young Russians, but how cores and peripheries continued to structure the supposedly global flow of cultural forms; Western popular musics are available as never before at the traditional peripheries, but while that makes it easy to buy Madonna in China, it is much harder to find Cui Jian in the United States (Taylor 1997, 199).

However, young people generally did not perceive Russian culture as becoming "Americanized" or "Westernized" as a result of the increased openness to the West. In other modern societies, the dominance of American cultural forms has been challenged through the recognition of distinctive cultural versions of originally American forms. For French rap artists, for example, the articulation of a "vision of rap that is French not American" is important (Huq 1999, 140), while in Japan American products have been heavily "domesticated" at the same time as Japanese cultural products, such as anime (Japanese animation) and manga (comic books), have been exported back to America (Fehrenbach and Poiger 2000). In Russia, there have been no such claims to the production of new, authentically Russian versions of Western cultural forms through a process of "reworking."[3] Rather, as young Russians have become increasingly exposed to Western cultural forms, they have maintained a distinction between the global and the local. Western cultural forms were perceived as global precisely because they could be reproduced successfully in different localities. Russian culture, however, was considered to be "not global" because it could not be understood outside Russia. This, however, was cited as evidence not of its parochialness, but of its intrinsic value. In young people's narratives of cultural exchange, global (Western) culture was seen to be fun but superficial, whereas Russian culture was spiritually rich and accessible only to Russians. Thus young people were happy to *consume* Western ("other," "global") culture, while remaining confident that that which was Russian ("ours," "local") would remain untarnished by global intrusion. This repositioning required the disaggregation of positive attitudes toward the West at the socioeconomic level (articulated via the "high standard of living" in the West) from negative attitudes at the sociocultural level (evident in references to the West as "spiritually impoverished" or "empty") and was clearly present in young people's talk about their music use. While almost all young people listened to both Russian music and Western music, different musics were drawn upon to satisfy different moods or needs. Thus Western (dance or pop) music was considered to be "music for the body" (that is for dancing or as background), whereas Russian (rock, folk or even pop) was "music for the soul."

Understanding the perceived sanctity of that which is "Russian" is central to evaluating the potential of theories of cultural hybridization to illuminate the way in which Western cultural forms and messages were appropriated in the everyday cultural practice of young people in Russia. Notions of hybridization as the outcome of cultural globalization are difficult to transpose to Russia because hybridization jars with the Russian narrative of self. In this narrative, Russia is the site of an alternative source of cultural production, whose content is primarily spiritual rather than material and, despite the manifest poverty of cultural production in the post-Soviet space—young people continued to profess that the spiritual wealth of Russia was an untapped global resource that might be ignored by the West, but was not undermined by it.

It is this self-narrative that prevents young Russians from recognizing themselves as part of the "peripheralised local" (Bauman 1998a) destined to be only consumers rather than producers of cultural commodities. Although young Russians affirmed the economic and technological superiority of the West, and desired the material comfort brought by economic prosperity, they did not subscribe automatically to the designation of "center" and "periphery" according to economic power alone. They voiced a feeling that Russia could, and should, retain an important global role commensurate with the country's spiritual and cultural wealth and potential. This was reflected in concrete cultural practices by young people's eagerness to adopt and enjoy global cultural commodities and forms for the physical pleasure they gave, while at the same time peripheralizing them in their wider value systems. The desire for Western prosperity was in this way combined with a conviction that the spiritual or moral gains ensuing from interaction with Western cultures were few (Howell 1995, 166).

Does this constitute a cultural practice of *resistance* to global cultural forms? Have young Russians ceased to "look West"? Certainly the "special relationship" of Russian youth with the West—rooted in the past importance of the West in providing an authentic youth cultural "other" which might be borrowed and reenacted in the margins of Soviet Russian culture—is being renegotiated as a consequence of the increasing experience of Western cultural forms as imposition rather than forbidden fruit. To talk about this process as a practice of resistance, however, presumes a deeper project of cultural homogenization inherent in globalization. In fact, cultural globalization cannot deliver cultural homogenization, nor can it eradicate diversity. However, as Wilk argues, globalization may organize that diversity such that different cultures vary in increasingly uniform ways (Wilk 1995, 118). It is in this sense that Russia's response to globalization continues to throw up challenges to Western hegemony, for its "local" specific lies in its rejection of the logic of cores and peripheries underpinning Western understandings of globalizing processes.

APPENDIX

The data drawn upon in this book were generated in the course of a research project designed and conducted by the authors to integrate three types of data: qualitative research in the form of interviews and focus groups; quantitative data from a small representative survey; and textual analysis of media products targeted at youth, supported by expert interviews with media professionals and cultural producers. This appendix outlines briefly how the data were collected and reflects on some of the issues raised by the field experience.

Qualitative Research: A Social Profile of Respondents

The qualitative research was the main focus of empirical work. A total of 270 young people took part in either a focus group or an ethnographic interview. Of these, 107 respondents were interviewed: 80 were interviewed once; 27 were involved in repeat interviews. The qualitative research was weighted toward the provinces: 41 percent of respondents came from Samara, 38 percent from Ul'ianovsk and 21 percent from Moscow.[1]

No representative sample was employed for the selection of respondents in the qualitative element of the research. Respondents at the end of the interview completed a short questionnaire containing basic sociodemographic questions or focus group, however. These data allowed at least a post factum analysis of the respondent group. The analysis of these data showed that a broad gender balance of respondents was maintained: 52.2 percent of respondents were male, 47.8 percent were female. Of respondents taking part in focus groups and interviews, 50 percent were aged 15–17, 25 percent were aged 18–20, and 18 percent were aged 21–25.[2] The relative overrepresentation of 15–17 year olds was largely due to the way in which the focus groups were constituted (see Table A.1) but was beneficial to the qualitative part of the research; since younger respondents were generally less articulate, their greater number ensured their experiences were not underrepresented. Seventy-five percent of respondents were ethnically Russian—that is both parents were Russian—14 percent were of mixed parentage, with one parent ethnically Russian, and 6 percent were of non-Russian parentage (half of these were Tatar).[3]

At the time of interview, most respondents were completing secondary school: 56 percent of Ul'ianovsk respondents, 53 percent of Samara respondents, and 30 percent of Moscow respondents were in this situation. Only a small proportion of respondents were in vocational secondary education (1 percent of Ul'ianovsk, 2 percent of Moscow, 0 percent of Samara respondents). However, of those who had already completed secondary education, 8 percent of Ul'ianovsk and 4 percent of Samara respondents had finished vocational colleges. Twenty-one

Table A.1
Profile of focus groups

Focus group	*Text*	*Place*	*Profile*	*Age*	*Female*	*Male*
FG1 (64–68)	Advertising	Moscow	School	14–16	3	2
FG2 (69–73)	Advertising	Moscow	*Izvestiia* employees	20–25	2	3
FG3 (74–78)	Advertising	Moscow	School	15–16	2	3
FG4 (79–81)	Advertising	Moscow	Bank employees	22–25	2	1
FG5 (82–84)	Advertising	Ul'ianovsk	Manual workers	17–19	2	1
FG6 (85–89)	Advertising	Ul'ianovsk	School (rural)	15	4	1
FG7 (90–94)	Advertising	Ul'ianovsk	School (central)	15–16	3	2
FG8 (95–99)	Advertising	Ul'ianovsk	School (central, elite)	15–16	3	2
FG9 (100–102)	Advertising	Ul'ianovsk	Bank employees	23–24	2	1
FG10 (103–7)	Advertising	Ul'ianovsk	Student	17–24	2	3
FG11 (108–11)	Advertising	Samara	Manual workers	17–21	1	3
FG12 (112–17)	Advertising	Samara	School (central, elite)	16–17	3	3
FG13 (118–23)	Advertising	Samara	Private business	19–25	4	2
FG14 (124–28)	Advertising	Samara	School (central)	15	3	2
FG15 (129–33)	Advertising	Samara	Student	16–19	2	3
FG16 (134–39)	Advertising	Samara	School (central)	16	3	3
FG17 (140–45)	Cultural text	Ul'ianovsk	School (central)	15–17	3	3
FG18 (88, 146–49)	Cultural text	Ul'ianovsk	School (rural)	16–17	3	2
FG19 (100,101, 102, 150)	Cultural text	Ul'ianovsk	Bank employees	21–24	3	1
FG20 (151–53)	Cultural text	Ul'ianovsk	Workers	19–21	2	1
FG21 (154–59)	Cultural text	Ul'ianovsk	School (central)	15–16	3	3
FG22 (160–63)	Cultural text	Ul'ianovsk	Student	17–20	2	2
FG23 (243–46)	Cultural text	Ul'ianovsk	School (central, elite)	15–17	2	2
FG 24 (247–49)	Cultural text	Ul'ianovsk	Bank employees	20–23	2	1
FG25 (164–69)	Cultural text	Samara	School (central)	15–17	3	3
FG26 (170–75)	Cultural text	Samara	School (central)	15–16	3	3
FG27 (176–81)	Cultural text	Samara	Worker	18–24	3	3
FG28 (182–87)	Cultural text	Samara	Student	18–20	3	3
FG29 (188–93)	Cultural text	Samara	Private business	21–23	2	4
FG30 (194–99)	Cultural text	Samara	School (central, elite)	15–17	3	3
FG31 (200–205)	Cultural text	Samara	School (rural)	15–16	3	3
FG32 (255–59)	Cultural text	Moscow	School	15–16	2	3
FG33 (260–64)	Cultural text	Moscow	School	15–16	4	1
FG34 (265–70)	Cultural text	Moscow	Private business and bank	19–24	2	4

Note: The numbers in brackets indicate the ACCESS database code numbers assigned to individual participants in the group. It is these numbers that are cited where respondents are quoted in the text.

percent of Moscow, 11 percent of Samara, and 6 percent of Ul'ianovsk respondents had higher education. A further 21 percent of Ul'ianovsk, 13 percent of Moscow, and 20 percent of Samara respondents were studying in higher educational institutions at the time of interview. The social status of respondents was determined by employment of parents, taking the higher status, if both were employed. The social status of respondents in Samara and Ul'ianovsk proved to be broadly similar: 6 percent came from the business sector, 15 percent from managerial backgrounds, 33–36 percent had parents employed in white-collar positions requiring higher education, 13–15 percent had families working in white-collar jobs requiring secondary education, 21–22 percent had manual-worker backgrounds, 2 percent had parents who were retired, and 3 percent had parents who were unemployed.[4] Moscow data on social background were quite different, however, showing a greater degree of polarization: 13 percent of respondents came from families engaged in business, and 40 percent came from families in white-collar "professions" (requiring higher education). Only a small proportion of respondents were from families employed in manual jobs (9 percent) but the percentage from unemployed families was higher than in the provincial cities (6 percent). Disposable income was primarily a privilege of respondents from Moscow: 43 percent of Moscow respondents had a monthly income of 1,000 rubles (approx. $150 at the time of research) or more, compared to 20 percent of Samara respondents and just 9 percent of Ul'ianovsk respondents.[5] At the other end of the scale 73 percent of Ul'ianovsk respondents had an income of less than 200 rubles ($30) per month, compared to 41 percent of Samara and 35 percent of Moscow respondents. The tendency toward polarization suggests the difference between those in school and those working as well as the relative lack of opportunity for young people to gain part-time employment.

Since the primary focus of the research was the interaction of young people with the West, the short questionnaire also asked respondents whether or not they had traveled abroad and, if so, to which countries. Of the 270 respondents, 129 (48 percent) had traveled abroad.[6] Of those, however, 62 had traveled only within the former Soviet Union and an additional 16 had traveled only within the former Soviet Union or former socialist "bloc" (that is former socialist countries of Eastern Europe and the wider "socialist bloc" including Mongolia and Cuba).[7] Thus only 50 respondents (19 percent) had traveled to a country outside the former Soviet Union or socialist bloc while 53 percent had not traveled outside Russia at all.[8] Of the 50 who had traveled outside the former Soviet Union or socialist bloc, 6 had been to the United States; 42 had been to Western Europe (mainly to Finland, Sweden, Germany, Britain, the Benelux countries, Spain, and Portugal). Moscow respondents were most likely to have traveled abroad: 77 percent had done so. Of the Samara respondents 44 percent had traveled abroad and of the Ul'ianovsk respondents 36 percent had traveled abroad. Of those having traveled beyond the former Soviet Union and socialist bloc, however, 54 percent came from Moscow, 32 percent from Samara, and just 14 percent from Ul'ianovsk.[9] There was no significant gender difference with regard to travel abroad.

Respondents were also asked whether they had friends from abroad.[10] Thirty-eight percent of respondents had friends from abroad, and once again, Moscow respondents featured disproportionately: 61 percent of Moscow respondents had friends from abroad, 32 percent of Samara respondents had friends from abroad, and 33 percent of Ul'ianovsk respondents had friends from abroad. Many respondents did not list where their friends came from, so it is difficult to establish just what proportion of these "friends" were in the West. It is clear, however, that young people were much more likely to have Americans among their friends from abroad than to have traveled to America. Sixty-two percent of respondents, however, said they had no friends from abroad at all.

Qualitative Research: In-depth Interviews

Interview respondents were not selected by sociodemographic criteria but by cultural activity. Contact with a cross-section of youth was sought by using a range of sites of access to young people at leisure. These sites included the *dvor* (yard), organized after-school activity (sports clubs, aerobics classes, modeling classes, civic culture training), cafes, discos, nightclubs, well-known *tusovka* sites, pop and rock concerts, folk or bard (*KSP*) clubs, and schools or colleges. Individual contacts of the researchers were employed in the first instance to establish the key *tusovka* sites in each city and, in some cases, to act as informants and guides. Because of the less structured nature of selection of respondents for in-depth interviews, such interviews were occasionally conducted with respondents outside the target age range; and although all were asked to complete the short questionnaire about social background, the context of interviews—which might be held in clubs, discos, in yards or at concerts—meant that it was not always possible to ensure that adequate data had been given.

A team of four Russian and two British researchers conducted the qualitative research. The relatively large number of respondents demanded a fairly structured approach to the interviewing. Nonetheless, observation and informal meetings in which roles of interviewer and interviewee were often exchanged supplemented the interviews. In Ul'ianovsk and Samara, at least in the smaller clubs, the research became part of the club life itself, and informal communication assisted reflection back on the research process. Respondents were generally extremely responsive and positively disposed toward the research, although respondents referred to as normals (see Chapter 5) sometimes took longer to feel comfortable with the interviewing process. This was partially because the sites of interview were more likely to be formal (such as sports clubs, schools, or colleges) but also because of respondents' less frequent interaction with people outside their normal spheres of friends.[11] The Russian researchers have maintained contact with some respondents (mainly in Samara and Ul'ianovsk), since fieldwork was completed through attending local events and delivering photographs taken during the fieldwork to respondents. Some contact by email has taken place between the British researchers and respondents.

Qualitative Research: Focus Groups

A total of thirty-four focus groups were conducted, fifteen using television commercials and nineteen using a range of cultural texts (music videos, film clips). One hundred sixty-three young people took part in a focus group; 89 participated in the focus groups on cultural texts; 70 took part in those on television commercials, and 4 took part in both. In each of the three cities, focus groups were selected according to a number of criteria: age cohort, type of educational establishment or form of employment, and gender. In the 15–17 age cohort, respondents were selected from three educational establishments, including one central (generally considered "elite") school, and one from the "periphery" (outskirts of the city or outside the city). In the older age cohort (18–25 years), one group was drawn from a higher educational institution, one from the manual employment sector, and one from the private sector/professional employment. A gender balance was sought in each group. The constitution of individual focus groups is detailed in Table A.1. The focus groups were designed to provide visual and audio stimulation to facilitate discussion of "images of the West." Since respondents' thoughts were thus context-specific, the notes to Chapter 4 (where responses are cited) indicate where respondents were reacting to a specific commercial or clip. The scenarios for these clips are detailed below. The inclusion of respondent data base numbers in Table A.1 also allows readers to trace individual respondents back to specific focus groups.

Focus Group Scenario 1: Advertising

The following commercials were used in the first round of focus groups:

1. Holsten (beer)
This commercial was developed in the Holsten Hamburg office together with the advertising agency Medder and Associates Ltd, Advertising and Promotions of Cape Town. Shooting was directed by this agency, and all the sets and outdoor scenes were filmed in Cape Town. The commercial used consciously global images symbolized by the prominence of young people and the slogan "one world, one beer." It begins with a picture of a divided TV screen in which young people at leisure are depicted alongside bottles of Holsten beer. In the background (and throughout the commercial) a song with the words "One World, One Beer" is audible. The commercial features a map of the world upon which the names of different cities appear and disappear. The final scene is set in a bar, where two young couples are pictured dancing, drinking, and talking. At the end of the commercial the words "German Art of Brewing" appear, followed by the Russian words *mirovoe pivo* (world beer) and the Holsten beer logo.

2. Sprite (soft drink)
The commercial used a combination of images, which might have been construed as a Western nightclub or as a Moscow nightclub frequented by "new Russians," to present a humorous view of the importance of "image." The main actors are

archetypal "new Russians" or Hollywood film stars; this was depicted by extravagant dress, mobile phones, and contrived gestures and behavior. The commercial focuses on the falseness of the relationships and communication between the people. The commercial has a voice-over in Russian about the importance of image, money, and expensive toys. At the end the words "Imidzh—nichto, zhazhda—vse" ("Image is nothing, thirst is everything") appears on the screen and is followed by the Sprite logo and bottle and the words "Ne dai sebe zasokhnut'" ("Don't go dry").

3. *Mars* (chocolate bar)
The commercial had mixed images, which might have been interpreted as being set in a modern Russian school or a Western school; it was created by DNB&B and was filmed in Russia. The action focuses on a number of different scenes depicting the school day, and the main actor is a young female school teacher. The surroundings of the school are modern, bright, and airy. Pupils are pictured roller-skating down the corridor past the young teacher, who drops her books and is reprimanded by the "traditional" headmistress. The commercial concludes with a scene of the young teacher marking school books. When a football comes flying in through the window, the teacher kicks it out and goes to the window to look out as the words "Mars, *vse luchshee v tebe*" ("Mars—the best is in you") are spoken.

4. *Wash and Go* (shampoo and conditioner)
This commercial was modeled on Western advertising of Wash and Go but included clear Russian cultural referents; hiking in the countryside, the style of clothes, and the physical appearance of the young people themselves. The commercial used Russian actors but was filmed in Spain. The commercial begins with a shot of two young couples hiking in the countryside (mountainous, barren terrain), wearing shorts and T-shirts, and carrying old rucksacks. The two girls try to wave down a passing car for a lift while the guys hide behind a bush. When the car does not stop, the girls decide to wash their hair with Wash and Go under a waterfall. The commercial then shifts to an image of Wash and Go and a verbal description (in Russian) of the shampoo. The girls are then shown with clean, shiny hair against a backdrop of mountains. They try again to wave down a car, and a male driver stops. The two young men then appear and all four climb in to the car, to the apparent disappointment of the driver.

5. *Legendary Harley Davidson* (aftershave)
This commercial employed overtly American images. It opens with the words "Legendary Harley Davidson—free space" and a view from a motorcycle being ridden by a woman. The commercial was shot in a desert location with views of canyons, and these scenes are interspersed with images of a bottle of Legendary Harley Davidson aftershave. After the opening shots, the commercial shifts to a focus to a man and then to this man and the woman embracing in a waterfall, with a view of a canyon in the background and a condor flying over it. Throughout the commercial the words "free space—Legendary Harley Davidson" are

spoken in English, and "prostranstvo, svoboda" (space, freedom) in Russian. At the end of the commercial the words "dukh svobody" (spirit of freedom) are heard and the final image is of the woman and man, on individual motorcycles, driving into the distance.

Focus Group Scenario 2: Cultural Texts

The following music video and film clips were used in the second round of focus groups:

1. Valerii Meladze, "Samba belogo motil'ka" (Samba of the white butterfly). The video clip focuses on the murder of a young, wealthy (possibly "new Russian") couple and the subsequent investigation by a group of detectives (sporting FBI badges), interspersed with images of the male singer Valerii Meladze. The clip shifts between scenes of the young, attractive couple talking, embracing, and dancing in a luxurious apartment and pictures of the investigation and examination of the murder scene by the detectives. The actual killing of the young couple is not shown until the end of the clip; two men are depicted bursting into the apartment and shooting the couple. The final scene is of two detectives discovering a case full of dollar bills.

2(a) The Spice Girls, "Stop!"
The clip is shot in a "traditional" British street of terraced houses, reminiscent of the 1950s. The members of the group (all female) are pictured at the beginning of the clip coming out of a number of the houses to sing together in the middle of the street watched by a variety of onlookers. A sense of strong community spirit is portrayed; men are drinking together in pubs, young girls are skipping, there is a man and boy on a horse-drawn cart, and a young boy pulling a handcart. The clip moves on to a scene set at a fair, which involves the members of the band taking part in different events and joining in the community spirit. The final scene is set in a bar/community center where the band appears on stage and sings to an audience made up of young and old people.

2(b) Blestiashchie, "Gde zhe ty, gde!" (Where are you, where!)
The clip is filmed, reportedly on location somewhere in the West, in a luxurious (country) cottage and focuses on a Christmas or New Year celebration. The focus of the clip is one of the members of Blestiashchie (an all-female Russian band) who sings the majority of the song while moving from one room of the house to another. Her friends (the other members of the band, and their boy friends) arrive and are shown celebrating, giving presents, drinking. The girls are also shown in a large Jacuzzi wearing Santa Claus hats. The main character remains peripheral to these celebrations waiting for a man to arrive. The clip finishes with a view from outside the cottage of the snowy environment and a snowman.

3(a) Savage Garden, "Truly, Madly, Deeply"
The story running through this clip is of a young woman and man looking for each other in a European city (Paris). The clip shifts between scenes of the two main characters, and the band Savage Garden (an all-male band from Australia)

playing in a small cafe. The clip starts with a scene of the young woman getting off the train looking for the young man, and the camera then follows the young woman around Paris in her search. She eventually comes across him by chance, and they are reunited. In the final scene the couple walk arm in arm down a Paris street as the group Savage Garden emerge from a cafe.

3(b) All-4-One, "I Swear"
The clip begins with the group "All-4-One" (an all-male American band) singing on top of a building located in a typical American inner city with a view of skyscrapers, large apartment blocks, buses, and wide streets. They see a beautiful young girl walking on the street below them and decide to go down to try to meet her. The whole clip follows the group around the streets of the city as the different members of the group try to attract the girl's attention. The girl responds in a friendly way, talking and dancing with them. At the end of the clip a bus arrives, and the girl runs to get it while the band members beg her to stay.

4. *Clips from films*
(a) *Trainspotting* (United Kingdom, 1996)
The clip selected was from the very beginning of the film during which the main characters of the film are introduced. It begins with a scene of two of the main characters running down a city street away from two policemen after a robbery. The characters are introduced one by one against different scenes of them first playing football and then of the main character taking drugs in a rundown apartment. The voice over throughout the scene is by the main character first talking about "choosing life, a job, a family," which he then rejects, "choosing not to choose life." The clip ends with the group sitting in one of the rooms of the apartment preparing to shoot up.

(b) *Kids* (United States, 1995)
The clip selected from the controversial film *Kids* is a scene where the young people, mainly male, are gathering around a fountain in a New York park. Most of the characters are wearing T-shirts, baggy jeans, and baseball caps. The two main characters in the scene are two boys who approach the group to greet their friends—shaking hands, hugging them, etc. One of the main characters has a conversation with one of the other boys about their plans for the evening. The scene includes shots of the different members of the group drinking out of bottles in brown paper bags, smoking, and chatting and a young couple kissing. The final part of the clip is of one boy showing the others how to roll a joint, which they then smoke.

Quantitative Research: Survey on Sources of Information About the West

A small-scale representative survey was conducted in the two Volga cities of Ul'ianovsk and Samara during the first two weeks of November 1997 following a pilot study in Ul'ianovsk. The survey was designed to capture, at the start of the empirical work, the range of media used by young people in provincial Russia and their relative popularity. It also asked questions about use of leisure time (see Diagram 6.1) and about general perceptions of "Russia" and "the West" (see Table 4.1). The following themes were covered in a mixed set of closed and open questions:[12]

1. Which youth television programs do you watch, and which youth magazines do you read, and how often?
2. What are your favorite films, music videos, groups, singers, actors/actresses, and computer games? (Respondents were asked to give their favorite "Russian" and "Western" ones.)
3. Where and with whom do you usually spend your free time?
4. What youth cultural movements (*tusovki*) are you aware of? Do you belong yourself to any such *tusovka*? With what do you associate these groups? Which of them are Western, which of them are purely Russian, and which originally came from the West but have become Russian?
5. Which regions of the world would you include in the term "the West"? With what do you associate "the West"? Are these characteristics of Russia also?
6. Name the five characteristics you associate most strongly with Western men, and with Western women.
7. Which are the most important sources of information about the West for you?
8. Do you feel positive, negative, or indifferent about the increasing visibility of Western things (material goods, magazines, videos, advertising, night clubs, "subcultural" styles, fashion, values) in Russia?

The total number of questionnaires returned was 982. The noncompletion rate was 1.8 percent. Five hundred completed questionnaires were from Samara and 482 from Ul'ianovsk. The survey was based on a representative sample of young people in the two cities constructed on three age cohorts (15–17, 18–20, and 21–25), gender, and residence. Representative age sampling meant that 27 percent of respondents were 15–17 years old, 30 percent were 18–20 years old, and 41 percent were 21–25 years old. Of those interviewed, 50.2 percent were male and 49.8 percent female. In Samara all eight city districts and two "peripheral" districts (the towns of Novokubyshevsk and Bereza) were included in the sample. In Ul'ianovsk all four city districts and two peripheral districts (the village of Isheevko and the peripheral suburb of Uchkhoz) were included. The questionnaire was designed using a mixture of closed and open-ended questions. Coding, data entry, and analysis was conducted using SPSSX.

Media Analysis: Textual Analysis and Expert Interviews

Textual analysis of a range of youth media was conducted over a three-year period. The decision to conduct most extensive analysis on Russian youth magazines and newspapers was taken following the analysis of data from the survey and is explained in Chapter 3. The publications *OM*, *Ptiuch*, *Rovesnik*, *Shtuchka*, *Spid-Info*, *Sobesednik*, *Ia Molodoi*, *Aida*, *COOL!*, and *Cosmopolitan* were analyzed over the period 1996–98, and *COOL!* and *Cool Girl* from the beginning of publication (January 1998). The titles of magazines chosen for analysis and periods over which the magazines were studied are detailed in Table A.2. The youth television programs selected for analysis were *Do 16 i starshe*, *Rok-urok*, *Tin-tonik*, *Dzhem*, and *Tet-a-tet*. Russian MTV had not begun transmission at the time of analysis and so could not be included. We analyzed the television commercials shown before, during, and after the youth programs on the main Russian TV channel *ORT* from 10 October to 11 November 1996 and all the television commercials shown over four days on the two main Russian TV channels—*ORT* and *Rossiia*—from 12 to 18 September 1997. Commercials for both Western and Russian products were included. Further relevant details concerning the analysis of television advertising and youth television programs are included in the notes to Chapter 3 and in Figure 3.1.

Table A.2
Youth magazines: Sampling details

Magazine	*First analysis*	*Protocol*	*Second analysis*	*Protocol*
*OM**	April 1996–April 1997	A	July 1997–June 1998	B
*Ptiuch**	April 1996–April 1997	A	May 1997–June 1998	B
*Rovesnik**	March 1996–June 1997	A	July 1997–May 1998	B
*Shtuchka**	April and June 1996; February 1997	C	July 1997–June 1998	B
*Cosmopolitan**	March, April, June, and December 1996	C	October 1997–June 1998	B
*Ia Molodoi ***	November 1996–June 1997	C.	March 1997–June 1998	B
*Spid-Info**	December 1996–June 1997	B	September 1997–June 1998	B
*Sobesednik***	October 1996–July 1997	B	September 1997–June 1998	B
*Aida**	—	—	August 1997–March 1998	B
*COOL!***	—	—	May and June 1998	General analysis

** = published monthly.*
*** = published weekly.*
A. Every fourth issue both qualitative and quantitative analysis.
B. Every issue qualitative analysis. Every fourth issue quantitative analysis.
C. Every issue both qualitative and quantitative analysis.

Expert interviews with media professionals and cultural producers were used to test preliminary hypotheses from the media analysis and to elicit editorial views. Expert interviews were conducted with the following people:

1. Vladimir Zabavskii, head of the creative group, senior artistic director, Moscow office of Young and Rubicam Europe (Moscow).
2. Aleksandr Filiurin, creative director, Melekhov i Filiurin advertising group (Novosibirsk).
3. Igor' Krylov, professor of the faculty of social and economic sciences, Academy of the Economy, under the auspices of the government of the Russian Federation, member of the board of the Russian Association of Advertising Agencies (Moscow).
4. Viacheslav Cherniakhovskii, executive creative director of ARTAMS, advertising, public relations (Moscow).
5. Aleksandr Shevelevich, vice-president, creative director, Kayn advertising agency (Minsk).
6. Ania Koncheva, chief editor for youth programs, *Komsomol'skaia pravda* (Moscow).
7. Aleksandr Kachalov, director, Kachalov i kollegi advertising agency (Moscow).
8. Evgenii Lungin, editor, youth programs, NTV (Moscow).
9. Igor' Grigor'ev, former editor-in-chief, *OM* (Moscow).
10. Igor' Chernyshkov, editor-in-chief, *Rovesnik* (Moscow).
11. Petr Oleinikov, first deputy director, TV-6 (Moscow).
12. Iurii Grymov, editor of video advertisements, head of the Master advertising studio at VGIK (Moscow).
13. Oleg Stukalov, head of advertising, Ul'ianovskaia sotovaia sviaz', ORT-reklama (Ul'ianovsk).
14. Igor' Rozhkov, editor, *Ia-molodoi* (Moscow).
15. Anzor Kankulov, current editor-in-chief, *OM* (Moscow).
16. Dmitrii Churov, editor of journal *Set*, Ul'ianovsk.
17. Dmitrii Ezhev, leader of youth movement "Kul'turnaia Initsiativa," Ul'ianovsk.
18. Maksim Matuk (DJ E), Dmitrii Sugreff (DJ Sugreff), Vasilii Markel (DJ Art), DJs, Ul'ianovsk.
19. "Adam," leader of Adam & ko. breakdance group, Ul'ianovsk.
20. Stanley Williams, DJ at Golodnaia Utka, Moscow.
21. DJ Antis, Club Sandra, Samara.
22. DJ Jump, DJ Slem, Club Aladdin, Samara.
23. Elena Sergienko, youth issues editor, "*Chisla*" newspaper, Samara.
24. DJ Balu, Club Tornado, Samara.

NOTES

Introduction

1. The discursive construction of Russia (and Eastern Europe more generally) in the West since Peter's "eruption into Europe" (Malia 1999, 17) has been traced successfully by historians in recent times (see, for example, Malia 1999 and Wolff 1994). The discursive configuration of the West in Russia, however, has not.

2. The book is based on the findings of a collaborative research project between The University of Birmingham and Ul'ianovsk State University entitled "Looking West? Images of the West among Russian Youth" and was financially supported by the Leverhulme Trust (F/94/BJ), March 1996–June 1999. The principal investigators were Hilary Pilkington and Elena Omel'chenko. The other coauthors of the volume were researchers employed on this project.

3. In the Soviet period, the "imitative" nature of youth cultural forms was explained by Soviet social scientists by the fact that the social conditions for the emergence of youth subcultures were absent in the Soviet Union. Young people's full integration into Soviet society was "evidenced" by repeated surveys of youth "attitudes" and "values" that showed ideological conformity.

4. Yurchak, although born and brought up in Russia, is included here as a Western scholar, since the work referred to was written in the West and published for a mainly Western audience.

5. Earlier ethnographic studies, while providing authentic accounts of youth cultural practices of the period, have been based in one or the other of Russia's capital cities—Moscow and St. Petersburg—and have focused on a small number of contemporary youth cultural formations (*stiliagi*, punks, skinheads, bikers, rock music *tusovki*, *Sistema*, Indianists, Tolkienists, rave) or specific practices (graffiti, rock music). See, for example, Bushnell 1990, Pilkington 1994 and 1996a, Cushman 1995, Rayport Rabodzeenko 1998, and Yurchak 1999.

6. The terms "glocal" and "glocalization" indicate that cultural "globalization" is always accompanied by processes of "localization." See, for example, Robertson 1995.

Chapter 1

1. It should be noted here that while Held and colleagues recognize homogenizers ("hyperglobalizers") as one party in the debate, the other is not "heterogenizers" but "globalization skeptics," those who suggest that global cultures lack the depth and wealth of national cultures.

2. Such a distinction falsely presumes that messages from Western mass media and popular culture are uncritically absorbed, however.

3. The critical exception here is Zygmunt Bauman.

4. Held and colleagues refer to these societies as States in Advanced Capitalist Societies (Held et al. 1999).

5. This point about the history of exposure to globalizing forces is made at a more abstract level by Held and colleagues (Held et al. 1999, 328).

6. The arguments that follow are based on the analysis of social science writing (1995–2000) relating primarily to *cultural* globalization. It is recognized that in some disciplines—such as economics—there may be greater, and more positive, engagement with globalization theories.

7. In fact, not only a Western idea but an integral part of Western *ideology*: "The discourse of globalization . . . can be seen also as an attempt at ideological indoctrination by certain groups for their own self-interested purposes" (Molchanov 1999, 98).

8. Its replacement by "foreign aid," increasingly perceived as Western arrogance and interference, consolidates rather than mitigates this anti-Westernism.

9. Data from VTsIOM as reported by http://www.russiavotes.org.

10. This sentiment, moreover, was evenly spread across all social groups, including youth.

11. Thirty-four percent of those surveyed thought they were "probably," European, 29 percent that they were "probably not" European (VTsIOM as reported by http://www.russiavotes.org).

12. The United Kingdom is the only other significant source of popular music recordings.

13. Richard Hoggart was concerned that American-style "milk bars" and juke-boxes springing up across Britain in the post–Second World War period would undermine more authentic working-class youth cultures (Hoggart 1957, 250).

14. Lash suggests, however, that where such taste communities develop shared meanings, practices, and obligations, they might "begin to be a community" (Lash 1994).

15. For a more detailed discussion, see D. Chaney, *Cultural Change and Everyday Life* (Basingstoke: Palgrave, 2002).

16. See, for example, papers submitted to the panel "The Global and the Local in Contemporary Youth Cultures," parts 1 and 2, Third International Crossroads in Cultural Studies Conference, University of Birmingham, June 2000.

17. Newitz argues that the attraction of Japanese anime in the local American context might indeed be that it constitutes a means of "stealing back" a Japanese product heavily influenced by Hollywood (Newitz 1994, 2). The content is also important, however. The consumption of anime allows mainly male fans to consume nonsexual romance stories and escape the hypersexuality of American media culture by reimagining romance as a relationship that goes beyond the purely sexual and is focused on female figures that do not correspond to Western postfeminist "correctness" (4).

18. We are grateful to Kyongwon Yoon for making us aware of this discursive configuration of "globalization" in Korean debates.

19. As in the case, for example, of Japan (see Condry 2000).

Chapter 2

1. Empirical data referred to in this context are drawn primarily from interviews with experts in the fields of media, advertising, and youth leisure.

A list of interviewees is included in the Appendix.

2. The idea of the "secret power" of television has been developed, for example, in the writings of Postman, who envisaged television as the "gentle smiling enemy" (Postman 1985).

3. The new reality created by television's unprecedented penetration of social life is described with remarkable accuracy and irony by Viktor Pelevin in his popular new novel *Generation "P."*

4. Collage involves working heterogeneous cultural and artistic texts and devices into a whole, which acquires meaning over and above its constituent parts. Styles and genres may be mixed to convey a new meaning. Bricolage is the use of signs from one subculture in a "reversed" or changed sense within a different subculture (mixing or replacing cultural meanings, meaning-traps, meaning mystification). Pastiche implies shifting meaning from the tragedy genre to the comedy genre and vice-versa, thus departing from the concept of the "purity" of the genre.

5. One of the authors, Elena Omel'chenko, experienced this first-hand, when as a young lecturer, she published an article critical of the Institute's "Science Day" in the Institute's own, internally circulated, paper. The criticism (which concerned the head of the department of scientific communism) was interpreted as "blatant subversion," and she was subjected to interrogation by the Institute's party committee. The latter's decision to dismiss her was overturned only after the unexpected intervention of the then first secretary of the regional party committee, Genadii Kolbin.

6. An episode in Andrei Tarkovskii's famous film *Zerkalo* (Mirror) illustrates this. The heroine (the mother) is responsible for proof-reading at a publishing house. One night she suddenly remembers (or thinks she remembers) that she has made a spelling mistake in one of the key names. She rushes to the office in fear. When they hear about her worries, some of her colleagues say their good-byes to her, knowing full well that not only her career, but her life, was over; such mistakes were unforgivable and interpreted as deliberate sabotage.

7. This battle affects many parts of the media but was most notoriously evident in the struggle for influence played out between Berezovskii's ORT television channel, which backed Putin for president, and Gusinskii's NTV channel, which supported Iavlinskii.

8. This program had proved remarkably resilient throughout the twists and turns of Soviet and post-Soviet history. It was first broadcast during the Khrushchev "thaw" of the early 1960s; and although it was shown only infrequently during the late 1980s, it underwent a revival in the 1990s. Essentially (by design) *KVN* provided a space for amateur artistic and creative performances, although it had also hosted satirical shows, mainly performed by students. At the time of research, the program had become increasingly commercial and akin to "real" show business.

9. It had been possible to receive MTV in some parts of Russia since 1989, but MTV Russia was not launched until September 1998 (after the fieldwork for this project was completed). At the time of writing, it was available to about a third of the Russian population in forty-five cities of the country, but still not in Ul'ianovsk.

10. Respondents could name up to five films they had particularly enjoyed.

11. This research was based on the study of film viewing of young people in Moscow during one month.

12. This film was particularly popular among fifteen to seventeen year olds and among young men.

13. For a more detailed analysis of gender representation—one of the ingredients of the success of the Russkoe radio project—see Shaburov 1999.

14. This is another example of intertextuality, being a play on the (rather unsuccessful) advertising slogan "Bread and Rama were made for each other." Rama is a margarine, which had been extremely heavily advertised on Russian television, in an, unsuccessful, attempt to replace ordinary butter on the Russian market. The saturation of prime time television with this commercial made it particularly unpopular.

15. The proposal by a member of parliament, A. Shakhrai, to limit the number of foreign programs on state-controlled television was made in the same spirit. His proposal involved freeing up 71 percent of television time for domestically produced programs. Viktor Chernomyrdin (then prime minister) rejected the proposal, believing that such limitations would only increase the popularity of Western films.

16. Expenditure on advertising per capita in Russia remained at U.S.$12, however, which was the lowest in Europe (V. Evstaf'ev 1998).

17. "Western-produced" indicates advertisements that were either simply translated or in some way adapted for the Russian market, but nonetheless produced entirely in the West. In print media there was greater parity; around 50 percent of advertising was Russian and 50 percent Western.

18. However, 61 percent of the respondents remained dissatisfied with the way the advertising market in Russia was developing ("U reklamy tozhe est' reiting" 1998).

19. The "most active" users are defined as those who spend at least three hours per week on the Internet. See http://www.monitoring.ru/internet/archive/1999/IV/1/sostav.

20. See, for example, the rave site chat room at http://www.chillout.net.ru.

21. See, for example, http://ravecity.circle.ru/; http://www.samara.ru/~grushinsky.

22. See, for example, http://www.tarunz.org/~vassilii/ru-rock-in-il and http://little-russia.uthscsa.edu/Music/Rock.

23. See, for example, http://www.musica.mustdie.ru.

24. Full details of interviewees are included in the Appendix.

25. This was confirmed by an analysis of readers' letters to the magazines. Readers of *OM* and *Ptiuch*, for example, often categorically demanded that their favorite magazines refuse to promote pop music, threatening that otherwise they would stop buying it. Analysis of concrete youth cultural practice also showed that these kind of "progressive" young people interpreted mass appeal ("poppiness") to pose a threat to their cultural space (see Chapter 7).

26. Editors themselves tended to avoid this label for fear of limiting their readership and deterring new readers through a pretension to exclusivity. On the contrary, these interviewees framed their exclusive interests as universal ones and portrayed their "struggle" against pop as an inevitable price of their mission to enlighten. *OM* and *Ptiuch*, however, clearly fell within this

category, as did a number of more specific youth publications (for bikers, heavy metal fans, and so on).

27. Despite this magazine's editor assurances that the magazine was for everybody, in this statement he expressly defined it as being for young men.

28. These singers are among the best-known figures in contemporary Russian pop.

29. In the case of *OM* for example, despite the fact that the magazine's authors and editors strenuously denied the fact, the magazine appeared to target a gay male audience.

30. As a rule, of course, editors who suggested this were referring to rival publications rather than their own magazines.

31. One example of a "norm" in the West which was considered not to work in Russia was the widespread use of youth media to promote sex education, or as the editor-in-chief of *OM* phrased it, "teaching schoolchildren to put a condom on a banana with a straight face," which, he claimed, would be totally impossible in Russia.

32. Indeed, the idea of "common advertising" has proven to be very tenacious. The view of many advertising executives at the Eighth International Moscow Festival of Advertising (1998) was that "a good advertisement" would be understood in any country.

33. However, the cultural sensitivity of marketing of the product as something to be eaten "with vodka" has been questioned, since vodka in Russia is drunk on its own or with gherkins or herring and onion, certainly never with pancakes ("Taking It to the Buyer" 1996).

34. The first two drinks are made by Pepsi, the second two by Coca-Cola.

35. An example of this approach in youth-oriented advertising could be seen in Fanta ads.

36. *Eralash* is a series of short, comic television films about the lives of children and teenagers. It remained popular, although it had been broadcast since Soviet times.

37. This character in a military hat represents a member of the light cavalry in the prerevolutionary Russian army. Its reference was to the 1812 war when starving Russian light cavalry men demanded food from the local French population *bystro* (quickly). The term *bistro*, to mean a place to eat quickly, is said to be derived from the French appropriation of the Russian term.

38. This, it was suggested, might make people remember the product, but would certainly not instill brand loyalty (Igor' Krylov, Russian Association of Advertising Agencies; Oleg Stukalov, ORT-reklama).

Chapter 3

1. The youth magazines analyzed were *OM*, *Ptiuch*, *Rovesnik*, *Shtuchka*, *Spid-Info*, *Sobesednik*, *Ia Molodoi*, *Aida*, *COOL!*, and *Cosmopolitan*. The term "magazine" is used throughout, although it should be noted that *Spid-Info*, *Ia Molodoi*, and *Sobesednik* are produced in a newspaper format. The main period of analysis was from April 1996 to June 1998, although some magazines were not available during the whole of this period. Details of the periods of analysis for the individual magazines are included in the Appendix, see Table A.1.

2. The youth television programs analyzed were *Do 16 i Starshe*, *Rok-*

Urok, *Tin-Tonik*, *Dzhem*, and *Tet-a-Tet* for the period 10 October–10 November 1996. Had the study been conducted at the time of writing, radio would have made a useful contrast, however, the revival of youth use of radio occurred after the empirical work for this study was complete.

3. Youth-targeted advertising was studied by analyzing those commercials shown before, after, and between youth programs on the main Russian TV channel ORT during the period 10 October–10 November 1996. This was supplemented by the analysis of all commercials shown during a period of four days (12–18 September 1997) on the two main Russian TV channels—ORT and Rossiia.

4. Although television and magazines were both widely used media among Russian youth (see Diagram 2.1), the very different foci of individual youth television programs and the fact that they often ran nonconcurrently made them a difficult medium to analyze systematically. Youth-targeted programs tended to be watched primarily by the younger cohort (15–17 year olds) of the age group being studied, the most popular programs among youth were not "youth" programs at all, and the vast majority of those watching programs "frequently" or "sometimes" in fact watched them only "sometimes." For these reasons, the content analysis focused on Russian youth magazines.

5. "Global" images included scenes of young people enjoying a range of leisure activities (in discos, bars, at the beach, in the street) as used, for example, in commercials for Wrigley's and Holsten beer. Other global images focused on general scenes of family life, the workplace, and the outdoors (e.g., Head and Shoulders, Timotei, Johnson and Johnson).

6. *Spid-Info* and *Sobesednik* were ranked first and third in terms of how frequently they were read by young people according to the representative survey of youth in Samara and Ul'ianovsk (see Diagram 2.3).

7. "House music" is a dance music that originated in the New York underground disco scene of the early 1970s and the Chicago gay clubs of the late 1970s.

8. "Trip-hop" is a non-dance electronic music style that originated in Bristol in the mid-1990s. Its sound is epitomized in the music of the bands Portishead and Massive Attack. "Jungle" music derives its name from the Tivoli Gardens area of Kingston, Jamaica, known as "the jungle." It emerged as a musical subgenre in London in 1991 and was sustained through the early 1990s as an underground music before achieving mass-market success in 1994 (Back 1996, 232–33). "Speed garage," also known as "UK garage," emerged in 1993 and became widely known in 1996–97. It combines traditional garage music—a mellower and more vocal strain of house music—with a heavy bass line.

9. *Rovesnik* wrote primarily about British and American rock, and although the magazine referred to other countries such as Australia and South America, there was almost a complete absence of any discussion of Russian rock.

10. Gabber is an extremely hard, dark, and fast subgenre of techno associated with the Rotterdam scene (Monroe 1999, 148).

11. On the Russian scene "hard core" refers to hardcore-techno, understood as hard, fast, and purely instru-

mental electronic music that emerged in the early 1990s.

12. "Goa trance" is a form of electronic dance music originating on the beaches of Goa (India) in the mid 1980s. It became a world phenomenon in the early 1990s.

13. Mumii Troll' was discussed in *OM* in the context of the band's relationship to Britpop and British culture. The group originated in Vladivostok, recorded its music in London, and enjoyed widespread popularity in the Russian Federation.

14. When the discussion moved to commercial rock and pop, the boundary was less clear, and thus in magazines such as *Spid Info* and *Sobesednik*, *Ia Molodoi*, *Aida*, and *COOL!*, such divisions were less apparent.

15. Russian rock was rarely discussed in *Rovesnik*. *OM* and *Ia Molodoi* did refer to it on occasion but primarily to note its "difference." *Ia Molodoi*, for example, stated that Russian rock was not at all similar to Western "types" of rock (*Ia Molodoi*, May 1998, 5).

16. Two of the five television programs analyzed were music programs—*Rok Urok* and *Dzhem*. *Rok Urok* was interview based, usually with a Russian (pop) artist, while *Dhzem* provided information and music clips from primarily Western rock artists.

17. The most famous of these was DJ Vadim, a Russian DJ based in London. Vadim, however, had left Russia at the age of four and despite claims that his Russian background meant he felt "less compelled to conform to the values given by the music industry . . . than if I was English" (Schaefer 1998), he could not really be considered a Russian "export" to the West.

18. While the discussion of music in these two journals presented Russia as a producer in and contributor to the global music scene, when fashion and style were discussed, the West was always the sole site of production.

19. At the end of the 1990s, there were a growing number of second-hand "charity" shops where designer clothes from Europe could be found.

20. This did not rule out influence from the East on the global fashion industry. The recent success of Japanese designers in providing new styles for a marketplace tired of the Western fashion industry, was noted, for example.

21. Frequent reference was made to the serial *Santa Barbara*, which was broadcast in forty-eight countries around the world including Russia. The series ceased to be broadcast in Russia following the August financial crisis because of financial constraints upon the Russian television company Rossiia.

22. VIVA-2 was only available on satellite TV.

23. *Disk-kanal* was not shown in Ul'ianovsk. It had previously been shown in Samara on TV-6, but at the time of research it was available only in Moscow.

24. Readers' letters printed in both *Ptiuch* and *OM* illustrated its importance for young people in the regions whose own access to the club scene was limited but who viewed the magazines as important channels for distributing information and providing horizontal links to other "similar" youth in different regions of Russia.

25. Across all the magazines the only foreign language used was English.

26. The analysis of word usage for the magazines covered the following periods: *Sobesednik*, nos. 42, 46,

49–50 (1996); no. 33 (1997); nos. 5, 21 (1998); *Shtuchka*, nos. 1, 2 (1996); nos. 2, 7, 9, 10 (1997); nos. 2, 6, (1998); *Cosmo*, March, June, December (1996); June (1997); January (1998); *Aida*, nos. 8, 9, 12 (1997); *Rovesnik*, nos. 3, 4, 7, 11 (1996); nos. 3, 6, 7, 9, 10 (1997); no. 4 (1998); *Ia Molodoi*, nos. 36, 40, (1997); nos. 1, 2, 6, 10, 14, 18, 19 (1998); *OM*, April/May, July/August, October/November (1996); January/February, April, July/August, October (1997); January, May (1998); and *Ptiuch*, nos. 1, 8, 9, 11 (1996); nos. 1/2, 4, 5, 10, (1997); nos. 1, 5 (1998). *Spid-Info* was not included in the analysis because of the almost complete absence of English language usage. The English words or expressions were counted for every article in the publication and the orientation of the article (Western, Russian, Eastern, mixed, neutral) where the word or expression was located was noted. The words and expressions were then tabulated and arranged according to the context in which they were located (i.e., music, art, business, sexuality, gender, mass media, and so on).

27. Although most words borrowed from English were rendered into Cyrillic script, sometimes they were written in Latin script. Quotation marks are used here to indicate where Latin script was used in the magazine.

28. There were no page numbers in this issue of the magazine.

29. Although *Cosmopolitan* is an American magazine, the magazine published in Russia was a Russian variant, not just a translated version (a policy of the magazine worldwide).

30. *OM* and *Ptiuch* demonstrated a cynical attitude to any traditional, accepted values, not only those associated with American society.

31. The view that in the West, but particularly America, any "normal" interaction between a man and a woman might be construed as "sexual harassment" was widespread.

32. The articles relating to American youth in *Rovesnik* were all translated versions of articles written by English or American authors.

33. The aim of new American music was seen by *OM* as being to deconstruct established American values. The new alternative cinema, where money was no longer the main concern, was seen as the champion of previously marginalized groups in society.

34. The magazine *Sobesednik* presented no coherent image of Britain, but contained random references to unconnected themes.

35. Thus, in *Ptiuch* and *OM*, New York was presented favorably in relation to America but unfavorably in relation to London.

36. The analysis of the magazines was conducted in the period immediately following the release of *Trainspotting*.

37. The response to the death of Princess Diana received substantial attention in the magazines.

38. In a more positive tone, the magazine also referred to everyday, normal British youth—as free and independent, sexually liberated, but with a serious attitude toward their education, career prospects, and money.

39. Diagram 3.1 indicates the proportion of articles in each magazines with a Western, Russian, and Eastern focus.

40. Advertising also rarely employed images of the East; the youth-targeted television advertising analyzed showed just 4 percent of commercials contained an image related to the East.

41. In the descriptions of Hong Kong, a clear distinction was drawn between Hong Kong City and the provinces, which were seen as being under the influence of Chinese ideology (*Ptiuch* 1998, no. 1, 45).

42. Russian images were used in 27 percent of television advertisements analyzed in the research, although mainly to sell Western products (e.g. Mars and Sprite).

43. *OM* and *Ptiuch* (which mainly referred to Britain) distinguished between different parts of the West in their discussion of gender and sexuality. Other publications, however, tended to refer to "Western" practices in more general terms.

44. Numerous publications referred to a trend toward Western men seeking Russian wives, who would have the qualities lacked by contemporary Western women (*Rovesnik*, *Sobesednik*).

45. The cases cited concerned incidents when, subsequently, children had been abused.

Chapter 4

1. All respondents participating in in-depth interviews or focus groups were asked to complete a short questionnaire about their sociodemographic background. These details were entered into an ACCESS database, and each respondent was assigned a number in that database. It is these numbers that are cited after quotations from interviews or focus groups alongside the city in which the respondent was interviewed.

2. See Diagram 2.1 and Chapter 2 for further discussion of sources of information about the West.

3. The concepts of "them," "over there," and "where they live" were used by virtually all respondents in the first instance to define attitudes toward the West. While such terms were undoubtedly products of the Soviet era, they echoed less Soviet *ideology* than they reflected the absence of reliable information about the West in the Soviet period. Without such real knowledge, identities became reduced to the most primitive level of "us" and "them" (*svoi* and *chuzhie*).

4. At the time of research, many Russian textbooks continued to carry remnants of Soviet ideology especially in the fields of history (where the place of the history of the CPSU remained unclear), in literature (where the list of writers and poets for study had been retained from the Soviet period), and in social sciences.

5. This study considers the changing nature of images of the West in their specific sociocultural contexts; any consideration of the psychological mechanisms, origins, and means by which primary stereotypes and images are formed lies beyond the scope of the study.

6. The table includes only those countries or regions selected by a significant number of respondents. Totals do not add up to 100 percent because the "don't knows" are omitted. North America, Japan, Australia, and Eastern Europe were considered to "belong to the West" by respondents from Samara more often than they were by respondents from Ul'ianovsk.

7. The qualitative data suggested that respondents associated first of all the United States, second Europe, and third England with the West in general. This priority of association differed slightly from the quantitative data. The absence of England from the latter is explained simply by the absence of this option in a closed question. The inver-

sion of the primacy of America and Western Europe, however, is probably explained by the fact that qualitative research was conducted in Ul'ianovsk, Samara, and Moscow, while the questionnaire survey was carried out in Ul'ianovsk and Samara only.

8. This remark was made during a focus group, in response to a video clip by the group Savage Garden set in an unidentified European city.

9. The term "abroad" was used more often with reference to Western Europe than to the United States.

10. The exception to this rule was the reference by a number of respondents to the persistence of racial tensions in the West (usually the United States).

11. Some respondents noted the diversity of people in the West (51, Moscow; 72, Moscow). Others, though, subscribed to the view that people were "the same everywhere," especially "rich" or "elite" sections of society.

12. Only one respondent defended Western people in this respect (65, Moscow).

13. This comment was made during a focus group in response to video clips of the Spice Girls and the Russian girl band Blestiashchie.

14. A number of commercials and video clips involved couples and romance narratives (see Appendix for details) and provoked discussion of gender relations.

15. This was said during a focus group in response to video clips of the bands Savage Garden and All 4 One.

16. This remark was made during a focus group and with reference to a video clip by Savage Garden.

17. A remark made after watching a commercial for the shampoo and conditioner Wash and Go during a focus group.

18. A remark made after watching a commercial for Harley Davidson aftershave during a focus group.

19. This remark was a response to\ the video clip by Savage Garden during a focus group.

20. The numbers shown in parentheses represent the total number of times these or equivalent qualities were mentioned in answer to the open question: "Name the five qualities which you think best describe Western women."

21. This remark was prompted by the video clip by Blestiashchie.

22. This remark was made during a focus group following a video clip by the Spice Girls.

23. It was only for men that "business-like" qualities were interpreted as unambiguously positive, however.

24. This remark was made during a focus group in response to a commercial for Sprite.

25. Although in most cases this was noted in an approving way, positive comments about Russian women's ability to always look as if they were going out no matter what their circumstances appear to contradict this.

26. For some respondents this film was about all teenagers, for others it was a clear example of how and why their own parties differed from those in the West.

27. It should be noted that Ul'ianovsk respondents most frequently evaluated Western parties in this way.

28. This rejection of the low-key approach of young Westerners might be conditioned by both traditional Russian village attitudes to "going out in style, wholeheartedly" [guliania na vsiu katushku i ot vsei dushi] and the painstaking preparation of Soviet mass

celebrations "designed" for (compulsory) shared enjoyment.

29. The full list of countries mentioned spontaneously by respondents when describing their images of the West in in-depth interviews was the United States, England, France, Germany, Greece, Ireland, Finland, Belgium, Italy, Switzerland, Sweden, Spain, Canada, and Turkey.

30. It is worth noting that images of America recounted during focus groups (in response to visual and audio stimuli) were significantly more positive than spontaneous references emerging during in-depth interviews.

31. This relates specifically to the low-grade American films which overwhelmed Russian screens at the end of the 1980s and beginning of the 1990s and consisted of predominantly violent action movies featuring scenes from mafia life and street fighting.

32. This respondent of course reproduces racial stereotypes while seeking to critique the state of race relations in the United States.

33. Given the growing number of young Russians seeking education in America, this disparaging attitude would appear to act as a defense mechanism to some degree. Articles in the press reinforced the image, however, drawing on comparative research that suggested that Russian pupils outperformed American, and the majority of European, children in mathematics and natural sciences ("Dognali i peregnali Ameriku" 1997).

34. In particular England was perceived to be "like Russia" in controlling young people, whereas Germany was closer to America in allowing them a great deal of freedom.

35. This was a representative survey of young people across twelve economic regions of the Russian Federation. It employed control groups of members of the older generation (excluding pensioners) to illuminate peculiarities in youth attitudes.

36. These findings were broadly in line with those for the older generation, although they suggested that young people were slightly more kindly disposed toward America; 24 percent of the older generation considered America to be "hostile," whereas 9 percent considered America to be a "friendly" state.

37. In addition to the reasons noted above for the prominence of England in respondents' narratives, it is also worth remembering that although all interviews were conducted in Russian, the interviewer was often British.

38. This remark was made during a focus group discussion of a video clip by the Spice Girls.

39. Interestingly enough, this order of preference was the same for the control group of adults surveyed (although the absolute proportions of people wishing to travel abroad were lower).

40. This finding confirms what Liebes and Katz found in their study of the readings of the television series *Dallas* by ethnic Russians. In their comparative study of different national groups, Russians (living in Israel) were the only ethnic group interviewed to "retell" episodes according to themes (as opposed to plot development). This was interpreted by the authors as evidence of the Russians' "feeling that the program is about messages of capitalism which serve the hegemonic interests of the producers or of American society" (Liebes and Katz 1993, 75).

Chapter 5

1. "Global" and "Western" are used as loosely interchangeable in this chap-

ter, recognizing, as Taylor notes, that although the United States "is beginning to share its core status with other areas, the globally influential *cultural* cores remain largely in the U.S." (Taylor 1997, 199). The specific contents of "global" and "Western" images, as perceived by both image makers and consumers, are discussed in Chapters 2 and 3.

2. This chapter was written by Hilary Pilkington but comments on a first draft as well as updates on the youth scene in Samara and Ul'ianovsk by Elena Starkova have been incorporated by the author.

3. "Peripheral" is used here to indicate a scene that lies beyond those of late-modern Western societies. It is the latter that are generally considered to be culture producers rather than receivers, and upon the study of which "post-subcultural" theory is being developed.

4. In fact, since respondents were specifically asked about their leisure time activities, their friends and the places they hung out, Diagrams 5.1–5.3 represent not all of the cultural space young people inhabit, but that part which is relatively uncontrolled by the social institutions that shape their lives (school, college, family, workplace). Although the authors consider domestic, work, and educational spaces important (possibly the most important) sites of youth existence, they anticipated a *continuity* between "domestic," "work/school," and "youth cultural" spheres of life rather than any use of the youth cultural sphere to undermine or rupture the "dominant" culture.

5. Respondents were not selected by sample but accessed by visiting a broad range of sites used by young people for leisure, such as the street or yard (*dvor*), organized after-school activities (sports clubs or training sessions, aerobics and "shaping" classes, modeling courses, choral and skating groups, after-school civic education courses), cafes, discos, nightclubs, well-known *tusovka* sites (squares, yards, underground stations, cafes), pop and rock concerts, folk (*KSP, Klub Samodeiatel'noi Pesni*) clubs and young ramblers groups (*turisty*), schools, and colleges. Personal contacts of the researchers were used initially to establish the key *tusovka* sites in each city and, in some instances, to locate individuals who could act as informants and guides. Some contacts were "blind" (turning up at a club, concert, cafe or other site of "hanging out," meeting people and arranging interviews for another time), some came via contacts (individuals already known, contacts given), some came from "natural" acquaintances made while hanging out at clubs and cafes, and a few ensued from more formal arrangements (visits to colleges or schools). A broad gender balance was sought alongside an equal representation of those interviewed from school, *dvor*, or formal leisure organizations and those from *tusovki* sites, cafes, and clubs. Despite the danger of pre-classifying respondents in this way, such a strategy was important to ensure that the research did not become skewed toward *tusovka* respondents who tended to be easier to "access" and more willing to introduce researchers to other potential respondents.

6. In the course of the research, 134 in-depth interviews, with a total of 107 respondents, were conducted (twenty-seven respondents engaged in repeat interviews). Nineteen focus

groups, exploring responses to Western and Russian music videos and excerpts from films popular among youth, were also held. Further details on the composition and content of these focus groups are contained in the Appendix.

7. The maps remain, of necessity, incomplete and uneven, since the prioritization of validity over representa-tiveness in the conceptual frame of the research meant only those groups in which our respondents participated, or with whom they had close (friendly or hostile) contacts, were mapped.

8. Kharkhordin, for example, suggests that informal groups were very close to Dick Hebdige's conception of subculture, although Soviet subcultures had to adopt a more formalized existence—usually as "clubs"—in order to keep up an appropriate public appearance (Kharkhordin 1999, 316).

9. This approach is reminiscent of the current debate on globalization (see Chapter 1). A key difference between the two debates is that alternative approaches to the dominant critique of globalization can be found and there is open access to Western literatures with quite different perspectives.

10. The plausibility of reappropriating the term "subculture" was achieved by distinguishing "counterculture" from "subculture." The former was used to refer to those cultural formations in the West in the 1960s which constituted a "conscious opposition to norms and ways of the dominant culture," while "subculture" was used more widely to define cultural communities—*kul'turnaia obshchnost'* (Kuchmaeva 1987, 5–7)—which existed and functioned within culture as a *normal* part of it (Matveeva 1987, 16). The term "subculture," in this way, could be utilized to classify different groups in society according to their ways or styles of life, with the proviso that socially threatening subcultures such as fascist movements, terrorist groups, and subcultures of declassed elements of society (criminals, idlers, and "psychedelic subcultures") were declared to be unacceptable to society (Orlova 1987, 8). Since these ways of life were seen to be born of common interests rather than class position, the acknowledgment of the existence of subcultures did not challenge the accepted version of the fundamental social structure of Soviet society. In fact it was fully consistent with the emphasis during perestroika on the need to identify and harness different professional interests for the general improvement of the economy.

11. This conceptualization was adopted not only by mainstream Soviet sociologists but also by those engaged in the critical interpretation of the relationship between youth and the "dominant culture." The latter interpreted youth cultural practice as shaping an alternative "nonofficial" sphere to which young people "escaped" and "evaded" the unwelcome interventions of the state and its ideology.

12. The classifications related to the degree to which the practice of the groups engaged with the tasks of reconstructing socialism.

13. *Tusovki* are centrally located, often style-based youth cultural formations, which became particularly visible in urban centers in the late 1980s. Their members are not necessarily from privileged backgrounds but their claiming of space in the center of cities signifies an upwardly and outwardly oriented strategy, and desire to escape the territorial gang formations of the periphery.

14. This is defined by Yurchak as "ironic treatment of ideological symbols, but so subtle was the ridicule that it was often almost impossible to tell whether the symbols were supported or subverted" (Yurchak 1999, 84)

15. Yurchak's inclusion in this category suggests that it is not strictly a matter of a "Western" approach but that of an outsider's gaze; in Yurchak's case this is a product of an anthropological approach.

16. The volumes are quite different in nature. The Omel'chenko text—written four years before its publication date—was intentionally designed primarily to introduce Russian students to original English-language texts on the theory of youth culture and subculture. The other two volumes are more empirically oriented and contain case studies of a number of post-Soviet youth "subcultures," including Slavic neo-paganists, Indianists, Tolkienist and other role playing gamers, Buddhists, squatters, football fans, Aikdoists, naturists, Sorokomany, hippies, students, and far-right political groups.

17. The edited volume in which these texts appear, however, suffers from a rather mechanistic analysis of "subcultures" as constituted in a number of perceived characteristics—possession of distinct rituals, language, mythology, internal structure—and adopts a functionalist notion of subcultural identities as little more than alternative "scripts" for youth socialization.

18. The subculture—being an extension of the peer group—is seen to act as an alternative development route to the construction of an integrated "fixed" sense of self in society which will later facilitate the discarding of the alternative identity which is "no longer them."

19. Muggleton is developing an "ideal type" here; his own empirical work only partially confirms these hypotheses.

20. Hereafter, for stylistic reasons, these terms are used without quotation marks. At all times, however, the terms are used in the way young people themselves used them. Thus, for example, "normal" indicates "ordinary," that is, unexceptional not nondevient.

21. The absence of skinheads in smaller industrial cities where "new Russians" were also relatively rare was confirmed by Tarasov (Tarasov 2000a, 50).

22. A similar classification ("romantic-escapist subcultures") is employed by Islamshina and colleagues (1997, 72).

23. Although respondents were not specifically asked about participation in organized religion, in Ul'ianovsk such practice was mentioned spontaneously as a site of youth cultural practice in relation to both orthodoxy ("the church circle") and Buddhist groups (*buddisty*). Although the association of those involved in religious groups with other groups of "romantics" might appear logical, given their common concern with the spiritual as opposed to the material aspects of life, it was not repeated elsewhere. In Samara, for example, the only spontaneous mention of religious groups was an articulated antipathy to a "Christian Students group" on the part of respondents involved in the bard movement (also positioned within the "romantics").

24. One respondent, who had been involved in the movement for a number of years, classified the games movement as having three constituent parts: open-air games where teams act out either a

historical event (such as the Hundred Years' War) or some work of fantasy (Tolkien or a self-constructed fantasy); indoor games such as *Dungeons and Dragons*; and historical reconstructions of daily life or battles, conducted primarily by chivalry clubs.

25. Gatherings of Tolkien followers had a relatively long history in Russia and were nationally organized. The first Hobbit Games were organized by the official All-Union Council of Clubs of Fantasy Lovers and has been an annual national summer event since 1990 (Rayport Rabodzeenko 1998, 402).

26. This was a club that involved children in fencing, sailing, and chivalry.

27. *Gopniki* was not a term of self-identification but one used (mainly by "alternative" youth) to refer to provincial (or capital peripheral) "louts" who gathered around the courtyard of their blocks of flats, close to their school, or in the basements of houses. *Gopniki* were antagonistically disposed toward "alternative" (*tusovka*) youth, and this often brought the two groups into physical conflict.

28. *Fen'ki* are woven bands worn around the wrist and traditionally associated with the hippie or *Sistema* movement in Russia, although now the term may be applied to a range of youth cultural accessories.

29. *Satanisty* primarily inhabited the world of "doom" and "black" rock and metal music; see, for example, the Samara-based web site http://www.musica.mustdie.ru.

30. Valerii Grushin, after whom the festival is named, was a great fan of Russian folk music (*avtorskaia pesnia*) and the "promoter" and organizer of the Samara trio Poiushchie bobry (The Singing Beavers).

31. The festival celebrated its thirtieth anniversary in 1998. In 1999, 362 groups and singers participated in the festival (see: http://www.samara.ru/~grushinsky/).

32. In addition to the weekly club meetings at which invited singer songwriters performed and talked about their music and songs, there were regular bard concerts in the city.

33. The bard movement was characterized by a generational continuity unusual for other parts of the scene, however; a number of respondents noted that their parents had been involved in the movement as well.

34. He estimated the number in Samara to be "a few hundred."

35. In particular the anti-Caucasian policy in Moscow following the shelling of parliament in October 1993 and the subsequent military action against Chechnya.

36. By February 2001, Tarasov's estimate of the number of skinheads in Moscow had risen to 3,500–3,800. An attack on a market near Tsarytsino metro station by 400 young people—mainly football fans and skins—on 30 October 2001 confirms the growing skinhead activity in Moscow. Three people were killed in the attack.

37. For this reason, members of the group expressed great concern about being involved in any kind of group interview in case a false "collective view" was elicited from it.

38. Although the Russian rave scene had its origins in St. Petersburg, a series of rave parties in Moscow from 1991 shifted the center of the scene to the capital. See Yurchak 1999 for a detailed account of the formation of the club scene in Russia.

39. The club scene changed rapidly as individual clubs opened, closed, and

often reopened again overnight. The clubs referred to here were those being frequented by young people in Moscow in January 1998, Samara in April 1998, and Ul'ianovsk in September–October 1997.

40. This is a light, commercial variant of house that came to Russia primarily via Germany, where it was the most popular dance music in 1993–94.

41. At the time of fieldwork "Russian jungle" was being promoted in particular by DJs Dan and Groove via the project "Storm Crew"; by the end of the fieldwork these DJs were already considered to have become "commercial."

42. A British-based dance music of the late 1990s based on jungle beats.

43. See Chapter 3, note 10.

44. See Chapter 3, note 11.

45. An early subgenre of techno, which became particularly popular on the Frankfurt and London (in its popular Goan variant) club scenes (Monroe 1999, 148).

46. This was housed in clubs such as Krizis Zhenra, Vermel', 4 komnati, Ne bei kopytom, and Propaganda, which prided themselves on providing a space for live bands to play and a relaxed, unthreatening, even semi-intelligentsia atmosphere.

47. The gay scene in January 1998 was found in the clubs Shans, Chameleon, Kino Imperiia, and increasingly, Luch, while the expatriate scene was centered in the infamous Canadian-owned Golodnaia Utka and the more expensive Mankheten Ekspress.

48. Such systems allowed the club management to restrict access to those in possession of distributed fliers and those considered suitable clientele at the door. I discuss this further in Chapter 7.

49. This was reported in an interview with an Ul'ianovsk DJ, who had recently returned from Moscow, in July 1999.

50. Of these subdivisions, the junglists were seen to be the most concerned with "being cool," while the hard core listeners were often looked down on by other dance scene members.

51. All clubs in Samara also operated special rates for students via a "student disco card" scheme.

52. Both Aladdin and Tornado have since closed but two new clubs subsequently opened, taking both managers and crowds from the former. Mapping a rapidly changing club scene was further complicated in Russia by the tendency of clubs to close during the summer; during the summer of 1999 only two established clubs—Dzhungli and Aisberg—were open in Samara.

53. One example was the Apix located in the Kirov House of Culture in Bezymianka district.

54. The fact that this was seen as a "way of life" is evident in the frequent reference to the club and dance scene as "techno-culture" (*tekhno-kul'tura*).

55. Fieldwork was conducted in Ul'ianovsk in September–October 1997. Since then, Sensatsiia and Pilot have closed although a new club—Orbit—replaced the latter in the new city (situated on the opposite side of the Volga river from all the other clubs). U Ivanoff remained open but had begun to cater primarily to students, while a new club for those with money opened in autumn 1998 (Nautilus). Paradoxically—since it catered to a musically unsophisticated but wealthy crowd—Nautilus was the only club in the city to have turntables as well as compact disk players.

56. The term "clubbers" (*klabera*) used in Samara, for example, was not current among respondents in Ul'ianovsk.

57. In autumn 1997 even these makeshift discos and clubs were under threat from a new directive from the regional governor, who sought to return the buildings to their original uses.

58. Leading DJs from Samara had participated in an intercity festival held at the U Ivanoff club in January 1998. Sponsorship by companies had facilitated a number of dance events in the city, and beginning in the summer of 1998 a magazine devoted to club and youth life in the city began to be published periodically.

59. Maffesoli, drawing on the linguistic research of Berque, suggests that cultures may be lococentric—where the immediate surroundings or context are paramount—or egocentric—where the individual's identity and her/his actions take on a primary significance (Maffesoli 1996, 138).

60. This was less true of Moscow, where identities such as "raver" and "rapper" had become so mainstream that they marked the basic division between Moscow peripheral youth. This is discussed in the following section of the chapter.

61. *Byk* is literally a male horned animal, but was used colloquially to refer to brainless "toughs" usually involved in small-scale semi- or illegal economic activities.

62. A common synonym for *gopniki* in Moscow has always been *urla*, and this would appear to be true also of St. Petersburg; Aleksandr Fain refers to the city's many "*urlovie*" *tusovki*, which are becoming increasingly integrated into semicriminal commerce (Shul'gina 1996, 26). At the end of the 1990s, the term was still used in Moscow but not encountered in the provincial cities of the study.

63. This was a practice, which had evolved out of traditional village against village and *dvor* versus *dvor* fighting.

64. This practice reached its height in the late 1980s and is best expressed by the youth slang *naezdy* (*naekhat'*), or "picking a fight," "giving grief" to those perceived to be "different."

65. *Byki*, although frequenting expensive night clubs, are not depicted as overlapping with the dance or club scene (see Diagram 5.3), since their use of clubs was not related to any interest in dance music.

66. This term was used to signify tough, small-time racketeers or other "businessmen" somewhere in the process of moving from ordinary *gopniki* to the better heeled, but equally "uncultured," *byki*. In Samara "iz brigad" was used rarely, being replaced by the term "lysie," which referred to "hard" young men whose close cropped hair signified an anti-*neformal* disposition but who were more "grown up" than the average *gopnik*.

67. There was less readiness to identify all those with money as anti-*neformaly* in Samara and Moscow where the term *bogatie* ("the rich") was used sometimes in a relatively value-free context.

68. Tamagochi are virtual pets—able to eat, sleep, and play—originally invented by the Japanese toy company Bandai.

69. Heavy metal fans, in particular, were caricatured as people who got drunk and then engaged in "mad dancing" (215, Samara; 230, Samara).

70. Although one seventeen-year-old rapper from Samara said he had partic-

ipated in conflicts between rappers and punks and *metallisty* when the former had been insulted by the punks (242, Samara).

71. This adopted "blackness" is a common, though not the only, form of engagement with hip hop among white European youth. See Bennett 2000, 150–65.

72. As with many other youth cultural groups the plural form may be indicated in the usual way with an "y" or, more colloquially, with an "a" (e.g., *rokery/rokera*, *liubery/liubera*).

73. The term *kislotniki* (literally "acid heads") (see Diagram 5.1) referred more to dress style (bright colors) than to drug use.

74. The emergence of mainstream "ravers" alongside cool "clubbers" mirrors a pattern on the British club scene from mid 1989 when, in Sarah Thornton's words, there emerged "a second-wave of media-inspired, sheep-like acid house fans" (Thornton 1997, 205). However, the degree of slippage in the term "ravers" in Russia has been remarkable; in just a couple of years a term which described the trendiest youth of Moscow and St. Petersburg (Yurchak 1999, 77) had reconstituted itself at the *gopnik* end of the dance scene.

75. Indeed, there were also antagonisms between *neformaly* in the 1980s when bikers and rock fans (*rokery*) reportedly picked fights (*naekhali*) with those groups they could easily dominate (Pilkington 1994, 271–76).

76. For example, whereas clubbers played down the necessity of dancing well or looking the part, rappers, break beat, and hip hop youth engaged in the dancing competitions (*peretantsovki*), which had been central to the early hip hop culture of New York (Stapleton 1998, 220).

Chapter 6

1. Young people in Ul'ianovsk were slightly more likely to spend time at friends' houses and in "entrance ways," while young people in Samara were somewhat more prone to spending time in organized sports sections and clubs, but also "on the street with friends."

2. A process which Maffesoli refers to as one of the "disindividuation" of postmodern society (Maffesoli 1996, 6). There is an apparent contradiction between this and Beck's understanding of late-modern society as being characterized by "individualization." If one understands Maffesol, he is talking about agency (cultural response), while Beck is referring to the social environment in which subjects move, then the apparent contradiction between the two is diminished.

3. That is the removal of "collective" support mechanisms (extended family, work or union collectives, social organizations, state welfare, class or community collectivities), which traditionally mediated these risks.

4. The forms taken by this embodied communication are discussed in more detail in Chapter 7.

5. *Otaku* was a term coined in the mid 1980s to describe an emergent type of technologically highly skilled but socially inept young person in Japan who spent large amounts of time at home engaged in or seeking information about his/her particular interest, usually anime (cartoons), manga (comic books), video games, or teen-idols (Grassmuck 1999).

6. Indeed, these circles need not be mutually compatible; young graduates, especially, often distinguished between "intellectual" and other acquaintances (57, Moscow; 223, Samara; 224, Samara).

7. For some progressives, "friends" and *tusovka* were incompatible and characterized by mutual jealousy. This was especially true of clubbers, possibly because of the greater importance of "image" among club *tusovki* (251, Ul'ianovsk). Among rock *tusovki*, and among older respondents, however, there appeared to be less tension. Such respondents even noted that long-term close friends might emerge out of the *tusovka* (4, Ul'ianovsk; 220, Samara; 32, Ul'ianovsk) or that different friendship circles had successfully "merged" (221, Samara).

8. In the case of newly urban youth, this "home" might be the home village (235, Samara).

9. The porous border between progressive and normal strategies was evident, however, in a number of respondents' descriptions of their communicative practice and friendship groups. Two respondents, who in other respects adopted normal strategies, had friends from across the city based on common interests or attitudes rather than location (238, Samara; 12, Ul'ianovsk). In two instances respondents noted that their friends were older than themselves and already in higher education or working in private business (238, Samara; 27, Ul'ianovsk); such friends appeared to give young people access to the wider (albeit mainstream as opposed to youth cultural) world in a similar way to the *tusovka* for progressive youth.

10. The "Samara Corporation of Street Dance" (*Samarskaia Korporatsiia Ulichnikh Tantsev, SKUT*) developed out of the initiative of the breakdance group in Samara mentioned above.

11. This, she explained, was the result of the coincidence of two unusual factors: a very large crowd (100) having turned up; and the run up to Moscow's 850th anniversary celebrations.

12. Alongside the problem of young people not being able to afford expensive drinks and meals, the clubs had to pay for security and safety personnel and lost up to 15 percent of their profits in "cover" (*krysha*) payments against extortion from organized criminals.

13. Even the entrance to the club was threatening; it was not until you had passed the bouncers and were inside that you were among your own (237, Samara).

14. A number of progressives (all young men) retained strong connections with the *dvor* group. One respondent from Samara described how he moved between *tusovka* and *dvor* groups, sitting with the *dvor* group in the yard when he had nothing else planned for the evening, and, in the summer, dragging them out to discos especially at local summer resorts and parks (230, Samara).

15. Although Diagram 6.1 shows the average attendance across weekdays and weekends, the single greatest difference in leisure practice shown by the representative survey of young people in Ul'ianovsk and Samara was that between how weekdays and weekends or holidays were spent; across all sections of respondents, young people were more than twice as likely to go to discos on the weekend than during the week.

16. This is a gender difference that cuts across progressive and normal strategies (see Chapter 7).

17. As indeed did a number of the younger progressive respondents from Ul'ianovsk (37, Ul'ianovsk; 38, Ul'ianovsk; 39, Ul'ianovsk).

18. It is in autumn when domestic obligations are most likely to encroach, especially since everyone in the family has to pitch in to gather the harvest from the dacha (4, Ul'ianovsk; 13, Ul'ianovsk).

19. Although another noted that one benefit of living at home was that, unlike in a student hostel, there was always somebody to open the door, no matter what hour of the morning you returned (237, Samara).

20. All respondents involved in martial arts were male, although one kickboxing trainer interviewed said he did have one girl who attended regularly.

21. This respondent was a young woman involved from early childhood in a figure skating group at the local House of Culture. The group had developed into a broader performance group appearing at local venues at the weekends and was self-financing; money earned from concerts was used for costumes and to pay directors. This was an important evolution for the respondent, since the performance element allowed her to think of the activity as a creative art rather than strictly "sport," and to gain some real experience of arts management.

22. For progressives, in contrast, success at school (1, Ul'ianovsk), attendance at private university (224, Samara), or lucrative employment (57, Moscow) had opened their horizons to travel (or the prospect of it) to the West.

23. Ketamine is a pharmaceutical medicine (used "officially" mainly as an anaesthetic for animals), which is generally injected intravenously by drug users in Russia for hallucinogenic effects. Ketamine is also often mixed with amphetamines in the production of home-made Ecstasy look-alike pills.

24. This was a slang word for a kind of porridge (*kasha*) made from hashish.

25. This clearly problematic drug use was reported among young people associated with the punk movement. The centrality of drug use to punk (Shapiro 1999, 21) is often forgotten amidst current concern over the "normalization" of drug use among clubbers.

26. A recent study of drug use among clubgoers (mean age 22.8 years) in northern England in 1998 showed that over 50 percent of those interviewed had used Ecstasy in the past three months (Measham, Aldridge, and Parker 2001, 96).

27. At the time of interview, in Samara one Ecstasy tablet cost four times the price of a dose of heroin.

28. A study of drug use among school-age children in Ul'ianovsk suggested that the most popular drugs used were cannabis (70 percent of those saying they had used drugs at least once had used some form of cannabis), heroin (47 percent), toxic substances such as glue and paint (30 percent), and pharmaceutical preparations such as antidepressants (30 percent) (Omel'chenko 1999b, 14).

29. A high level of heavy alcohol use is confirmed by a study of teenagers hanging out on the streets of St. Petersburg, which found that 10 percent of teenagers used alcohol daily (Shul'gina 1996).

30. Since our fieldwork was completed, there has been a noticeable increase in the use of hard drugs among Russian youth. In Ul'ianovsk, for example, 47 percent of school students reporting having used drugs at least once said they had used heroin (Omel'chenko 1999b, 14).

31. Clearly questions could have been devised which would have encouraged young people to talk about gender relations within the group. Since this was not the primary object of the research, however, gender issues were followed through in interviews only where respondents themselves raised them.

32. Of all progressive *tusovki*, rappers were the most involved in violent encounters with other youth groups.

33. Some respondents, it should be noted, were uncertain about the concept of unisex style and confused and conflated it with transvestism (230, Samara).

Chapter 7

1. Grunge is a rock music emanating from Seattle and most frequently associated with the band Nirvana. Musically it draws from heavy metal but its "attitude" is punk-inspired "alternative." Both grunge and alternative rock in the United States are considered to be musics of suburban youth, also known as "Generation X." The suicide of the lead singer of Nirvana, Kurt Cobain, following a drug overdose provoked widespread concern about such suburban teenage "no-hopers" (see Epstein 1998, 18).

2. Amongst these respondents Grinders and Dr Martens, Adidas and Nike footwear and Gas, Naf Naf, Diesel, Kangol, Calvin Klein, Gucci, Gap and Levi labels were all mentioned positively (215, Samara; 228, Samara; 227, Samara; 237, Samara; 242, Samara; 254, Ul'ianovsk; 253, Ul'ianovsk). It was also noted that "unisex" style could only work in its designer format (237, Samara). At the same time, those who walked round with their jumpers tucked into their jeans just to show off the labels on them were mocked (253, Ul'ianovsk). Moreover, a significant section of progressive youth, primarily those from the "romantics" wing (see Chapter 5) actively denied the significance of labels in particular, but style consciousness in general. Instead they emphasized the importance of practicality (51, Moscow; 210, Samara; 220, Samara), affordability (51, Moscow), tastefulness (57, Moscow; 231, Samara), and quality (206, Samara) in choosing clothes.

3. Although another two respondents, who associated themselves with the hippie movement, used visual symbols—such as the traditional woven bracelets (*fen'ki*) but also specific colors—to express certain affections, moods, and attitudes (233, Samara).

4. Although a number of respondents noted that when they had first started on the scene there had been a much greater concern with creating a certain "acid look" (*kislo*).

5. One such individual was described as wearing only tennis shoes, short trousers with a white fringe sewn on, and a T-shirt even in the Moscow winter and sporting a child's panama hat decorated with pom poms (54, Moscow).

6. This is particularly significant, given the way rap acted as a vehicle facilitating normal to progressive strategy border crossings (see Chapter 5).

7. These clothes markets (referred to colloquially often as *tolkuchki*) were the prime sales point for the shuttle

traders who set up in the open spaces around the central markets of provincial cities.

8. In Ul'ianovsk a number of clubbers had tried to make a distinctive mark on the local scene by designing and making their own clothes, but the impact had been short-lived, and they no longer succeeded in surprising anyone (251, Ul'ianovsk; 252, Ul'ianovsk, 23, Ul'ianovsk).

9. Around $1.50 at the time of interview.

10. This was actually mentioned by only one Moscow respondent—who explicitly stated that she had not engaged in shoplifting herself—and her explanation suggested that the theft had been not out of necessity but for the thrill (54, Moscow).

11. Indeed, by the end of the 1990s, it had become difficult to get a rise out of parents, who in the past at least could have been relied upon to complain about what might be "read into" a young man sporting an earring. This new tolerance, or rather passive disapproval, on the part of parents was explained variously as a recognition that their children were of an age where they made decisions for themselves (210, Samara), that they could not "make" them change their look (38, Ul'ianovsk), or more intriguingly, a result of the "normalization" of earrings for "normal" men following the popularity of the film *Pulp Fiction* (Expert interview with DJs, Ul'ianovsk). The only real confrontation with parents noted over clothes was recounted by a Moscow rapper whose father had objected to the way he wore his trousers "round the ankles" (63, Moscow).

12. Progressives, for example, bought second-hand clothes rather than buy at the rag markets while second-hand buying was not mentioned by any normal respondents. One normal respondent did say she made many of her own clothes, however (236, Samara).

13. The difference between what might be defined as "global" and as "Western" music appears to hinge on distribution rather than production. "Global" music continues to be produced primarily in the West; it is simply considered to have reached consumers on a global scale. Music actually produced outside the West, in contrast, tends to be referred to as "ethnic" or "world" music.

14. The data here are not directly comparable with those in the West, since the Western research is specifically youth related and thus includes teenagers as opposed to the 18–35 youth bracket used by the public opinion polls. The Western research also considers music use in a range of youth practices rather than asking how people "usually" spend their time.

15. The one respondent who claimed to have fixed preferences, nevertheless fixed those preferences diversely, in an unwavering liking for "various music" (60, Moscow).

16. By 1993 the rave scene had transmuted into a post-rave urban dance scene fueled by implosion of the techno music scene and its reemergence in a wide range of subgenres. According to Monroe this fragmenting process in the techno scene is determined by the interface of extremely rapid technological and creative development and the need of postmodern cultural production to invent and reinvent niche markets to service (Monroe 1999, 153).

17. Nautilus Pompilius was the most popular of Russian rock bands

cited in the representative survey conducted in Ul'ianovsk and Samara.

18. The German band Scorpions was the most popular Western *rock* group cited in the representative survey conducted in Ul'ianovsk and Samara and the second most popular Western group overall.

19. The clearest example of this in relation to East European music is the success of Deep Forest's *Boheme* album, which won the World Music Grammy in 1995 (Taylor 1997, 12).

20. Favorite singer-songwriters included Mitiaev, Sergeev, Ivashchenko, and Vasil'ev.

21. In particular, rock music fans were likely to criticize all kinds of dance music as "uninteresting" (206, Samara), "commercial" (225, Samara), "unnatural" (38, Ul'ianovsk), and "dead" (11, Ul'ianovsk), while within the dance scene "hard core" fans were subjected to ridicule.

22. A well-known club in Moscow in January 1998; see Chapter 5.

23. A dance scene *tusovka* meeting at Teatral'naia metro station (see Chapter 5).

24. This marks a clear continuity of *tusovka* values from an earlier decade as well as indicating a distaste for commercial clubs.

25. One Ul'ianovsk DJ, however, said he had noted a preference among young women in the clubs for "softer" and more "danceable" musics such as garage music.

26. Nowhere has this fact been more apparent than in the United Kingdom, where the Sixties' generation is firmly in office; cabinet ministers attend the Brit awards and Oasis band members pass through the central offices of power.

27. A term used widely among *tusovki* in the 1980s to describe those "pretenders" to the scene who did not have real knowledge or cool.

28. Respondents interviewed reported their own involvement in composing and singing their own folk music, playing rock music or rap music in bands, and composing their own "independent" electronic music.

29. This fueled a broader critique of the club scene as "a site of depravity . . . a swamp of drugs" (206, Samara), and clubs themselves as first and foremost pick-up joints (23, Ul'ianovsk; 24 Ul'ianovsk; 251, Ul'ianovsk) and places antagonistic to rock *tusovki* (207, Samara).

30. This explains the claim by one respondent in Samara that punks and rappers shared a "happy disposition" reflected in their "slamming" (241, Samara).

31. Although, as was noted in Chapter 6, young men developed a distinctive "sporting" narrative of dance, this was a way of overcoming the disruption to masculine identity caused by dance practice. Respondents often talked about friends back in the *dvor* who were prevented from taking up breakdance by their "male pride" and fear of failure (33, Ul'ianovsk).

32. Interestingly, the term used to describe DJs who played in different clubs was *guliat* with its implication of sexual infidelity (228, Samara; 215, Samara). The smallness of the Ul'ianovsk scene, however, made this a negative, not positive, characteristic, since the result was that an individual would hear the same set from a particular DJ in different places (251, Ul'ianovsk; 252, Ul'ianovsk).

33. This refers to a practice associated with restaurant culture in Russia; meals are eaten over a long period of time in between which guests dance

to a live restaurant band. Requests are frequently made of the performers encouraged by a tip.

34. This related to both the lack of turntables, which prevented the use of "scratch" techniques, and the lack of access to digital technologies. However, DJs were able to create their own unbroken sound experience for clubbers. The concern to distinguish the creative practices of dance music from commercial issues, however, is a very Russian understanding of the genre and rather ironic, given the centrality of dub to Chicago House music and thus the whole dance scene. Dub was a technological innovation designed above all to facilitate the production of multiple sound system versions of recorded music to meet a consumer demand beyond the capacity of the Jamaican record industry of the 1950s (Bakari 1999, 108; Ingham 1999, 126).

35. The other is held in St. Petersburg. Events at the Berlin "Love Parade" were often also discussed as they were covered in the music magazines.

36. See http://kazantip.cityline.ru.

37. The only exception was a reference to DJ Groove by two Moscow respondents (42, Moscow; 43, Moscow).

38. One exception was a young teacher interviewed in Ul'ianovsk who noted a tendency among her pupils for girls to like "weepy" pop and boys to favor more "aggressive" music such as rave and *blatnie pesnie* (1, Ul'ianovsk).

39. However, pop itself had its own "alternative" voices, and some respondents expressed conscious preferences for singers such as Linda and Boris Moiseev, because they were "unusual people" (236, Samara). Other respondents noted a growing commercialism in Russian pop, in contrast to Soviet *estrada* (209, Samara, 12, Ul'ianovsk), that the mass popularity of bands was temporary and linked to a high degree of peer pressure exerted among younger teenagers (187, Samara; 12, Ul'ianovsk) or, taking a more critical stance, that the mass media (television and radio) "created" such phenomena by drowning out "alternative" musics (13, Ul'ianovsk).

40. Although one respondent suggested that there was a generational difference; younger people (those around fourteen years old), it was suggested, listened to more Western music and more remixes (234, Samara).

41. This respondent made the comment with specific reference to the group Prodigy.

42. Frankie Knuckles—the founder of Chicago house music—also notes the perception of acid house (rave) to be one of a "soulless machine music" making the older generation react negatively to it and seek "something more soulful and meaningful" (cited in Tomlinson 1998, 204).

Chapter 8

1. One exception was a concern that young people increasingly prioritized "ends" over "means," for example, not caring *how* they "make money" as long as they do (210, Samara).

2. Sociological research published in 1997 found 80 percent of students in their final two years of school enjoyed American film while only 10 percent rejected it (Poluekhtova 1997, 78). However, Russian films were regarded highly also and considered to be well received abroad.

3. This narrative of course draws heavily on Soviet depictions of the

United States as an aggressive imperial force (Petrov et al. 1979, 11–12).

4. These binaries were constructed by the authors, but all concepts and categories used were taken directly from the opinions expressed by respondents themselves.

5. The question asked whether respondents considered a number of youth cultural trends (from punks to Russian folk singing clubs) to be primarily "Western" (*zapadnie*), "Russian" (*nashi*) or hybrids (*smeshannie*).

6. The vagueness of young people about the *content* of Russian identity is noted by Oushakine (Oushakine 2000a). As was argued in Chapter 7, however, the current authors see this problem as primarily one of verbal articulation; in the cultural practice of young people, this content was apparent.

7. The examples of bard and *blatnie* songs indicate that what Russians perceive to be incomprehensible about Russian culture to the West is both the *dushevnaia* (spiritual) and the "earthy." While Westerners cannot understand the former because they are too pragmatic, they cannot penetrate the latter because it concerns situations peculiar to Russian "reality."

8. This of course is typical of migration patterns worldwide; those without dependents are much more likely to contemplate migration, since the costs of both leaving and of resettling are significantly reduced.

Conclusion

1. It should be noted here that this survey was of the general adult population, not of youth.

2. This was partially borne of increasing personal interaction with the West, especially among Muscovites. Personal travel to the West and having friends from the West were correlated with the articulation of critical attitudes toward the West in general and its impact upon Russian culture in particular. This correlation was particularly evident in focus groups where groups of young people most bound to their locality (those from provincial cities, and in particular from peripheral schools of those cities), showed distinctly less critical faculty in relation to images of the West.

3. Arguably, the Tolkienist movement is such an example. Its lack of visibility in the West, however, makes it an unusual example.

Appendix

1. This was a conscious decision. Although the Moscow-based research was important for establishing a base line for the studies in Samara and Ul'ianovsk, the focus of the research was essentially urban, provincial Russia.

2. Four percent of respondents were under fifteen years of age (all being fourteen), 1 percent was over twenty-five, and data were missing for 2 percent of respondents.

3. Data were missing for 5 percent of respondents.

4. The only significant difference between Samara and Ul'ianovsk was that in the latter city there was a particularly high proportion of people employed in the military or police (10 percent compared to 4 percent 0in Samara).

5. It should be borne in mind here that Moscow respondents were also the oldest and those from Ul'ianovsk were the youngest. The cost of living in Moscow was also significantly higher than in Ul'ianovsk.

6. "Abroad" was defined as anywhere outside Russia, including the former Soviet republics.

7. Accurate information was missing for one respondent, who claimed to have traveled abroad but did not list which countries.

8. It is possible, of course, that more respondents had traveled within the former Soviet Union—for example to the popular holiday destinations in Crimea and the Baltic states—without recognizing it as travel abroad.

9. This is even more striking, given the general weighting toward respondents from the provinces.

10. This was defined as, for example, Ukrainians from Ukraine but not Ukrainians living in Russia.

11. Both Russian and British researchers experienced this; indeed in some respects the barriers for the former were greater.

12. These are not the precise questions asked, but provide an indication of the questions covered

REFERENCES

Abrams, M. 1959. *The Teenage Consumer*. London: London Press Exchange.

Adorno, T. 1991. *The Culture Industry: Selected Essays on Mass Culture*. Edited by J. M. Bernstein. London: Routledge.

Akhiezer, A. S. 1993. "Rossiia kak bol'shoe obshchestvo." *Voprosy filosofii*, no. 1:3–19.

———. 1994. "Samobytnost' Rossii kak nauchnaia problema." *Otechestvennaia istoriia*, no. 4–5:6.

———. 1997a. *Kak "otkryt" zakrytoe obshchestvo?* Moscow: Institut "Otkrytoe Obshchestvo," Magistr.

———. 1997b. "Nravstvennost' v Rossii i protivostoianie katastrofam." *Obshchestvennie nauki i sovremennost'* 6:26–37.

———. 1997c. *Rossiia: Kritika Istoricheskogo Opyta (Sotsiokul'turnaia Dinamika Rossii)*. Vols. 1 and 2. Novosibirsk: Sibirskii khronograf.

Althusser, L. 1994. "Selected Texts." In *Ideology*, ed. Terry Eagleton. London: Longman.

Anisimov, A. 1996. "Sistema tsivilizatsionnikh kodov i global'naia dinamika." *Rossiia XXI* 1–2:42–64.

Appadurai, A. 1990. "Disjuncture and Difference in the Global Cultural Economy." *Theory, Culture and Society* 7:295–310.

Arnason, J. 1993. *The Future That Failed: Origins and Destinies of the Soviet Model*. London: Routledge.

Avraamova, E. M. 1998. "Formirovanie novoi rossiiskoi makroidentichnosti." *Obshchestvennie nauki i sovremennost'* 3:73–85.

Back, L. 1996. *New Ethnicities and Urban Culture: Racisms and Multiculture in Young Lives*. London: UCL Press.

Bakari, I. 1999. "Exploding Silence: African-Caribbean and African-American Music in British Culture Towards 2000." In *Living Through Pop*, ed. A. Blake. London: Routledge.

Bassin, M. 1991. "Russia Between Europe and Asia: The Ideological Construction of Geographical Space." *Slavic Review* 50(1): 1–17.

Baudrillard, J. 1988. *America*. London: Verso.

Bauman, Z. 1998a. *Globalization: The Human Consequences*. New York: Columbia University Press.

———. 1998b. *Work, Consumerism and the New Poor*. Buckingham: Open University Press.

Beck, U. 1994. "The Reinvention of Politics: Towards a Theory of Reflexive Modernization." In Beck, Giddens, and Lash 1994, 1–55.

———. 2000. *What Is Globalization?* Cambridge: Polity.

Beck, U., A. Giddens, and S. Lash. 1994. *Reflexive Modernization: Politics, Tradition and Aesthetics in the Modern Social Order.* Cambridge: Polity Press.

Bennett, A. 1999a. "Hip hop am Main: The Localisation of Rap Music and Hip Hop Culture." *Media, Culture and Society* 21(1): 77–91.

———. 1999b. "Subcultures or Neo-tribes: Rethinking the Relationship Between Youth, Style and Musical Taste." *Sociology* 33(3): 599–617.

———. 2000. *Popular Music and Youth Culture.* Basingstoke: Macmillan.

Bergson, A. 1994. *Dva Istochnika Morali i Religii.* Moscow: Kanon.

Besov, A. 1998. "Ispovedim li tsivilizatsionnii put' Rossii v mirovoi istorii?" *Rubezhi* 2:66–84.

Bestuzhev-Lada, I.V. 1997a. *Perspektivy Razvitiia Kul'tury v Problematike Sotsial'nogo Prognozirovaniia: Lektsii. Uchebnoe Posobie.* St. Petersburg: SPBUP.

———. 1997b. "Rossiia: kontury budushchego." *Rossiia i sovremennii mir* 2:20–27.

Bhabha, H., ed. 1990. *Nation and Narration.* London: Routledge.

Bliumfel'd, R. 1997. "Tekhno-proryv!" *Venets* (Simbirskaia ezhenedel'naia gazeta—biznes, kul'tura, molodezh'), 29 August, 1, 6 and 8.

Bocharova, O., and N. Kim. 2000. "Rossiia i zapad: obshchnost' ili otchuzhdenie?" At http://www.polit.ru, 3 March.

Brake, M. 1985. *Comparative Youth Culture.* London: Routledge & Kegan Paul.

Brutents, K. V. 1998. "V poiskakh pax americana." *Svobodnaia mysl'* 6:57–67.

Burganov, A. Kh. 1995. "Rossiia i Zapad: sootnoshenie putei istoricheskogo razvitiia." In *Zapad i Vostok: Traditsii, vzaimodeistviia i novatsii,* Tezizy Vserossiiskogo nauchno-prakticheskoi konferentsii, Vladimir, 15–17 March.

Bushnell, J. 1990. *Moscow Graffiti: Language and Subculture.* Boston: Unwin Hyman.

Caryl, C. 1998. "Rapping in Red Square." *U.S. News and World Report,* May 18.

Castells, M. 1998. *End of Millennium: The Information Age: Economy, Society and Culture.* Vol. 3. Oxford: Blackwell Publishers.

Chaney, D. 2001. "Lifestyle and Cultural Citizenship." Paper presented in the ESRC Research Seminar Series "Citizenship and Its Futures," University College Northampton, 23 February.

Cherniakhovskii, V. S. 1994. "V Rossiiu s reklamoi." *Reklama,* no. 5–6:47–48.

Cheshkov, M. 1996. "Nezapad: stanovlenie istoricheskogo sub ekta?" *Mirovaia ekonomika i mezhdunarodnie otnosheniia* 12:13–18.

———. 1999. "Globalizatsiia: Sushchnost', nyneshniaia faza, perspektivy." *Pro et Contra* 4 (Autumn): 1–13 (accessed at http://pubs.carnegie.ru/p&c/vol4-1999).

Clarke, J. 1976. "Style." In *Resistance Through Rituals: Youth Subcultures in Post-War Britain,* ed. S. Hall and T. Jefferson. London: Hutchinson.

Clifford, J., and C. Marcus, eds. 1986. *Writing Culture.* Berkeley and Los Angeles: University of California Press.

Condry, I. 2000. "The Social Production of Difference: Imitation and Authenticity in Japanese Rap Music." In *Transactions, Transgressions, Transformations: American Culture in Western Europe and Japan*, ed. H. Fehrenbach and U. Poiger. New York: Berghahn Books.

Cushman, T. 1995. *Notes from Underground: Rock Music Counterculture in Russia*. Albany: SUNY Press.

Davies, J. 1999. "It's Like Feminism, But You Don't Have to Burn Your Bra: Girl Power and the Spice Girls' Breakthrough, 1996–7." In *Living Through Pop*, ed. A. Blake. London: Routledge.

Davydov, Iu. P., ed. 1977. *SShA—Zapadnaia Evropa: Partnerstvo i sopernichestvo*. Moscow: Nauka.

Diligenskii, G. G. 1996. "Rossiiskie arkhetipy i sovremennost'." *Segodnia*, 5 July, 5.

———. 1997a. "Chto my znaem o demokratii i grazhdanskom obshchestve?" *Pro et Contra* 2 (Autumn) (accessed at http://pubs.carnegie.ru/p&c).

———. 1997b. "Rossiiskii arkhetip." *Rubezhi* 2:127–52.

"Dognali i peregnali Ameriku." 1997. *Argumenty i Fakty* 40:20.

Ellis, F. 1999. *From Glasnost to the Internet: Russia's New Infosphere*. Basingstoke: Macmillan.

Ellwood, D. 2000. "Comparative Anti-Americanism in Western Europe." In *Transactions, Transgressions, Transformations: American Culture in Western Europe and Japan*, ed. H. Fehrenbach and U. Poiger. New York: Berghahn Books.

Epstein, J., ed. 1998. *Youth Culture: Identity in a Postmodern World*. Oxford: Blackwell Publishers.

Evstaf'ev, D. 1997. "Novaia evrazia ili 'dikoe pole'?" *Novaia Rossiia* 2:67–76.

———. 1998. "Neskol'ko myslei ob Amerike: Zametki predvziatogo cheloveka." *Novaia Rossiia* 1:36–48.

Evstaf'ev, V. 1998. "Otechestvennii rynok reklamy demonstriruet stabil'nii rost'." *Finansovie izvestiia*, 26 March, 5.

Fain, A. 1990. "Specific Features of Informal Youth Associations in Large Cities." *Soviet Sociology* 29(1): 20–42.

Fardon, R., ed. 1995. *Counterworks, Managing the Diversity of Knowledge*. London: Routledge.

Featherstone, M. 1995. *Undoing Culture, Globalization, Postmodernism and Identity*. London: Sage.

Featherstone, M., and S. Lash. 1995. "Globalization, Modernity and the Spatialization of Social Theory: An Introduction." In *Global Modernities*, ed. M. Featherstone, S. Lash, and R. Robertson. London: Sage.

Fedorov, I. 1999. "Kriticheskii vyzov dlia Rossii." *Pro et Contra* 4 (Autumn): 1–13 (accessed at http://pubs.carnegie.ru/p&c/vol4-1999).

Fehrenbach, H., and U. Poiger. 2000. "Introduction: Americanization Reconsidered." In *Transactions, Transgressions, Transformations: American Culture in Western Europe and Japan*, ed. H. Fehrenbach and U. Poiger. Oxford: Berghahn Books.

Fel'dshtein, D., and L. Radzhikhovskii, eds. 1988. *Psikhologicheskie Problemy Izucheniia Neformal'nikh Molodezhnikh Ob"edinenii.* Moscow: APN SSR.

Ferdinand, P. 1992. "Russia and Russians After Communism: Western or Eurasian?" *The World Today* 48(12): 221–25.

Fond Obshchestvennogo Mneniia. 1999. Cited in http://www.fom.ru/week, January 2000.

Fornäs, J., and G. Bolin, eds. 1995. *Youth Culture in Late Moderntity.* London: Sage.

Friedman, J., and A. Weiner. 1999. "Between a Rock and a Hard Place: Holy Rus" and Its Alternatives in Russian Rock Music." In *Consuming Russia: Popular Culture, Sex, and Society Since Gorbachev,* ed. Adele Marie Barker. Durham: Duke University Press.

Frisby, D., and M. Featherstone, eds. 1997. *Simmel on Culture: Selected Writings.* London: Sage.

Frith, S. 1983. *Sound Effects: Youth, Leisure, and the Politics of Rock'n'Roll.* London: Constable.

Furlong, A., and F. Cartmel. 1997. *Young People and Social Change.* Buckingham: Open University Press.

Fursov, A. 1996. "Kolokola istorii (voina i mir mirov i sistem)." *Rubezhi* 8:3–28.

Giddens, A. 1994. "Living in a Post-Traditional Society." In Beck, Giddens, and Lash 1994, 56–109.

Godina, A. 1999. "Vzaimodeistvie subkul'tury i kul'tury (na primere dvizheniia indeanistov)." In *Molodezhnie Dvizheniia i Subkul'tury Sankt-Peterburga (Sotsiologicheskii i antropologicheskii analiz),* ed. V. Kostiusheva. Saint Petersburg: Izdatel'stvo Norma.

Gorshkov, N. K., A. V. Avilova, A. L. Adreev, et al. 1996. "Massovoe soznanie rossiian v period obshchestvennoi transformatsii: real'nost' protiv mifa." *Mir Rossii* 2:75–117.

Gorsuch, A. 2000. *Youth in Revolutionary Russia: Enthusiasts, Bohemians, Delinquents.* Bloomington: Indiana University Press.

Grassmuck, V. 1999. "Eine Lebensform der Zukunft? Der Otaku." In *Neue, schöne Welt? Lenbensformen der Informationsgesellschaft,* ed. D. Matejovski. Herne: Heitkamp Edition. Accessed electronically at: http://waste .informatik.huberlin.de/Grassmuck/Texts/otaku99.html.

Greenfeld, K. 1993. "The Incredibly Strange Mutant Creatures Who Rule the Universe of Alienated Japanese Zombie Computer Nerds." *Wired,* March–April.

Grinchenko, Wells L. 1994. "Western Concepts, Russian Perspectives: Meanings of Advertising in the Former Soviet Union." *Journal of Advertising Research* 23(1): 85–93.

———. 1996. "The Role of Professional Advertising Associations in Russia." *International Journal of Advertising* 15:103–15.

Gromov, A. V., and O. S. Kuzin, eds. 1990. *Neformaly: Kto est' kto?* Moscow: Mysl'.

Gubman, B. L. 1994. "Evraziiskii sindrom." In *Rossiia i Zapad: dialog Kul'tur. Sbornik nauchnikh trudov*, ed. B. Gubman. Tver': Tver' gosudarstvenni universitet.

Guseinov, A. 1996. "Slovo ob intelligentsii." *Novaia Rossiia* 32:18–26.

Hall, S. 1990. "Cultural Identity and Diaspora." In *Identity: Community, Culture, Difference*, ed. J. Rutherford. London: Lawrence & Wishart.

Hanke, R. 1998. " 'Yo quiero mi MTV!' Making Music Television for Latin America." In *Mapping the Beat. Popular Music and Contemporary Theory*, ed. T. Swiss, J. Sloop, and A. Herman. Malden and Oxford: Blackwell Publishers.

Hannerz, U. 1990. "Cosmopolitans and Locals in World Culture." *Theory, Culture and Society* 7:237–51.

———. 1992. *Cultural Complexity*. New York: Columbia University Press.

———. 1996. *Transnational Connections*. London: Routledge.

Harter, S. 2000. "Life on planet.ru. The Internet in Russia." Unpublished paper for the BASEES Annual Conference, Fitzwilliam College, Cambridge, 1–2 April.

Hebdige, D. 1988. *Hiding in the Light*. London and New York: Comedia, Routledge.

Held, D., A. McGrew, D. Goldblatt, and J. Perraton. 1999. *Global Transformations: Politics, Economics and Culture*. Stanford: Stanford University Press.

Henderson, P. 1999. "Russia Rocks to MTV Beat." Russian Intercessory Prayer Network. News Release, 30 September, on http://www.ripnet.org/mtv.htm

Hetherington, K. 1998. "Vanloads of Uproarious Humanity: New Age Travellers and the Utopics of the Countryside." In Skelton and Valentine 1998, 328–42.

Hingley, R. 1977. *The Russian Mind*. London: The Bodley Head.

Hodkinson, P. 2001. "Subculture as Substance: The Identities, Values, Practices and Infrastructure of the Goth Scene." Ph.D. diss., University of Birmingham.

Hoggart, R. 1957. *The Uses of Literacy*. London: Chatto & Windus.

Hosking, G. 1988. "A 'Great Power' in Crisis." Reith lecture no. 1. *The Listener*, 10 November, 16–19.

Howell, S. 1995. "Whose Knowledge and Whose Power? A New Perspective on Cultural Diffusion." In *Counterworks, Managing the Diversity of Knowledge*, ed. R. Fardon. London: Routledge.

Howes, D., ed. 1996. *Cross-cultural Consumption: Global Markets—Local Realities*. London: Routledge.

Humphrey, C. 1995. "Creating a Culture of Disillusionment: Consumption in Moscow, a Chronicle of Changing Times." In *Worlds Apart: Modernity Through the Prism of the Local*, ed. D. Miller. London: Routledge.

Huq, R. 1999. "Living in France: The Parallel Universe of Hexagonal Pop." In *Living Through Pop*, ed. A. Blake. London: Routledge.

Ikonnikova, S. 1974. *Molodezh': Sotsiologicheskii i sotsial'no-psikhologicheskii Analiz*. Leningrad: Leningradskii Gosudarstvenii Universitet.

———. 1976. *Kritika Burzhuaznikh Kontseptsii "Molodezhnoi Kul'tury."* Moscow: Obshchestvo "Znanie" RSFSR.

Ingham, J. 1999. "Listening Back from Blackburn: Virtual Sound Worlds and the Creation of Temporary Autonomy." In *Living Through Pop*, ed. A. Blake. London: Routledge.

Islamshina, T. G., R. S. Tseitlin, A. L. Salagaev, S. A. Sergeev, O. A. Maksimova, and G. R. Khamzina. 1997. *Molodezhnie Subkul'tury*. Kazan: Kazanskii gosudarstvennii tekhnologicheskii universitet.

Iusupovskii, A. 1997. "Verit' . . . ili unichtozhat'." *Novaia Rossiia* 3:17–23.

Jameson, F. 1998. "Notes on Globalization as a Philosophical Issue." In Jameson and Miyoshi 1998.

Jameson, F., and M. Miyoshi, eds. 1998. *The Cultures of Globalization*. Durham: Duke University Press.

Jefferson, T. 1973. "The Teds—A Political Resurrection." *CCCS Stencilled Occasional Paper* 22.

Jourdan, C. 1995. "Masta Liu." In *Youth Cultures: A Cross-Cultural Perspective*, ed. V. Amit-Talai and H. Wulff. London: Routledge.

Kedrov, K. 1996. "Evropa i Amerika prochtut 'Onegina' po 'Internetu.' " *Izvestiia*, 15 May, 7.

Kentavr pered sfinksom. 1995. Moscow: Gorbachev-fond Tsentr problem kul'tury, April.

Kerr, D. 1995. "The New Eurasianism: The Rise of Geopolitics in Russia's Foreign Policy." *Europe-Asia Studies* 47(6): 977–88.

Kharkhordin, O. 1999. *The Collective and the Individual in Russia: A Study of Practices*. Berkeley and Los Angeles: University of California Press.

Kholodkovskii, M., ed. 1996. *Grazhdanskoe Obshchestvo v Rossii: Zapadnaia Paradigma i Rossiiskaia Real'nost'*. Moscow: Institut mirovoi ekonomiki i mezhdurarodnikh otnoshenii, RAN.

Khoros, V. G. 1995. " 'Stolknovenie' ili 'kontsert' tsivilizatsii v obshchemirovom modernizatsionnom protsesse?" *Politicheskie Issledovaniia* 1:79–80.

Khudaverdian, V. 1977. "O nekotorikh novikh tendentsiiakh v sovremennoi burzhuaznoi sotsiologii molodezhi (kriticheskii analiz)." *Sotsiologicheskie Issledovaniia* 3:71–77.

———. 1986. *Sovremennie Al'ternativnie Dvizheniia (Molodezh' Zapada i "Novii Irratsionalizm")*. Moscow: Mysl'.

King, A. 1995. "The Times and Spaces of Modernity (or Who Needs Postmodernism?)." In *Global Modernities*, ed. M. Featherstone, S. Lash, and R. Robertson. London: Sage.

———, ed. 1991. *Culture, Globalization and the World System*. London: Macmillan.

Klishina, S. 1998. "Russkaia ideia v postmodernistskom prostranstve." *Rossiia XXI* 1–2:144–56.

Kopylov, D. I. 1995. "Rossiia i mirovoi istoricheskii protsess." In *Zapad i Vostok: Traditsii, vzaimodeistviia i novatsii*, Tezizy Vserossiiskogo nauchno-prakticheskoi konferentsii, Vladimir, 15–17 March.

Kosals, L., R. Ryvkina, and Iu. Simagin. 1996. "Rynochnie reformy glazami raznikh pokolenii." *Mirovaia ekonomika i mezhdunarodnie otnosheniia*, no. 7:134–43.

Kostiusheva, V., ed. 1999. *Molodezhnie Dvizheniia i Subkul'tury Sankt-Peterburga (Sotsiologicheskii i antropologicheskii analiz)*. Saint Petersburg: Izdatel'stvo Norma.

Kovalenko, Iu. 1996. "Andrei Bitov: Ia nikogda ne byl s masterami kul'tury." *Izvestiia*, 15 May, 5.

Krasil'shchikov, V. A. 1996. "Zavisimost' i otstalost' v razvitii Rossii." *Mir Rossi* 4:67–97.

Kuchmaeva, I. 1987. "Molodezhnie subkul'turnie ob"edineniia kak faktor dinamiki kul'tury." In *Subkul'turnie Ob"edineniia Molodezhi: Kriticheskii Analiz*, ed. I. Kuchmaeva. Moscow: AN SSSR Institut Filosofii.

Kurbanova, A. 1985. "Fenomen 'subkul'tur' i ideologicheskaia bor'ba." In *Problemy Kul'tury v Sovremennom Kapitalisticheskom Obshchestve (Tsennostnie Aspekty)*. Moscow.

———. 1986. "Protsess samorealizatsii lichnosti v molodezhnikh subkul'turakh." In *Kul'tura i Lichnost' v Kapitalisticheskom Obshchestve*. Moscow.

Kustarev, A. 1997. "Sovok i zapadnia (o knige Zinov'eva *Zapad*)." *Rubezhi* 7:116–40.

Kutkovets, T. I., and I. M. Kliamkin. 1997. "Russkie idei." *Polis* 2:118–41.

Kvitsinskii, Iu. 1996. "Rossiia: kontseptsiia bytiia (grustnie razmyshleniia)." *Novaia Rossiia* 4:7–11.

Lash, S. 1994. "Reflexivity and Its Doubles: Structure, Aesthetics, Community." In Beck, Giddens, and Lash 1994, 110–73.

Lash, S., and J. Urry. 1994. *Economies of Signs and Space*. London: Sage.

Lee, R. 1994. "Globalisation and Cultural Change." *Current Sociology* 42(2): 26–33.

Leonard, M. 1998. "Paper Planes: Travelling the New Grrrl Geographies." In Skelton and Valentine 1998, 101–18.

Leslie, D. 1995. "Global Scan: The Globalization of Advertising Agencies, Concepts and Campaigns." *Economic Geography* 71:402–26.

Levada, Iu. 1993. *Stat'i po Sotsiologii*. Moscow.

Levanov, E., and V. Levicheva. 1988. "Eti mnogolikie 'neformaly.'" *Orientiry* 12:20–24.

Levanov, E., V. Levicheva, and N. Rubanova. 1989. "Samodeiatel'nie ob"edineniia molodezhi kak obshchestvennoe iavlenie." *Aktual'nie Problemy Ideino-politicheskogo Vospitaniia Molodezhi*. Moscow: VKSh pri TsK VLKSM.

Liebes, T., and E. Katz. 1993. *Export of Meaning: Cross-Cultural Readings of Dallas*. Cambridge: Polity Press.

Liechty, M. 1995. "Modernization, Media and Markets: Youth Identities and the Experience of Modernity in Kathmandu, Nepal." In *Youth Cultures: A Cross-Cultural Perspective*, ed. V. Amit-Talai and H. Wulff. London: Routledge.

Lipkin, A. 1995. "Dukhovnoe iadro kak sistemoobrazuiushchii faktor tsivilizatsii: Evropa i Rossiia." *Obshchestvennie nauki i sovremennost'* 2:57–68.
Liu Kang. 1998. "Is There an Alternative to (Capitalist) Globalization? The Debate About Modernity in China." In Jameson and Miyoshi 1998.
Lull, J. 1995. *Media, Communication, Culture: A Global Approach*. Cambridge: Polity Press.
Madden, N. 1996. "Cross-Cultural Miscommunication Can Mar Western Advertising Campaign." *Transition*, 19 April, 9.
Maffesoli, M. 1996. *The Time of the Tribes: The Decline of Individualism in Mass Society*. London: Sage.
Maksimenko, V. 1999. "Proiskhodit li 'globalizatsiia'?" *Pro et Contra* 4 (Autumn): 1–13 (accessed at http://pubs.carnegie.ru/p&c/vol4-1999).
Maksimychev, I. F. 1997. "Rossiia kak sostavnaia chast' obshcheevropeiskogo tsivilizatsionnogo prostranstva." *Obshchestvennie nauki i sovremennost'* 6:85–97.
Malbon, B. 1998. "Clubbing: Consumption, Identity and the Spatial Practices of Every-Night Life." In Skelton and Valentine 1998, 266–88.
———. 1999. *Clubbing. Dancing, Ecstasy and Vitality*. London: Routledge.
Malia, M. 1999. *Russia Under Western Eyes. From the Bronze Horseman to the Lenin Mausoleum*. Cambridge: Harvard University Press.
Markowitz, F. 1999. "Not Nationalists: Russian Teenagers' Soulful A-politics." *Europe-Asia Studies* 51(7): 1183–98.
———. 2000. *Coming of Age in Post-Soviet Russia*, Urbana: University of Illinois Press.
Massey, D. 1994. *Space, Place and Gender*. Cambridge: Polity Press.
———. 1998. "The Spatial Construction of Youth Cultures." In Skelton and Valentine 1998, 121–29.
Matveeva, S. 1987. "Subkul'tura v dinamike kul'tury." In *Subkul'turnie Ob"edineniia Molodezhi: Kriticheskii Analiz*, ed. I. Kuchmaeva. Moscow: AN SSSR Institut Filosofii.
McLuhan, M. 1964. *Understanding Media*. London: Routledge.
McRobbie, A. 1994. *Postmodernism and Popular Culture*. London: Routledge.
Measham, F., J. Aldridge, and H. Parker. 2001. *Dancing on Drugs: Risk, Health and Hedonism in the British Club Scene*. London: Free Association Books.
Mignolo, W. "Globalization, Civilization Processes and the Relocation of Languages and Cultures." In Jameson and Miyoshi 1998.
Mikhailova, B. V., ed. 1994. *Grazhdanskoe Obshchestvo i Perspektivy Demokratii v Rossii*. Moscow: RNF.
Mikheev, V. 1999. "Logika globalizatsii i interesy Rossii." *Pro et Contra* 4 (Autumn): 1–13 (accessed at http://pubs.carnegie.ru/p&c/vol4-1999).
Mitchell, T. 1996. *Popular Music and Local Identity: Rock, Pop and Rap in Europe and Oceana*. London: Leicester University Press.
———. 1999. " 'Doin' Damage in My Native Language': The Use of Resistance Vernaculars in Hip Hop in France, Italy and Aotearoa/New Zealand." Paper abstract for Conference "Protesting 'Globalization': Prospects for

Transnational Solidarity," December 10–11, located at http://www.transforming.cultures.uts.edu.au/conferences/prot_glob/pg_home.htm
Molchanov, M. 1999. "Istoki rossiiskogo krizisa: globalizatsiia ili vnutrennie problemy?" *Polis* 5:94–108.
Monroe, A. 1999. "Thinking About Mutation: Genres in 1990s Electronica." In *Living Through Pop*, ed. A. Blake. London: Routledge.
Morley, D., and K. Robins. 1995. *Spaces of Identity*. London: Routledge.
Muggleton, D. 2000. *Inside Subculture: The Postmodern Meaning of Style*. Oxford: Berg.
Nazarov, M. M. 1999. *Massovaia kommunikatsiia v sovremennom mire: metodologiia analiza i praktika issledovaniia*. Moscow: URSS.
Newitz, A. 1994. "Anime otaku: Japanese Animation Fans Outside Japan." *Bad Subjects* 13 (April).
Oleshchuk, Iu. F. 1994. "Evropa i sovetsko-amerikanskie otnosheniia." In *Rossiia i budushchee evropeiskoe ustroistvo*, ed. N. A. Kosolapov, part 2. Moscow: RAN, Institut mirovoi ekonomiki i mezhdunarodnykh otnoshenii.
Omel'chenko, E. L. 1996. "Young Women in Provincial Gang Culture." In Pilkington 1996c.
———. 1999a. " 'Telo drug cheloveka': Provintsial'naia molodezh' posle seksual'noi i nakanune gendernoi revoliutsii. Opyt izhucheniia molodezhnoi seksual'nosti v gorode Ul'ianovske." Paper presented to BASEES Annual Conference, Fitzwilliam College, Cambridge, March.
———. 2000. *Molodezhnie Kul'tury i Subkul'tury*. Moscow: Institut Sotsiologii RAN.
———, ed. 1993. *Reklama v Rossii: Problemy i perspektivy*. Ul'ianovsk: Izdatel'stvo MGU-Ul'ianovsk.
———, ed. 1999b. *Podrostki i narkotiki. Opyt issledovaniia problemy v shkolakh Ul'ianovska*. Ul'ianovsk: Izdatel'stvo Ul'ianovskogo gosudarstvennogo universiteta.
Orlik, E. N. 1995. "Obraz zhizni ot sovetskogo k zapadnomu: massovie predstavleniia." In *Zapad i Vostok: Traditsii, vzaimodeistviia i novatsii*, Tezizy Vserossiiskogo nauchno-prakticheskoi konferentsii, Vladimir, 15–17 March.
Orlova, E. 1987. "Subkul'tury v strukture sovremennogo obshchestva." In *Subkul'turnie Ob"edineniia Molodezhi: Kriticheskii Analiz*, ed. I. Kuchmaeva. Moscow: AN SSSR Institut Filosofii.
Oswell, D. 1998. "A Question of Belonging: Television, Youth and the Domestic." In Skelton and Valentine 1998, 35–49.
Oushakine, S. 2000a. "In the State of Post-Soviet Aphasia: Symbolic Development in Contemporary Russia." *Europe-Asia Studies* 52(6): 991–1016.
———. 2000b. "The Quantity of Style: Imaginary Consumption in the New Russia." *Theory, Culture and Society* 17(5): 97–120.
Panarin, A. S. 1995. *Rossiia v Tsivilizatsionnom Protsesse*. Moscow: Institut filosofii RAN.

———. 1997. "Est' li spasenie na dne otchaianiia?" *Novaia Rossiia* 4:23–28.

———. 1998. "Vostok-Zapad: Tsikly bol'shoi istorii." *Novaia Rossiia* 1:65–72.

Parker, D. 1998. "Rethinking British Chinese Identities." In Skelton and Valentine 1998, 66–82.

Parker, H., J. Aldridge, and F. Measham. 1998. *Illegal Leisure: The Normalization of Adolescent Recreational Drug Use*. London: Routledge.

Parrish, S. 1995. "Poll Surveys Attitudes Towards US." OMRI (online news journal), pt. 1, no. 191, 2 October.

Pelevin, V. 1999. *Generation "P."* Moscow: Vagrius.

Peters Hasty, O., and S. Fusso. 1988. *America Through Russian Eyes, 1874–1926*. New Haven: Yale University Press.

Petrov, N., et al. 1979. *SShA i NATO: Istochniki voennoi ugrozy*. Moscow: Voenizdat.

Petterson, J. 2000. "No More Song and Dance: French Radio Broadcast Quotas, Chansons, and Cultural Exceptions." In *Transactions, Transgressions, Transformations: American Culture in Western Europe and Japan*, ed. H. Fehrenbach and U. Poiger. New York: Berghahn Books.

Pieterse, J. 1995. "Globalization as Hybridization." In *Global Modernities*, ed. M. Featherstone, S. Lash, and R. Robertson. London: Sage.

Pilkington, H. 1994. *Russia's Youth and Its Culture: A Nation's Constructors and Constructed*. London: Routledge.

———. 1996a. "Farewell to the Tusovka: Masculinities and Femininities on the Moscow Youth Scene." In Pilkington 1996c.

———. 1996b. "Young Women and Subcultural Lifestyles: A Case of 'Irrational Needs'?" In *Women in Russia and Ukraine*, ed. R. Marsh. Cambridge: Cambridge University Press.

———. 1998. " 'The Future Is Ours': Youth Culture in Russia, 1953 to the Present." In *Russian Cultural Studies: An Introduction*, ed. C. Kelly and D. Shepherd. Oxford: Oxford University Press.

———, ed. 1996c. *Gender, Generation and Identity in Contemporary Russia*. London: Routledge.

Plaksii, I. 1988. *Molodezhnie Gruppy i Ob"edineniia: Prichiny Vozniknoveniia i Osobennosti deiatel'nosti*. Moscow: Znanie.

Poiger, U. 2000. *Jazz, Rock and Rebels: Cold War Politics and American Culture in a Divided Germany*. Berkeley and Los Angeles: University of California Press.

Polhemus, T. 1997. "In the Supermarket of Style." In Redhead 1997.

Poluekhtova, I. 1997. "Amerikanskie fil'my kak faktor sotsializatsii molodezhi v Rossii 90-x." *Rossiiskie obshchestvennie nauki: novie perspektivy*, no. 8:57–82.

Pomerants, G. 1998. "Pereklichka vremennogo i vechnogo v dialoge kul'turnykh mirov." *Rubezhi* 1:3–16.

Popov, V. A., and O. Iu. Kondrat'eva. 1998. "Narkotizatsiia v Rossii—shag do national'noi katastrofy." *Sotsiologicehskie Issledovaniia* 8:65–68.

Postman, N. 1985. *Amusing Ourselves to Death*. Harmondsworth: Penguin.

Rashkovskii, E. B. 1993. "Opyt totalitarnoi modernizatsii Rossii, 1917–1991. V svete sotsiologii razvitiia." *Mirovaia ekonomika i mezhdunarodnie otnosheniia*, no. 7:88–105.

Rausing, S. 1998. "Signs of the New Nation: Gift Exchange, Consumption and Aid on a Former Collective Farm in North-West Estonia." In *Material Cultures: Why Some Things Matter*, ed. D. Miller. London: UCL Press.

Rayport Rabodzeenko, J. 1998. "Creating Elsewhere, Being Other: The Imagined Spaces and Selves of St. Petersburg Young People, 1990–95." Ph.D. diss., Department of Anthropology, University of Chicago.

Redhead, S. 1990. The End-of-the-Century Party. Youth and Pop Towards 2000. Manchester: Manchester University Press.

———, ed. 1997. *The Clubcultures Reader. Readings in Popular Cultural Studies*, Oxford: Blackwell Publishers.

Reimer, B. 1995. "Youth and Modern Lifestyles." In *Youth Culture in Late Moderntity*, ed. J. Fornäs and G. Bolin. London: Sage.

Richard, B., and H. Kruger. 1998. "Ravers' Paradise? German Youth Cultures in the 1990s." In Skelton and Valentine 1998.

Richard, L. 1995. "Ex-Soviet States Lead World in Ad Cynicism." *Advertising Age*, 5 June, 3.

Riordan, J. 1989. "Teenage Gangs, 'Afgantsy' and Neofascists." In *Soviet Youth Culture*, ed. J. Riordan. London: Macmillan.

Robertson, R. 1995. "Glocalization: Time-Space and Homogeneity-Heterogeneity." In *Global Modernities*, ed. M. Featherstone, S. Lash, and R. Robertson. London: Sage.

Robinson, D., E. Buck, and M. Cuthbert. 1991. *Music at the Margins: Popular Music and Global Cultural Diversity*. London: Sage.

Rogov, S. 1998. "Rossiia I SShA ispytanie krizisom." *Mezhdunarodnaia Zhizn'*, no. 10:97–112.

Rondeli, L. D. 1995. "Kinomeniu shkol'nikov," *Sotsis* 3:92–94.

Roniger, L. 1995. "Public Life and Globalization as Cultural Vision." *Canadian Review of Sociology and Anthropology* 32(3): 259–85.

Rosbizneskonsalting 2001. "V Moskve proshel miting antiglobalistov." *RBK*, 11 February (accessed at www.rbc.ru).

Rose, T. 1994. *Black Noise: Rap Music and Black Culture in Contemporary America*. Hanover: Wesleyan University Press.

Rossiiskii nezavisimii institut sotsial'nikh i natsional'nikh problem (po zakazku moskovskogo predstavitel'stva Fonda im. F. Eberta). 1998. "Molodezh novoi Rossii: Kakaia ona? Chem zhivet? K chemu stremitsia?" Moscow. (Cited as RNISiNP.)

Rozhkov, I. Ia. 1994. "Tsivilizovannaia reklama—nasushchnaia neobkhodimost' tsivilizovannogo rynka." *Reklama*, no. 5–6.

Sakwa, R. 1996. *Russian Politics and Society*. London: Routledge.

Salagaev, A. L. 1997. *Molodezhnie pravonarushenniia i delinkventnie soobshchestva skvoz' prizmu amerikanskikh sotsiologicheskikh teorii*. Kazan': Ekotsentr.

Sazonov, V. 1994. "Russians: The West, Friend or Foe?" *Segodnia*, December 6, 10. Translated in *Current Digest of the Post-Soviet Press* 46(49): 14–15.

Schade-Poulson, M. 1995. "The Power of Love: Rai Music and Youth in Algeria." In *Youth Cultures: A Cross-Cultural Perspective*, ed. V. Amit-Talai and H. Wulff. London: Routledge.

Schaefer, M. 1998. "Getting Perpendicular with Dj Vadim." *Ink*, 19 April (accessed at http://neurosis.hungry.com/~matthew/dj_vadim.html).

Semennikova, L. I. 1996. "Tsivilizatsionnie paradigmy v istorii Rossii. Stat'ia 1." *Obshchestvennie nauki i sovremennost'* 5:107–19.

Shaburov, O. V. 1999. " 'Russkoe Radio'—samoe muzhskoe v Rossii." In *Russkaia zhenshchina—2. Zhenshchina glazami muzhchiny*. Ekaterinburg: Izdatel'stvo Ural'skogo universiteta.

Shapiro, H. 1999. "Dances with Drugs: Pop Music, Drugs and Youth Culture." In *Drugs: Cultures, Controls and Everyday Life*, ed. N. South. London: Sage.

Shapovalov, V. F. 1998. " 'Kak poniat' Rossiiu? (Etiudy o 'rossiiskoi ekzotichnost")." *Obshchestvennie nauki i sovremennost'* 1:89–103.

Shchepanskaia, T. 1991. "The Symbols of the Youth Subculture." *Soviet Education* 33(10): 3–16.

Shiner, M., and T. Newburn. 1999. "Taking Tea with Noel: The Place and Meaning of Drug Use in Everyday Life." In *Drugs: Cultures, Controls and Everyday Life*, ed. N. South. London: Sage.

Shlapentokh, V. 1989. *Public and Private Life of the Soviet People: Changing Values in Post-Stalin Russia*. Oxford: Oxford University Press.

Shliapentokh, V. 1994. "Zapad kak osnovnaia problema dlia Rossii i ee budushchego." In *Rossiia i Zapad: dialog Kul'tur. Sbornik nauchnikh trudov*, ed. B. Gubman. Tver': Tver' gosudarstvenniye universitet.

Shuker, R. 1994. *Understanding Popular Music*. London: Routledge.

Shul'gina, E. 1996. "Tusovka: ili v bandity ili v biznesmeny." *Ogonek* 1:26–27.

Simoniia, N. A. 1996. "Dogoniaiushchee razvitie Nezapada versus zapadnoi modeli." *Mirovaia Ekonomika I Mezhdunarodnie Otnosheniia* 12:5–10.

Skelton, T., and G. Valentine, eds. 1998. *Cool Places: Geographies of Youth Cultures*. London: Routledge.

Smith, G. 1999. *The Post-Soviet States: Mapping the Politics of Transition*. London: Arnold.

Smolian, G. I., D. S. Chereshkin, O. N. Vershinskaia, et al. 1997. *Puti Rossii k informatsionnomu obshchestvu: predposilki, indikatori, problemi, osobennosti*, Moscow: Institut sistemnogo analiza RAN.

Sokolov, M. 1999. "Subkul'turnoe izmerenie sotsial'nikh dvizhenii: kognitivnii podkhod." In *Molodezhnie Dvizheniia i Subkul'tury Sankt-Peterburga (Sotsiologicheskii i antropologicheskii analiz)*, ed. V. Kostiusheva. Saint Petersburg: Izdatel'stvo Norma.

Solonitskii, A. S. 1996. "Preuspevaiushchii Nezapad i Rossiia pered litsom zapadnoi modeli razvitiia." *Mirovaia ekonomika i mezhdunarodnie otnosheniia* 12:10–13.

Stapleton, K. 1998. "From the Margins to Mainstream: The Political Power of Hip-Hop." *Media Culture and Society* 20 (April): 219–34.

Stratton, J. 1985. "On the Importance of Subcultural Origins." From "Youth Subcultures and Their Cultural Contexts." *Australian and New Zealand Journal of Sociology* 21(2). Reprinted in *The Subcultures Reader*, ed. K. Gelder and S. Thornton. London: Routledge, 1997.

Sundiev, I. 1987. "Neformal'nie molodezhnie ob"edineniia: Opyt ekspozitsii." *Sotsiologicheskie Issledovaniia* 5:56–62.

———. 1989 "Samodeiatel'nie ob"edineniia molodezhi." *Sotsiologicheskie Issledovaniia* 2:56–62.

"Taking It to the Buyer." 1996. *Russia Review*, 21 October.

Tarasov, A. 2000a. "Porozhdenie reform: britogolovie, oni zhe skinkhedy." *Svobodnaia Mysl'* 4:40–53.

———. 2000b. "Porozhdenie reform: britogolovie, oni zhe skinkhedy." *Svobodnaia Mysl'* 5:39–56.

Taylor, T. 1997. *Global Pop: World Music, World Markets.* New York: Routledge.

Thornton, S. 1995. *Club Cultures: Music, Media and Subcultural Capital.* Cambridge: Polity Press.

———. 1997. "The Social Logic of Subcultural Capital." In *The Subcultures Reader*, ed. K. Gelder and S. Thornton. London: Routledge.

Tolstykh, V. 1997. "Ni panslavizm, ni evraziistvo, ni pravoslavnoe edinstvo." *Rodina* 8:15–20.

Tolz, V. 1998. "Conflicting 'Homeland Myths' and Nation-State Building in Postcommunist Russia." *Slavic Review*, no. 57: 2.

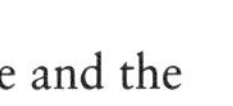

Tomlinson, L. 1998. " 'This Ain't No Disco' . . . Or Is It? Youth Culture and the Rave Phenomenon." In Epstein 1998.

Tsygankov, P. A. 1995. "Identifikatsiia Evropy vo vneshnei politike Rossii." *Sotsial'no-politicheskii zhurnal* 6:3–21.

"U reklamy tozhe est' reiting." 1998. *Ekonomika I Zhizn'* 26:13.

Ule, M. 1998. "The Lifeworld of Young People." In *Youth in Slovenia: New Perspectives from the Nineties*, ed. M. Ule and T. Rener. Ljubljana: Youth Department of the Republic of Slovenia.

Utkin, A. I. 1995. *Rossiia i Zapad: problemy vzaimnogo vospriiatiia i perspektivy stroitel'stva otnoshenii.* Moscow: RAN Institut Istorii.

———. 1996. *Vyzov Zapada i Otvet Rossii.* Moscow: Magistr.

———. 1997. "Konflikt tsivilizatsii?" *Novaia Rossiia* 2:77–84.

Vishnevskii, A. 1998. "Postsovetskoe demograficheskoe prostranstvo: Vostochnaia Evropa ili integral'naia chast' Evropy." *Mirovaia ekonomika i mezhdunarodnie otnosheniia*, no. 5: 122–32.

Volodin, A. G., and G. K. Shirokov. 1999. "Globalizatsiia: istoki, tendentsii, perspektivy." *Polis* 5:83–94.

———. 1997. "Mirovaia sistema: peregruppirovka sil." In *Kosmopolis: Al'manakh*, ed. T. V. Shmachkova. Moscow: Polis.

Wallace, C., and S. Kovatcheva. 1998. *Youth in Society: The Construction and Deconstruction of Youth in East and West Europe*. Basingstoke: Macmillan Press.

Ware, V., and L. Back. 2001. *Dark Thoughts on Whiteness*. Chicago: University of Chicago Press.

Waters, M. 1995. *Globalization*. London: Routledge.

Wilk, R. 1995. "Learning to Be Local in Belize: Global Systems of Common Difference." In *Worlds Apart: Modernity Through the Prism of the Local*, ed. D. Miller. London: Routledge.

Willems, H. 1995. "Right-Wing Extremism, Racism or Youth Violence? Explaining Violence Against Foreigners in Germany." *New Community* 21(4): 501–23.

Willis, P. 1978. *Profane Culture*, London: Routledge & Kegan Paul.

Wolf, J. 1991. "The Global and the Specific: Reconciling Conflicting Theories of Culture." In *Culture, Globalization and the World-System*, ed. A. King. London: Macmillan.

Wolff, L. 1994. *Inventing Eastern Europe: The Map of Civilization on the Mind of the Enlightenment*. Stanford: Stanford University Press.

Wulff, H. 1995. "Introduction: Introducing Youth Culture in Its Own Right: The State of the Art and New Possibilities." In *Youth Cultures: A Cross-Cultural Perspective*, ed. V. Amit-Talai and H. Wulff. London: Routledge.

Yanoshak, N. 2000. "*Mr West* Mimicking Mr. West." Paper presented to BASEES Annual Conference, Fitzwilliam College, Cambridge, 1–2 April.

Yeltsin, B. N. 1992a. "Vystupleniia El'tsina na VI s"ezde narodnikh deputatov 21 aprelia 1992." *Diplomaticheskii Vestnik* 9–10 (5 May): 3.

———. 1992b. "Poslanie El'tsina uchastnikam nauch-prakt. Konferentsii 'Preobrazhennaia Rossiia v novom mire.' " *Diplomaticheskii Vestnik* 6 (31 March): 29–45.

Yovovich, B. 1995. "Youth Market Goes Global." *Advertising Age*, 27 March, 10.

Yurchak, A. 1999. "Gagarin and the Rave Kids: Transforming Power, Identity and Aesthetics in Post-Soviet Nightlife." In *Consuming Russia: Popular Culture, Sex, and Society Since Gorbachev*, ed. Adele Marie Barker. Durham: Duke University Press.

Zinov'ev, A. A. 1995. *Zapad: Fenomen zapadnizma*. Moscow: Tsentrpoligraf.

———. 1998. *O Rossii, o Zapade, o zagranitse i o sebe . . .*, stenogr. sovmest. zasedaniia Akad. sotsial. nauk, Mosk. intellektual.-delovogo kluba, kluba "Realisty" i Instituta sotsial-polit. issled RaN, 29 October 1997, IN-t sotsial-polit.issled. RAN, Akad.sotsial. nauk, Moscow.

Zlokazova, E. I. 1996. "Mass Consciousness of Youth and Cinema." In *Youth in Changing Societies*, ed. V. Puuronen. Joensuu: University of Joensuu.

Zobov, R. A., and V. N. Kelas'ev. 1995. *Mify rossiiskogo soznaniia i puti dostizheniia obshchestvennogo soglasiia*. St. Petersburg: Sankt Petersburgskii gosudarstvennyi universitet, Sankt Peterburgskii Iazykovoi tsentr.

INDEX